THE GREAT COMMISSION

Evangelicals and the History of World Missions

EDITED BY
Martin I. Klauber
& Scott M. Manetsch

ACADEMIC

Nashville, Tennessee

127 Ninth Avenue, North
Nashville, TN 37234
www.bhpublishinggroup.com

ISBN 13: 978-0-8054-4300-4

Unless otherwise noted, Scripture quotations are from the Holman Christian Standard Bible® copyright © 1999, 2000, 2002, 2003 by Holman Bible Publishers. Used by Permission.

Scripture quotations designated as NIV are from the Holy Bible, New International Version, copyright © 1973, 1978, 1984 by International Bible Society.

Dewey Decimal Classification: 266
Subject Heading: MISSIONS--HISTORY

Printed in the United States of America
1 2 3 4 5 6 7 8 13 12 11 10 09 08
VP

CONTENTS

VOLUME CONTRIBUTORS

Fred W. Beuttler
Deputy Historian,
United States House of Representatives

D. A. Carson
Research Professor of New Testament,
Trinity Evangelical Divinity School

Richard R. Cook
Assistant Professor of Mission History and Global Christianity,
Trinity Evangelical Divinity School

Timothy George
Professor of Divinity and Dean,
Beeson Divinity School of Samford University

Bradley J. Gundlach
Associate Professor of History,
Trinity College of Trinity International University

Jon N. Hinkson
Fellow of the Rivendell Institute and
Staff Worker for Campus Crusade for Christ,
Yale University

Martin I. Klauber
Adjunct Professor of Church History and the History of Christian Thought,
Trinity Evangelical Divinity School

Erwin W. Lutzer
Senior Pastor of Moody Memorial Church and
Adjunct Professor of Homiletics,
Trinity Evangelical Divinity School

Scott M. Manetsch
Associate Professor of Church History and the History of Christian Thought and
Chairman of the Church History Department,
Trinity Evangelical Divinity School

Thomas J. Nettles
Professor of Historical Theology,
Southern Baptist Theological Seminary

Alice Ott
Doctoral Student in Historical Theology,
Trinity Evangelical Divinity School

J. Daniel Salinas
Director and Lecturer,
International Fellowship of Evangelical Students (Paraguay)

Glenn S. Sunshine
Professor of Early Modern European History and
Chairman of the History Department,
Central Connecticut State University

Douglas A. Sweeney
Associate Professor of Church History and the History of Christian Thought and
Director of the Carl F. H. Henry Center,
Trinity Evangelical Divinity School

Tite Tiénou
Professor of Theology of Mission and
Senior Vice President of Education and Academic Dean,
Trinity Evangelical Divinity School

PREFACE

This book represents the literary harvest of a conference held at Trinity Evangelical Divinity School in April 2006 on the theme of the Great Commission, Evangelicals, and the History of World Missions. This conference was held in honor of John D. Woodbridge, research professor of Church History at Trinity Evangelical Divinity School, on the event of his sixty-fifth birthday. For more than thirty-five years, John has been an esteemed professor, cherished mentor, and wise advisor for hundreds, indeed thousands, of graduate students at Trinity. John's love for the gospel and the Christian Church has left an indelible mark on several generations of men and women who now serve Christ around the world as pastors, missionaries, campus ministers, and local church leaders. John's commitment to a life of intellectual labor and scholarly engagement *coram deo* has also inspired scores of men and women to embrace vocations in the academy, desiring to live out their Christian discipleship through ministries of teaching, research, and writing. We, the editors of this book, are among John's students who were thus inspired, and our academic work bears the mark of his gentle but significant example. More than twenty years later, we continue to recognize God's enormous kindness in giving us John as a teacher and mentor, and now as a colleague and friend.

John Woodbridge is both historian and storyteller. As masters' students at Trinity in the late 1970s and early 1980s, we were captivated by his lectures in which the strands of historical analysis and lively biographical detail were woven together to create fascinating accounts of Christians through the centuries, men and women who like the faithful of Hebrews 11 were "foreigners and temporary residents on earth . . . they now aspire to a better country—a heavenly one." John helped us see that their story was our story as well, that we too belonged to the great company of the redeemed, called by God to be faithful disciples of Jesus Christ. John regularly reminded us that we too live our lives under the providence of God. At the same time, John always had an arsenal of personal anecdotes and stories to share with his students, accounts of manuscript chases, rare books, and adventures in the French archives, that taught us that the discipline of history was both craft and science, and intensely interesting.

More importantly, John is a man who has experienced God's grace through faith in Christ. As a doctoral student in Toulouse, France, in the 1960s, John's confidence in Marxist materialist explanations for human behavior was decisively undermined by an unexpected spiritual encounter with the person of Jesus Christ. John's new life as a Christian disciple was thereafter shaped in a profound manner through the example of a wonderful Christian wife, Susan, and the wise counsel of several close friends, especially evangelical leaders Kenneth Kantzer and Carl F. H. Henry. As the recipient of grace, John has spent his adult life sharing God's gracious love with other people. We remember fondly his affection for his students, his office door open to visitors, his home as a place of warm hospitality. Through his writing and teaching, John has frequently reminded the Church that the good news of God's grace in Jesus Christ is a message that must be proclaimed in word and loving action. Given John's life story and driving passion for the gospel, it seemed particularly appropriate that we honor our professor and friend with a conference, and this book, devoted to evangelical history and the Great Commission.

We would like to thank Ryan Finnelly and the Trinity Alumni Association, who partnered with us in hosting the conference in honor of John Woodbridge. In addition, we are very grateful for the substantial financial support and sponsorship provided by the Carl F. H. Henry Center for Theological Understanding and the Dean's office of Trinity Evangelical Divinty School, making both the conference and this book possible. We express our thanks as well to graduate students Jacob Yates, who assisted in the compiling of the index, and David Barshinger, who leant an attentive eye to editing a final draft of this volume. The organizing committee for the conference was a true collaboration between the faculties of the undergraduate and graduate schools of Trinity International University, with Bradley Gundlach of the undergraduate school and Douglas Sweeney of the graduate school joining us. Finally, we wish to thank the scholars who contributed essays to this volume, who join with us in honoring our colleague and friend John D. Woodbridge. This volume is dedicated to him with our gratitude and love.

Martin I. Klauber
Scott M. Manetsch
Pentecost 2007

FOREWORD: PROVIDENCE, HISTORY, AND EVANGELICAL MISSIONS

By Erwin W. Lutzer

The book you hold in your hands, written in honor of Dr. John D. Woodbridge, combines the best of scholarship with a holy zeal to see the gospel reach to the ends of the earth. In these pages, history is used as a mirror to reflect how well the Church has carried out Jesus' mandate to go into the whole world to preach the gospel.

How fitting that these historians have chosen the topic of missions to honor their colleague and friend John Woodbridge on the event of his sixty-fifth birthday. He is a scholar admired well beyond the confines of Trinity Evangelical Divinity School. For him, academics has never been an end in itself but a means to a much grander goal, namely, the spread of the Good News around the world.

As I read these pages, I was struck with the diversity of the eras covered, a panorama beginning with Martin Luther and continuing all the way to present-day missionary work in Latin America, Asia, and Africa. I was also intrigued by the various attitudes evangelicals have had toward the Great Commission—some practically ignored it, others saw it merely as a side job, and still others made it the thrust of their whole ministry. So, amid many failures and hard won successes, the gospel has, with varying degrees of clarity, gone to the four corners of the world. As Count Zinzendorf said, "It is always He.... We are nothing but poor tools."

It is difficult to read these pages without seeing in them the providence of God. The Puritans were not the only ones to discern "the missionary designs of God" in dark providences, such as persecutions that thrust them into the New World. The Bible clearly teaches that God's Hand guides history, directing it toward an appointed end. In Old Testament times, Israel looked upon its history as the record of God's leading, directing, and orchestrating. The nation's successes and failures were all attributed to the good pleasure of the Divine Hand.

So it is with the history of God's people throughout the ages. There has always been a confluence of the will and purposes of God with the will and abilities of men. Amid man's sin and limitations, God has honored the efforts of those who have seen beyond their own locality to devote themselves to the greater vision of impacting the world. We can profit from history not simply to be motivated by the courage of those who have gone before us, but also to be encouraged by those special evidences of God's providence that inspire us to be faithful to the Great Commission in our time.

This book will keep past missionary endeavors in perspective. It is important for historians not to be so enamored with the reformers and missionary leaders of the past that they ignore the obvious failures and blind spots evident along the winding history of the Christian Church. It is also important not to be so critical of the past that we see nothing redeemable in the lives and methodology of those who have preceded us. This book avoids both extremes.

In these pages I discovered there is much to learn about evangelical missions even though we live at a different time and in vastly different cultures. We cannot turn the clock back, and even if we could it would not be wise to do so. But we can build on the past. We can learn from the successes and mistakes of those who have gone before. The past can be profitable if it is a rudder that guides us rather than an anchor that weighs us down.

And we can rejoice that all the people represented in this volume did the best they could with what they had. The God who sees the heart is the ultimate arbiter of the impact of each. We stand on their shoulders and say, "We promise, by God's grace, to follow you in finishing the task you so bravely undertook."

This history of missions also reminds us of what changes and what does not. Personalities change—Martin Luther and Jonathan Edwards are no more. Methods change—today we travel over oceans with jet planes and use computer programs to help translate primitive languages. Our spiritual forefathers could not have envisioned the burgeoning technological revolution that has made it possible for us to penetrate even so-called "closed countries" via radio, television, and now the Internet. Yet the biblical message remains unchanged. Here at the Moody Church in Chicago we have a large sign at the front of the sanctuary, "Jesus Christ is the same yesterday, today, and forever" (Heb 13:8).

Given this span of centuries and the radical changes of contemporary culture, what binds history together? Whence its continuity? The eternality of God and His Word give the individual events of history their focus and meaning. The same Jesus who confronted the Apostle Paul on his way to Damascus is the same Jesus who has saved us; the God who called Martin Luther is the same God who called John Woodbridge to Himself and chose him to touch the lives of thousands of students through his teaching and mentoring.

Generations come and generations go, but God is there. Buildings are built and destroyed, but God is there. Nations rise, and nations fade into oblivion, but God is there. Isaiah reminds us that the generations are like grass and then continues, "The grass withers, the flowers fade, but the word of our God remains forever" (40:8).

The fact that God is the final author of history gives us the settled confidence that the past is never lost. The best historians—such as are those who have compiled this book—are unable finally to evaluate the impact (either positive or negative) of any leader in the past. Only God knows the hidden connections, those cause-effect relationships that are unknown to us. Heaven no doubt will judge history differently than we do. Numerous books have been written about Dwight L. Moody, but we know little about Edward Kimball, who led him to faith in Christ. We all know who Billy Graham is, but who was Mordecai Ham, the man who preached that sermon in a tent meeting outside of Charlotte, North Carolina, in the spring of 1934 when Graham was converted?

My point is that much of the past is lost to us, but none of it is lost to God. He alone is privy to the impact of a praying mother such as Susanna Wesley or the impact of David Brainerd, whose biography of faithfulness in the midst of hardship has inspired millions. Sermons, seminary lectures, and random encounters long forgotten to us are ever present to the Almighty and will be faithfully rewarded. He takes our feeble efforts and is careful to "establish the work of our hands" (Psa 90:17).

Finally, since God is both the author and preserver of history, we can be sure that the missionary task will continue until Christ returns. No doubt people wondered who would step in and take leadership after the Protestant reformers passed from the scene, but God had other reformers waiting to take their place. After William Carey died, a host of missionaries went to India and beyond. Who will step in when this generation of seminary professors and missionaries have finished their work? Again, God is quietly growing His next generation of leaders, and they will become known in due time.

Which brings us to our own individual histories. It is sobering to realize that God has already chosen the people who will succeed us in our positions as leaders and teachers in this generation. But because we are convinced of the continuity of God's purposes, we can rejoice that the future of the church and her mission is in capable hands. God assures us that it will be brought to completion. As the old adage says, "God buries His workman, but the work continues."

John Woodbridge lives and breathes confidence in a great God who oversees history and will complete what He has purposed. Anyone who has heard John speak on America's Great Awakenings knows that he is captivated by God, the God who has made Himself known in Christ and is well able to bless individuals, churches, and, yes, even nations in unpredictable and transforming ways. John wants to run the race with confidence and end well, leaving behind a generation of trained historians and evangelists to carry on the work of defending and spreading the gospel. John knows, as we all do, that each of us has only a short window of time to make a small contribution to the completion of the missionary task.

Every time I've met with John, I have been inspired by his warm affection for all who serve Christ. Scott Chapman, John's pastor, told me that he was not only impressed with John's deep humility, but his genuine love for all people regardless of their stature. "Even if he was not a historian or never taught a class, I'd have lunch with him as often as possible," Scott said. "He motivates me to be more like Jesus." And that, at the end of the day, will be John's greatest legacy in the lives of his many students and friends—*motivating others to be like Jesus.*

Be assured that you will benefit from this volume, even as I have. But we must remember that information alone is not what is needed. We need to have the spiritual determination and faith to follow the hard path of those who have shown that seemingly insurmountable obstacles should not hinder us from doing what Jesus commanded us to do.

Congratulations to our friend John Woodbridge for more than thirty-five years of teaching and to all who wrote these pages intending to motivate the rest of us to run the race with faithfulness and joy.

INTRODUCTION

By Douglas A. Sweeney

The 11 disciples traveled to Galilee, to the mountain where Jesus had directed them. When they saw Him, they worshiped, but some doubted. Then Jesus came near and said to them, "All authority has been given to Me in heaven and on earth. Go, therefore, and make disciples of all nations, baptizing them in the name of the Father and of the Son and of the Holy Spirit, teaching them to observe everything I have commanded you. And remember, I am with you always, to the end of the age."

—Matthew 28:16–20

The "Great Commission" found in Matthew 28 has shaped our evangelical movement as much as any passage of Scripture.Though entrusted by the Lord Jesus Christ to His disciples before His ascension, it suffered sore neglect from most believers through the ages. During the past few hundred years, however, thanks in large part to the work of evangelical missionaries, it has played a powerful role in the rapid spread of the Christian faith—numerically, culturally, and geographically. Whereas in 1500, only 19 percent of the world's population was Christian and more than 83 percent of the world's Christians lived in Europe, by the year 2000 more than 32 percent of the world's population was Christian and most Christians were non-Western people of color. From 1750 to 1900, the very period when the evangelical movement came of age, the world's Christian population nearly quadrupled. In 1750, 160 million people claimed to be Christian, roughly 22 percent of the world's inhabitants. By 1900, however, more than 558 million people claimed to follow Jesus, over 34 percent of the global family.[1]

---

[1] Statistical estimates taken from the *World Christian Encyclopedia: A Comparative Study of Churches and Religions in the Modern World, A.D. 1900–2000*, ed. David B. Barrett (Nairobi: Oxford University Press, 1982), 796–97.

What is this potent movement that has exerted such a vital force in world evangelization? This question can be difficult to answer. The term "evangelical" has gained a wide currency over the past several decades, as the evangelical movement has proliferated globally. Today, there may be more than 800 million evangelicals spread throughout the world (including Pentecostals and Charismatics). Not surprisingly, then, the evangelical movement is diverse, and the term "evangelical" is slippery. Baptist leader Timothy George, a contributor to this volume, defines evangelicals as "a worldwide family of Bible-believing Christians committed to sharing with everyone everywhere the transforming good news of new life in Jesus Christ, an utterly free gift that comes through faith alone in the crucified and risen Savior." Scottish historian David Bebbington has the most popular definition: "there are . . . four qualities that have been the special marks of Evangelical religion: *conversionism*, the belief that lives need to be changed; *activism*, the expression of the gospel in effort; *Biblicism*, a particular regard for the Bible; and what may be called *crucicentrism*, a stress on the sacrifice of Christ on the cross. Together they form a quadrilateral of priorities that is the basis of Evangelicalism."[2]

I prefer to describe evangelicalism with more specificity as a movement that is based in classical Christian orthodoxy, shaped by a Reformational understanding of the gospel, and distinguished from other such movements in the history of the church by a set of beliefs and behaviors forged in the fires of the eighteenth-century revivals—the so-called "Great Awakening," discussed more fully below—beliefs and behaviors that had mainly to do with the spread of the gospel abroad.[3]

This volume offers a survey of the efforts of evangelicals to fulfill the Great Commission, making disciples everywhere. It fills a gap in the textbook literature on the history of the church by focusing closely on the history of the Protestant missions movement. It also reflects the chief passions of Professor John D. Woodbridge—to whom this book is dedicated—for gospel proclamation and the history of the church. "What higher commission," Woodbridge asks, "could a human being have than to be Christ's ambassador, His personal representative? Amazingly enough, that is the very mission to which each one of us as a Christian has been called: to be an ambassador for Christ. We are all on an awesome assignment in this life."[4] As Woodbridge himself has demonstrated in a host of publications, many unsung spiritual heroes have fulfilled this calling faithfully. Their labors in God's vineyard have contributed significantly to the global network of Christians taken for granted in our time and accounted for historically in the chapters found below.

In Part One of this volume, devoted to "Early Protestant Missions," we see that evangelical missions started slowly. Reformers such as Luther thought that

---

[2] For George's definition, see *Christianity Today* (August 9, 1999): 62. For Bebbington's, see David W. Bebbington, *Evangelicalism and Modern Britain: A History from the 1730s to the 1980s* (London: Unwin Hyman, 1989), 2–3.

[3] For historical and theological analysis of these and other definitions, see Douglas A. Sweeney, *The American Evangelical Story: A History of the Movement* (Grand Rapids, Mich.: Baker Academic, 2005), esp. 9–26.

[4] John D. Woodbridge, "Foreword: Ambassadors for Christ," in *Ambassadors for Christ*, ed. John D. Woodbridge (Chicago: Moody Press, 1994), 10–11.

the end of the world was near and that their job as Protestant pastors was to purify and strengthen the church before the Lord's return. They favored missions, to be sure, in pursuit of this urgent goal. By the early seventeenth century, Protestant missionaries were active on every continent in the world. However, by most Christian standards their activity was slight before the modern missions movement coalesced in the eighteenth century.[5]

Glenn Sunshine opens his chapter on sixteenth-century Protestant missions by granting that "'[m]issions' is not a word that . . . springs to mind when discussing the . . . Reformation." As a matter of fact, he continues, "foreign missionary activity was . . . distinctly lacking among all Protestants in the sixteenth century." Compared to Roman Catholic leaders, early Protestants had precious little access to the colonies and trading posts that served as gospel beachheads overseas. Thus they focused first and foremost on the Christianization of Europe. Making use of the printing press, engaging Catholics in debate, and working to purify their parishes and regional governments, magisterial Protestant leaders won control of much of Europe. Their "vision of church and state collaborating to produce a Christian society led them to embrace a missions approach that used the existing social and political structures to introduce Protestant ideas to both the masses and the elites." They launched missions, to be sure. One might label them with the later designation, "home missionaries." But they did not attempt too much outside of Christendom.[6]

Rather, the Puritans and the Pietists were the leading pioneers of the kind of work that paved the way for the modern missions movement. It was not until the Puritans' work with New England's Native Indians that Protestants projected a major international missions plan, expecting great results. And it was not until the Pietists' work in the early eighteenth century that Protestant missionaries reaped a bumper crop of converts.

As Jon Hinkson reports in his chapter on the Puritans and Pietists, both groups took on enormous gospel projects. The Puritans who populated Massachusetts Bay claimed that the "principal" goal of their colony was to Christianize the Indians. They never launched a comprehensive campaign to meet this lofty

---

[5] During the past generation, church historians and others working on Luther and the early German Lutheran Reformation have worked hard to retrieve what they can of early Protestant missiological concern. Most of this work has been done in German, but some of it has been translated. See especially Volker Stolle, *The Church Comes from All Nations: Luther Texts on Mission*, trans. Klaus Detlev Schulz and Daniel Thies (St. Louis: Concordia Publishing House, 2003), orig. *Kirche aus allen Völkern, Luther-Texte zur Mission* (Erlangen: Verlag der Ev.-Luth. Mission, 1983); *Lutheran Contributions to the Missio Dei*, trans. William O'Hara (Geneva: Department of Church Cooperation of the Lutheran World Federation, 1984), orig. *Lutherische Beiträge zur Missio Dei* (Erlangen: Martin-Luther Verlag, 1982); and Robert Kolb, "Late Reformation Lutherans on Mission and Confession," *Lutheran Quarterly* 20 (Spring 2006): 26–43.

[6] The term "Christendom" refers to the territory and the ideal of state-sponsored Christian nationalism, both of which date back to the conversion of the Roman Emperor Constantine (in A.D. 312), the establishment of Christianity by Emperor Theodosius I as the only legal religion of the ancient Roman Empire (in A.D. 380), and the geopolitical agenda of the Holy Roman Empire (which emerged in A.D. 800, lasted in one form or another until the early nineteenth century, and gave to Christendom its definitive, medieval shape). During the age of Christendom, Christians often assumed that the best way to spread the Christian faith was by spreading Christian territory (and Western cultural forms). As Christendom declined and evangelicalism arose, however, a much more voluntaristic approach to missions was developed.

goal. By the early eighteenth century, in fact, many regretted this failure. In the words of Solomon Stoddard, one of the region's leading pastors:

> There has been a neglect to bring the Indians to the Profession of the Gospel. Something has been done through the Piety of particular Men, and at the Cost of some in Old-England; But we are reproached abroad for our Negligence. Many Men have been more careful to make a Prey of them, than to gain them to the Knowledge of Christ. The King in the CHARTER says, that the Undertakers did profess it to be their principal design to bring the Natives to the Knowledge of GOD. But we have very much failed of prosecuting that Design to Effect. . . . We have reason to fear that we are much to blame for their continuance in their Heathenism.[7]

Nevertheless, the Puritans did make several attempts at Indian missions. John Eliot founded a series of "praying towns" for Indian converts and worked diligently on his well-known Algonquian Bible (not to mention his translation of several other Christian texts). The Mayhew family spread the gospel among the natives of Martha's Vineyard. David Brainerd later gave his life for the cause of Indian missions, inspiring thousands of young Christians to do the same.

More significantly, perhaps, Europe's continental Pietists were missions pioneers. The Danish-Halle Pietist missionaries thrived in Tranquebar. Bartholomew Ziegenbalg performed astounding feats in Tamil, translating Scripture, sharing the gospel, and making a way for European students of South Indian culture.[8] The later Moravian Pietist followers of Nicholas von Zinzendorf excelled at foreign missions, traversing the globe and founding tight-knit gospel communes. Because they did not represent a European state church, moreover, Moravians could preach a gospel free of national politics. Their message retained elements of European culture. Still, they played a greater role than any other group before them in developing the methods that would prevail in foreign missions after the end of Christendom.

These early efforts to spread the gospel came to fruition in the wake of the major eighteenth-century revival known to some as the Great Awakening,[9] giv-

---

[7] Solomon Stoddard, *An Answer to Some Cases of Conscience, Respecting the Country* (Boston: Green, 1722), 11–12. Stoddard later wondered aloud "whether God is not angry with the country for doing so little towards the conversion of the Indians." See Solomon Stoddard, *Whether God Is Not Angry for Doing So Little towards the Conversion of the Indians?* (Boston: Green, 1723), 6.

[8] For a report on the recent tercentennial celebration of the Tranquebar mission, see Robert Kolb, "The Three-Hundredth Anniversary of Lutheran Mission in India," *Lutheran Quarterly* 21 (Spring 2007): 95–101, who notes: "the landing of Ziegenbalg and Plütschau in Tranquebar marked the beginning of a new era in the proclamation of the gospel, and it deserves to be remembered. Such an act of remembering took place on July 9, 2006, as the three million Indian Lutherans of the early twenty-first century gave thanks to God for the blessings that Ziegenbalg and those who followed him have brought to their land."

[9] American scholars, especially, have debated the accuracy, analytical utility, and theological import of the term "Great Awakening" for years. For information on this debate, see the essays by Allen C. Guelzo, "God's Designs: The Literature of the Colonial Revivals of Religion, 1735–1760," in Harry S. Stout and D. G. Hart, eds., *New*

ing birth to a massive, international movement of mission agencies and full-time missionaries. Like the Moravians, these newly awakened evangelical missionaries collaborated across historic denominational boundaries. But positioned as they were so close to the end of Christendom—especially in America, where the colonial state churches were undergoing disestablishment—they enjoyed a greater freedom than their European forebears to forge broad coalitions of evangelistic Christians bent on taking Christ to the nations. They also completed a crucial shift in missions methodology begun in fits and starts by earlier Protestant leaders: a transition from doing evangelism by means of purifying Catholic Europe's state churches and then spreading Protestant territorial interests overseas to doing evangelism by calling people to genuine conversion that transcends all prior confessional allegiances. In short, they harnessed the energy of the eighteenth-century Awakening in the service of what we have come to recognize as modern missions.

In his chapter on the revival and the rise of modern missions, Timothy George details the story of this transition. Emphasizing English Baptists like the redoubtable William Carey, George unpacks the ways in which the new revival-based ecumenism boosted and, in turn, received a boost from modern missions (and from missionaries focused less on institutional differences than on the global spread of the gospel message). "The missionary awakening," writes George, "flamed forth from the sparks ignited in the 1730s and 1740s at Aldersgate, Northampton, Cambuslang, Moorfield, and Bristol." These revivals yielded a literature of gospel expectation, a theology of missions that guided the course of the missions movement, and an ecumenical spirit that enabled it to flourish.

Part Two of this volume, on "Modern Anglo-American Missions," brings the story of the missions movement all the way up to the present, zooming in on the roles played by evangelicals in America. Bradley Gundlach leads the way with a chapter on missions in the United States, from independence through the middle decades of the nineteenth century. Focusing closely on the ministries of white Protestant missionaries to Indians, slaves, and residents of the Sandwich Islands (later Hawaii), Gundlach stresses that such ministries "went largely from the developed world to the undeveloped world, mixing the spread of Western civilization with the spread of the gospel—and doing so in situations of decidedly unequal power relations." Indeed, from the slaughter of Christian Delawares by patriot militiamen in 1782 to the "extreme cultural makeover" of Hawaii by New Englanders, the story of mission expansion throughout early modern America is rife with sin and struggle for socio-cultural preeminence. Or in Gundlach's weighty words, "the realities of a sin-sick world make for a story of burgeoning missions that is not all sweetness and light. Not only did existing powers and interests complicate and compromise missionary success..., but the

---

Directions in American Religious History (New York: Oxford University Press, 1997), 141–72; and Christopher Grasso, "Appendix 3: A Note on the Historiography of the Great Awakening," in Grasso, *A Speaking Aristocracy: Transforming Public Discourse in Eighteenth-Century Connecticut* (Chapel Hill, N.C.: University of North Carolina Press, 1999), 495–98.

very structures that made the sudden spread of Christianity possible also encumbered it with difficulties. The story of early American missions is a perplexing combination of divine appointments and human dilemmas."

Tom Nettles highlights the roles of Anglo-American Baptist leaders in the modern missions movement. Featuring the efforts of England's Calvinistic Baptists to come to terms with what they called the "modern question," which asked if Christians were *obligated* to use *means* to spread the gospel through the non-Christian world, Nettles demonstrates the important role that Jonathan Edwards played in helping them answer the question affirmatively—igniting their holy fire for global missions. Edwards' writings had been raising a global missionary consciousness in Britain since the middle of the eighteenth century. His understanding of the human will and his commitment to world evangelism had softened hyper-Calvinist resistance to such work.[10] But in the 1780s and 90s, Edwards found two Baptist champions, Andrew Fuller and William Carey, among Great Britain's evangelicals. Fuller's well-known book, *The Gospel Worthy of All Acceptation* (1785), became the (Edwardsean) magna charta of the English missions movement. Carey's better-known *Enquiry into the Obligations of Christians to Use Means for the Conversion of the Heathens* (1792), in its turn, became the (Edwardsean) *vade mecum* of many early missionaries. Both books proved influential among American Baptists, too, Southern Baptists in particular, who by the late nineteenth century proved the world's most numerous missionaries. In sum, then, for Nettles, "the mission efforts of the English Baptists rode on the back of a mammoth struggle for the use of means in worldwide propagation of the gospel." And Edwards' role in addressing England's vexing "modern question" led to a boom in Baptist missions that reverberates today, as "Southern Baptist foreign mission work presently maintains over 5,000 missionaries in over 100 countries."

Fred Beuttler treats the history of missions in America from the time of the Civil War through the end of the twentieth century. Concerned that we contextualize the history of Christian missions in relation to secular history, Beuttler places it in broader frames of reference. He notes that "[m]issionary activity does not take place in a vacuum, for it is embedded in the historical context as the faith is incarnated into a new culture." Historians of missions, then, should flee from the temptation to isolate their subjects from the rest of world history, treating missionaries as disembodied ministers of the gospel. Beuttler heeds his own advice, reaping great rewards for readers mainly interested in interpreting the history of missions in light of modern political life and the forces of globalization.

Part Three of this volume, entitled "Majority Church Missions," offers the most original contribution found in the pages below. Traditionally, historians who specialized in missions paid the most attention to missionaries sent

---

[10] Important in this regard were Edwards' example as a missionary to Native American Indians and three major treatises he wrote on related topics: *An Humble Attempt to Promote Explicit Agreement and Visible Union of God's People in Extraordinary Prayer for the Revival of Religion and the Advancement of Christ's Kingdom on Earth* (1747); *The Life of David Brainerd* (1749); and *Freedom of the Will* (1754).

by Western agencies to non-Western lands. In recent decades, however, two developments have occurred that have begun to alter the orientation of this field of study: 1) the "majority church" has overtaken the Western church in size;[11] 2) the rise of social history, which focuses closely on the history of "previously marginalized groups," has yielded a "new missions history" in which non-Western peoples are receiving increased attention, both as hosts of Western missions and as missionaries themselves.[12] All three contributions to Part Three of this volume bear the marks of this new approach. They stress the roles played by Asians, Latin Americans, and Africans in the history of missions—and in global evangelicalism.

Daniel Salinas charts the history of missions and missionaries coming from Latin American countries. Noting the paucity of sources for the study of their work, he challenges up-and-coming historians "to sort through the scarce oral traditions and to find local deposits of documents scattered throughout the continent to uncover the rich and multifarious webs of personal and denominational stories" of their labors. While most scholars still assume that the Latin American mission movement arose only recently, Salinas makes clear that "Latin Americans have been involved as missionaries since the very beginning of the history of the evangelical church in the continent in the nineteenth century." They have also been involved in the theology of missions. In fact, according to Salinas, Latin American reflection on "holistic" Christian missions—i.e., missions to the whole person, body, soul, and spirit—has yielded their most important contribution to the modern missions movement. "Integral or holistic mission is, to date, the major contribution of Latin America to the theory and practice of evangelism and cross-cultural missions. . . . It is not an exaggeration to say that integral or holistic mission has been a theory of mission that Latin America has exported to the whole globe."

Richard Cook has undertaken the daunting task of summarizing the history of missions by and from the Christians of Asia. The size and scope of this assignment is made clear by Cook himself, as he notes:

> Between 1900 and 1970 the number of Christians in Asia rose from just over 20 million to a remarkable 96 million. Then, after 1970, the churches exploded. By 2000, the Christian Church had grown to over 300 million adherents and growth continued with an estimated 344 million by 2005. Projections are that by 2025 there will be nearly 500 million Christians in Asia alone.

---

[11] "Majority church" is a recent term that refers to the church in the non-Western world. Since the early 1970s, the majority of Christians has lived outside the West. Today, moreover, most full-time missionaries come from outside the West. For useful analysis of these trends, see Philip Jenkins, *The Next Christendom: The Coming of Global Christianity* (New York: Oxford University Press, 2002).

[12] See especially John Halsey Wood Jr., "John Livingston Nevius and the New Missions History," *Journal of Presbyterian History* 83 (Spring/Summer 2005): 23–40; and the entire "Special Issue on Missionaries, Multiculturalism, and Mainline Protestantism," *Journal of Presbyterian History* 81 (Summer 2003).

Such numbers stagger the minds of Christians living in the West, where most churches are declining. However, Cook does not exaggerate. Nor does he inflate the magnitude of Asian missions. The number of full-time missionaries has been shrinking in the West, but is expanding in parts of Asia—and expanding exponentially. "The number of missionaries from Korea," for example, "is rocketing, as the churches are sending out 1,100 new missionaries each year, as many new missionaries annually as all the countries of the West combined." This surge in Asian missions soon will register in the West and then will change the ways we think about the face of world evangelism. Indeed, as Cook avers, "evangelical churches in Asia may soon lead the world in missionary activity." They have much to do at home, for there are still billions of non-Christians living in Asian countries. But given the growth of Asian economies and evangelistic passions, it is only a matter of time before they are recognized as leaders of the global missions movement.

Tite Tiénou treats the topic of Christian missions from African nations, contending that African missions started as soon as the gospel found a home among the people of the continent. Such missions "focused primarily on the evangelization of [Africa] in the nineteenth and early part of the twentieth centuries," but also "extended to the rest of the world in the latter part of the twentieth century." Many in the West are unaware of this history. But scholars are now working diligently to overcome this problem and to tell the stories of missionaries from multiple parts of Africa—William Wadé Harris, Julius the Cobbler, Bokari Saba, Jacques Diassana, Mary Prow, and Ba Hawa, for example. As Tiénou makes clear, moreover, these are only the best-known of the early African missionaries. "They represent numerous other African Christians throughout the continent, known and unknown, who labored for the cause of the Christian faith with full confidence in the gospel, personal sacrifice, and much suffering." Our volume calls on scholars to incorporate such stories into their classrooms and their textbooks on the history of the Church.

Although this book is about the past, it would be woefully inadequate as a primer on the legacy of evangelical missions—and as a tribute to Dr. Woodbridge—without a word or two in conclusion about the ongoing imperative of global gospel witness. The last word is given, then, to a biblical theologian, D. A. Carson, who addresses this theme from Scripture. Stressing "three fundamental biblical truths" that should perpetuate the practice of world mission—the "sheer desperate lostness of human beings," the "sheer glory of God," and the "sheer power of the gospel of Christ crucified"—Carson concludes with a summary of the truths that have compelled sacrificial Christians' witness through the ages:

> Christians know, above all people, that by nature we were all objects of God's wrath (Eph 2:3). But we have been reconciled to God by Christ Jesus, and we urge others to be reconciled to Him, too (2 Cor 5:11–21), for in the cross, "God made him who had no sin to be sin for us, so that in him we might become

the righteousness of God" (2 Cor 5:21). . . . We have tasted so much; there is so much more to come. The power of God in the cross of Christ has begun its transforming work, but we long for the consummation of all things, the dawning of the new heaven and new earth, the home of righteousness. We long for consummated resurrection existence, when the sheer God-centeredness of everything will be our incalculable delight. . . . Until then, precisely because we have tasted something of the power of the cross, we implore men and women from every tribe and language and people and nation, "Be reconciled to God."

And so we trust that Christians will witness till their Lord returns in glory. True disciples have always done so—requiring no other reason than to fulfill the Great Commission.

PART ONE:
EARLY PROTESTANT MISSIONS

Chapter One:

PROTESTANT MISSIONS IN THE SIXTEENTH CENTURY

By Glenn S. Sunshine

"Missions" is not a word that generally springs to mind when discussing the Protestant Reformation. According to much of the literature on sixteenth-century missions, among the Protestants, only the Anabaptists took any real interest in evangelism. For example, Wolfgang Reinhard's article on "Missions" in *The Oxford Encyclopedia of the Reformation* discusses Catholic and Anabaptist missions, but says nothing about the "magisterial" Reformers.[1] James Thayer Addison comments that "The foremost leaders [of mainstream Protestantism]— men like Luther, Melanchthon, Bucer, Zwingli, and Calvin—displayed neither missionary vision nor missionary spirit."[2] Littell adds, "[W]hen Luther referred to a mission to the heathen world, he was almost always referring to the so-called Christian world. 'We have among us too many Turks, Jews, heathen, non-Christians, with both public false teaching and exasperating, scandalous life.'"[3] He contrasts this with the missionary zeal of the early Anabaptists, who traveled around as itinerant preachers, bringing the gospel wherever they went. This presumed indifference to foreign missions was not a new charge, nor is it limited to Anabaptist criticism of the magisterial reformers. Cardinal Bellarmine, for example, accused the Protestants (including the Anabaptists) of a complete failure to engage in missionary activity of any kind except to pervert the faith of good Christians (i.e., Roman Catholics). In response, Neill notes, the Protestant reformers had remarkably little to say; in fact, the sum total of their defense can be summarized in a scant three pages.[4]

---

[1] The term "magisterial" raises its own set of historiographic issues which extend well beyond the scope of this chapter. Suffice it to say that here it is used interchangeably with "mainstream" reformers to refer to Lutheran and Reformed Protestant theologians and churches.

[2] Quoted in Franklin Hamlin Littell, *The Anabaptist View of the Church: A Study in the Origins of Sectarian Protestantism*, 2nd edition, revised and enlarged (Boston: Starr King Press, 1958), 114.

[3] Ibid., 115.

[4] Stephen Neill, *A History of Christian Missions*, The Pelican History of the Church, revised edition (New York: Viking Penguin, 1986), 188–89, citing H. W. Gensichen, *Missionsgeschichte der neueren Zeit* (1961), 5–7.

These are serious charges, but the question is, are they fair? This chapter will discuss briefly the problem of Protestant foreign missions in the sixteenth century and then will address missions within Europe during the period, focusing in particular on the differences between the Anabaptists and the magisterials in their attitudes and their approaches to spreading the gospel.

Foreign Missions

It must be said that foreign missionary activity was in fact distinctly lacking among all Protestants in the sixteenth century, even among Anabaptists. In fact, Littell's complaint that Luther was more concerned with evangelizing nominally Christian Europe strikes a discordant note considering Anabaptist missionaries rarely ventured out of the confines of their own ethno-linguistic groups and never tried to convert the Jews in Europe or the Turks just beyond the borders of the Holy Roman Empire. For example, Claus Felbinger, one of the better-known Hutterite missionaries, said that the Anabaptists would go to people anywhere *that spoke their language* to spread their faith[5]—hardly a world-embracing vision! Most of the itinerant Anabaptist missionaries had regional ministries and worked exclusively to convert Catholics or magisterial Protestants to their particular vision of the gospel. The differences between the Anabaptists and the magisterials in terms of foreign missionary activity have thus been greatly exaggerated.

Several reasons for this general lack of foreign missions work by Protestants have been suggested. The worst, perhaps, was the argument offered by some of the magisterial reformers themselves, that the Great Commission in Matthew 28 applied only to the Apostles and thus that missions activity was no longer necessary for Christians.[6] On the other hand, both the Anabaptists and some magisterial reformers argued that the Great Commission was still binding, though they understood it in different ways. The Anabaptists argued that it applied to all Christians at all times and in all places. On the magisterial side, Calvin, for example, argued that the Great Commission applied only to ministers of the Word, since it was originally addressed to the Apostles.[7] Yet even while acknowledging that the Great Commission was still in effect, none of these groups or individuals engaged in foreign missions; the rejection of the Great Commission by some magisterials is thus not an adequate explanation for the lack of missionary activity.

A second line of defense focuses on the fact that the Protestants were busy fighting for their lives in Europe, with the Schmalkaldic Wars (1546–47), the French Wars of Religion (1562–98), the Dutch Revolt (1566–1609), the Thirty Years' War (1618–48), and the ever-present threat of the Turks. They thus had

---

[5] William R. Estep, *The Anabaptist Story* (Grand Rapids, Mich.: William B. Eerdmans Publishing Co., 1975), 189.

[6] Neill, *A History of Christian Missions*, 189.

[7] John Calvin, *Calvin's New Testament Commentaries*, vol. 3, *A Harmony of the Gospels Matthew, Mark and Luke*, trans. A. W. Morison, edited by David W. Torrance and Thomas F. Torrance (Grand Rapids, Mich.: William B. Eerdmans Publishing Company, 1972), 250–53.

little time or attention to spare for foreign missions. While there may be some truth to this, it still misses the mark. The Spanish were involved in the Dutch Revolt, the Armada campaign against England, the Lepanto campaign with Venice and the papacy against the Turks, the Thirty Years' War, etc., yet they also engaged in missions work in the New World and Asia. Involvement in multiple, often simultaneous, wars did not stop Spanish missionaries. While it can be argued that the Spanish Empire's resources were vastly greater than what was available to the Protestant states, the Spanish crown would be driven to bankruptcy multiple times during the long sixteenth century, however great its resources seemed to be. Further, as we will see below, magisterials did engage in evangelism within Europe, stereotypes to the contrary notwithstanding. If it was simply war or the threat of war that kept them from foreign fields, would that not also have kept them from evangelizing Europe as well?

The best explanation for the lack of foreign missions is simply the Protestants' lack of access to mission fields. Put simply, for most of the sixteenth century, Catholic powers such as Spain, Portugal, and the Italian city-states had trading connections and colonies in Asia, Africa, and the New World, while the Protestant powers did not. So while Catholics were able to engage in extensive missionary activity around the globe in the sixteenth century, Protestants had little opportunity to do so until later. In the few instances where they did have access to mission fields, the Protestants were involved in cross-cultural evangelism. In 1556, Huguenot colonists sent by Admiral Coligny to Brazil developed relationships with the native population and sought to evangelize them at the first opportunity.[8] The suppression of the Huguenots by the Catholic colonists and the subsequent collapse of the colony prevented ongoing Protestant missionary activity in that region. The English, who were attempting to establish colonies in the sixteenth century, granted a charter to Sir Humphrey Gilbert in 1578 that called for the conversion of the "poor infidels" in America.[9] It does not appear that this resulted in any missionary activity, however. It may simply have been window-dressing to make the commercial enterprise more palatable. Nonetheless, even if this is true, the fact that the clause was included in the charter indicates that the Anglicans were sufficiently aware of the opportunity and responsibility to evangelize the Native American tribes that they felt obligated at the very least to pay lip service to it, and possibly even to plan to carry it out. In practice, it seems that the first attempts to bring the gospel to the native tribes in the English colonies did not occur until twenty-six years later, and even then it began with the Puritan John Eliot.[10] Given the scarcity of Protestant colonial efforts during the sixteenth century, these examples suggest that as opportunities arose, mainstream Protestants did take an interest in foreign missions, even if the follow-through was inconsistent.

---

[8] For a full account of the colony, see Jean de Léry, *History of a Voyage to the Land of Brazil*, trans. and introduction by Janet Whatley (Berkeley, Calif.: University of California Press, 1990), especially pp. 146–47.

[9] Neill, *A History of Christian Missions*, 191–92.

[10] Neil, *A History of Christian Missions*, 191–92. On John Eliot, see chapter two below.

Foreign missions were thus a weakness for the sixteenth-century Protestants, largely because their circumstances did not give them many opportunities to evangelize unreached peoples. But what about internal missions? How did Protestants do within Europe itself? Again, the usual view is that the Anabaptists engaged in evangelism and the mainstream reformers did not. Several explanations for this difference have been suggested. First, as we have seen, the Anabaptists believed that the Great Commission was still in effect and applied to Christians, including the laity. This encouraged informal evangelistic efforts among friends and neighbors and permitted the more charismatic among the Anabaptists to begin preaching more extensively without the kind of official training or sanction that the magisterials would have required. A second explanation that has been suggested is that the Anabaptists were scattered by persecution, and this served to broaden the geographic range of their evangelistic efforts. Third, and much less commonly discussed, is the millenarianism of many of the Anabaptists. Historically, millenarianism is frequently accompanied by evangelistic fervor, and although pro-Anabaptist scholars may not want to emphasize this point, it was clearly a significant motivating factor for early Anabaptist missions. Hans Hut, for example, was described as "one of the most zealous and successful Anabaptist preachers," but Estep and others try to distance his evangelistic efforts, which they praise, from the millenarianism that motivated it.[11] The convergence of millenarianism and evangelism is evident in a number of other prominent Anabaptist missionaries as well.

Missions within Europe

While all of these elements may have contributed to Anabaptist evangelism, they are not in themselves an adequate explanation for the differences between Anabaptist and magisterial missions within Europe. First, not all the mainstream reformers believed that the Great Commission only applied to the Apostles. As noted above, Calvin saw it as part of the paradigm for ministers of the Word. Magisterial views of the Great Commission were rooted primarily in their objections to the Catholic clergy, many of whom never preached and often were not even attached to a specific church. For the magisterials, one of the primary responsibilities of ministers of the Word was preaching; further, the magisterials argued that as pastors, ministers of the Word were not to wander around but were to serve in a specific church. Itinerant Anabaptist evangelists thus fell afoul of a practical reform aimed at abuses by the Catholic clergy. Further, since the magisterial vision of the Reformation hinged on recovering proper doctrine, the mainstream reformers believed that permitting untrained lay preaching was courting disaster. Although the Anabaptists may have believed that "the common man can be better informed by [lessons from] the creatures than through writing,"[12] the magisterials emphatically did not. Thus Calvin argued that since

---

[11] Walter Klaasen, "A Fire that Spread," *Christian History* 4.1 (1985): 7–9; Estep, *The Anabaptist Story*, 76.
[12] Littell, *The Anabaptist View of the Church*, 113.

the Great Commission was given to the Apostles, only properly trained ministers of the Word—the successors of the Apostles—should preach. His vision for how the Great Commission should be carried out was thus different from that of the Anabaptists, but he certainly did not believe that the church no longer needed to be involved in preaching the gospel. The mainstream reformers used different means, but their goal was essentially the same as that of the Anabaptists: to convert people to their doctrine and practice.

As for the idea that persecution drove the Anabaptists to scatter and thus expand the geographic range of their evangelistic activities, the range of that spread can be greatly exaggerated. Again, they tended quite naturally to "scatter" primarily within their own ethno-linguistic regions. Further, persecution may explain the dispersion of Anabaptist preachers, but it does not explain the source of their missionary zeal in the early years of the movement; if anything, persecution occurred because of their evangelistic efforts, not the other way around. Indeed, persecution has also been used to explain why the Anabaptists eventually *stopped* doing missions and withdrew into their communities. For example, Latourette comments that, "[I]n the course of their history the Mennonites and other descendants of the Anabaptists became ingrowing. Originally vigorously missionary, persecution caused them to largely withdraw within themselves and to perpetuate themselves by birth rather than conversion."[13] If persecution is the cause of both the spread of Anabaptist missionary activity and its cessation, this raises the question of why one cause had two opposite effects. If persecution was the root cause of both phenomena, something must have changed within the Anabaptist communities to prompt these different responses. One possible explanation is changing millenarian expectations: as apocalyptic hopes were delayed, evangelistic zeal may have declined. More research will be needed to determine if this was in fact the case, but even taking the effects of millenarianism into account, persecution by itself does not seem to be an adequate explanation for both the rise and decline of Anabaptist missions. For example, some of the most successful Anabaptist communities were founded in Moravia, where they had been driven by persecution. But those communities thrived largely because the local nobility protected them from further persecution by the Hapsburgs, in keeping with the area's tradition of religious toleration going back to the Hussites.[14] In other words, the success of these communities depended not on persecution, but on its absence.

Thus far, none of the discussions have hit upon the crucial point that distinguishes Anabaptist and magisterial concepts of missions. The real difference between them in this as in almost all other points is their divergent ecclesiologies, particularly their understandings of the relationship of church and society. Anabaptists saw the church as an elite minority in a corrupt and evil world. To

---

[13] Kenneth Scott Latourette, *A History of Christianity*, vol. 2, *Reformation to the Present*, revised edition (New York: Harper and Row, 1975), 786.

[14] James M. Stayer, "The Radical Reformation," in *Handbook of European History 1400–1600: Late Middle Ages, Renaissance, and Reformation*, vol. 2, *Visions, Programs, and Outcomes*, edited by Thomas A. Brady Jr., Heiko A. Oberman, James D. Tracy (Grand Rapids, Mich.: Eerdmans Publishing Co., 1995), 260–62.

the Anabaptists, the church was to live out its description in Scripture as the pure and spotless bride of Christ, and most of the distinctive characteristics of the Anabaptists come from their efforts to put this principle into practice. Thus if the church is to be pure it must be made up only of those who can make a credible confession of faith and back it up by the evidence of holy lives. Since baptism is the rite by which people are brought into the church, infants obviously should not be baptized since they have neither the faith[15] nor the fruit to demonstrate that they belong to Christ. Since infant baptism is invalid, people who do come to faith should be re-baptized, or, as the Anabaptists would describe it, they should be baptized properly. In other words, the most visible distinctive of Anabaptist practice in the sixteenth century was a product of their ecclesiology. Further, to the Anabaptists, the church of necessity had to be a voluntary association, made up of people who chose to come out from the sinful world into the community of the righteous. As a result, Anabaptists rejected the idea that church and state were in any way connected; in fact, many Anabaptists questioned whether a Christian could be a magistrate at all.[16] Further, the church had high membership standards, both to get in and to remain in. Those violating the group's norms risked severe sanctions, including the ban (or "shunning"). This was the second major area of controversy between the Anabaptists and the magisterials in the sixteenth century, with the magisterials arguing that Anabaptist disciplinary practices were far too harsh. The Anabaptists responded that without these strict standards, they would allow the ungodly into the church and so introduce a stain onto the bride of Christ.

In contrast to this "Christ against culture" view,[17] the mainstream reformers believed that church, state, and society were closely interrelated. Though they differed on how these relationships should be defined, mainstream Protestants did agree on a number of foundational principles. First, they argued that the Anabaptists had confused the church on Earth with the church in heaven. Ultimately, the Church Triumphant will be pure and spotless, but the church in this world will not be. The earthly church is always and inevitably a mixed body, made up of both true and false believers. Any effort to create a "pure church" on earth is doomed to failure: true believers will inevitably be wrongly excluded, and false believers will slip through the net because it is impossible to see into the human heart. The reformers commonly cited the parable of the weeds to support this view of the church (Matt 13:24–30, 36–43). In Jesus' own explanation of this parable, not even the angels can separate the "sons of the kingdom" from the "sons of the evil one" in this world because of the harm this would do

---

[15] The idea that infants were incapable of faith was itself challenged by some mainstream theologians.

[16] The main exception to this point is arguably the disaster at Münster in 1535, where the "Revolutionary Anabaptists" took over the government and forced their laws on the entire city. This has led some critics of George Huntston Williams's distinction between magisterials and radicals to argue that the real difference was not that the magisterials believed in a state church and that the radicals didn't, but that the magisterials succeeded in setting up an alliance with the state while the radicals failed and so withdrew from society.

[17] See H. Richard Niebuhr's classic discussion in *Christ and Culture* (New York: Harper and Row, 1951), 45–82. Although he does not use the Anabaptists as an example of this position, it is an apt description of their thought on the relationship of the church and society.

to believers. Rather, the separation must wait until the final judgment; only then will the church be completely pure. The mainstream reformers thus rejected the strict membership requirements and the harsh discipline of the Anabaptists in favor of a more inclusive view of church membership, since they argued it would inevitably lead to some people being cut off from the church who nonetheless were true Christians, while others slipped through the net because we are incapable of seeing into the human heart.

This view of church membership led the mainstream reformers to a different conception of the church's role in society. These reformers drew their model for the relationship of church and state from the Old Testament. They argued that just as Israel was to be a godly society, where proper worship of God was mandated and where church and state worked together, the same should be true in their day as well.[18] Functionally, for the magisterials, this meant state churches. These took a wide range of forms, from Erastianism, in which the state controlled the church, to Calvin's Geneva, where the church had far more autonomy with respect to the civil government. Even in Geneva, however, the church was a branch of the state. Far from being a theocracy, the civil and church governments of Geneva were designed to give each authority within its own sphere and to cooperate with each other in areas where they both had a legitimate interest. Among other things, by Calvin's own regulations the pastors (including Calvin himself) were paid civil servants and could be fired on 24 hours' notice. In all areas controlled by Protestants, native born residents (except Jews) were considered members of the church and were baptized as infants, even while recognizing that this in no way guaranteed their membership in the Church Triumphant.[19]

Since the church was effectively coterminous with the state, the magisterials saw their program as a reform not simply of the church but of society as a whole. While the reformers accepted that the state would always be imperfect just as the church on Earth would never be completely pure, they nonetheless believed that it was possible to create a society built on fundamentally Christian principles. Church and state each had a role to play in promoting godliness within the society. The state was generally seen as being responsible for external behavior, including taking over from the Catholic church courts such areas as probate, family law, and contract law. The church was typically seen as being responsible for the inner life, including spiritual and moral formation and tending the consciences of believers. Each political unit worked out its own system for balancing the interests and responsibilities of church and state, but they all agreed that the two should work together toward the goal of producing a godly society. This ideal manifested itself in a myriad of ways. In keeping with humanist assumptions that education was the road to moral and spiritual reform, school systems were established, generally directed by the

---

[18] The Anabaptists, who based their theology almost exclusively on the New Testament, argued that the magisterials were Judaizers for relying on the Old Testament for their view of church-state relationships.

[19] The theology is, of course, more complex than this suggests, but for purposes of contrast with Anabaptists this oversimplification is sufficient.

churches. Churches also set up different forms of discipleship training, whether through Bible lectures, academies, or informal programs such as Martin Bucer's "Christian fellowships."[20] Reformers also addressed family life, teaching that the household, the fundamental unit of society, was a mini-church, with the father acting as pastor for the family. New institutions rationalized and consolidated the chaotic tangle of Catholic religious orders and confraternities that had earlier handled social welfare in the cities. These were generally part of the state, though the church frequently claimed an interest in charity as well. And, of course, in Geneva and other Reformed areas, church and state cooperated in social discipline with the intention of dissuading people from sin and encouraging righteous behavior. In short, the mainstream Protestants sought to engage and transform culture, with the goal of producing a godly society. The Anabaptists thought this was a fool's errand; the only godly society would be one made up exclusively of the godly, not the "mixed church" that the mainstream reformers advocated.

Given these divergent visions of the church, the missions strategies of the Anabaptists and the magisterials naturally took radically different forms. For the Anabaptists, the church's mission could only be fulfilled through intentional evangelism,[21] that is, by fulfilling the Great Commission by calling people out of the world into their churches. Although some groups had pastors and missionaries, Anabaptists in general had a less formal leadership, with little or no requirements for theological education. As a result, Anabaptists did not view evangelism as being the job of professionals; all members of the congregation were to share the faith with the people around them.[22] And as they were scattered by persecution throughout South Germany, Austria, the Low Countries, and beyond, they preached their vision of Christianity and established new church communities with a fervor born from their millenarian expectations. Although there was a great deal of diversity among Anabaptist groups, the sacral community was at the heart of nearly everything that they did. Thus, for example, during the Counter-Reformation in Austria, some Hutterites agreed to convert to Catholicism as long as they were permitted to continue as lay religious communities. The commitment was thus to sacral community, not to specific doctrine or practice. Once their churches and communities were established and millenarian expectations declined, the Anabaptists lost much of their missionary fervor. They withdrew into their communities, living largely apart from the world that they had rejected.

The early Anabaptist approach to missions thus followed a pattern modern missiologists recognize: personal evangelism, calling people into a new belief system and a new community, and so on. The magisterial strategy was quite different from this and thus has gone unrecognized by many missiologists. The

---

[20] See Amy Nelson Burnett, *The Yoke of Christ: Martin Bucer and Christian Discipline*, Sixteenth Century Essays and Studies 26 (Kirksville, Mo.: Sixteenth Century Journal Publishers, 1994), 180–207.

[21] Estep, *The Anabaptist Story*, 193.

[22] Wolfgang Schaufele, "The Missionary Vision and Activity of the Anabaptist Laity," in *Anabaptism and Mission*, ed. Wilbert R. Schenk (Scottdale, Pa.: Herald Press, 1984); cf. Nanne van der Zijpp, "From Anabaptist Missionary Congregation to Mennonite Seclusion," in *Anabaptism and Mission,* 121.

magisterials sought to sway both public opinion and governments toward their belief and practice. A complete picture of this process is, of course, impossible in a chapter of this length, and would involve not simply evangelism but political and economic considerations, anti-Italian sentiment in Germany, and a host of other issues.[23] For present purposes, however, it is important to recognize the means magisterial Protestants used to spread their ideas. The initial spread of the Reformation, particularly in the cities, illustrates three important tools used by Protestants to win people to their cause. The first of these was the effective use of printing. The Reformation was triggered by the vernacular publication of the 95 Theses, and Luther and other reformers continued to use broadsides, tracts, and treatises as a powerful means of attacking the Catholic Church and generating support for their vision of reform.[24] A second approach involved getting Protestant preachers into parish churches to preach the gospel. To pick just one obvious example, this was how Zwingli began the reform in Zurich. These two approaches together created a groundswell of popular opinion which put pressure on governments to adopt "evangelical" reforms. Governments were sometimes reluctant to go along with these changes, but popular pressure pushed them to pass legislation insisting that the "pure gospel" be preached in the churches, though it is far from clear what that meant either to the populace as a whole or to the government.[25] A third route that led town governments to adopt Protestantism was public debates between the undertrained local Catholic clergy and very highly trained Protestant pastors. Sometimes these occurred after the town was already leaning toward Protestantism, sometimes not, but in the first decades of the Reformation, the effect was almost always the same: a vote would be taken, the Protestants would win, and the city would officially break with Rome. Whatever the route, however, once the reforms were adopted, the new ideas sank deep roots into the cities.

One thing that should be noticeable in this greatly oversimplified summary of the process is the central role of trained theologians and pastors, whether as writers, preachers, or debaters. This emphasis on a professional ministry in turn led to another approach to evangelism within some magisterial churches: training and sending out missionary pastors. Calvin's Geneva is the best example of this practice. More than any other Protestant state, Geneva welcomed refugees fleeing religious persecution in their home countries. Early in the Reformation,

---

[23] Even where these other factors came into play, however, once Protestant churches were established the process of teaching the people "proper" doctrine and practice began. These secular influences on the Reformation are thus not sufficient to explain the movement toward Protestantism, since the "religious" elements were a very prominent part of the follow-up once the new churches were established.

[24] Later on, printing would continue to play a role in Protestant evangelization. For example, Calvinism initially spread in France primarily through Calvin's French language theological treatises (see e.g. Francis Higman, *Censorship and the Sorbonne: A Bibliographical Study of Books in French Censured by the Faculty of Theology of the University of Paris, 1520–1551*, Travaux d'Humanisme et Renaissance 172 [Geneva: Librairie Droz, 1979], 62, and "Index of Authors and Titles of Works in French," 181–89). The German nobleman Hans Ungnad von Sonneck attempted to spread Reformation ideas into the Balkans by publishing books in the South Slavonic languages, and thus hoped to reach the Turks as well (Neill, *A History of Christian Missions*, 190).

[25] See the discussion in Euan Cameron, *The European Reformation* (Oxford: Oxford University Press, 1991), 234–39.

the city had established a school to train pastors, which in 1559 became the Genevan Academy, the ancestor of the University of Geneva. In addition to training pastors for Geneva, however, the Academy also trained refugees and sent them back to their own countries (or in some cases to other countries) to establish Protestant churches. Most of the refugees came from France, and most of the missionaries were sent there as well, but other countries were also represented, including the Netherlands, Scotland, and England. For example, in 1561 alone, it appears that 142 missionary pastors were sent to France on 151 separate missions.[26] Not all of these were refugees: francophone areas of Berne and Geneva itself supplied so many missionaries to France that there was a shortage of pastors in these parts of Switzerland.[27] One particularly prominent example of this is Pierre Viret, who was from the Pays de Vaud and had been recruited into the ministry by Guillaume Farel. He was sent with Farel by the Bernese authorities to help protestantize Geneva prior to Calvin's arrival in the city. Once Calvin arrived in Geneva in 1536, he became fast friends with Viret. After Calvin was kicked out of Geneva in 1538 in a dispute over church discipline, Viret played a pivotal role in negotiating Calvin's return in 1541. In 1559, Viret was named one of Geneva's pastors, and his reputation at this point was comparable to Calvin's within the French Protestant community. In 1561, he seems to have become gravely ill, and so he was sent to Languedoc in the hope that it would aid his recovery. He traveled to Nîmes, where he experienced a remarkable recovery. He then began a vigorous campaign of evangelism and church-building activities in Nîmes, Montpellier, and Lyons. The evidence suggests that the illness may have been feigned, and that in any event Viret had secretly been planning an extended trip throughout France to promote the Protestant cause and strengthen the churches.[28] That so prominent a figure in the Calvinist ministry should choose to devote his later years to missionary work, together with the depletion of pastors in Geneva and the Pays de Vaud to provide missionaries to France, makes it abundantly clear that the Anabaptists were not the only Protestants concerned about missions and evangelism.

Although many of the missionary pastors from Geneva served in local churches, some of them also took positions as chaplains to Protestant nobles. This highlights yet another element of magisterial missionary strategy: working with the existing elites to spread the gospel. In keeping with the hierarchical nature of sixteenth-century society, Protestant reformers typically saw the elites as the key to advancing the Protestant cause. On one level, these were the people that ran the governments and who thus needed to be won over if states were to accept Protestant preaching. Beyond that, however, in areas such as France where the Huguenots were being actively persecuted, nobles acted as patrons for pastors and churches, provided armed protection for preaching services, and had access to the corridors of power, enabling them to win concessions for

---

[26] Robert M. Kingdon, *Geneva and the Coming of the Wars of Religion in France 1555–1563* (Geneva: Droz, 1956), 79.

[27] Ibid., 79–80.

[28] Ibid., 82–83.

Protestants from the monarchy. On a more informal level, Protestantism spread through the nobility by traveling up and down patronage networks. To give just one indication of how effective these networks could be, Janine Garrisson has demonstrated that a significant percentage of the five hundred people condemned for heresy by the Parlement of Bordeaux in 1569 were the clients of a single Protestant nobleman, Pons de Polignac.[29]

This last point highlights a final element in magisterial Protestant evangelism. Although formal preaching was supposed to be left to professionals, average believers were also active in sharing their faith. As we have seen, colonists tried to share their faith with Native Americans, and Protestants tapped into their social network as a way of spreading their faith. Once again using the example of France and Geneva, many French refugees who became residents and bourgeois of Geneva returned to France, bringing with them their new-found faith.[30] This was particularly true of the nobility, with all that implies for spreading of their faith up and down the patronage networks. And within every household, the magisterial reformers expected the father to fulfill the role of pastor, responsible for evangelizing them, leading prayers and devotions, and maintaining Christian standards of behavior. Again, the difference between Anabaptists and magisterials in lay evangelism is not as great as it is often portrayed to be. The magisterials may not have called what the lay people did preaching or evangelism, but they encouraged them to share their faith nonetheless.

There is much more that could be said about Protestant evangelism, particularly within Europe, but the major trends are clear. Lack of access to mission fields kept virtually all sixteenth-century Protestants from engaging in any systematic foreign missions; internal missions are a different matter, however. Contrary to the stereotypes, both magisterial and Anabaptist Protestants actively evangelized within Europe, though differences in their theologies, particularly their views of the relationship of the church with society, produced very different evangelistic approaches. The sectarian ecclesiology of the Anabaptists led them to reject engagement with government (for the most part) and culture, thus promoting personal evangelism and separation from the world. The magisterials' vision of church and state collaborating to produce a Christian society led them to embrace a missions approach that used the existing social and political structures to introduce Protestant ideas to both the masses and the elites, though they clearly focused more on the latter as the most effective way (as they saw it) to reach and transform their culture. Although the magisterials emphasized an educated, professional ministry, both they and the Anabaptists also encouraged lay people to spread their faith as they had opportunity. Although I have not found any reformer who exegeted the Great Commission this way, the only verb in Greek that is an imperative is "make disciples"; all the others are participles, including "go." The sense, then, is "as you go," or "wherever you go" make disciples—something that all sixteenth-century Protestants, Anabaptists and magisterials alike, certainly tried to do.

---

[29] Janine Garrisson, *Protestants du Midi 1559–1598* (Toulouse: Edouard Privat, Editeur, 1980), 22–28.

[30] Kingdon, *Geneva and the Coming of the Wars of Religion*, 84–85.

Chapter Two:

MISSIONS AMONG PURITANS AND PIETISTS

By Jon Hinkson

This chapter provides an account of missionary initiatives among English Puritans and Continental Pietists during the seventeenth and eighteenth centuries. While English Puritans made efforts to reach their own island, penetrating pagan frontiers in Wales and the Scottish Highlands, I shall examine their missionary concern for native peoples of North America—a truly cross-cultural encounter. Rather than a comprehensive yet superficial study of this enterprise, I will focus on three significant figures, John Eliot, Thomas Mayhew, and David Brainerd, looking especially at their missionary motivations and methods. In the second part of this chapter, I turn to missionary efforts among European Pietists. This is really a tale of two cities: Halle and Herrnhut. Halle was the center of the German Pietist movement that supplied the first Protestant missionaries who brought the gospel to the Orient. Particular attention will be given to Bartholomew Ziegenbalg, who was the unmistakable leader and pioneer of this mission to India. Finally I take up Herrnhut and the Moravians, who from 1732 supplied so many missionaries to the world they might almost be considered a Protestant missionary order. My focus here is on Count Zinzendorf, the leader of the Moravians, whose convictions concerning missions largely defined the nature of their efforts. In the pages to follow we will certainly see broken vessels and methods that appear far from perfect. But God has never been constrained by human inadequacy or limited by less-than-perfect methods. These missionaries themselves were well aware that their success ultimately depended on Another. God was no doubt honored by their faith as they witnessed His divine Word to the larger world.

PURITANS AND THE MISSIONARY TASK

The body of English Protestants known as "Puritans" are not usually celebrated for their missionary endeavors, and by most accounts their efforts on behalf of foreign missions seem scanty.[1] Puritan communities did not depart for foreign lands with the sole purpose of reaching non-Christians with the gospel of Christ. This is not to say they did not have a sense of urgency to herald the message of salvation, rather that this zeal found expression in home missions-preaching in parish pulpits to what they perceived to be a largely un-regenerate population. What turned Puritans into prospective cross-cultural missionaries was migration to the New World in the seventeenth century. Among their expressed motives for migration, missionary ambition is not ab-sent, but it is mentioned as simply one among many, and never seemingly the leading impulse, for moving beyond their homeland.[2] While the Massachusetts Bay Charter proclaimed the ambition "to wynn and incite the Natives of that Country to the Knowledg and Obedience of the onlie true God and Savior of Mankinde" as the "principall Ende of this Plantacion," several decades elapsed between the founding of the first settlements and the earliest missionary out-reach to neighboring native peoples.[3] This certainly argues against a primacy of missionary intent. Ameliorating this perhaps is the fact that these first settlers were largely absorbed in sustaining and stabilizing a precarious existence in a hostile wilderness. It has also been urged on their behalf that what may appear an early neglect of missions may merely have been a more passive, "simply shine" strategy-whereby natives would be drawn to the gospel by the settlers' godly comportment.[4] It is doubtful, however, that such was a conscious mis-sions strategy. For when the Puritan John Eliot finally initiated missionary work among the Indians and they asked him why the settlers had taken so long to proclaim these glad tidings, his response made no reference to any strategy but rather confessed remiss—"We doe repent."[5] Experience Mayhew described this failure as "unaccountable and inexcusable." Indeed this lassitude was all the more egregious in light of the missionary zeal of the Roman Catholic Church: "It is what more particularly calls for our Lamentation, that the Churches of the Reformation have done so little . . . while the Missionaries of Antichrist are more than can be numbered, and the Bigots are at prodigious Pains to propa-gate the Romish Idolatries."[6] Neither were New Englanders insensitive to the charge voiced in Old England by critics that not more was being done toward

---

[1] The title "Puritan" was applied to a group of Protestants within the English Church who, from the reign of Elizabeth I on, sought to eradicate "papal practices" and implement Calvinistic reforms in England.

[2] See David Cressy, *Coming Over: Migration and Communication between England and New England in the 17th Century* (Cambridge: Cambridge University Press, 1987), 74–106.

[3] Cited in Michael P. Clark, ed., *The Eliot Tracts*, Contributions in American History, Number 199 (Westport, Conn.: Praeger, 2003), 1. Plymouth Colony was established in 1620, while the Massachusetts Bay Colony was founded in 1630.

[4] Richard Cogley has dubbed this approach an "affective model." Cogley, *John Eliot's Mission to the Indians before King Philip's War* (Cambridge: Harvard University Press, 1999), 5. A better description might be "centrip-etal," whereby outsiders are drawn by the enviable blessedness of covenant privileges-akin to missions in the Old Testament. This contrasts with a New Testament "centrifugal" model, where witnesses do not simply shine, but are sent out into all the world.

[5] John Eliot, *The Clear Sun-shine of the Gospel Breaking Forth upon the Indians in New England* (1648), reprinted in Michael P. Clark, ed., *The Eliot Tracts*, 129. Hereafter *Clear Sunshine*.

[6] Experience Mayhew, *Indian Converts: or, Some Account of the Lives and Dying Speeches of A Considerable Number of the Christianized Indians of Martha's Vineyard, in New England* (Boston: Samuel Gerrish, 1727), xiv.

the conversion of the Indians. In 1642, Thomas Lechford, after briefly visiting the New World and returning to England, complained in print that no member of any Massachusetts Bay congregation had yet been commissioned to learn the native tongue or instruct the Indians in religion.[7] In response to this and similar charges, a pamphlet appeared in 1643 entitled *New England's First Fruits*, which recorded the first efforts that had been taken, admittedly mere "sprincklings of God's Spirit upon a few Indians," but hopefully "an earnest-penny of more to come."[8] The instrument of much of that "more to come" was the minister of the Roxbury congregation John Eliot, whose copious gospel labors would earn him the title "Apostle of the Indians."

John Eliot

The Puritan historian Cotton Mather reported that Eliot's first sense of calling to missionary work among the Native Americans was prompted by the seal of the Massachusetts Bay Colony, with its image of a native echoing the Macedonian's plea: "Come over and help us."[9] As a conscientious pastor of a sizable congregation, John Eliot (1604–90) had only limited time and energy for this missionary task. His zeal more than compensated for these limitations, however, and he soon acquired a working knowledge of Algonquian, the dialect of the local Massachusetts tribe. Because faith in Christ came by hearing, Eliot made preaching the center of his mission, an enterprise that began on October 28, 1646, when he preached to a gathering of natives at Waaubon's wigwam.[10] Thus was inaugurated fortnightly visits that included preaching, simple catechizing of the children, and response to questions. And the Indians had many questions for Eliot, including the painful query "What took you so long?" More encouragingly: "How may wee come to know Jesus Christ?" The answer given was to read the Bible, but since they did not have one, they were encouraged to meditate on the missionary's instruction and pray to God—"sigh and groane, and say thus: Lord make mee know Jesus Christ. . . ."[11] Modern commentators have sometimes questioned whether these Native Americans were truly converted to Christianity, pointing to how few and faint are the analogies between Puritan and native religion.[12] Eliot and his colleagues were very mindful of the

---

[7] Thomas Lechford, *Plaine Dealing: or Newes from New-England* (London, 1642), reprinted in *MHSC* 3:3 (1833): 80.

[8] [Thomas Weld, Hugh Peter, Henry Dunster?], *New Englands First Fruits* (London, 1643), in Clark, ed., *The Eliot Tracts*, 62, 67. Hereafter *First Fruits*.

[9] Cotton Mather, *The Great Works of Christ in America* (1702; reprint, Edinburgh: Banner of Truth Press, 1979), 1.556–57. Hereafter *Magnalia*. The biblical text is found in Acts 16:9.

[10] [Thomas Shepherd?], *The Day-Breaking, if not the Sun-Rising of the GOSPELL with the INDIANS in New-England* (1647), in Clark, ed., *The Eliot Tracts*, 83. Hereafter *Day-Breaking*.

[11] *Day-Breaking*, in Clark, ed., *The Eliot Tracts*, 84–85.

[12] Charles L. Cohen elucidates the alien nature of reformed Christianity to Indian conceptualities and experience and finds such prospects for acculturation unlikely: ". . . no bear-greased Augustine poured out his heart in New England's woods." See Cohen, "Conversion among Puritans and Amerindians: A Theological and Cultural Perspective," in Francis J. Bremer, editor, *Puritanism: Transatlantic Perspectives on a 17th Century Anglo-American Faith* (Boston: Northeastern University Press, 1993), 223–56, here citing 247. The question of the difficulty of "conversion" is not a new one; indeed, it was raised by Jesus' disciples: "Who then can be saved?" Jesus provided a ready response: "With man it is impossible, but with God all things are possible" (Matthew 19:25–26). Puritans believed that more

great gulf that divided their own faith and life from that of the Massachusetts. Indeed it was generally held that they could not be converted apart from being first, or at least concurrently, acculturated. As contemporary Cotton Mather expressed the challenge Eliot faced: "[H]e had a double work incumbent on him: he was to make men of them, ere he could hope to see them saints; they must be *civilized* ere they could be *Christianized*. . . ."[13]

Such language grates upon the sensibilities of our post-colonial, "enlightened" age. And rightly so. Was this concern with "civilizing" nothing other than English pride and prejudice—akin to the old insistence that Gentiles become Jews before they could be Christian?[14] Doubtless there was a good measure of this, which contributed to a limited exercise of the missionary imagination as to what an authentically native Christianity might look like. But when he did exercise such an imagination, Eliot did not see how "church" could be accomplished without at least some form of permanent, "civilized" settlement. The Indians needed to be "brought from their scattered and wild course of life, unto civill Co-habitation" to sustain a permanent pastor and practice effectual church discipline.[15] Accordingly Eliot sought to gather and settle "praying Indians" (as Indian converts real or hopeful came to be called) in their own towns so that civilization might serve as a stepping stone—"a preparative to imbrace the Law & Word of God."[16] They were to be gathered into society so God could gather them into salvation. The first "Praying Town" was established at Natick (1650), and six more would follow during Eliot's lifetime.[17]

---

transpired in conversion than acculturation. Fundamentally, it was a regenerating work of God that would manifest itself in more than "learned" responses, but in "turning doctrines into their own experience." The Spirit's "first special work is application," they believed. *Tears of Repentance, or A Further Narrative of the Progress of the Gospel Amongst the Indians of New England* (1653), in Clark, ed., *The Eliot Tracts*, 261. Hereafter *Tears of Repentance*.

[13] Mather, *Magnalia*, 1.560.

[14] Thus, James P. Ronda asserts: "The Indian who embraced Christianity, was compelled in effect to commit cultural suicide." In Ronda, "We are Well as We Are: An Indian Critique of 17th Century Christian Missions," *William and Mary Quarterly* 34 (1977): 66–82, here citing 67. James Axtell has made a similar charge in his *The Invasion Within: The Conquest of Cultures in Colonial North America* (Oxford: Oxford University Press, 1985), 330. Most extreme, George Tinker has depicted this as a form of cultural genocide. See *Missionary Conquest: The Gospel and Native American Cultural Genocide* (Minneapolis, Minn.: Fortress Press, 1993). David Howlett provides a helpful response to Tinker in "Historians on Defining Hegemony in Missionary-Native Relations," *Fides et Historia* 37.1 (2005): 17–24.

[15] John Eliot, *A Late and Further Manifestation of the Progress of the Gospel amongst the Indians in New England* (1655) in Clark, ed., *The Eliot Tracts*, 303. Hereafter *Late and Further*. The reality of this challenge is still faced by missionaries today among nomadic peoples. Jonathan Bonk, director of the Overseas Missions Study Center at Yale University, notes: "Church does not always work that well off the back of a camel" (Seminar, April 13, 2007).

[16] *Clear Sunshine*, in Clark, ed., *The Eliot Tracts*, 124.

[17] John Eliot, *A Brief Narrative of the Progress of the Gospel amongst the Indians in New-England* (1671) in Clark, ed., *The Eliot Tracts*, 402–406. Hereafter *Brief Narrative*. This resettling strategy of Eliot's Indian mission has come under the charge of being nothing more than a religious veneer for expropriating Indian lands. See, for example, Francis Jennings, *The Invasion of America: Indians, Colonialism, and the Cant of Conquest* (Chapel Hill, N.C.: University of North Carolina Press, 1975), 251, and Neal Salisbury "Religious Encounters in a Colonial Context: New England and New France in the 17th Century," *American Indian Quarterly* 16.4 (1992): 507. But as Richard W. Cogley has shown, "The mission, in fact, increased rather than diminished the property rights that praying Indians held in legal theory," for they were granted legal title to lands without having to plant or build on it. And not only in legal theory but in actuality "the mission probably expanded, rather than reduced, the territory the Massachusett and Pawtucket proselytes occupied within the bay colony." Cogley, *John Eliot's Mission*, 234, 236. Furthermore, to cast Eliot as a willful agent of Indian expropriation fits ill with his repeated defense of their land claims and his repeated warnings to colonists to do the Indians no injustice in regard to land (see ibid., 238).

These Praying Towns were organized according to a social and political model Eliot drew from Scripture and involved a civil covenant to receive religious instruction and abide by certain civil rules.[18] This, it was judged, would be conducive to the operation of the means of grace. As Eliot wrote in his *Christian Commonwealth*, "[H]e that is willing to serve Christ by the Polity of the second Table civilly, is in some Degree of Preparation to serve him by the Polity of the first Table ecclesiastically."[19] But a civil covenant to live under God's rule was not yet a church, which required careful examination of the Indians' religious convictions. Not until 1660, fourteen years after Eliot's first preaching at Waaubon's wigwam, was an Indian church gathered. "God's works among men, doe usually go slowly," remarked Eliot, not one to rush in a matter so important, "and he that goeth slowly, doth usually goe most surely. . . ."[20] A substantial source of encouragement to Eliot in his labors was his surmise that the Indians were plausibly the posterity of the lost tribes of Israel.[21] Understanding the Scriptures to hold out a restoration of Israel in the last days (based on such passages as Ezek 37; Zech 12:10; Rom 11:23), Eliot thought the Indians were included in these eschatological hopes. "If these people be under Covenant and Promise," he writes, "it is a ground of faith to expect mercy for them."[22] And the implications of this identification could be pushed both ways. For if Indians were indeed of Jewish stock, their turning to Christ could mean the ingathering of the Jews had dawned and the final glorious stage of history was at hand. The effect of these possibilities upon Eliot was the prosecution of his work, as Mather put it, "more cheerfully, or at least more hopefully."[23] If such hopes made missionary labor less laborious, it also made funding more forthcoming.

---

[18] In Eliot's mind the Praying Towns as the embodiment of scriptural society were "an experimental rehearsal" for the millennial transformation of English society. See James Holstun, "John Eliot's Empirical Millenarianism," *Representations* 4 (1983): 142.

[19] Eliot, *Christian Commonwealth*, facsimile edition (New York: Arno Press, 1972), 144.

[20] *Day-Breaking*, in Clark, ed. *The Eliot Tracts*, 81. Salisbury questions the quality of Eliot's conversions, finding native conversion narratives lacking. He notes: "There is no indication that the converts understood . . . the most basic tenets of Puritan theology." See "Red Puritans: The 'Praying Indians' of Massachusetts Bay and John Eliot," *William and Mary Quarterly* 31 [1974]: 49–50. Neither does Salisbury think that Native Americans were expected in their conversion experience "to measure up to those of the English" (ibid., 50). But as Cohen observes, having compared native and English confessions of the same period, "these tribesmen proved at least as conversant with essential doctrines as did the goodmen and goodwives of Puritan Massachusetts." See his "Conversion among Puritans," 254–255. James Axtell even contends that "admission standards of the Indian churches not only began higher than English colonial standards but remained higher throughout the seventeenth century." See his *After Columbus: Essays in the Ethnohistory of Colonial North America* (Oxford: Oxford University Press, 1988), 115. This corroborates Cotton Mather's testimony: "The churches of New England have been very strict in their admissions to church fellowship.... But they seemed rather to augment than abate their usual strictness, when the examination of Indians were to be performed." *Magnalia*, 1.512.

[21] This identification was based in part upon what were considered striking similarities between Indian and Israelite practices and characteristics such as circumcision, fondness for parable, delight in dancing, wailing in bereavement, and even aversion to swine. The argument was forwarded most intricately by Thomas Thorowgood (a delegate to the Westminster Assembly) in his *Jews in America, or Probabilities that the Americans be of that Race* (London, 1650).

[22] *Light Appearing more & more towards the perfect Day or a farther discovery of the present state of the Indians in New England*, in Clark, ed., *The Eliot Tracts*, 185. Hereafter *Light Appearing*.

[23] *Magnalia*, 1.561. For discussion on the bearing of eschatology upon Eliot's missionary endeavors, see J. A. DeJong, *As the Waters Cover the Sea: Millennial Expectations in the Rise of Anglo-American Missions 1640–1810*

In the very year Eliot would despair that the Indian work "sticks in the birth for want of means," a bill was passed in England's Parliament, energized by his and other accounts of the mission and the tantalizing possibility of the natives' Israelite heritage.[24] The result was the establishment of "The Society for the Propagation of the Gospel in New England," which has the distinction of being the oldest English Protestant missionary society.[25] For well over a century, until the War of Independence, it canvassed parishes across England and Wales for contributions, provided salaries to missionaries and provisions for Indians, printed tracts for the field and reports for the home front. Many a laborer—Eliot among them—was sustained by the offerings of London merchant and cottage dweller. By 1660, nearly £16,000 had been contributed to the Indian work. The number and range of donors does honor to England and provides a good index to the interest in North American missions at that time. That no financial contributions stemmed from New England is a puzzle and probably ought to be an embarrassment.

It was the New England Company that financed the great work of Eliot's life—the Algonquian Bible. Often he had answered the Indian query, "How may I get faith in Christ?" with the admonition: "Pray and read the Bible." And yet they had no Bible they could read. There was no way around this necessity. Eliot became the first missionary since Ulfilas in the fourth century to translate the Scriptures into an unwritten language and then teach the people how to read it.[26] Eliot spent fourteen years on the project, completing it in 1663. As he had written upon the final page of his *Indian Grammar Begun*: "We must not sit still, and look for miracles; up and be doing, and the Lord will be with thee. Prayer and Pains, through faith in Christ Jesus, will do anything."[27]

The decade after the Bible appeared was one of great spiritual harvest. But a withering frost was to descend and sweep away almost everything Eliot had accomplished: King Philip's War (1675–1678). "Praying Indians" were the especial victims of the conflict, for they were slaughtered both by their kinsmen embittered by their refusal to join them on the warpath and by many of the English incapable in crisis of making distinctions between "praying" and "preying" Indians. Eliot did all he could to preserve his native brethren, but by war's end the mission was in shambles.[28] At the age of 74 he had to begin again. And so he labored on till an age so ripe he feared his old friends, long safe in heaven ahead of him, might soon suspect by his non-appearance he had gone the wrong

---

(Kampen: J.H. Kok, 1970) and Cogley, *John Eliot's Mission*, 76–104.

[24] *Light Appearing*, in Clark, ed., *The Eliot Tracts*, 186.

[25] See William Kellaway, *The New England Company 1649–1776* (London: Longmans, 1961).

[26] Accordingly he composed *The Indian Primer, or the way of training up our Indian Youth in the good knowledge of God, in the knowledge of the Scriptures, and in an ability to Reade* (1654).

[27] *Glorious Progress of the GOSPEL amongst the Indians in New England* (1649), in Clark, ed., *The Eliot Tracts*, 95.

[28] Eliot sought not only to preserve his Praying Indians, but also to protect native war captives from being sold into slavery: "The designs of Christ in these last dayes is not to extirpate nations, but gospelize them. When we came, we declared to the world... that the indeavor of the Indians conversion, not their extirpation, was one great end of our enterprize in coming to these ends of the earth.... To sell soules for money seemeth to me a dangerous merchandize." Cited in Samuel Eliot Morison, *Builders of the Bay Colony* (Boston: Houghton Mifflin, 1930), 317.

way! At the last it was the Indian work that was upon his heart with the prayer, "Lord, grant it may live when I am dead."[29]

Eliot knew very well that all missionaries have feet of clay and those in square buckled shoes are no exception. As he confessed himself: "My doings, alas, they have been poor and small.... I'll be the man that shall throw the first stone at them all.[30]" One stone commonly thrown is that Eliot was less than an acute observer of Indian culture. But criticism must go deeper than his failure as a cultural anthropologist. For all this "Apostle to the Indians" was able to accomplish among the natives, he was ever only a part-time missionary, with the bulk of his energies expended upon the English Roxbury congregation. Even to the Praying Settlements he created he was only a periodic visitor. "Wee never thought it fit to send any of our English to live amongst them," wrote John Cotton.[31] This diminished presence greatly limited Eliot's ability to identify with the people he sought to reach. The Puritans would produce no Hudson Taylor. Happily, love covers a multitude of sins, and, on that score, in Eliot's case the Indians had no doubts. As several of them expressed to their aging spiritual patriarch:

> God hath made you to us and our nation a spiritual father, we are inexpresably ingaged to you for your faithful constant, Indefatigable labours, care and love, to and for us, and you have alwaies manifested the same to us as wel in our adversity as prosperity, for about forty years makeing known to us the Glad tidings of Salvation of Jesus Christ.[32]

Thomas Mayhew Jr.

Eliot's missionary endeavors are often compared with those of his contemporary, Thomas Mayhew Jr., (c.1620–57) upon Martha's Vineyard.[33] The Mayhew family settled on the Vineyard in 1641, and Thomas, Jr., having acquired competency in the native dialect began preaching to the local Massachusetts by 1643 (three years before Eliot first preached at Waaubon's wigwam). A native, John Hiacoomes, found himself especially drawn to "the English God," and began to meet with Mayhew every Lord's day to hear him explain the Christian faith. One of the great obstacles for the gospel on the Vineyard was the fear exerted upon the tribe by the "Pawwaws," native diviners who exercised spiritual and healing power, or in the description of the Puritans: "such as cure by devilish sorcery and to whom the devil appears sometimes."[34] While many Indians were attracted to the Creator God proclaimed by Mayhew, few thought they could afford to cut themselves off from the Pawwaws' curative powers, much

---

[29] *Magnalia*, 1.578, 577.

[30] Ibid., 1.577.

[31] John Cotton, *The Way of the Congregational Churches Cleared* (London: Matthew Simmonds, 1648), 1.79.

[32] John Ford, ed., *Some Correspondence between the Governors and Treasurers of the New England Company in London and the Commissioners of the United Colonies in America* (London: Spottiswoode & Co., 1896), 74.

[33] For Mayhew's life see Lloyd C. M. Hare, *Thomas Mayhew, Patriarch to the Indians* (New York: Appleton, 1932).

[34] *Glorious Progress*, in Clark, ed., *The Eliot Tracts*, 148–49. See also Experience Mayhew, *Indian Converts*, 9.

less expose themselves to their terrible wrath if offended. Others simply reckoned the Englishman's God a poor exchange: "Shall I throw away these thirty-seven gods for one?" The decisive breakthrough came when Hiacoomes, who had been edging toward faith, took a public stand, declaring that he did *not* fear the Pawwaws and that "because he did believe in God and trust in him . . . all the Pawwaws could not do him any hurt...." This courageous step emboldened his fellows: "Though before I was afraid of the Pawwawes," testified one, "yet now because I hear *Hiacoomes* his words, I do not fear them, but believe in God too."[35] Such defection the Pawwaws did not let pass unavenged, and Hiacoomes was made the special object of their malice and magic. One Pawwaw later testified to "having often employed his God, which appeared . . . in the form of a snake, to kill, wound, or lame . . . *Hiacoomes* . . ., all which prov'd ineffectual." Indeed, discovery that the old gods' powers were impotent against this greater might prompted the Pawwaw to declare himself for "the true God."[36]

And so the gospel advanced upon the Vineyard, with what the natives perceived as real spiritual power.[37] But if the gospel came in power, it seems significant that its spokesman did not. Whereas Eliot was identified as part of the Massachusetts Bay power structure, behind which was a well-armed, rapidly growing English population with expanding land needs, Mayhew's situation was very different. When he began his missionary efforts in the 1640s, there were only 65 English settlers on the Vineyard, in contrast to between 1,500 and 3,000 Wampanoags. By the eve of King Philip's War, the settlers on the Vineyard had increased to 180, but the native population was still over 1,000.[38] Further, Martha's Vineyard, as a largely isolated offshore island, was not caught up in King Philip's War, and so escaped the ravages that virtually destroyed Eliot's work by poisoning native-settler relations. That the community of Praying Indians on Martha's Vineyard would become the largest in New England, perhaps has much to do with the fact that the natives there did not feel threatened by the settlers, neither were they killed or incarcerated in a terrible and deadly conflict.

As with Eliot, Thomas Mayhew Jr., (and later his father Thomas Mayhew Sr.) gathered Indian converts into their own native churches rather than assimilating them into English congregations. This lack of integration naturally raises the question of bigotry, even racism.[39] But it appears the reason for not integrating congregations was neither cultural contempt nor racial prejudice, but rather linguistic necessity. Few Indians understood English; fewer English

---

[35] *Light Appearing*, in Clark, ed., *The Eliot Tracts*, 178.

[36] Experience Mayhew, *Indian Converts; Or Some Account of the Lives & Dying Speeches of a considerable Number of the Christianized INDIANS of Martha's Vineyard* (1727), 7. Hereafter *Indian Converts*.

[37] It is not clear that Mayhew intentionally targeted the Pawwaws as a missionary strategy. In the providence of God, Mayhew's prayers for the sick proved effectual, whereas the Pawwaws' efforts were unavailing, and the public challenge to harm Hiacoomes failed despite their concerted efforts. Clearly this power encounter of Pawwaw and Puritan was the lynchpin, but it seems more a matter of Hiacoomes' chutzpa than Mayhew's method.

[38] Statistics from James P. Ronda, "Generations of Faith: The Christian Indians of Martha's Vineyard" *William and Mary Quarterly* 38.3 (1981): 370. See also *Magnalia*, 2.430.

[39] Simmons describes these native churches on the Vineyard as "separate" and "subordinate," remarking that "neither the father, nor the son, nor the converts themselves discussed the possibility of integrating converts within the English community." See his "Conversion from Indian to Puritan," *William and Mary Quarterly* 52.2 (1979): 214.

could comprehend Algonquian, and, as the substance of the Sabbath assembly was hearing and heeding the Word of God, comprehension was critical. English settlers on the Vineyard professed that but for the language barrier, they would gladly have received Indian pastors,[40] and we know of an instance when English pastors were not at hand, an English congregation "very chearfully" received the Lord's Supper administered by John Tackanosh—ordained teacher of the Indian church of which Hiacoomes was pastor.[41] For all their foibles, the Puritans did not have the coherent option in their theology for racism, for aborigine was no less a human and creature of God than Englishman, neither any less an heir of salvation upon faith and repentance. There was never a need in Puritan New England to argue for the humanity of the native peoples as was required of Bartolomé de Las Casas in Spanish America.[42] Neither did they hesitate (it seems) to move toward indigenization of Indian missions. By the end of the seventeenth century there were 37 Indian preachers in Massachusetts.[43]

In 1657 Thomas Mayhew Jr., and an Indian convert boarded a ship bound for England that was never seen or heard from again. Mayhew's father could not endure the thought of the loss of both his son and the Indian work. So at the venerable age of sixty-five, Thomas Sr., took up the mantle of his son. He preached to the Native Americans every week for the rest of his life—another 25 years. The patriarch spared no pains or fatigues, "sometimes traveling on Foot nigh twenty Miles thro' the Woods to preach and visit."[44] When Thomas Mayhew Sr., died, the work was taken up by grandson John (1652–88), and in turn by great grandson Experience (1673–1758). By that time there were around sixteen hundred professing Christian Indians on Martha's Vineyard.[45] Thomas Mayhew Jr.'s prayer that the Indian ministry would "be a fruitful glorious spreading Vine" had been answered.[46]

David Brainerd

While Thomas Mayhew Jr., was the most successful among Puritan missionaries, none would possess the subsequent celebrity of David Brainerd (1718–47). Brainerd's missionary career had a peculiar origin. Intending to become a pastor, he entered Yale College and, bouts of malady and melancholy notwithstanding, managed to attain the promise of top academic rank. But just prior to graduation he made the indiscreet remark that his tutor had "no more grace than a chair," and he found himself expelled with all prospects for a pastoral post lost.[47] Instead, Brainerd resolved to devote his life to the salvation of

---

[40] *Magnalia* 2.432.

[41] Experience Mayhew, *Indian Converts*, 16.

[42] See Pierce Beaver, "Methods in American Missions to the Indians in the 17th and 18th centuries: Calvinist Models for Protestant Foreign Missions," *Journal of Presbyterian History* 47.2 (1969): 147.

[43] Ford, ed., *Some Correspondence*, 84.

[44] Experience Mayhew, *Indian Converts*, 298.

[45] *Magnalia*, 2.430.

[46] *Light Appearing*, in Clark, ed., *The Eliot Tracts*, 184.

[47] See Norman Petite, "Prelude to Mission: David Brainerd's expulsion from Yale," *New England Quarterly* 49.1 (1986): 28–50.

the Indians, and he was thereafter commissioned by the Society in Scotland for the Propagation of Christian Knowledge (SSPCK) in 1742. The commissioners found their man "armed with a great deal of self-denial and animated with noble zeal."[48] He had need of every bit of both, for in the four short years of his missionary career he would often labor under strain of solitude and sickness, indeed he was already slowly dying of tuberculosis contracted during his college days. Brainerd began his labors among the Housatonics in western Massachusetts. He was determined to "burn out in one continued flame for God,"[49] even while placing no hope of success in his own sacrificial exertions: "To the eye of reason, everything that respects the conversion of the heathen is as dark as midnight; and yet I can't but hope in God for the accomplishment of something glorious among them."[50]

By hope of "something glorious," Brainerd referred to a sovereign and mighty work of God for the conversion of the Indians. The stirrings of spiritual awakening were evident in many corners of New England in the 1730s and early 1740s. Churches were witnessing a great ingathering of souls, with men and women experiencing deep conviction and professing renewed commitment to Christ. "God seemed to have gone out of His usual way in the quickness of His work," noted Jonathan Edwards. "When God in so remarkable a manner took the work into His own hands there was as much done in a day or two, as at ordinary times, with all endeavors that men can use, and with such a blessing as we commonly have, is done in a year."[51] This "Great Awakening" (as it was later called) changed missionary strategy. The flames of revivalism demonstrated that "civilization" need not precede salvation, but rather could proceed out of it. This insight brought with it newfound confidence that conversion, even of the Indians, need not be a long process if God should will it. Who knew but that God might work Indian conversion suddenly?[52]

Brainerd's missionary hope was remarkably fulfilled after two years of largely fruitless itinerant preaching. In August 1745, as Brainerd preached among the Delaware Indians at Crossweeksung (New Jersey), he noted among his hearers an unusual earnestness, a hanging upon his words as though they knew them to be their very life. As he daily declared the love of Christ and entreated sinners to come to the Savior, he found his voice almost drowned out by penitent sobs and

---

[48] Cited in R. Pierce Beaver ed., *Pioneers in Mission* (Grand Rapids, Mich.: Eerdmans,1966), 108. For the SSPCK, see Frederick V. Mills Sr., "The Society in Scotland for the Propagation of Christian Knowledge in British North America 1730–1775," *Church History* 63.1 (1994): 15–30.

[49] Cited in Joseph Conforti, "Jonathan Edwards' Most Popular Work: 'The Life of Brainerd' and 19th Century Evangelical Culture," *Church History* 54 (1985): 195.

[50] Jonathan Edwards, "The Life of David Brainerd," in *The Works of Jonathan Edwards*, vol. 7, ed. Norman Pettit editor (New Haven: Yale University Press, 1985), 254. Hereafter *Life of Brainerd*.

[51] Jonathan Edwards, "Faithful Narrative of the Surprising Work of God" (1737), in *The Works of Jonathan Edwards*, vol. 4., edited by C. C. Goen (New Haven: Yale University Press, 1972), 159.

[52] As John Freeman writes of Brainerd: "Consigning the 'civilization first' argument to the devil, he placed his dependence on God, looking upon Indian culture as a hindrance only to the missionary." See his "The Indian Convert: Theme and Variation" *Ethnohistory* 12.2 (1965): 122. This shift in missions strategy away from "civilization first" is also observed by Laura M. Stevens, *The Poor Indians: British Missionaries, Native Americans and Colonial Sensibilities* (Philadelphia: University of Pennsylvania Press, 2004), 141.

anguished groans of souls in travail. Some fell to the ground "much melted," others cried out for mercy and a new heart. As his journal records:

> The power of God seemed to descend upon the assembly 'like a rushing mighty wind,' and with an astonishing energy bore down all before it. I stood amazed at the influence that seized the audience almost universally, and could compare it to nothing more aptly than the irresistible force of a mighty torrent, or a swelling deluge, that with its insupportable weight and pressure bears down and sweeps before it whatever is in its way![53]

So "surprising" and "so entirely supernatural" was this work, it attested, in Brainerd's mind, to God's utter sovereignty in salvation: "I never saw the work of God appear so independent of means.... And although I could not but continue to use the means I thought proper . . . yet God seemed (as I apprehended) to work entirely without them: so that I seemed to do nothing, and indeed to have nothing to do but to 'stand still and see the salvation of God.'. . ."[54]

Brainerd baptized those who seemed soundly converted, and they became the beginning of a growing flock. But while a new people were being raised up to spiritual life, the missionary was dying in the final stages of tuberculosis. His brother John took his post while Brainerd sought medical help in Boston. But it was too late. He died at 29 years of age in the home of Jonathan Edwards. Edwards' eighteen-year-old daughter Jerusha, nursing him at the end, contracted the dreaded disease and followed Brainerd to the grave.

But Brainerd's service in the cause of missions was by no means over. He left at his death a diary that inspired countless numbers of men and women to the cause of missions. Brainerd's example was not simply a stimulus to become a missionary, but a pattern of how to carry out the missionary task. Just as the spiritual harvest at Crossweeksung vindicated Edwards' theology of awakening, so Brainerd's life exemplified Edwards' theology of true spirituality—it supplied an answer incarnate to the question, "What are distinguishing signs of truly gracious and holy affections?"[55] Many a novice missionary would set off to the field armed with Bible and Brainerd. And many a seasoned veteran kept a worn copy near at hand. William Carey voiced common sentiment when he called the *Life of Brainerd* "almost a second Bible."[56] Yet an irony has been identified at the heart of Brainerd's legacy—that his elevation of faithfulness displaced fruitfulness as the goal of the missionary, and so made success irrelevant if only the

---

[53] Edwards, *Life of Brainerd*, 311, 308.

[54] Ibid., 310, 315.

[55] Jonathan Edwards, *Religious Affections*, edited by John Smith (New Haven: Yale University Press, 1959), 191.

[56] See Joseph Conforti, "Jonathan Edwards' Most Popular Work," 188–201; Andrew Walls, "Missions in Historical Memory: Jonathan Edwards and David Brainerd," *Jonathan Edwards at Home and Abroad*, edited by David W. Kling and Douglas A. Sweeney (Chapel Hill, N.C.: University of North Carolina Press, 2003). On the impact of *Life of Brainerd* on missionary strategy, see Jan Douglas Maxwell, "Civilization or Christianity? The Scottish Debate on Missions Methods, 1750–1835," *Christian Missions and the Enlightenment*, edited by Brian Stanley (Grand Rapids, Mich.: Eerdmans, 2001), 123–140.

course of self-denial be endured.[57] There is evidence from Brainerd's example, however, that faithfulness may well have affected the fruitfulness of his labors. One of Brainerd's first Indian converts is reported to have said, accounting for how she came to faith, "Brainerd loved his Heavenly Father so much that he was willing to endure hardships, travelling over mountains, suffering hunger and lying on the ground, that he might do [our] people good. . . ."[58] As this testimony suggests, at least some Indians were able to believe that Christ suffered for them because Brainerd suffered to tell them so.

PIETISTS AND THE MISSIONARY TASK

The Danish-Halle Mission

On November 29, 1705, Bartholomew Ziegenbalg (1683–1719) and Heinrich Plutschau boarded the Princess Sophia Hedwig bound for India.[59] It was an historic moment, for in their departure they became the first Protestant missionaries to embark for non-Christian lands for the single design of winning them to Christ. Though subsequently celebrated, their action was at the time quite controversial. Missions ran against the grain of Lutheran belief and practice of the day. Lutheran theologians deemed evangelistic enterprise as "meaningless . . . if not directly heretical."[60] It is thus ironic that initiative in missions would emerge from within Lutheranism, and not at the initiative of clergymen, but through the leadership of King Christian IV of Denmark.

At the dawn of the eighteenth century, Denmark was the only Lutheran territory that possessed foreign dominions composed of "heathen" peoples. Tranquebar, the destination of Ziegenbalg and Plutschau, was a colony on the Coromandel coast of India comprising some 250 Europeans, but 25,000 local Tamils. King Christian believed it his royal obligation to bring the gospel to this non-Christian population. Accordingly, in one sense the mission may be

---

[57] See David L. Weddle, "The Melancholy Saint: Jonathan Edwards' Interpretation of David Brainerd as a Model of Evangelical Spirituality," *Harvard Theological Review* 81 (1988): 317. Note Brainerd's statement on this subject: "[W]as satisfied that if not one of the Indians should be profited by my preaching . . ., yet I should be accepted and rewarded as faithful." Edwards, *Life of Brainerd*, 285.

[58] Reported in a letter of Rev. Cutting Marsh (July 1, 1864), cited in Thomas Brainerd, *The Life of John Brainerd, the Brother of David Brainerd and His Successor as Missionary to the Indians of New Jersey* (Philadelphia: Presbyterian Publishing Co., 1865), 461.

[59] The best modern narrative accounts in English of the Danish-Halle Mission to India are E. Arno Lehman, *It Began At Tranquebar* (Madras: Christian Literature Society, 1956) and Erich Beyreuther, *Bartholomaeus Ziegenbalg* (Madras: Christian Literature Society, 1955).

[60] Jens Glebe-Møller, "The Realm of Grace Presupposes the Realm of Power: The Danish Debate about the Theological Legitimacy of Mission to the Heathen," in *It Began in Copenhagen: Junctions in 300 Years of Indian-Danish Relations in Christian Mission,* edited by George Oomen and Hans Raun Iversen (Delhi: ISPCK, 2005), 161. For orthodox Lutherans, foreign missions were suspect on at least three counts: First, it was held that the gospel had already been preached in all the world (Rom 10:18), leaving no further obligation; second, it was judged impermissible to preach the gospel in territories under control of another sovereign; finally, it was held that legitimate ministry required a prior "call" from the existing flock of a region, something that pioneer missionaries could not obtain. On these prevailing convictions, see ibid., 169–172.

seen as an expression of the prevailing principle of "cuius regio eius religio."[61] But while this territorial principle established the theological warrant, both king and missionaries had a vision not restricted to the colony, and in this they diverged from Lutheran orthodoxy. Ziegenbalg and Plutschau, along with the royal chaplain Lütkens who held King Christian's ear, belonged to a renewal movement within Lutheranism known as Pietism. The Pietists found the solid but often arid doctrinal exactitude of Wittenberg—the centre and symbol of Lutheran orthodoxy—lacking in spiritual vitality and barren of works expressive of real Christian faith. Halle—the home of Pietism—by contrast promoted warm-hearted devotion abounding in enterprises of practical charity. So when the king sought missionary candidates, it was to Halle he turned, and to the Pietist leader August Hermann Francke.[62] Francke recommended two of his students for this challenging assignment, Ziegenbalg and Plutschau. His discernment in this matter proved excellent, for the thirty-year-old Plutschau would show patient tenacity, and Ziegenbalg (though seven years his junior) would demonstrate natural leadership and a fiery ardor. In this collaboration of royal Danish sponsorship and Halle manpower the Danish-Halle Mission was born.

The two missionaries arrived in Tranquebar in early September 1706. Although they carried the king's commission, they received no cooperation from the local authorities, as the colony was governed by the Danish East India Company, which operated strictly for economic interests, caring not the slightest for the promotion of Christianity. Indeed Hassius the governor regularly opposed the missionaries when he thought their actions might threaten profits, and on one occasion he even imprisoned Ziegenbalg for four months. The missionaries wondered whether the mission would not fare better under a Muslim governor; they feared martyrdom, not at the hand of the Tamils, but through the complicity of Hassius. Yet this persecution by the authorities bore providential fruit, for the more the missionaries fell foul of their European hosts, the more the local Indians tended to look upon them with sympathy.

"Our chief care," wrote Ziegenbalg only days after landfall, "was now to learn the Malabarian language."[63] Here the younger of the missionaries was in his element, and with enormous energy and singular ability he applied himself to Tamil. Inviting a 70-year-old Hindu teacher to hold his class in the missionary lodgings, Ziegenbalg took his place with the young pupils and formed his letters in the sand alongside them. In a matter of only months Ziegenbalg attained tolerable fluency, and in less than a year spoke so masterfully that locals listened in amazement. In the months that followed, he also began to amass and digest classic works of Tamil culture, 112 texts during his first two years, and 300 by the

---

[61] "Whoever reigns establishes religion for the realm." Anders Nørgaard makes this point in "The Missions Relationship to the Danes" in It Began in Copenhagen, 46–49. See also page 45 below.

[62] August H. Francke (1663–1727) was the successor of Philipp Jakob Spener as leader of Lutheran Pietism. Through his leadership, Halle emerged as a center of Pietist theology and as the home of a multitude of charitable endeavors, including the far-famed orphanage.

[63] Letter of Sept. 12, 1707 in Ziegenbalg, Propagation of the Gospel in the East: Being an account of Two Danish Missionaries Lately sent to the East-Indies for the conversion of the Heathens in Malabar ... (London: J. Downing, 1709), 66.

next. This reading and research culminated in his encyclopedic *Genealogie der malabarischen Götter*.[64] He also sent courteous letters to thoughtful, respected Hindus, soliciting their impressions and objections to Christianity.[65] Their responses made it clear that the message of the missionaries would have to make its way against powerful prejudices. "One of the most obstinate prejudices," writes Ziegenbalg, "is the *abominably wicked Life of Christians here*. This has inspired [Hindus] with an utter Detestation & Abhorrency of all Notions, that seem to border upon Christianity; supposing the Christians to be the vilest and most corrupted People under the Sun."[66] He dubbed the colonists "Atheistical Christians" and "our false Christians and superficial Pretenders." But an even greater obstacle to evangelization was the issue of caste.[67] Any Hindu who converted to the Christian faith was rendered an outcast, which meant they could no longer converse, eat or drink with anyone, "so that such must, in a true literal Sense," writes Ziegenbalg, "*forsake Wife, Children, Houses, Lands, Friends, &c.* which is a Degree of Faith, few or none of them could ever arrive to." And "as for the rich & great," the cost of conversion was so steep "*that it is easier for a camel,* &c."[68] Ziegenbalg's first baptized convert was Watthiar Kanabadi who, when his family discovered his conversion, locked him up, threatened him with death, and even tried to poison him.

What strategies did the missionaries employ in the face of such challenges? While they preached to all and any who would give them a hearing, they determined to focus upon the young, "for those who are grown up in their Idolatry, I conceive that in the main, no great Good can be done upon them." But, "those who are train'd up in the Christian Religion from their Youth, it is to be hoped, may prove good Christians in their Age. . . ."[69] Accordingly, within two years of their arrival in India, the Pietist missionaries opened a "Charity School," com-

---

[64] Francke declined to publish the manuscript, declaring that the missionaries had been sent out to supplant heathen superstition, not spread it in Europe. The work was not printed until 1867. For an English translation, see *Genealogy of the South Indian Deities* (London: Routledge Curzon, 2005). On Ziegenbalg's achievement see Hans-Werner Gensichen, "'Daring, in order to Know': the Contribution of Christian Missionaries to the Understanding of Hinduism, 1550–1850," *Indian Church History Review* 20.2 (1986): 92–94.

[65] Many of the replies received along with the dialogues which transpired are found in Ziegenbalg's *34 Conferences between the Danish Missionaries and the Malabarian Bramans (or heathen priests)*(London: H. Clements, 1719).

[66] Ziegenbalg, *Propagation of the Gospel* (1709), 57. And apparently Hindus regarded the colony Christians not simply wicked but disgusting: "The Law of the Christians is holy, just and good," wrote one Hindu remarkably, "and did you but abstain from your eating of cow's flesh, spitting in your Houses, and some other daily nastiness committed by you; and on the contrary accustom yourselves to washing your Bodies more often . . . we assure you the whole Nation would have nothing to say against your discipline . . ." Ziegenbalg, *34 Conferences*, 324.

[67] Ziegenbalg, *Propagation of the Gospel* (1709), 55–56. Ziegenbalg's attitude toward caste is somewhat controverted. Stephen Neill opines that while Ziegenbalg did not think that the caste system could be completely abolished, he refused to let it prevail within the church. *A History of Christianity in India 1707–1858* (Cambridge: Cambridge University Press, 1985), 36. And yet in the New Jerusalem church (built 1718) seating was by caste, Sudras occupying the center nave, the transcept left to Pariahs, who also only followed their caste superiors to the Lord's Table. For other perspectives, see Duncan Forrester, *Caste and Christianity: Attitudes and Policies on Caste of Anglo-Saxon Protestant Missions in India* (London: Curzon Press, 1980), 18, and Brijraj Singh, *The First Protestant Missionary to India: Bartholomaeus Ziegenbalg (1683–1719)* (Oxford: Oxford University Press, 1999), 60.

[68] Ziegenbalg, *Propagation of the Gospel in the East: Being a Collection of Letters from the Protestant Missionaries* (London: J. Downing, 1718), 58.

[69] Ibid.

mitted to cultivate literacy, provide Christian instruction, and train prospective laborers such as catechists and teachers. Ziegenbalg was hopeful that such an instance of indiscriminate neighbor love as a charity school would do much to subvert diehard prejudice against Christianity. In the first years, children for the school were recruited from the Tamil congregation or "purchased" from families or kidnappers.[70]

The curriculum was certainly Christian, with a heavy dose of Bible and Luther, but not exclusively Christian, for the Tamil classics were taught notwithstanding their Hindu worldview.[71] Eager to affirm Tamil culture where he could, Ziegenbalg did not shy from challenging it either. The Bible used was Ziegenbalg's own translation of the New Testament in colloquial Tamil, completed in November 1711.[72] The charity school's classrooms were cross-caste, and the same food was consumed by all together. Radically divergent from the surrounding culture was also the equal inclusion of girls (similar curriculum, separate classroom). This "may well have been the first school in India for girls' education," perhaps even "the first girls' school in Asia."[73] About five years into their educational enterprise the missionaries had five schools running with nearly 100 children enrolled.[74]

With schools established, the missionaries turned their sights to founding a theological seminary—"our greatest hope."[75] Ziegenbalg's vision was to raise up indigenous gospel laborers who would be far more effective than foreign missionaries. The doors opened to the "College of Missionaries" on October 23, 1716, with eight students enrolled. In the years that followed, the seminary trained many Tamils who went on to exercise leadership in the Indian church, including Aaron of Cuddalore, the first native to be ordained (1733).[76] With five schools, one seminary, two printing presses, and a growing number of converts (many cut off from a livelihood and in need of support), the resources required to keep such a full-service mission operating were substantial. And they would also of necessity be almost entirely foreign. "We have indeed put up an *Alms-Box* in our House," writes Ziegenbalg, "but we find nothing in it but what we put in ourselves."[77] The financial lifeline with Europe was maintained through an extensive correspondence. Letters elaborating the mission were directed to

---

[70] "We must buy such Children (and this now and then at a high Rate too)," writes Ziegenbalg, ibid. This sounds horrific but was actually a humane act, for the unwanted children who were being sold were likely to be far better off acquired by the missionaries, and so enrolled in the school-orphanages.

[71] See Ziegenbalg, *Propagation of the Gospel in the East* (1718), 83–99.

[72] Ziegenbalg also completed an Old Testament translation through the book of Ruth by the time of his death. See ibid., 101.

[73] Singh, *The First Protestant Missionary to India*, 3, and Iversen, *It Began in Copenhagen*, 10.

[74] Letter of Jan. 3, 1714, indicates 92 children spread across five schools, three Tamil, one Portuguese, and one Danish. Ziegenbalg, *Propagation of the Gospel in the East* (1718), 112.

[75] Ibid., 157.

[76] Both Ziegenbalg's curriculum for his schools and his commitment to a seminary have been hailed as reflecting an instinct for indigenization. It appears that Ziegenbalg believed that natives could embrace Christianity without entirely giving up cultural roots. For the degree to which a distinctively Indian Christianity did indeed emerge, see D. Dennis Hudson, *Protestant Origins in India: Tamil Evangelical Christians 1706–1835* (Grand Rapids, Mich.: Eerdmans, 2000).

[77] Ziegenbalg, *Propagation of the Gospel* (1709), 38.

Halle, where Francke would collect, edit, and print them as *Remarkable Reports from East India*. By their regular appearance (both in German and English translation) they constituted "the first Protestant missionary magazine in the world."[78] They were widely consumed with great interest and resulted in all manner of contributions—money, medicines, even a printing press. Especially popular was the opportunity to sponsor a child at the orphanage.

But not everyone on the home front was eager to support the expansive needs of the Danish-Halle Mission. Some challenged the missionaries and their strategy behind this plethora of kingdom enterprises. The most significant critic was Christian Wendt, who as chairman of the Danish Mission College and controller of the funds, could not be ignored. Wendt had a clear and dogmatic sense of what Ziegenbalg and his team needed to do, namely return to an "apostolic" pattern, which meant, for Wendt, being unencumbered by private property and foreign finance. Rather than be consumed in costly services, missionaries should restrict themselves to itinerant preaching and live off the alms of converts. "Everything which hinders you from going out among the non-Christians and from orally proclaiming the Gospel must be destroyed, must fall away & disappear," Wendt insisted.[79] In keeping with this philosophy, Wendt withheld the funds directed to the mission by the Danish king and other donors, convinced that European financing would inevitably reproduce "European Christianity" in India.[80] Ziegenbalg, too, was convinced that significant principles were at issue. For him both the nature of man and the call of the gospel demanded a wide-ranging ministry. "As the body is bound to the soul," wrote Ziegenbalg,

> so precisely is the service of the body connected with the service of the soul, and these cannot be separated from each other. This work demands the service of the whole man. If I deny such service, I deny that in which the Scripture places the proper manner of faith and love.[81]

Into this gridlock of principles the king finally intervened, Wendt was removed, and the crisis averted. But the long conflict had taken a heavy toll on Ziegenbalg, and by all accounts was the chief factor in his death on February 23, 1719, at age 36. He left behind a church of 250 baptized members, two small sons, and a young wife, who five months later gave birth to a third child. While on the field he had consulted daily a memorandum that stated: "For this reason

---

[78] Lehman, *It Began at Tranquebar*, 103. The first publication of missionaries' letters by Francke was in 1707 under the title "Halle Correspondence" and subsequently "Halle Reports," which appeared in nine thick volumes from 1713 to 1767, containing 108 issues.

[79] Cited in Beyreuther, *Bartholomaeus Ziegenbalg*, 74–75.

[80] There is a ring of modern missiological wisdom to Wendt's concern, and it is possible that Ziegenbalg was a little too ready to open mission coffers to those who claimed to be needy converts. On the substance of such concerns, see Jon Bonk, *Missions and Money: Affluence as a Western Missionary Problem* (Maryknoll, N. Y.: Orbis, 1991). In his defense, surely Ziegenbalg was right to insist that those who by their conversion lost all lifesupport ought not to be allowed to starve. It is also difficult to direct wisely a mission from halfway around the world, with next to no knowledge and absolutely no experience of local conditions.

[81] Letter to Wendt, Aug. 15, 1718. Cited in Lehman, *It Began at Tranquebar*, 87.

we are made Christians, that we should be more bent upon the Life to come, than upon the present."[82]

For all Ziegenbalg and his colleagues accomplished, they saw their labors as merely preparatory. "We do nothing as yet but break the Ice, that those who come after us, may find a Way beat out for them," he wrote.[83] The way they did beat out proved in many ways a promising path. "Much of the 'indigenization' and 'contextualization' that became commonplace in late twentieth-century missions," asserts one scholar, "had been developed by the first Lutheran missionaries at Tranquebar on their own pietistic terms over 200 years earlier."[84] An Indian scholar has posed the question of how Ziegenbalg could have been so vehement a critic of Hinduism and yet have been so well-loved by Hindus, and answers that he was "totally free of considerations of race, colour, nationality or any other such divisions that exist between human beings," and that in a colonizing world "Ziegenbalg was not a colonist."[85] Not a bad legacy for a path-breaker.

Moravian Missions

One place Ziegenbalg's Tranquebar letters were read was in the hearing of an eight-year-old boy, the young Count Nicholas von Zinzendorf (1700–60), in whom they stirred an early missionary impulse that would come to extraordinary fruition. But it would not be as an individual missionary like Eliot or Brainerd, or even as the leader of a small team like Ziegenbalg that his impact would be exerted. It would be as captain of a great missionary host. In the early 1720s Zinzendorf began to grant asylum on his estate in Saxony to a group of religious refugees from Bohemia. The settlement came to be called "Herrnhut" (meaning "The Lord's Protection") and the community the "United Brethren" or Moravians. There was a deep piety and spiritual joy to the Herrnhutters. They loved to sing at work and worship. "We are the Savior's happy people," Zinzendorf once declared.[86] As much as Herrnhut afforded a cherished refuge for the community, their maxim bred a foundational commitment to Christ's service: "Where there is presently most to do for the Savior; that becomes our home."[87]

The first place the Moravians found something to do for the Savior was the Caribbean island of St. Thomas. The call arose in the form of a negro slave named Anthony Ulrich, whom Zinzendorf had met at the coronation of King Christian VI of Denmark. Anthony had told the Count of his people in St. Thomas without Christ and, as slaves, without hope of being reached unless one were willing to assume their condition. This fearful prospect did not discourage the Herrnhutters, and on August 21, 1732, a potter named Dober and a car-

---

[82] Ziegenbalg, *Propagation of the Gospel* (1709), 55.
[83] Ziegenbalg, *Propagation of the Gospel in the East* (1718), 77.
[84] Iversen, *It Began in Copenhagen*, 9.
[85] Singh, *The First Protestant Missionary to India*, 2, 163.
[86] Cited in A. J. Lewis, *Zinzendorf the Ecumenical Pioneer* (London: SCM Press, 1962), 73.
[87] Cited in Karl-Wilhelm Westmeier, "Zinzendorf at Esopus: The Apocalyptical Missiology of Count Nicolaus Ludwig von Zinzendorf—A Debut to America," *Missiology* 22.4 (1994): 431, note 29.

penter named Nitschmann were commissioned and left for St. Thomas, sent off with hymns and prayers. Thus Moravian missions were born. When they arrived, they stammered to the slaves in broken Creole that they were precious in God's sight and that He had shed His blood for their salvation. Their amazed hearers clapped their hands for joy in what proved a great responsiveness on the island. But as many a Caribbean slave found the Savior, many a Moravian missionary found the grave—160 in the first 50 years.[88] Yet as swiftly as they fell they were followed by more, eager to fill their ranks.

Zinzendorf was especially concerned, not of the death toll, but of the response rate. In the first six years of ministry on St. Thomas, 300 people, comprising one-tenth of the total inhabitants, had become Christians. The source of anxiety for the Count was that mass conversion, as had been the pattern in Europe, made not *Christians*, only *Christendom*. The last thing Zinzendorf wanted was to duplicate the situation in Europe. Such would simply "do the greatest Piece of Service to the Devil."[89] Furthermore, Zinzendorf's expectations for conversion were governed by his eschatology. Large-scale genuine conversion would not take place before the full ingathering of the Jews, brought on by the appearance of Jesus the Messiah whom they had pierced (Zech 12:10).[90] Given that this eschatological epoch had not yet been reached, Zinzendorf believed that all one could expect to gain among unbelieving Jews and Gentiles was a small number of converts, a "First Fruits"—a prior advance on the full harvest to come.[91]

How then were these first fruits to be gleaned? At the heart of the Moravians' missions methodology was the conviction that it is the Holy Spirit who both sends out missionaries and stirs up seekers. The Moravians believed the Spirit went out in advance of them to find single souls chosen by God to be the Bride of the Lamb. The classic biblical models for Zinzendorf were Cornelius and the Ethiopian eunuch (Acts 10 and 8, respectively), in whom "the Holy Spirit has done everything beforehand; everything invisible, . . . out of which faith may arise. . . . The word falls into prepared soil, . . . and is nothing other than the explanation of the truth which already lies in the heart."[92] Accordingly the missionary goes out to discover where the Spirit has done His prior drawing work and simply explains that work to the seeker. This perspective was reflected in Zinzendorf's first encounter with Shikellimy, a tribal chief of the Oneida Indians. Claiming an intimate acquaintance with God, Zinzendorf informed him he had come to reveal this knowledge to the Indians. "Where, or in what tribe I would

[88] J. E. Hutton *A History of Moravian Missions* (London: Moravian Publications Office, 1922), 49.

[89] Zinzendorf, "Zinzendorf's Account of His Experience among the Indians," in *Memorials of the Moravian Church*, ed. and trans. by William C. Reichel (Philadelphia: J. B. Lippincot, 1870), 1.118.

[90] On Christ's appearing to the Jews, see Zinzendorf's homily "Du Zeichen des Menschen-Sohns, Erscheine dem Israel nach dem Fleisch, ehe Du in den Wolken kommst" (Aug. 8. 1747) in *Texte zur Mission*, ed. Helmut Bintz (Hamburg: Friedrich Wittig Verlag, 1979), 110–113, especially page 111.

[91] Zinzendorf writes "We believe in general that the Time of the Heathen is not yet come. For it is believed in our Church that the Conversion of the Jews, & of all Israel must needs go before, ere the proper Conversion of the Heathen can go forward. And we look upon all what has been done hitherto, even by ourselves among the Heathen, *as first fruits only*...." Zinzendorf, "Zinzendorf's Account," 1.116.

[92] Zinzendorf, *Nine Public Lectures on Important Subjects in Religion Preached in Fetter Lane Chapel in London in the Year 1746*, ed. and trans. by George W. Forell (Iowa City, Iowa: University of Iowa Press, 1973), 51.

begin to teach, I had not yet determined; it being my custom . . . to instruct only such as God Himself had already addressed, and who felt the need of someone to interpret to them the meaning of the words He had spoken."[93]

Armed with this conviction that the Spirit was everywhere wooing a bride for the Lamb, Moravians went throughout the world in search of converts. Their missionaries endured the chilling frosts of Lapland and the sweltering heat of Guinea, they journeyed to the Samoyeds and the shores of Ceylon, they proclaimed glad tidings to Buddhist Calmucks and Persian Kurds, to Tartars and Hottentots. Few of these missionary ventures were fruitful, but the Moravian Brethren were not overanxious about results. "[W]e are not to be very concerned about the bride which the Holy Spirit courts in this world for Jesus Christ. . . . He is sure of her." Neither did the missionary carry the burden of spiritual awakening, for this is "never the responsibility of the preacher."[94] Accordingly if the Spirit does not turn resistance to responsiveness, the missionary may legitimately withdraw and move on. As Zinzendorf directed in "Method with the Jews" (1742), "don't engage in disputation, rather read in the person's face whether the veil still lies over the heart, and if so let him go."[95] The same went for the unbelieving Gentiles: "Work directly with no heathen," writes Zinzendorf, "in whom you fail to find a favorable disposition toward a righteous nature...." For it is to seekers like the biblical character Cornelius that "Christ sends His messengers. . . ."[96]

The practices of Moravian missionaries did not always conform to Moravian mission strategy, however. Many missionaries demonstrated remarkable perseverance even when ready-ripened fruit was not apparent. This was the case in their mission to Greenland, which began in 1733. The icy climate seemed mirrored in the Eskimo hearts, and in five years the missionaries still had not a single sheaf of first fruits to show for their troubles. A final breakthrough did come, and in a manner that helped to clarify what became the distinctive of the Moravian way. One of the missionaries was busily translating a passage from the Gospels when some Eskimos asked him what he was doing. He proceeded to explain, but then stopped, picked up the manuscript and began to read aloud—it was Matthew's account of Christ's agony upon the cross. The Greenlanders listened transfixed. Previously, the missionaries had discoursed about the fall of man and the plan of salvation, and their hearers had merely wondered, but through the bare recounting of Gethsemane and Golgotha, they wept. It was the first fruits of Greenland. "Henceforth," concluded the missionaries, "we shall preach nothing but the love of the slaughtered lamb."[97]

This experience and lesson drawn confirmed Zinzendorf's suspicion that the reason why many missionaries fail is that rather than preaching Christ they give lectures in theology, and he directed the Brethren straightway to set forth

---

[93] Reichel, ed., *Memorials of the Moravian Church*, 87.

[94] Zinzendorf, *Nine Public Lectures*, 30, 517.

[95] Cited in Peter Vogt, "The Attitude of 18th Century German Pietism towards Jews and Judaism: A Case of Philo-Semitism," *Covenant Quarterly* 56 (1998): 23.

[96] Zinzendorf, "Brief an den Missionar Johann Ernst Geister," in Bintz, ed., *Texte zur Mission*, 36.

[97] Cited in Hutton, *A History of Moravian Missions*, 73.

Christ, especially and evocatively dwelling on his passion.[98] Like an "audacious" artist, "we paint before people's eyes portraits of the cross," urged Zinzendorf. "What happened to Thomas must befall them. They must be thunderstruck by the Passion Story; by the doctrine of the wounds...."[99]

This method of simply narrating Christ's passion found vindication for Moravians by its seeming success upon the field. When Henry Rauch arrived among the Mohicans in Shekomeko (1740), he straightway told them of the shed blood of Christ, then lay down before them, exhausted from his journey, and fell asleep. Tschoop, one of his Indian hearers, later reminisced: "I could not get rid of his words. They continually recurred to me; and though I went to sleep, yet I dreamed of the blood which Christ had shed for us." Rauch's words of the cross proved effectual for Tschoop, and he himself drew the lesson for the missionaries: "[B]rethren, preach to the heathen, Christ, & his blood, & his death, if ye would wish to produce a blessing among them."[100]

When they preached, they proclaimed the blood of Christ, but Moravians did not typically begin their missionary work with public preaching. As Zinzendorf directed his missionaries: "Do not begin with public preaching, but with a conversation with individual souls who deserve it, who indicate the Saviour to you. . . . If it is desired of you, then also witness to each man the Gospel publically."[101] Zinzendorf's own practice conformed to this principle, which was in conscious contrast with the Puritan model. On his first meeting with the Iroquois Indians in 1742, he told them he had "a different method" from the others who came. "[I] begged them to have patience with me, in case I failed at once to preach long sermons." Instead he asked to be permitted "simply to sojourn" among them "until such time as we should have mutually learned each other's peculiarities."[102]

This mutual learning Zinzendorf thought necessary to reverse the Indians' negative impressions of Europeans. The hope was that the winsome behavior of the missionaries would prompt their native hosts to ask, "How is it that you are not like the other people?", affording the opportunity to tell of "what our Lord Jesus does for and with poor humans. . . ."[103] This approach was more than mere show, for Zinzendorf directed missionaries never to act in a culturally superior way. They were never to rule over non-Christians, even "in the smallest of externals," but rather to look for every opportunity to "humbly place themselves under

---

[98] Zinzendorf's successor Spangenberg described and defended this approach in his *An Account of the Manner in which the Protestant Church of the Unitas Fratrum, or United Brethren, preach the Gospel and carry on the Missions among the Heathen* (London: H. Trapp, 1788). Intriguingly, he finds support for the Moravian approach in the experience of the Danish-Halle missionaries at Tranquebar (ibid., 69–80).

[99] Zinzendorf, "Homily" (August 8, 1747), in Bintz, ed., *Texte zur Mission*, 112. "Passion" here is literally "torture" (*Marter*)—a typically Moravian intensification of the language of Christ's physical suffering. See, for example, *The Moravian Mission Diaries of David Zeisberger 1772–1781*, ed. Herman Wellenreuther and Carola Wessel (University Park, Pa.: Penn State University Press, 2005), 266.

[100] Spangenberg, *An Account of the Manner*, 63.

[101] Cited in David A. Schattschneider, "'Souls for the Lamb': A Theology for the Christian Mission According to Count Nicolaus Ludwig von Zinzendorf and Bishop August Gottlieb Spangenberg" (Ph.D. Diss., University of Chicago, 1975), 77.

[102] Zinzendorf, "Zinzendorf's Account," 65.

[103] Cited in Westmeier, "Zinzendorf at Esopus," 427.

them."[104] Neither were they to measure according to the cultural norms present at Herrnhut. Apart from the demands of the gospel, the Indians were to be allowed to remain Indians. This proved difficult, of course, for cultural assumptions and prejudices cling like shadows. But the Moravians did try. At the first Moravian mission in Shekomeko the missionaries lived in wigwams, the chapel was made of birch bark, and the Herrnhutters were even occasionally mistaken for Native Americans. But quite soon the settlements were laid out in straight German rows, with a tight schedule kept to the sound of a bell. And yet many Indians were drawn to the Moravians and to the Christian Savior by their witness. David McClure, a SSPCK missionary among the Delaware, reckoned the Moravians had "the best mode of Christianizing the Indians."[105] And indeed, their mission settlements in colonial America flourished and multiplied until caught in the crossfire of the French and Indian War, when the progress and promise burnt to ashes.

Yet taken globally, Moravian efforts were remarkably fruitful. Before William Carey set sail for Serampore in 1792, Moravian missionaries had already gathered 14,976 souls for the Lamb (as they put it).[106] Given such prodigious results, four years after Zinzendorf's death in 1760, the Moravians officially rejected his "First Fruits" doctrine. As his successor Spangenberg reflected: "[I]t was not for us to limit the grace of our Lord Jesus Christ."[107] Zinzendorf, too, had come to realize his notion of first fruits had been far exceeded. As he lay dying he joyfully exclaimed: "I only asked for the first fruits among the heathen, and a thousand have been granted me. What a grand caravan there must be now before the throne of the Lamb."[108]

Equally impressive was the number of Moravian missionaries who traveled around the world to gather this spiritual harvest. In most Protestant churches of the eighteenth century, if missionaries were known at all they were an exotic, largely isolated singularity. Not so the Moravians. Theirs was a missionary congregation in which each and every person was mobilized for ministry, with perhaps one in every twelve members of the Moravian community becoming a foreign missionary.[109] Thus it was that the greatest missions impact of the eighteenth century was paradoxically exerted by one of the smallest churches with negligible resources. But there was no place given to pride. "For who are we," Spangenberg reminded his Brethren, "that God should count us worthy to make any use at all of us? . . . we are unprofitable servants, we have done that which was our duty to do."[110]

---

[104] "Brief an den Missionar Johann Ernst Geister" (1732) in Bintz, ed. *Texte zur Mission*, 37. For Zinzendorf's cultural sensitivity, see David A. Schattschneider, "Moravians' Approach to the Indians: Theories and Realities," *Unitas Fratrum* 21/22 (1988): 41.

[105] Franklin B. Dexter, ed., *Diary of David McClure* (New York, 1899), 46.

[106] The Moravian General Synod of 1789 listed conversion numbers as follows: Danish West Indies: 6,690; British West Indies: 6,820; South America: 312; North America: 200; Greenland: 891; Labrador: 63. This list was not comprehensive of all the fields. See Hutton, *A History of Moravian Missions*, 202.

[107] Spangenberg, *An Account of the Manner*, 52.

[108] Cited in Hutton, *A History of Moravian Missions*, 186.

[109] See J. Herbert Kane, *A Concise History of the Christian World Mission* (Grand Rapids, Mich.: Baker, 1978), 79.

[110] Spangenberg, *An Account of the Manner*, 109.

Chapter Three:

EVANGELICAL REVIVAL AND THE MISSIONARY AWAKENING

By Timothy George

At the end of the sixteenth century, Robert Bellarmine, the famous Counter-Reformation controversialist, drew up a list of eighteen marks of the true church, one of which was its missionary outreach. Writing one hundred years after the voyages of Christopher Columbus and Vasco de Gama, in the wake of the Council of Trent and the reinvigoration of various religious orders—the Franciscans, Dominicans, Augustinians, and above all the newly created Society of Jesus—Bellarmine could rightly claim that the Catholic faith, formerly confined largely to Europe, had indeed spread to the four corners of the world. By contrast the Protestants, Bellarmine said, lagged far behind. The "heretics," as he called the Protestants, were good at subversion and perversion but not conversion.

> But in this one century the Catholics have converted many thousands of heathens in the New World. Every year a certain number of Jews are converted and baptized at Rome by Catholics who adhere in loyalty to the Bishop of Rome; and there are also some Turks who are converted by the Catholics both at Rome and elsewhere. The Lutherans compare themselves to the Apostles and the evangelists, yet though they have among them a very large number of Jews, and in Poland and Hungary have the Turks as their near neighbors, they have hardly converted even so much as a handful.[1]

Though there had been missionary impulses within the Protestant Reformation, it would be another two hundred years before the launching of

---

[1] Robert Bellarmine, *Controversiae*, Book 4; quoted in Stephen Neill, *A History of Christian Missions* (Baltimore, Md.: Penguin Books, 1964), 221.

the worldwide missionary movement. This missionary movement would usher in what Kenneth Scott Latourette has called "the great century" of Christian advance, the most concentrated and expansive extension of the world Christian movement in the history of the church. It would also challenge the constitutional basis of the Reformation settlement, the famous principle of *cuius regio, eius religio*[2] agreed upon at the peace of Augsburg in 1555, and further confirmed in the Treaty of Westphalia which ended the Thirty Years' War in 1648.

Andrew Walls has said that "the modern missionary movement is an autumnal child of the Evangelical Revival."[3] The purpose of this chapter is to explore some of the connections between these two renewal impulses, especially as they came together in the life and work of William Carey, the Baptist shoemaker-pastor whose forty-year ministry in India opened up a new epoch in the history of Christian missions. Carey himself was a keen student of the history of missions, and he saw his own efforts not as something new and totally unheard of, but rather as a part of the extension of Christ's Kingdom represented by the earlier missions of Augustine to England, Patrick to Ireland, Columba to Scotland, Boniface to Europe, Cyril and Methodius to the Slavs, and the more recent breakthrough among the Pietists.

The Pietists, especially the Moravians, were the true missionary pioneers of the eighteenth century. They carried the gospel to Greenland, translating the New Testament into Eskimo in 1766; to the West Indies where they preached without discrimination to slaves and took up the cause of their liberation; to South India and Ceylon where they planted churches, established schools, and encouraged the development of small-group Bible studies (*collegia pietatis*) on the model of Philipp Jakob Spener and August Hermann Francke in Germany. Back in England, Susanna Wesley heard about the work of the Danish Pietist missionaries in South India at Tranquebar, and in her weekly instruction of her children she made them aware of this outpost of Christian witness. When her son John was appointed as a missionary to Georgia under the Society for the Propagation of the Gospel, she remarked, "Had I twenty sons, I should rejoice that they were so employed, though I should never see them more."[4] Susanna's instruction bore fruit not only in John Wesley's ill-fated missionary career in Georgia, but also in his lifelong support for the missionary cause throughout the world. When the founder of West Indian Methodism, Nathaniel Gilbert, visited England in 1756, he brought with him several recently converted products of the mission. When Wesley met them on a preaching mission in London, he noted in his *Journal* that Gilbert's converts, "two negro servants and a mulatto," appeared to be "much awakened." "Shall not God's saving help be made known to all nations?" Wesley asked.[5]

---

[2] "Whoever reigns establishes religion for the realm."

[3] Andrew Walls, "The Evangelical Revival, the Missionary Movement, and Africa," in *Evangelicalism*, eds. Mark A. Noll, David W. Bebbington, and George A. Rawlyk (New York: Oxford University Press, 1994), 310.

[4] Quoted, Walter J. Noble, "Wesleyan Evangelicalism and the Modern Missionary Movement," in William K. Anderson, ed., *Christian World Mission* (Nashville, Tenn.: Commission on Ministerial Training, 1946), 46.

[5] Ibid.,48.

The Literature of Expectation

The missionary awakening of the 1790s and the early nineteenth century flamed forth from the sparks ignited in the 1730s and 1740s at Aldersgate, Northampton, Cambuslang, Moorfield, and Bristol. The rise of the missionary movement among evangelicals in the Anglo-American world is often marked by a sermon Carey preached in Nottingham at the annual meeting of the Northamptonshire Baptist Association on May 31, 1792. The text of Carey's "deathless sermon," as it came to be called, has not survived but there are several reports of it. By all accounts, it had a palpable effect on those who heard it. Taking his text from Isaiah 54 where God is portrayed as speaking to Israel as to a disconsolate widow, bereft of children, sitting in sackcloth and ashes at the gates of Jerusalem, God tells her to burst into song, to rejoice, to shake herself from the dust and to begin, as it were, an ambitious building program:

> Enlarge the place of thy tent, and let them stretch forth the curtains of thine habitations. Spare not, lengthen thy cords, and strengthen thy stakes, for thou shalt break forth on the right hand and on the left; and thy seed shall inherit the Gentiles, and make the desolate cities to be inhabited. Fear not (Isa 54:2–3).

The sermon came to a crescendo in a summarizing couplet, eight syllables, six words, "two plain, practical, pungent, quotable watchwords," as John Clifford once described them: "Expect great things. Attempt great things." Later biographers of Carey embellished his admonition by adding "from God" and "for God" to these two lines, but Carey's own God-intoxicated theology would not have required such explicit references to the deity. In a sense, both the "expecting" and the "attempting" were "*from* God" and both were also "*for* God," that is, for his praise, honor, and glory—*Soli Deo Gloria*!

In fact, Carey's famous sermon was merely one of several calls to missionary action during this period. Nine years earlier, Thomas Coke, the indomitable juggernaut of Methodist missions, had published his *Plan of the Society for the Establishment of Missions Among the Heathens* (1783). In the Anglican world, David Brown, a chaplain in the East India Company, and Charles Grant, one of the Company's officials, issued *A Proposal for Establishing a Protestant Mission in Bengal and Bihar* (1787), though chaplains who worked under the aegis of the East India Company were prohibited from evangelizing native peoples for fear that such work would be "bad for business." However, Carey's word "expectation" tapped into a deeper impulse stemming from the earlier revivals on both sides of the Atlantic.

The growing cult of literacy, and the opportunity of mass producing printed books and tracts inexpensively, helped to create an eager international readership of religious writings, a community of discourse eager to learn about recent movings of the Spirit in both familiar and faraway places. Jonathan Edwards' *Faithful Narrative of the Surprising Work of God*, describing the revival at

Northampton in the 1730s, was a best seller on both sides of the Atlantic. By the mid-eighteenth century, the postal system within the British empire was at least as good as ours is today and, though Amazon.com had not yet been conceived, local printers, booksellers, and colporteurs abounded. Thus arose a literature of expectation that helped to create a sense of solidarity and a world-visionary mentality among believers in disparate places touched by the spiritual impulses of the revival movement, including the passion and the theology of the three giants of the era—Wesley, Whitefield, and Edwards.

Let us look briefly at three classic works from this literature of expectation, each of which greatly influenced the missionary awakening. Two of these books originated in New England and came from the prolific pen of Edwards; the third is Carey's own plan and appeal for a new missionary initiative.

David Brainerd, like Robert Murray McCheyne in the nineteenth century, lived for Christ with such abandon in his few years on earth that he seemed in retrospect like a meteor against the night. Converted in 1739 during one of the Connecticut revivals inspired by Whitefield's preaching, Brainerd was expelled from Yale College for making an intemperate comment about the rector who had forbidden the students to attend Whitefield's meetings. Brainerd had said that this man had "no more grace than a chair." Still, he was ordained by the revivalistic Presbyterians and commissioned to preach to the Indians under the auspices of the Scottish branch of the Society for the Propagation of Christian Knowledge. Engaged to Jonathan Edwards' daughter, Jerusha, Brainerd died in Edwards' home, leaving behind his diary which recorded his missionary work among the Indians of New York, New Jersey, and Pennsylvania. Two years later in 1749, Edwards published Brainerd's story in his *An Account of the Life of the Late Reverend David Brainerd*.

It is hard to overemphasize the influence of Brainerd's biography on those who took up the missionary cause in subsequent generations. This was one of the few books Carey took with him on board the ship to India, re-reading it so often that he could quote it by heart. Edwards' account of Brainerd's labors in the "hideous and howling wilderness" of the New World also inspired Henry Martyn, a younger contemporary of Carey who, like Brainerd, never lived to see his thirty-third birthday, and whose own missionary exploits in India and Persia made him an evangelical icon throughout the nineteenth century. Martyn's journal, like Brainerd's, also became a classic of evangelical devotion. Martyn's indebtedness to Brainerd is reflected in these words:

> Read David Brainerd today and yesterday, and find as usual my spirit greatly benefited by it. I long to be like him; let me forget the world and be swallowed up in a desire to glorify God. Read Brainerd. I feel my heart knit to this dear man, and really rejoice to think of meeting him in heaven.[6]

---

[6] Constance E. Padwick, *Henry Martyn: Confessor of the Faith* (London: InterVarsity Fellowship, 1953), 49.

One year before Brainerd's diary came out, Edwards published another book that was to have an incalculable impact on the rise of the missionary movement. Its full title was

> *An Humble Attempt to Promote an Explicit Agreement and Visible Union of God's People Through the World, in Extraordinary Prayer, for the Revival of Religion, and the Advancement of Christ's Kingdom on Earth, Pursuant to Scripture-promises and Prophecies Concerning the Last Time.*

In this book, Edwards refers to a concert of prayer throughout the chief cities of Scotland and encourages others to support this effort. Thirty-six years after its initial publication in Boston, John Erskine, one of Edwards' correspondents in Scotland, included a copy of it in a parcel of books he sent to John Sutcliff, a Baptist pastor in Olney. The reading of Edwards' treatise ignited a fire in Sutcliff's heart. Sutcliff must have fastened on Edwards' commentary on this text: "Who knows but that the generation here spoken of, may be this *present* generation?"[7] In response to Edwards' challenge, Sutcliff called on his fellow Baptists to join in a concert of prayer, following the lead of "their Scottish brothers of the previous generation." Sutcliff brought out the first edition of Edwards' treatise published in England.

Though Sutcliff did not endorse every aspect of Edwards' eschatology, he did share a sense that his generation was indeed living on the very edge of time. (Significantly, Carey preached a series of weekly sermons on the Book of Revelation during his pastorate in Leicester prior to his departure for India.) Sutcliff projected a 250-year gradual advance of the gospel that, if carried out with "amazing and unparalleled progress," could conceivably usher in the millennium by the year AD 2000! According to this projection, the purity of the church would be restored among the Protestants in the half century from 1750 to 1800; the Roman Catholics would come to the full light of evangelical truth from 1800 to 1850; the Muslim world and the Jewish people would be converted from 1850 to 1900; and during the twentieth century the whole heathen world would be enlightened and accept the Christian faith (throughout all parts of Africa, Asia, America, and *terra australis*). Then all things would be so adjusted and settled that "the world thenceforth should enjoy a holy rest, or sabbatism."[8]

The Baptist churches of the English Midlands responded to Sutcliff's call to prayer and, for nearly ten years prior to Carey's departure for India, hundreds of believers, divided into small bands in their respective cities, towns, villages, and neighborhoods, met at the same time to offer up united prayers for the outpouring of God's spirit and the extension of the gospel unto the ends of the earth. These "praying societies" began within the Baptist fellowship, but soon encompassed believers across various denominations. Thus a treatise written

---

[7] *The Works of Jonathan Edwards* (Edinburgh: Banner of Truth Trust, 1974), 2:291.

[8] Iain H. Murray, *Jonathan Edwards: A New Biography* (Edinburgh: Banner of Truth Trust, 1987), 306.

by a New England Congregationalist in support of Scottish Presbyterians and reprinted by English Baptists inspired a new generation to launch a world missionary movement.

The deep-seated concern to carry the gospel to those who had never heard it gave urgency to the missionary call. A century after Carey's mission to India, Hudson Taylor, a former medical student who founded the China Inland Mission, reflected this view when he spoke to students in 1894: "There is a great Niagara of souls passing into the dark in China," he exclaimed. "Every day, every week, every month they are passing away! A million a month in China they are dying without God."[9]

Carey perused reports of the Moravians and collected much information from the private libraries of learned friends. The centerpiece of the *Enquiry*[10] was Carey's survey "of the present state of the world," divided by continent, country, and religion. Here he brought together in comprehensive overview the results of his reading and study over the past ten years. His survey was as complete and accurate as the best information available to him would allow. In this work he laid the foundations for the modern science of missiology. His survey was a forerunner of the *World Christian Encyclopedia*[11] and other indispensable resources for mission research today.

But Carey was concerned not only to present objective information for discussion and reflection; his treatise was a trumpet call to action. He called on his fellow Christians to "exert themselves to the utmost"—in fulfilling the Great Commission. He answered in detail the various objections he expected to be raised against such a far-flung missionary endeavor. The objections had to do with distance, the barbarism of uncivilized peoples, dangers to the missionary, the difficulties of making a living, and learning a new language so far away from home. He replied to each of these objections, combining an idealism of absolute commitment with the most practical realism possible. For example, the missionary is not simply to "trust the Lord"; he is also to know how to "cultivate a little spot of ground." He should understand husbandry, fishing, fowling, and the like. Preferably, married couples should be sent together to form a community of mutual support and care. In this way a self-supporting mission station could become the nucleus for the evangelization of an entire region or country. But above all, the missionaries must be persons "of great piety, prudence, courage, and forbearance; of undoubted orthodoxy in their sentiments," men and women of God who will "enter with all their hearts into the spirit of their mission."[12]

The *Enquiry* had a direct influence on the formation of the "Particular Baptist Society for the Propagation of the Gospel among the Heathen" at Kettering in October 1792. The following summer, on June 13, 1793, William Carey, his wife

---

[9] Quoted, Paul A. Varg, "Motives in Protestant Missions, 1890–1917," *Church History* 23 (1954): 71.

[10] *An Enquiry into the Obligations of Christians to Use Means for the Conversion of the Heathens.*

[11] *World Christian Encyclopedia,* 2 vols., 2nd ed., David Barrett, George Kurian, and Todd Johnson (New York: Oxford University Press, 2001).

[12] Carey's *Enquiry* has been published as an appendix in Timothy George, *Faithful Witness: The Life and Mission of William Carey* (Birmingham, Ala.: New Hope, 1991).

Dorothy, and their four children, including a nursing infant—baby Jabez—sailed from Dover on a Danish ship headed for India. At the commissioning service for the missionaries held at the Baptist meeting house in Olney, John Sutcliff's congregation, the closing hymn had sounded the note that would characterize not only the life of Carey but also thousands of others who would follow in his footsteps over the next two centuries:

> And must I part with all I have,
>   Jesus, my Lord, for Thee?
> This is my joy, since Thou hast done
>   Much more than this for me.
>
> *Yes, let it go:* One look from Thee
>   Will more than make amends
> For all the losses I sustain,
>   Of credit, riches, friends.[13]

Theology of Missions

One of the most famous incidents in Carey's early ministry occurred when he was still a young pastor trying to feel his way into Baptist circles. At a ministers' fraternal, he had proposed as a topic for discussion, "the duty of Christians to attempt the spread of the Gospel among heathen nations." The presiding minister, the venerable John Ryland, Sr., is reported to have said, "Young man, sit down. When God pleases to convert the heathen, he will do it without your aid or mine!" A later tradition says that the elder minister referred to Carey as a "miserable enthusiast" for even raising such an issue.[14]

To be called an "enthusiast" in the eighteenth century was about as derogatory a term as could be hurled against someone suspected of fanaticism, irrationality, and unconstrained zeal. When the Reverend Sydney Smith wanted to say something pejorative about the missionary movement, he declared that it was "enthusiastical." William Carey and all his cohorts were "canting hypocrites and raving enthusiasts."[15] However, Carey's brash suggestion that serious consideration should be given to taking the message of Christ halfway around the world was not only an over-the-top comment of a hot gospel preacher boy, it also posed a serious theological challenge to the reigning orthodoxy of the day.

In the first place, the missionary imperative as interpreted by Carey and others posed a hermeneutical crisis for those who had accepted the standard reading of the Great Commission, namely, that Jesus had given the original missionary commandment to His apostles and their immediate successors and that it was no longer binding on the contemporary church. This interpretation was

---

[13] Leighton Williams and Mornay Williams, eds., *Serampore Letters* (New York: G. P. Putnam's Sons, 1892), 13.
[14] Cf. George, *Faithful Witness*, 53. For more on this important encounter, see Tom Nettles' discussion in chapter five below.
[15] Stuart Piggin, *Making Evangelical Missionaries 1789–1858* (London: Sutton Courtenay Press, 1984), 65.

by no means peculiar to the leaders of English Dissent such as John Ryland, Sr. Martin Luther himself could be cited in favor of this interpretation, and in 1651 the University of Wittenberg went on record affirming that Jesus' command to evangelize the nations had been a special assignment restricted to His apostles accompanied by "special, immediate, extraordinary gifts" that had long since been exhausted in the history of the church.[16] So ingrained was this interpretation of the Great Commission that it had come to be reflected in the hymnody of the church, including this anti-missionary refrain:

> Go ye into all the world,
>> The Lord of old did say
> But now, where He hath placed thee,
>> There He would have thee stay.[17]

Carey and others rejected this "bloom where you are planted" mentality by arguing that there was no statute of limitations to the Great Commission. If Jesus' command to go unto all the world had been abrogated, Carey asked, what about the other parts of the Commission? Should we stop baptizing and teaching as well? Is the promise of Christ's presence limited to the apostles too? Yet He expressly promised the contrary—to be with us to the end of the world. No doubt this "new" interpretation of the Great Commission caught fire in part because of the demographic revolution occasioned by the new geography, especially by the discovery of the New World. Assuming the most energetic and effective missionary evangelism possible in the early church, there was clearly no explicit knowledge of the gospel among the aboriginal natives of the Americas (Joseph Smith had not yet been born, nor the Book of Mormon "revealed").

A new theology of mission arose out of the evangelical revival that allowed Wesleyans and Calvinists to cooperate in the task of world evangelization despite their different understandings of the divine decrees, predestination, perseverance and the other "distinguishing doctrines of grace," as Andrew Fuller called them. Fuller's *The Gospel Worthy of All Acceptation*, published in 1785, itself indebted to Edwards' distinction between natural and moral ability, provided theological ballast to challenge the anti-evangelistic, anti-missionary assumptions of hyper-Calvinism which had held a tight grip in the Baptist and Congregationalist denominations. Fuller's view can be summarized in these six propositions:

1. Unconverted sinners are commanded, exhorted, and invited to believe in Christ for salvation.
2. Everyone is bound to receive what God reveals.
3. The Gospel, though a message of pure grace, requires the obedient response of faith.
4. The lack of faith is a heinous sin which is ascribed in the Scriptures to human depravity.

---

[16] Anderson, *Christian World Mission*, 39–40.
[17] George, *Faithful Witness*, 39.

5. God has threatened and inflicted the most awful punishments on sinners for their not believing in the Lord Jesus Christ.

6. The Bible requires of all persons certain spiritual exercises which are represented as their duty. These include repentance and faith no less than the requirement to love God, fear God, and glorify God. That no one can accomplish these things apart from the bestowal of the Holy Spirit. Nonetheless the obligation remains. In this sense "man's duty and God's gift" are the same thing, seen from different perspectives.[18]

The kind of evangelical Calvinism spawned by Fuller emphasized *obligation* and *means*, both words found in the title of Carey's *Enquiry*. If sinners were *obliged* to repent and believe in Christ, as the Bible makes clear, was there not also another *obligation* to be considered? Were not Christians, themselves delivered from darkness into light, most urgently *obliged* to present the claims of Christ to those who have never heard? Another English Baptist leader, Robert Hall, put it this way: "The way to Jesus is graciously open for everyone who chooses to come to him."[19] The God who predestined the salvation of the elect also predestined the means by which they would be saved. The "means" God had chosen included the sending of missionaries, the raising up of evangelists, and the preaching of the gospel in every corner of the world.

John Wesley and the Methodists, of course, had a different way of relating divine sovereignty and human responsibility. Along with the General Baptists, who were greatly influenced by the Evangelical Revival and had re-organized themselves into a "New Connection" under Daniel Taylor in 1760, Methodism emphasized the theology of universal redemption. While the hyper-Calvinists were singing anti-missionary hymns, the Methodists were singing anti-predestinarian hymns, such as this one from the prolific pen of Charles Wesley:

> Thou has compell'd the Lost to die;
>   'Hast reprobated from thy Face;
> 'Hast Others sav'd, but them past by;
>   Or mock'd with only Damning Grace.'

> How long, thou jealous God, how long
>   Shall impious Worms thy Word disprove,
> Thy Justice stain, thy Mercy wrong,
>   Deny thy Faithfulness and Love.

> Still shall the Hellish Doctrine stand?
>   And Thee for its dire Author claim?
> No—let it sink at thy Command
>   Down to the Pit from whence it came.[20]

---

[18] See George, *Faithful Witness*, 56–57.

[19] Ibid.

[20] Timothy George, *Theology of the Reformers* (Nashville, Tenn.: Broadman & Holman Publishers, 1988), 231–32.

More often, however, the Wesleyan hymns convey a more positive thrust, emphasizing the fact that Christ had died for all:

> O, for a trumpet voice,
>   on all the world to call,
> To bid their hearts rejoice,
>   In him who died for all;
> For all my Lord was crucified,
>   For all, for all, my Savior died.[21]

The doctrinal wars over predestination could be divisive, ill-tempered, and destructive of Christian fellowship. But faced with the challenge of world evangelization, missionary leaders on both sides of this theological divide frequently found a way to collaborate in prayer, works of benevolence, and evangelism for the sake of sharing the gospel with the lost. Most evangelical Calvinists could appreciate Wesley's strong doctrines of original sin, objective atonement, and justification by faith alone, while most evangelical Methodists could resonate with George Whitefield's maxim: "Every man's damnation is of himself, and every man's salvation is all of God."[22]

This is not to say that there were no doctrinal tensions on the mission field, or that these divisive issues ceased to agitate the churches back home. Indeed, one of the reasons for the founding of the first Wesleyan Methodist Missionary Society in 1813 was the concern that Methodist money was being diverted toward organizations that did not favor Wesleyan theology. As Thomas Coke asked, "If we are to employ thousands of pounds in Asia, shall we employ them in establishing *Calvinism* in that immense country in preference to Methodism?"[23] The same concern was a factor in the rise of the General Baptist Missionary Society as well. However, the greater emphasis was toward cooperation based upon essential points of agreement focused on the gospel. In the end, *evangelical* Calvinism, and *evangelical* Arminianism preferred to give more weight to the adjective they shared in common than to the divergent theological systems that it qualified. As Stuart Piggin has put it: "Since moderate Calvinists emphasized man's accountability so as to refute the antinomianism inherent in Calvinism, and Wesleyans stressed the sovereignty of God to resist the Pelagianism inherent in Arminianism, it is not surprising that adherents of the two systems found themselves in substantial agreement."[24]

Mission and Christian Unity

Isaac Watts' hymn, "Jesus Shall Reign Where'er the Sun" with its millennial overtones and its universal appeal—"People in realms of every tongue dwell

---

[21] Anderson, *Christian World Mission*, 47.
[22] George Whitefield, *Works* (London, 1770–72), 2:363.
[23] Quoted, Piggin, *Making Missionaries*, 93.
[24] Ibid., 94.

on his love with sweetest song"—had long been a classic by the 1790s. And long before Edwards' *Humble Attempt* had inspired Baptists in the Midlands to organize the famous Prayer Call of 1784, Philip Doddridge, a distinguished Dissenting minister at Northampton, had set forth a plan for quarterly prayer meetings throughout England as a first step towards a foreign missionary movement.[25] We have earlier referred to the exemplary role of the Pietists and Moravians. Still, Brian Stanley is correct to observe that "In the period before the Evangelical Revival, there was no consistent acceptance of the missionary obligation by either Anglicanism or Dissent."[26]

The situation changed dramatically with the creation of the various missionary societies around the turn of the century. Chief among these were the Baptist Missionary Society (1792), the London Missionary Society (1795), the Church Missionary Society (1799), the British and Foreign Bible Society (1804), and, on the other side of the Atlantic, the American Board of Commissioners for Foreign Missions (1810) and the American Baptist Missionary Board (1814). Most of these societies were explicitly denominational in their origin and orientation. The General Baptists would organize their own society to parallel the earlier effort by their Particular or Calvinistic Baptist cousins. The CMS was Anglican. The ABCFM was largely Congregationalist, and there would be others—Methodists, Presbyterians, etc. The creation of such societies in the Anglo-American sphere set a precedent for similar efforts on the Continent with the formation of the Basel Mission in 1815, and the Berlin Society in 1824.

Of the earliest missionary societies only one, the London Missionary Society, formed in 1795, was explicitly ecumenical from the start. Its "Fundamental Principle" declared its intention "not to send Presbyterianism, Independency, Episcopalicy or any other form of Church Order and Government…but the glorious Gospel of the blessed God to the Heathen."[27] This was in line with Melville Horne's *Letters on Missions*, published in 1794, which projected a missionary society embracing evangelicals across the board: "Let liberal Churchmen and Conscientious Dissenters, pious Calvinists and pious Arminians, embrace with fraternal arms."[28] David Bogue, another early leader of the LMS, agreed: "Here are Episcopalians, Methodists, Presbyterians and Independents, all united in one society…behold us here assembled with one accord to attend the funeral of bigotry."[29]

In fact, the lofty interdenominational idealism of the LMS was never fully realized, as it came to be dominated by Congregationalists. Only one Baptist ever served under its aegis, and soon Anglicans, Methodists, Presbyterians, and others had their own missionary sending entities. But the ideal of a united evangelical enterprise in support of the global extension of the gospel message—a direct aftereffect of the revival preaching of Wesley and especially Whitefield—would

---

[25] Roger H. Martin, *Evangelicals United: Ecumenical Stirrings in Pre-Victorian Britain, 1795–1830* (London: Scarecrow Press, 1983), 23.

[26] Brian Stanley, *The Bible and the Flag* (Leicester: InterVarsity Press, 1990), 55–56.

[27] LMS, Board Minutes, May 9, 1796, quoted, Piggin, *Making Missionaries*, 107.

[28] Ibid., 108.

[29] Ibid., 109.

transform all of the societies over time and help make the missionary movement itself the matrix for the kind of ecumenism that came to fruition in the 1910 International Missionary Conference at Edinburgh.

To cite only two witnesses for this thesis, let us look briefly at these statements by John Philip and J. A. James. John Philip, originally a Congregationalist pastor in Aberdeen, spent thirty years in South Africa under the sponsorship of the London Missionary Society. He was married to a remarkable woman, Jane Philip who, unlike Dorothy Carey, was not only the wife of a missionary but a missionary wife.[30] After his death, Ralph Wardlaw said of his friend John Philip:

> He was a man of a *catholic*, or rather, let me say, of a *Christian* spirit...for whilst he was a thorough dissenter, he was distinguished alike for his love for the likeness of Christ in whomsoever he saw that likeness, and also for his willingness to cooperate with Christians of other denominations, in any or every work that had for its object either the amelioration of the social condition of the people or the extension of the religion of Christ at home and abroad.[31]

Throughout the nineteenth century advocates for the world mission enterprise increasingly turned to Jesus' prayer in John 17:21 as an important biblical text fraught with implications for Christian unity: "May they all be one, as You, Father, are in Me and I am in You. May they also be one in Us, so the world may believe You sent Me." Commenting on this text, the great Scottish church leader Thomas Chalmers declared that Christian unity was "the condition on which we are told that the world shall be converted."[32] Even more expansive is this statement by J. A. James, one of the prime movers in the formation of the Evangelical Alliance in 1846:

> A divided, alienated church cannot convert the world to God...it is Satan's object to keep us separated at home, that he may reign unmolested abroad...the effects of our union would be felt in every part of the earth, and the approach of the millennium may be accelerated...a united church must precede, and will soon introduce, a converted world.[33]

This is not to say that evangelical mission fields around the world did not sometimes become venues for renewed sectarian struggles. Indeed, the denomi-

---

[30] Natasha Erlank, "Jane and John Philip: Partnership, Usefulness and Sexuality in the Service of God," *The London Missionary Society in South Africa, 1799–1999*, ed. John de Gruchy (Athens, Ohio: Ohio University Press, 2000), 82–98.

[31] Ralph Wardlaw, *What is Death? A Sermon Delivered on the Occasion of the Recent Death of the Reverend John Philip, D. D.* (Glasgow, 1852), 49.

[32] Piggin, *Making Missionaries*, 107.

[33] Ibid.

national wars back home were frequently re-fought on far-flung islands and continents far removed from the original scenes of battle. A mini-war of sorts broke out within Carey's community at Serampore over the issue of the terms of communion, that is, whether non-Baptist Christians should be allowed to partake of the Lord's Supper. Imbued by the ecumenical spirit of their mission setting, the Serampore community, after studying the issue, came down on the side of open communion. "No one has a right to debar a true Christian from the Lord's Table," they reasoned. "We cannot doubt whether a Watts, an Edwards, a Brainerd, a Doddridge, a Whitefield, did right in partaking of the Lord's Supper though really unbaptized, or whether they had the presence of God at the Lord's Table?"[34] But when their Baptist friends back in England, especially Andrew Fuller, heard about this liberalizing of communion policy on the mission field, they reacted strongly, criticizing the missionaries' "wandering in the mazes of carnal reasonings." Fuller's rejoinder brought the issue to a close, as Carey and his associates reinstituted the stricter policy. Other controversies in other mission settings were not so easily resolved, and there are many records of bitter disputes over issues of church governance, ordination, predestination, the role of women in missionary service, and even Bible translation.

However, ironically enough, it was often the vigor and futility of such squabbles that prompted missionaries to yearn even more fervently for the demise of the sectarian spirit. To quote J. A. James again: "Perish for ever all envy and rivalry, and let the only contest be this, who shall most glorify God and bless the human race."[35] Here, as elsewhere, William Carey was a visionary leader who saw beyond the limits of his own age toward a new horizon. In 1806 Carey surveyed the growing competition of the various missionary societies that had sprung up since the founding of his own Baptist effort fourteen years earlier. Considering the need for a coordinated strategy for world evangelization, he set forth what has been called "the most startling missionary proposal of all time."[36] In a letter to Andrew Fuller he asked:

> Would it not be possible to have a general association of all denominations of Christians, from the four corners of the world, held there once in about ten years? I earnestly recommend this plan, that the first meeting be in the year 1810, or 1812 at furthest. I have no doubt but it would be attended with many important effects. We could understand one another better, and more entirely enter into one another's views by two hours' conversation than by two or three years of epistolary correspondence.[37]

---

[34] See Timothy George, "Controversy and Communion: The Limits of Baptist Fellowship from Bunyan to Spurgeon" in *The Gospel in the World*, ed. D. W. Bebbington (Carlisle, Pa.: Paternoster Press, 2002), 53.

[35] Piggin, *Making Missionaries*, 106.

[36] Ruth Rowse, "William Carey's 'Pleasing Dream,'" *International Review of Missions* 38 (1949): 181.

[37] Carey to Andrew Fuller, Calcutta, May 15, 1806.

Fuller admired Carey's "pleasing dream," as he called it, but he did not encourage its implementation. Such a meeting, he felt, could as easily be a seedbed for further dissention as a catalyst for the kind of united missionary action Carey envisaged. Carey's dream would be deferred but it would not die. Precisely one hundred years after Carey had proposed such a gathering, the first international mission conference convened in Edinburgh in 1910. Evangelicals today who, often with good reason, are suspicious and dismissive of the modern ecumenical movement should not forget that the modern quest for Christian unity was born on the mission field. It sprang from the godly desire of Bible-believing Christians to take seriously the words of Jesus which directly connect the visible oneness of His followers on earth with the mandate He gave to them to evangelize in His Name.

Why They Went

In Charlotte Brontë's popular novel, *Jane Eyre*, one of the characters is named St. John Rivers. An individual of noble bearing, he has dedicated his life for missionary service in India. Prior to his departure, Brontë has Rivers expound on his motivation for such a career:

> I burnt for the more active life of the world—for the more exciting toils of a literary career—for the destiny of an artist, author, orator...Yes, the heart of a politician, of a soldier, of a votary of glory, a lover of renown, a luster after power, beat under my curate's surplice. I considered my life was so wretched, it must be changed, or I must die. After a season of darkness and struggling, light broke and relief fell: my cramped existence all at once spread out to a plane without bounds—my powers heard a call from heaven to rise, gather their full strength, spread their wings, and mount beyond ken. God had an errand for me; to bear which afar, to deliver it well, skill and strength, courage and eloquence, the best qualifications of soldier, statesman, and orator, were all needed: for these all centre in the good missionary. A missionary I resolved to be.[38]

By the time *Jane Eyre* was published in 1847, the evangelical missionary had emerged as a cultural icon in popular imagination. In 1793 Carey and his family had sailed up the Hoogle River to Calcutta under cover of dark, entering the city clandestinely as illegal aliens. However, long before Carey's death in 1834, William Wilberforce and other friends in Parliament had passed the so-called Missionary Bill which opened up to missionary service not only India but the growing British Empire around the world. In the meantime, missionary heroism became immortalized through the retelling of the daring exploits of Carey and the Serampore Trio (Carey, the printer William Ward, and the school teacher

---

[38] Charlotte Brontë, *Jane Eyre* (London: Everyman, 1969), 363.

Joshua Marshman and his wife Hannah); Henry Martyn; Adoniram Judson and his remarkable wife Ann Haseltine Judson; Robert Morrison, the first Protestant missionary to China; Alexander Duff, a Scottish Presbyterian whose time in India overlapped briefly with that of Carey; Robert Moffat and his more famous son-in-law, David Livingstone, who carried the evangelical message to Africa. These are just a few of the more famous missionaries who fanned out across the globe in what they believed was literal obedience to the Great Commission.

Who were these people and why did they do what they did? What St. Paul said about God's elect in 1 Corinthians 1 could also be applied to the early missionary force—not many were wise by human standards; not many were influential; not many were of noble birth. Here again, God seems to have been pleased to choose the foolish things of the world to shame the wise, the weak things to shame the strong, the lowly and despised things, even things that are not, to nullify the things that are (1 Cor 1:26–28).

Stuart Piggin carefully studied the social location of several hundred missionaries and found that only a few of them came from the higher echelons of society. The majority, however, were from the artisan classes. With the coming of the Industrial Revolution, some of their jobs had been made obsolete, an early instance of "downsizing," and a number had gravitated toward teaching or the ministry. Hannah Marshman reflected this situation in a comment she made prior to her departure for India: "The distress is tenfold to what it used to be. The machines are the ruin of the country."[39] Other missionaries had held a variety of occupations back home, many of which were to prove invaluable in their new settings: cabinetmakers, grocers, drapers, farm laborers, weavers, bookbinders, coopers, carpenters, ironmongers, merchants, printers, stable boys, surgeons (which usually meant barbers), potters, glovers, shoemakers, master dyers, engravers, stonemasons, wheelwrights, and at least one mole catcher! Most, like Carey, Henry Martyn, and the Judsons, left behind families, friends, and whatever earthly possessions they had accrued to venture all in response to what they believed was the irrevocable call of Almighty God on their lives. Why did they do this?

Recent scholarship has continued to study missionary motivation, but much of it has confirmed the classic work by Johannes Van den Berg, a Dutch historian whose 1956 doctoral dissertation at Kampen was published under the title "Constrained by Jesus' Love: An Inquiry into the Motives of the Missionary Awakening in Great Britain in the Period Between 1698 and 1815."[40] In this study, Van den Berg identifies ten major motives of the great missionary awakening. While each of these deserves a full study of its own, we do well to list them here:

1. Political motives. It has become almost a shibboleth in certain circles of missiological research to assume that the evangelical missionary enterprise was, in the words of K. M. Panikkar, "merely an epiphenomenon of Western politi-

---

[39] Piggin, *Making Missionaries*, 41.

[40] Johannes Van den Berg, *Constrained by Jesus' Love: An Inquiry into the Motives of the Missionary Awakening in Great Britain in the Period Between 1698 and 1815* (Kampen: J. H. Kok, 1956).

cal and economic expansion."[41] According to Panikkar, the "great century" of evangelical missionary advance was both the logical extension and the culmination of what he called "the Vasco de Gama era," marching hand in hand with the colonial enterprise and suffering with the latter decline and discrediting over the past century. Brian Stanley, among others, has weighed this thesis in the balance and found it wanting, though not without significant support. As we have seen, Carey and the earliest missionaries to India were counter-cultural in the sense that they carried out their work in defiance of the laws of their country, even though they did see the hand of God in the rising tide of international commerce and trade that paved the way for the dissemination of the gospel. Van den Berg notes that during the Victorian era evangelicalism, especially in its Nonconformist posture, became politically respectable (perhaps not unlike evangelicalism in the United States has become over the past twenty-five years). This rapprochement between empire and missions had both positive and negative influences that continue up to the present time. Whenever evangelicalism has been truest to its deepest gospel instincts, however, it has always followed the wisdom of the great Lesslie Newbigin, a twentieth-century missionary to India, who declared that at the very heart of the biblical vision "is not an imperial power but the slain Lamb."[42]

2. Humanitarian-cultural motives. It is well known that the evangelical revival gave rise to numerous movements for social reform, from Whitefield's support for orphans to Wesley's concern for the health and safety of coal miners to the great campaign led by Wilberforce to end the slave trade within the British Empire. Most of the early evangelical missionaries were practitioners of holistic missions and incarnational evangelism. They knew that Jesus had given food to hungry people on the same occasion that He presented himself to them as the Bread of Life. Carey not only translated the Scriptures into dozens of languages and dialects, but he and his missionary team also planted schools, established the first newspaper in India, organized an agricultural society, and worked tirelessly to overturn the sati laws which permitted the burning alive of women who had lost their husbands. They were well aware that there was both a propositional and an incarnational dimension to the life and mission of the church. What the Methodist missionary, E. Stanley Jones, said in the twentieth century was well known by his predecessors: "A soul without a body is a ghost; a body without a soul is a corpse. The gospel is addressed to living persons, soul and body, in all of their broken humanity and need for wholeness."[43]

3. The ascetic motive. The ascetic ideal is usually associated with monasticism and other strains of Roman Catholic spirituality, best exemplified by the example of St. Francis. Yet self-denial and a lifestyle based on simplicity, frugality, and abstention from worldly pleasures is also a part of the Protestant ethos. As we have seen, the very act of leaving one's home and traveling far distances

[41] Quoted, Stephen Neill, *History of Missions,* 560.

[42] Lesslie Newbigin, *The Gospel in a Pluralist Society* (Grand Rapids, Mich.: Eerdmans, 1989), 159.

[43] E. Stanley Jones, *The Unshakable Kingdom and the Unchanging Person* (Nashville, Tenn.: Abingdon Press, 1972), 40.

around the globe itself required enormous self-sacrifice on the part of most missionaries. The disciplines of prayer, fasting, and celibacy are well attested in evangelical missionary history. Among Southern Baptists, one thinks of the great Lottie Moon, who gave up the opportunity for marriage and a comfortable domestic life in America for the strenuous life of a missionary in China.[44] Among the early missionaries, perhaps Henry Martyn best exemplifies the ascetic ideal. After reading the life of Francis Xavier, he wrote in his journal: "I was exceedingly roused at this astonishing example of that great saint, and began to consider, whether it was not my duty to live, as he did, in voluntary poverty and celibacy."[45] There were, of course, many missionaries whose lifestyle was far removed from anything ascetic and who lived in luxury compared to those to whom they had gone to present the gospel.

4. The motive of debt. Van den Berg refers here to the voice of the Christian conscience towards restitution for the wrongs inflicted upon other peoples of the world by the "empire-building" of Western rule. Carey and many other early missionaries revealed a deep-seated social conscience with reference to the slave trade in that they saw this evil business not only as a personal sin of individual slave traders, but also as something that benefited the entire nation, thus implicating everyone in its dirty business. While still in England, for example, Carey refused to eat sugar since he knew it had been produced by the labor of slaves in the West Indies. As Carey wrote in his *Enquiry:* "The vices of Europeans have been communicated wherever they themselves have been; so that their religious state of even heathens has been rendered worse by intercourse with them."[46] In addition to what might be called the cultural debt of all so-called civilized nations, there is the apostolic indebtedness Paul refers to in Romans 1:14 where he declares himself indebted to everyone, Jews and Greeks, barbarians and free persons, a debt he can discharge only by preaching the gospel at Rome and elsewhere.

5. Romantic motives. We have seen something of the romantic ideal already in the quotation from Charlotte Brontë's portrayal of the ideal missionary in *Jane Eyre.* No doubt, the myth of the "noble savage" and other fantasies of Enlightenment philosophers such as Jean-Jacques Rousseau contributed to the romanticism of a culture in which the evangelical missionary awakening was born. It would be surprising indeed if some of those committing their lives to serve in the South Sea Islands or some other quixotic locale were untouched by the romantic ideal. Still, Van den Berg notes, "Romanticism may sometimes have acted as a stimulus, but it is utterly wrong to try to explain the missionary awakening as a whole from the influence of the romantic movement."[47]

6. The theocentric motive. The missionary awakening was driven by a God-intoxicated theology, and William Wilberforce spoke for many of his fellow evangelicals when he declared that there are "many passages of Scripture, wherein the promoting of the glory of God is commanded as our supreme and

---

[44] For more on Lottie Moon, see chapter five below.
[45] Van den Berg, *Constrained,* 148–50.
[46] Ibid., 157.
[47] Ibid., 155.

universal aim, and wherein the honor due unto him is declared to be that in which he will allow no competitor to participate."[48] The evangelical missionary enterprise was rooted in the gracious, eternal purpose of the triune God, Father, Son, and Holy Spirit, to call unto Himself a redeemed people out of the fallen race of lost humankind. Before he decided to go to India, William Carey visited with John Newton in London. The former slave trader turned Anglican pastor and hymn writer understood well the role of Providence in the course of history. While we do not know what he said to Carey on the occasion of his visit, it may well have been something like these words just five years earlier:

> All changes, successes, disappointments—all that is memorable in the annals of history, all the risings and falls of empires, all the turns in human life—take place according to God's plan. In vain men contrive and combine to accomplish their own counsels. Unless they are parts of His counsel likewise, the efforts of their utmost strength and wisdom are crossed and reversed by the feeblest and most unthought-of circumstances. But when He has a work to accomplish and His time is come, however inadequate and weak that means He employs may seem to a carnal eye, the success is infallibly secured: for all things serve Him, and are in His hands as clay in the hands of the potter. Great and marvelous are Thy works, Lord God Almighty! Just and true are Thy ways, Thou King of saints![49]

7. The motive of love and compassion. Paul declared himself to be compelled, constrained as the KJV has it, by the love of Christ (2 Cor 5:14). No doubt the factor of love was an indispensable element in missionary motivation. Charles Simeon, the great evangelical preacher of Cambridge and mentor of Henry Martyn, was especially well known for his love for God, which manifested itself in his love for others. After hearing Simeon preach in Cambridge, Wilberforce wrote in his diary: "Simeon is with us—his heart glowing with love of Christ. How full is he of love, and of desire to promote the spiritual benefit of others."[50]

What about the fate of the unevangelized, those who had never heard the name of Christ or the gospel of grace? This question, hotly debated in our own day, was not unknown to the early evangelical missionaries. We should not think that either pluralism or syncretism are new ideas in our own age. The idea that salvation was attainable by sincerely following the tenets of pagan religion was rejected as contrary to the clear thrust of Scripture. At the same time, Henry Martyn, among others, was careful not to usurp the ultimate role of God Himself

---

[48] William Wilberforce, *A Practical View of the Prevailing Religious System of Professed Christians in the Higher and Middle Classes of this Country, contrasted with Real Christianity* (London, 1797), quoted in Van den Berg, *Constrained*, 155.

[49] Quoted, George, *Faithful Witness*, 170.

[50] E. Marshall Howse, *Saints in Politics, The Clapham Sect and the Growth of Freedom* (Toronto, 1952), quoted in Van den Berg, *Constrained*, 157.

in the final disposition of every person made in His image: "When I affirm my belief that those who reject the triune Jehovah will perish, of course I mean those who do this deliberately and not withstanding opportunities. I leave to God Almighty, the application of general threatenings to every particular case."[51]

8. The ecclesiological motive. Evangelicals, in the tradition of Augustine, Luther, and Calvin, have always stressed the reality of the church universal, the invisible church composed of all of the redeemed of all of the ages, whose definite membership is known only to God alone. This is the Body and Bride of Christ, the church for which Christ died and into which lost men and women were engrafted of the Holy Spirit. But this does not mean that evangelicals have been unconcerned with the reality of the visible church in its local manifestation. Evangelical missionaries not only preached the gospel to lost souls, they also planted local churches. The fact that they also represented different denominations with various polities, ordinances, disciplinary practices, and views of ordination and ministry led to tension and sometimes raucous disputes on the mission field. This was one factor in the various comity arrangements later devised in many mission settings. But this fact should not obscure the emphasis placed on indigenous church life among the early evangelical missionaries. Now, two centuries later, we witness the fruit of those early church-planting endeavors when we consider what John Stott has called "the many-colored wisdom of God" revealed in the worldwide evangelical church which prefigures the heavenly assembly of Revelation 5 from every tribe and language and people and nation.

9. The eschatological motive. We have referred already to the literature of expectation and the belief shared by many early evangelical missionaries that they were living on the edge of time, an age pregnant with great events that could well usher in the millennial reign of Christ. Carey continued to exude this "optimism of grace" until the end of his life. When he was past seventy years of age, two and one-half years before his death, he wrote to his sisters back in England:

> I expect the fulfillment of all the prophecies and promises respecting the universal establishment of a Redeemer's Kingdom in the world, including the total abolishment of idolatry, Mohammedanism, infidelity, Socinianism, and all the political establishments in the world; and the abolition also of war, slavery, and oppression, and all their ramifications. It is on this ground that I pray for, and expect, the peace of Jerusalem; not merely the cessation of hostilities between Christians of different sects and connections, but that genuine love which the Gospel requires, and which the Gospel is well calculated to produce.[52]

Now, at the dawn of the third millennium, we might be more cautious in expressing our hopes for the Lord's Kingdom to come and His will to be done on

[51] Martyn, *Journals and Letters*, quoted in Van den Berg, *Constrained*, 158.
[52] Quoted, Kenneth Scott Latourette, *These Sought a Country* (New York: Harper and Brothers, 1950), 35.

earth as it is in heaven. Islam remains vigorous and, in many places, resurgent; and while Socinianism, in its old-fashioned form, is largely confined these days to the Back Bay of Boston, a more insidious form of infidelity, which we usually call secularism, has made far deeper inroads into our culture than that of Carey's day. Thankfully, slavery no longer has the grip it once held on the world's soul but, as we all know, it still thrives in the Sudan and other places. War, oppression, and idolatry are still with us. Later, evangelical missionaries would turn to a less optimistic eschatology, premillennialism, often in its dispensational form, which saw the world in darker, more hard-headed ways. Yet it is wise always to take the longer view and to realize, perhaps, as Richard John Neuhaus has said, that when we look back from heaven to our present vantage point in history we may well discover that we were living in 2007 in the first days of the early church.

10. The command of Christ as a missionary motive. No doubt all of these motives played a role in the rise of the missionary awakening, but we come back to the theme of this volume: the Great Commission. It would be wrong to take Jesus' command out of context, as though the early missionaries were simply following a New Testament imperative without realizing its wider biblical and theological context. The Great Commission is an expression of the *missio dei* and must be understood within the context of the soteriological and eschatological thrust of biblical revelation, all of which reflects the character of the living God.

In the conclusion to his wonderful book, *These Sought a Country*, the great historian of missions, Kenneth Scott Latourette, wrote a chapter entitled "The Conclusion of the Whole Matter." In it he reminds us that the New Testament vision of the Great Commission is universal in its sweep. It declares that all things in heaven and on earth are to be united or summed up in Christ, that all the vast universe, God's creation, is groaning in travail eager for the liberation that is to come. In the meantime, Christians cannot but believe and know that the vision and the command of the Great Commission are from God.

> How and when they will be fulfilled they cannot know. In seeking to fulfill Jesus' command, his disciples will not always succeed. They will not always be able to persuade others; their judgment will be faulty; they will not be fully free from the taint of sin; physical weakness will thwart them; what men call death will come, early or late, to cut off the act before its final accomplishment, so far beyond the compass of human years has it been planned. Yet it is through daring to live now in the new age and not resting content until all their fellow creatures share it that God brings in his Kingdom. He is not ashamed to be called their God. In the eternity beyond this present span, we must believe, they will not be disappointed for they have ventured out in faith in him who is 'able to do far more abundantly than all that we ask or think.'[53]

---

[53] Latourette, *These Sought a Country*, 147.

PART TWO:
MODERN ANGLO-AMERICAN MISSIONS

Chapter Four:

EARLY AMERICAN MISSIONS FROM THE REVOLUTION TO THE CIVIL WAR

By Bradley J. Gundlach

On March 8, 1782, raiders attacked a peaceful village of Christian farmers, herding men into one building, women and children into another, where each group sang hymns to buoy their spirits as their captors scalped and killed them. As pacifists they offered no resistance. While no one knows the precise number of the dead, conservative estimates place it around ninety souls. We know the details of the massacre because one youth survived his scalping, hid under a pile of dead bodies, and later related the horrific story to a missionary.[1]

No, this was not one of the many Indian raids on the frontier that pepper early American history and haunted the imaginations of white settlers. This was the infamous work of patriot militiamen destroying a village of Christianized Delaware Indians along the Muskingum River in the Ohio Territory. Next to Wounded Knee it stands as the worst atrocity against Native Americans in American history.[2]

These Indians had responded to the gospel under the winsome preaching of David Zeisberger, a Moravian missionary in Pennsylvania. He organized his converts into peaceable farming villages, but pressure from white settlers forced them to move to Philadelphia, then westward to the banks of the Susquehanna, then further west to the Ohio region, beyond the frontier of white settlement. They were finalizing yet another move at the time of the slaughter. A remnant completed the relocation to Ontario, to a place they called, poignantly, "Shielded by Grace" (Gnadenhütten).[3]

---

[1] Earl P. Olmstead, *Blackcoats Among the Delaware: David Zeisberger on the Ohio Frontier* (Kent, Ohio: Kent State University Press, 1991), 55. This account comes from Zeisberger's contemporary description of the massacre as reported to him by survivors.

[2] *Ibid.*, 54.

[3] R. Pierce Beaver, *Church, State, and the American Indians: Two and a Half Centuries of Partnership in Missions Between Protestant Churches and Government* (St. Louis, Mo.: Concordia, 1966), 58–59; Olmstead, *Blackcoats Among the Delaware*, 56 ff.

Indian missions were the only American missionary activity at the time of the Revolution, and clearly that work was not going well. But soon things would change. Zeisberger's enormous disappointments came just a few short decades before a great explosion of missionary effort—the "Great Century" of missions in the 1800s—when the lone missionary was replaced by an institutionalization of missions that made possible a truly unprecedented spread of Christianity. Whole societies responded to the gospel in such exotic places as Burma and Hawaii as well as closer to home among the Cherokees and Choctaws of the American South. Large and influential missions took hold in India and South Africa under British colonial power. Americans joined Englishmen, Scots, and continental Europeans in Protestant mission work on a global scale.

This sudden unveiling of the way of salvation to large swaths of humanity is surely something to celebrate. At the same time, the realities of a sin-sick world make for a story of burgeoning missions that is not all sweetness and light. Not only did existing powers and interests complicate and compromise missionary success (as in the massacre of the Delawares and the subsequent history of American Indian missions), but the very structures that made the sudden spread of Christianity possible also encumbered it with difficulties.[4] The story of early American missions is a perplexing combination of divine appointments and human dilemmas, which I will illustrate by treating missions to the American Indians, slaves, and the Sandwich Islands.

Overview of Early American Missions

Between the Revolution and the Civil War, American evangelical missions advanced quickly in both scope and numbers, especially when compared to the colonial period. From small and sporadic attempts to civilize and evangelize the Indians (in that order), American evangelical missions burgeoned into well-organized and widely supported agencies that sent evangelists and educators to the Native Americans, to slaves in the Deep South, and overseas to Asia, Africa, and the Pacific Islands—not to mention home missions among immigrants and along the frontier.

What accounts for this sudden growth spurt? First, a heightened appreciation of the power of the gospel to transform lives and societies, joined with a heightened expectation of the Lord's return when the nations were gathered in,

---

[4] Oliver Wendell Elsbree sounded this note nearly eighty years ago in his *The Rise of the Missionary Spirit in America, 1790–1815* (1928; reprint, Philadelphia: Porcupine Press, 1980), 23. R. Pierce Beaver, don of the history of Native American missions, characterized his theme as "the glorious and often terrible story of the mission to the Indians" (*Church, State, and the American Indians*, 6). Indeed, while it may appear to casual readers that missions history has taken a postcolonial turn in the recent emphasis on missionaries as agents of cultural imperialism, missionaries themselves were often well aware of the problems that power structures and economic forces were creating for their evangelistic work, even as those structures and forces made global missions possible. This should come as no surprise, since early missionaries were often among the best educated and most reflective members of American society. See William R. Hutchison, *Errand to the World: American Protestant Thought and Foreign Missions* (Chicago: University of Chicago Press, 1987), 1, 9–12.

transformed attitudes toward mission work.[5] And just as important was *insti-tutionalization*—the founding of a myriad of sending organizations at the local, state, and national levels, with varying degrees of attachment to denominations. Economic and geopolitical changes, giving Europe and America unprecedented access to the world's peoples, constitute a third and fundamental reason. As a result of these factors, Christians in the early nineteenth century faced an awe-inspiring opportunity for global outreach. It was a great age of experimentation in structure and theory—a pioneering period, not just in sending the very first Protestant missionaries to many parts of the world, but in laying the founda-tion for the great period of missionary expansion that would follow after the 1850s.[6]

The American story is but a part of a larger transatlantic missionary awaken-ing, tied clearly to the evangelical awakenings of the mid-eighteenth century and early nineteenth century. Influences sailed back and forth among Americans, Englishmen, Scots, Moravians, and others, made possible by the improved communications of that era. Europeans read Jonathan Edwards' stirring *Life of David Brainerd*, a model of missionary devotion. Americans read evangelicals of the Scottish Enlightenment like Thomas Chalmers on the power of the gos-pel to transform societies—while Chalmers in turn learned from accounts of Moravian missions in Greenland and Labrador that evangelism did not need to await a preparatory stage of civilizing. And everybody read the English Baptist William Carey's forceful *Enquiry into the Obligations of Christians to Use Means for the Conversion of the Heathens* (1792).[7] "Missionary Intelligence" or news from the field became popular reading in the multiplying religious periodicals of the early 1800s, fanning the flames of missionary zeal and inspiring more people to contribute funds or to go themselves.[8]

The line between "home" and "foreign" missions in North America was in-distinct, due to Anglo conceptions as to who was an American and who was foreign. Indians enclosed within existing state boundaries or in unorganized territories to the West were foreign nations both in popular thought and legal practice. Also in the midst of white America were African and African-American slaves, a remarkably unevangelized population even in the early 1800s. After 1830, immigrant groups such as Catholics and Jews became targets of mission work in the cities and on the frontier. And a final target group, easily overlooked but hugely important in attracting (and diverting) attention and funds, were

---

[5] Hutchison, *Errand to the World*, 40. Other historians emphasize the role of Enlightenment notions of universal humanity and "the regenerative capacity of rational knowledge" in spurring evangelical confidence for undertak-ing global missions—see e.g. Brian Stanley, "Christian Missions and the Enlightenment: A Reevaluation" and "Christianity and Civilization in Evangelical Mission Thought, 1792–1857," both in *Christian Missions and the Enlightenment*, ed. Stanley (Grand Rapids, Mich.: Eerdmans, 2001), 8, 169–97. In my view evangelicals' debt to the Enlightenment is real but secondary. Their primary motivation and primary categories of thought concerning the spread of the gospel came from the Bible and Protestant doctrine.

[6] Kenneth Scott Latourette, *The History of the Expansion of Christianity*, vol. 4, *The Great Century in Europe and the United States of America, 1800 A.D. to 1914 A.D.* (1941; reprint, Grand Rapids, Mich.: Zondervan, 1970), chap. 2.

[7] Stanley, "Christianity and Civilization," 177–79; Sweeney, *The American Evangelical Story*, 85–87.

[8] Early examples are *The Methodist Magazine* (1818–1828, continued with varying titles throughout the nine-teenth century) and the journal of the American Colonization Society, *The African Repository* (1825–1892).

white Americans on the frontier. Indian missions and slave missions would suffer significantly when home missionary interest turned to frontier white communities.[9]

And of course there were foreign missions proper. Americans' most important missions overseas included work in Burma, where Adoniram Judson and others had great success among the Karen people; British India, where American Congregationalists, Presbyterians, Methodists, Baptists, and Lutherans joined a much larger force of British missionaries (and where offers of education perennially attracted more people than the gospel did); and the major missions of the interdenominational American Board of Commissioners for Foreign Missions: Turkey and Armenia, attracting converts from ancient Eastern churches; Lebanon, establishing an influential college; and the Sandwich Islands mission (Hawaii), where the ABCFM had stunning successes, building what was for a time the model of fruitful overseas missionary work.

Missions to American Indians

Evangelical missions in America clearly begin in New England, where the Puritans were the great exception to the general Protestant neglect of their professed colonial purpose of bringing the gospel to the natives in the 1600s. John Eliot established a mission to the Indians of Massachusetts that thrived up to the 1670s, when King Philip's War between the English settlers and the natives brought Indian relations to a permanent low. Two Thomas Mayhews (father and son) enjoyed success on the Massachusetts islands of Nantucket and Martha's Vineyard. Both of these missions received sponsorship from the colonial government, and both assumed the necessity of raising the "savages" to a state of European-style civilization before they would be ready for a Christianization that would last.

The connection of Native American missions with civil government would plague Indian missions through the nineteenth century, but the old assumption that civilization must precede evangelization dropped away in the mid-1700s, thanks to David Brainerd and Jonathan Edwards. These men championed a new appreciation of the power of the gospel in individual and social life. Regenerated people, however undeveloped their societies might be before evangelization, would have the power of God for righteousness at work in their lives to bring them quickly to a Christianized and civilized mode of existence. Such civilization included European ways of settled agriculture, private property, monogamous patriarchal families, literacy, and intellectual and aesthetic cultivation, as well as public righteousness in line with the Ten Commandments. The civilizing ideal clearly contained ideas and attitudes of cultural superiority, some more closely connected with biblical categories of sin and righteousness than others. But it also asserted the basic solidarity and moral equality of humanity, some-

---

[9] Here I follow Latourette's classification of American missions in *The History of the Expansion of Christianity*, vol. 4, chapters 6–9.

thing that later imperialism, based on ideas of essential racial difference, would not do.[10]

The Great Awakening prompted a revival of American Indian missions. The New England Company (based actually in England) sent a missionary to the Oneidas, one of the Six Nations of the Iroquois in central New York. A large part of the tribe converted in the 1760s. When white settlers in Connecticut, Massachusetts, and Long Island coveted the lands of Christianized tribes there, the Oneidas generously received them into their own territory. This began the policy of Indian removal that would take forcible, governmental form in the nineteenth century.[11] David Zeisberger's Christian Delawares put up with similar voluntary removals, as mentioned at the outset of this chapter, only to suffer massacre at the hands of hostile whites on the frontier. These Indians showed amazing humility and patience in the face of gross injustice, leading one to ask just which group showed itself more savage in its treatment of others. And the missionaries found themselves in the uncomfortable position of having to recommend removal for the very survival of their Christian brothers and sisters.[12]

When the Revolution cut off funds from England and Scotland, New Englanders led the way in founding missionary organizations on American soil, first on the state level (the Massachusetts Missionary Society, for instance, founded in 1799) and soon transcending state and denominational boundaries.[13] Church mission boards followed. As the nineteenth century dawned, much missionary vision would turn from Indian missions to the overseas field—but even the American Board of Commissioners for Foreign Missions, founded in 1810 to fund work in India, continued to include American Indians in its "foreign" missions work.

The Methodists provide a fine instance of denominational missions to the American Indians. The entire Methodist movement was in practice a kind of home mission, intent on making converts especially of the neglected and unreached, organizing them into the Methodist small-group system, and giving converts themselves roles of responsibility in spiritual oversight and further evangelism.[14] This pattern anticipated the "go in, train them, get out" strategy that would not take hold in mainline missions until a good century later. Especially in the late 1700s the Methodists were remarkable for their spiritual egalitarianism. The races mingled freely in early Methodist meetings, whites sometimes even sitting under black preaching. This would change in the early 1800s as the Methodists began to woo the slaveholding class, striking a com-

---

[10] R. H. Pearce, *Savagism and Civilization: A Study of the Indians and the American Mind,* cited in Stanley, "Christianity and Civilization," 177. Missionaries and church people continued to debate the relation of civilization and Christianization into the nineteenth century. At the first meeting of Princeton Seminary's Society of Inquiry on Missions (ca. 1814), students considered whether civilization must precede evangelization in American Indian missions, using a paper on John Eliot as their launching point. David B. Calhoun, *Princeton Seminary,* vol. 1, *Faith and Learning, 1812–1868* (Edinburgh: Banner of Truth Trust, 1994), 143.

[11] Beaver, *Church, State, and the American Indians,* 86–87.

[12] Latourette, *History of the Expansion of Christianity,* 4:300.

[13] Ibid., 4: 205–206; Beaver, *Church, State, and the American Indians,* 53.

[14] Elsbree, *Rise of the Missionary Spirit,* 118.

promise with worldly power structures in order to win souls at the top as well as the bottom.[15] But a striking example of egalitarianism in the early days is the first Methodist mission to Indians. In 1816 John Steward, an African American convert at a camp meeting in Ohio, felt called to preach to the Wyandot Indians. Welcomed by the Indians, Steward found among them a runaway Kentucky slave named Jonathan Painter—a providential opportunity for an interpreter. He led Painter to the Lord and together they began evangelizing the Wyandots. Soon the Methodist Church licensed Steward to preach, and in 1819 the Methodist Missionary Society was formed, sending trained missionaries to the area.[16]

The most important early Methodist missions leader, William Capers, ventured into the lands of the Creek Indians within Georgia in 1821 to scope out the possibilities for establishing a mission there. Capers felt acutely the sense of "entering a Pagan land" when he crossed the border into the Creek Nation. He also worried that whites in the region might deliberately "prejudice the Chiefs against us." He lamented, "Can it be that from a land of Bibles, they have come into this region of death—not to relieve its gloom, but to mingle with its shades a still deeper darkness?" For the sad fact was that whites interested in dispossessing Indians of their land often urged "fire-water" upon them, and in this case might well wish to prevent them from hearing the gospel at all, since their Christianization might lessen the chances of their removal.[17]

Capers was typical in his free use of language of moral degeneracy to describe heathen lands. He reported on seeing "nature in her naked naughtiness" and confessed, "I had not supposed that so close at the door of civilized man—just beyond sight of the Bible, and the sound of our sacred services—there could exist so gross a state of human degradation." Reports of heathen moral darkness were a stock in trade of missionary intelligence, reflecting a certain fascination with the exotic, forbidden world of idolatry, but more importantly moving Christian readers to sympathize with fellow humans thus degraded. While there was certainly an air of cultural superiority to it, such reporting always carried a basic sense of common humanity. Thus Capers would write from his visit to the Creek Nation, "Upon leaving my bed-room (which was dirty and ill-savoured enough to induce an early exit) I was pleased to see a happier instance of humanity . . . :—a young woman with the very looks of a mother and wife, was holding an infant on her bosom, while her husband, as he lay by her side, half-raised upon one elbow, with eager tenderness fondled the child, and smiled upon the mother. At once I thought of home; and at once I felt, the Indian is my brother."[18] Compared to rapacious settlers and dirty-dealing government

---

[15] See Christine Leigh Heyrmann, *Southern Cross: The Beginnings of the Bible Belt* (New York: Knopf, 1997).

[16] Ruth A. Tucker, *From Jerusalem to Irian Jaya: A Biographical History of Christian Missions* (Grand Rapids, Mich.: Zondervan, 1983), 96; Elsbree, *Rise of the Missionary Spirit*, 119.

[17] William Capers, "Mission Among the Creek Indians," *Methodist Magazine* (N.Y.) 5 (1822): 233.

[18] Ibid., 233, 272. Hiram Bingham described the Hawaiian mission as an effort "to raise that people from their degradation and barbarism, and convert them from their idols, their cruel superstitions, and their unbridled lusts." The Hawaiian people were "miserable captives of Satan, led by him at his will, [to] sacrifice even themselves or their children to devils, being given over to a reprobate mind, because they change the truth of God into a lie . . . ." Bingham, *Residence of Twenty-One Years in the Sandwich Islands, or, The Civil, Religious, and Political History of*

agents, the missionaries' sense of human solidarity and duty to children of one heavenly Father shone brightly.

In the case of both the Indians and the slaves, though, that Christian conviction came up against serious barriers. The missionaries sometimes struck compromises for the sake of evangelism, or found themselves ultimately powerless to prevent oppression—leaving brothers and sisters in the Lord without temporal justice.

It is a striking irony that the very popularity of foreign missions helped doom Indian and slave missions to involvement in temporal oppression. By the early 1800s the same institutionalizing movement that made possible concerted effort among the Indians was launching the first American missionaries to fields overseas. Churches and missionary societies found it much easier to excite interest in the foreign field abroad than in the "foreign" field at their doorsteps—where, after all, zeal for evangelism was entangled with national and even personal self-interest. And so the Indian and slave missions had to depend on financial support from powers having a definite conflict of interest in their evangelization.

In the case of the Indians, all kinds of church mission boards, including the Baptists, Methodists, and Presbyterians, gladly accepted government money—as did the many voluntary societies like the ABCFM. The United States Congress established in 1819 a "Civilization Fund" as the cheapest and most effective way to deal with the Indian problem. Indian nations that assimilated to white ways could be absorbed into white America—and who better to assimilate them than Christian missionaries, who worked for a pittance, accepted hardship cheerfully as the expected circumstances of their sacrificial ministry, resisted corruption, and applied themselves with, well, missionary zeal?[19]

But assimilation was not enough. The United States government intended to remove the Indians from lands desired by whites, in spite of previous treaties. Systematic removal began under President Monroe. The Wyandot Indians of Ohio, among whom Methodists were seeing some success, protested to the War Department. Their missionary, Methodist James Finley, argued forcefully that to remove them from their lands, where they were beginning to adopt Christianity and civilization, would cause converts to lose their faith. But Methodists ran their missions to Indians at the local conference level, where average Methodists were too closely identified with frontier settlers' anti-Indian attitudes and aims. The Wyandots were removed and removed again.[20] The majority of eastern and midwestern tribes suffered the same fate, so that very few of them live today upon their ancestral lands.

Those Islands, 3rd ed. (Canandaigua, N.Y.: H. D. Goodwin, 1855), v, 22. Another missionary to Hawaii, ex-slave Betsey Stockton, echoed Capers's assessment on seeing the islanders for the first time: "They were mostly naked except for a narrow strip of tapa around their loins. When they first came on board, the ladies retired to the cabin and burst into tears; and some of the gentlemen turned pale. . . . [M]y own soul sickened within me, and every nerve trembled. Are these, thought I, the beings with whom I must spend the remainder of my life? They are men and have souls—was the reply which conscience made." Quoted in Eileen F. Moffett, "Betsey Stockton: Pioneer American Missionary," *International Bulletin of Missionary Research* 19 (1995): 71–76.

[19] Beaver, *Church, State, and the American Indians*, 68–74.

[20] Ibid., 93–94.

The most notorious case of Indian removal was that of the Cherokees, whose forced eviction by the United States government not only remains a dark blot on the national honor, but also reveals the priority of economics and politics over the government's ostensible goals of Christianizing and civilizing the Indians. The Cherokees were the great success story of Indian missions, the nation that most quickly adopted European ways and the Christian religion. After 1785 they adopted settled agriculture. In the War of 1812 they fought in Andrew Jackson's army against the Creeks and the British. And when the missionaries came—Moravians in 1801, Baptists, Methodists, and the ABCFM in 1816/17— the Cherokees welcomed their preaching stations and schools. The ABCFM established among them a mission press that published a newspaper, the *Cherokee Phoenix*, and soon turned over the whole operation to the Cherokee Nation. A large proportion of the population converted and joined churches, especially Baptist and Methodist churches, where revival methods and easy terms of admission to membership prevailed. By 1825 the U.S. War Department (the branch of government tellingly entrusted with Indian relations) declared the Cherokees a Christian nation. In 1827 they even adopted a constitution modeled on that of the United States. Here was a people playing by all the rules of the civilize-and-Christianize ideal, a model of church-state cooperation in Indian affairs.

But the Cherokees intended to keep their lands and their sovereignty, and this the state of Georgia could not abide. Soon after the adoption of the Cherokee constitution, Georgia's legislature extended state law over Cherokee territory, declared Cherokee laws null and void, and pressed them to agree to emigrate. Settlers wanted the rich upcountry lands of the Cherokee nation, and the state wanted no foreign jurisdiction in its midst. The Georgia legislature passed punitive measures against missionaries who aided Cherokee resistance, blaming them for inciting the Indians to resist.[21]

ABCFM missionaries, joined by Moravians, Methodists and a Baptist, heroically stood for Cherokee rights. Officials arrested, chained, and abused several of them. Their cause in solidarity with the Cherokees became a national issue. Jeremiah Evarts, leader of the ABCFM, lobbied Congress and rallied his supporters to flood Washington with letters opposing Cherokee removal. They took the Cherokees' case to the Supreme Court and won in 1832: the Cherokees were a nation protected by the federal government and so immune from the laws of Georgia. But states' rights trumped everything. The state of Georgia simply ignored the Supreme Court decision. President Jackson refused to carry out the ruling, reportedly saying, "John Marshall [Supreme Court Chief Justice] has pronounced his judgment; let him enforce it if he can." In 1837 United States

---

[21] The fact that the ABCFM was headquartered in Boston, seat of William Lloyd Garrison's abolitionist journal, the *Liberator*, did not endear it to the Georgians. In 1831, the year of Nat Turner's slave uprising and the founding of the *Liberator*, Georgia's governor spoke to the legislature on the subject of Cherokee removal. "A most obstinate and perverse opposition has been made to the authority of the state, by certain persons representing themselves to be religious Missionaries, and particularly those who have acted under the direction of the Board of Foreign Missions in Boston." Note the omission of the term "American" and the substitution of "in Boston"—the governor clearly was playing on sectional and anti-abolitionist feeling. "Miscellanies: The Cherokees," *New England Magazine* 1 (July-Dec. 1831): 545.

Army troops forced the Cherokees from their lands and marched them westward across the Mississippi along the infamous Trail of Tears. Poor planning and bad weather resulted in many deaths along the way. But the miserable journey paled in comparison to the permanent loss described by a seventeen-year-old Cherokee girl. Her people had been "driven from a happy home and cultivated country to distant and desolate regions, which no light of civilization illumines and no association endears." Land-hungry Georgians held a lottery to assign the lands, making many new fortunes. The fine home and farm of John Ross, leader of the Cherokee delegation to Washington that pleaded against removal, became part of a new city named, of all things, Rome. In 1848 a visitor found the chief's former home occupied by the local Presbyterian minister, apparently with an untroubled conscience.[22]

So, while some missionaries took a heroic stand for Indian rights, they could not prevail against the self-interest of local whites and the theoretical scruples or political pragmatics of others, inside and outside the church. When two Methodist missionaries among the Cherokees opposed removal, and were jailed for it, the Tennessee Conference of the Methodist Church publicly rebuked them for meddling in politics. The conservative Presbyterian *Biblical Repertory* lamented the ill-treatment of the southeastern tribes, and arraigned the "cupidity" that motivated it, yet declared in the end that "right existed on the side of Georgia"—for the federal government had no constitutional right to meddle in a state's internal affairs, and had it done so, it might have provoked civil war.[23]

Not even missionaries to Indians could agree about Indian removal. The Baptists were in fact ardent advocates for it. Isaac McCoy, working in Indiana and faced with the nasty behavior of white settlers near his mission, believed it better for his charges to settle as far away from white influence as possible. He even took a government post in charge of surveying western lands to which to remove the tribes and had a large hand in devising the plan for removal that the government adopted in 1830.[24] McCoy understood the evil of removal, but believed it a better alternative than the evil of annihilation or corruption by whites.

After removal the American Indian missions continued, now largely in the "Indian Territory" stretching from today's Oklahoma to the Dakotas. Both church and state took a paternalistic approach to the missions, believing the only hope for Indians lay in adopting white ways and joining white society. To achieve this goal they turned to boarding schools as their favored method. According to missionary reports, dispirited Indian parents, seeing the doom of their old way of life, gladly sent their children to live entirely under white supervision. A missions executive reported in 1854:

---

[22] Beaver, *Church, State, and the American Indians*, 103–13; Latourette, *History of the Expansion of Christianity*, 4: 315–16.; A. A. Ross, "The Wrongs of the Cherokees," an examination essay for her New Jersey school printed in the Methodist *Ladies' Repository* 5 (1845): 169; Erskine Clarke, *Dwelling Place: A Plantation Epic* (New Haven: Yale University Press, 2005), 264–65.

[23] Beaver, *Church, State, and the American Indians*, 93–94; [Charles Hodge?], "Indian Affairs," *Biblical Repertory* 11 (1838): 513–18, 534.

[24] Beaver, *Church, State, and the American Indians*, 97–98.

The scholars in such institutions are trained up under Christian influence, instruction, and example. They live in the missionary household, and are clothed, plainly but comfortably, after our fashion. The boys are taught to work in the garden and on the farm; the girls to knit, sew, and attend to the common duties of housekeeping. They are taught the English language, and the usual branches of common-school learning. They are assembled morning and evening at family worship, and on the Sabbath they unite together in the services of the sanctuary. Thus they are in training for the duties of life under the happiest circumstances.[25]

—except, of course, for the fact of systematic separation from their own families at a very young age. Missionaries found "their chief encouragement" in boarding schools, where they had visible success in initiating young Indians into white Christian ways. Here was missionary paternalism at its height, absorbing Indians into the missionary household and supplanting the entire parental role. Now that the Indians were removed physically from their homelands, the missionaries with government assistance removed them culturally from their heritage as well. Missionaries found the results of the boarding school system cheering, well worth the considerable expense, for many students received Christ and some even went into the ministry themselves. All told, by 1854 there were 2,477 Indian children in mission boarding schools, and nearly ten thousand communicant church members. Yet the emotional damage to parents and children, and the outright cultural loss, was severe.[26]

Slave Missions

A recent book employs the phrase "slave missions" in its title (rather than "missions to slaves") for a very good reason: evangelism and discipleship among American slaves was not a just a white-to-black affair; slaves numbered among the missionaries themselves and indeed inspired the formalized white-led mission work that followed.[27]

African laborers in America predate the coming of the Pilgrims, yet for two hundred years the majority of American blacks remained non-Christian. Some owners did believe it their duty to evangelize their slaves, and in the mid- and

---

[25] John C. Lowrie, *A Manual of Missions, or, Sketches of the Foreign Missions of the Presbyterian Church* (New York: Anson D. F. Randolph, 1854), 21, 24.

[26] Ibid., 23, 71. The 259 missionary assistants include some natives. The boarding school system reached larger proportions after the Civil War and lasted into the twentieth century. A good deal of money was spent on the boarding school system, including substantial government annuities to tribes in compensation for removal. The missionary force (some 125 missionaries and 259 assistants in 1854) was large in proportion to the Indian population. Might these resources have been put to more effective and compassionate use?

[27] Janet Duitsman Cornelius, *Slave Missions and the Black Church in the Antebellum South* (Columbia, S.C.: University of South Carolina Press, 1999), 3.

late 1700s many slaves and freedmen responded to the Great Awakening and its Baptist and Methodist aftermath in the South—but still the bulk of the black population, especially in areas dominated by large plantations where slaves rarely interacted with whites other than the overseer, remained at best only remotely familiar with Christianity.[28]

Again the Methodists provide us a good example of this "home foreign" mission. Free blacks in the Methodist church of Charleston, South Carolina, "men of intelligence and piety, who read the Scriptures and understood them," went out to nearby plantations to hold meetings with blacks slave and free in the first decade of the 1800s. Similar informal evangelism by blacks was going on up the coast all the way to Baltimore. When William Capers, whom we met earlier as a missionary to the Creek Nation, took charge of the Charleston Methodist church in 1811, he decided to place slave missions under formal church control.[29] While Methodists were famous for not requiring higher education for their ministers, they worried that untutored leaders and unsupervised discipleship among African Americans might lead to syncretism, or the blending of paganism and Christianity. Formalized mission gave the work publicity in the *Methodist Magazine*, encouraged sustained and concerted effort, and placed the mission under white oversight—something very important given slaveholders' need to guard against uprisings. But it was also a step backward in mission effectiveness, converting an indigenous evangelization back into a "mission to."[30]

Slave missions got more complicated after 1822, when a free black named Denmark Vesey, himself a Methodist class leader, attempted to launch a slave revolt. Planters were now much more suspicious of black evangelists and disciplers. Even white missionaries to slaves had to tread carefully. To get access to the plantations, Capers established the Methodist Mission to Slaves by agreeing to a plan devised by a number of leading Christian plantation owners. The planters not only allowed the missionaries access, but funded their mission. A nice deal—except that they stipulated that evangelism and discipleship had to exclude talk of earthly freedom and even had to abandon the usual mission component of civilizing. A Methodist preacher taking part in the mission promised in 1831 "not to civilize them—not to change their social condition—not to exalt them into citizens or freemen—but to save them. . . . Sweeten their toil—sanctify their lives—hallow their deaths."[31] With this move Methodists gained the confidence of Southern slaveholders and launched upon an evange-

---

[28] Michael Gomez dates the overall Christianization of American blacks to the period between 1830 and 1860. This of course does not mean that every African American was converted by then, but rather that a Christianized African American culture had emerged—retaining strong ties to African belief and practice, he argues. Michael A. Gomez, *Exchanging Our Country Marks: The Transformation of African Identities in the Colonial and Antebellum South* (Chapel Hill, N.C.: University of North Carolina Press, 1998), 251–63.

[29] Cornelius, *Slave Missions*, 47–49.

[30] To secure right doctrine, Capers published a *Catechism for the Use of Methodist Missions* (Charleston, S.C.: John Early, 1853).

[31] Cornelius, *Slave Missions*, 50–51. She writes, "The symbol of the neglected slave, who could only be reached if missionaries accepted planters' conditions, forced into silence those Methodists who disliked slavery or who wanted converts to read the Bible."

listic mission of vast proportions. Black membership in the Methodist Church grew to 65,000 in 1835 and 217,000 by 1860.[32]

Another "apostle to the slaves," the Presbyterian Charles Colcock Jones, provides an equally instructive story. One of the planter elite from the Georgia low country, Jones applied the Edwardsean theology of "disinterested benevolence" he had learned at Andover Seminary to the slaveholding in which his family was deeply invested. As a young theological student he decided that slavery was an evil to be eradicated—but not immediately, as the abolitionists would have it. Slaves, he believed, needed well-educated white preachers to give them the gospel in its doctrinal purity. They needed Christian masters, too, who would model for them the Christian virtues and school them for eventual civilization—a civilization to then be carried back to Africa, so that the victims of American slavery might in God's redemptive purpose become the preachers and teachers to bring the "Dark Continent" into the light. It was a thoroughgoing paternalism, benevolent in its avowed purposes, but premised on the notion that Africans were incapable of self-government. Jones established preaching stations among the slaves of his own numerous plantations and throughout his home county, winning many planters to his vision of Christian slaveholding. He studied African culture carefully in order to understand his audience as best he could. He devised an admirable system of oral instruction (since it was illegal to teach a slave to read) that soon was adapted to many foreign mission fields, including a catechism and several topical series. Jones and the local churches enrolled slaves as "watchmen" in charge of reporting cases of church discipline to the white elders for action. He got to know personally, and love genuinely, scores of slaves, visiting them weekly in their settlements. He established and ran the Liberty County Association for the Religious Instruction of Slaves, writing numerous reports of his work for publication in the *Charleston Observer*. And in keeping with his mission's guiding paternalistic ideal, he sought to convert white planters to Christ, so that they would sincerely seek to improve the physical and moral circumstances of their slaves by supplying adequate housing, food, and clothing, and especially by hallowing slave marriage and family life. In these ways Jones worked to better the lot of people in bondage—without disturbing the system of bondage itself.[33]

There was a bitter irony in this approach to slave missions. The more fully planters lived up to Jones' benevolent slaveholder ideal, the more slavery seemed justified not only as an economic system but as a means to civilize and Christianize the African. Jones himself came to abandon his early antislavery sentiments, believing that he and others were providing for the slaves' spiritual and physical welfare in ways that blacks were incapable of themselves. The one-time antislavery missionary became a prominent advocate of proslavery argu-

---

[32] Ibid., 48.

[33] Jones's life and missionary efforts are richly presented in Erskine Clarke's marvelous new book, *Dwelling Place: A Plantation Epic*, cited above—made possible by the publication of the Jones family correspondence in Robert Manson Myers's monumental *The Children of Pride: A True Story of Georgia and the Civil War* (New Haven: Yale University Press, 1972). On benevolence and slave missions, see Larry E. Tise, *Proslavery: A History of the Defense of Slavery in America, 1701–1840* (Athens, Ga.: University of Georgia Press, 1987), 294–301.

ments, and this in good part because of, not in spite of, his missionary efforts.[34] Harriet Beecher Stowe, author of *Uncle Tom's Cabin*, saw it and made a public example of Jones: while he was "a man of the finest feelings for humanity, and for many years an assiduous laborer for the good of the slave," yet his case brought one to "see painfully how the moral sense of the finest mind may be perverted by constant familiarity with such a system." Benevolent masters only masked the fundamental sinfulness of chattel slavery, she argued, for reducing people to property and placing them under absolute power invited all kinds of degradation. Leaving a fundamental injustice intact, mission work within the slave system necessarily imparted an incomplete gospel.[35]

Even under these circumstances slave missions enjoyed remarkable success. The gospel of Jesus Christ the suffering servant had a raw appeal to people in bondage. Slaves found plenty to identify with in both the Old Testament and the New, and welcomed the promise of forgiveness and a home in glory where the last shall be first and the meek will inherit the earth. By 1851 Richard Fuller of South Carolina would report that missionary stations in the South had yielded "56,000 professed converts" joining the churches, and that black church membership in the slave states numbered about 350,000. In sheer numbers the slave missions far surpassed any other missionary effort in the world.[36] But it came at a cost. Missionaries set aside antislavery sentiments for the chance of bringing spiritual salvation to a population otherwise unreachable by formal missionary effort. Slaves heard a gospel message bereft of earthly justice and knew it. They slipped away to their "hush harbors" all the more, taking the gospel they heard from the missionaries and developing on their own the messages of the Exodus and the Day of Jubilee, of a church that is no respecter of persons and in which the humble have great things to offer to the high. While Southern whites committed themselves to a separation of the "spiritual" from the "political" (extending in the Presbyterian case to a well-defined doctrine of the "spirituality of the church"), blacks developed a powerful alternative emphasis that would speak with prophetic voice to Christian America in later generations.[37] The missionaries faced a choice between evils that God was still able to turn to good, though not in their lifetimes.

---

[34] Tise, *Proslavery*, 331–33.

[35] Harriet Beecher Stowe, *A Key to Uncle Tom's Cabin* (1853), quoted in Clarke, *Dwelling Place*, 298–99.

[36] Richard Fuller, *Our Duty to the African Race: An Address Delivered at Washington, D.C., January 21, 1851* (Baltimore, Md.: W. M. Innes, 1851), quoted in Cornelius, *Slave Missions*, 172–73. Interestingly, Lowrie did not include slave missions in his statistical overview of Protestant missions in 1854—perhaps because of the sensitivity of the subject in view of the sectional conflict over slavery, perhaps because American slaves did not fit in the category "unevangelized nations." But Fuller's figure of 350,000 church members clearly outpaces not only the nearest competitors (Guiana and the West Indies with 76,072 communicants; Pacific Islands with 42,518), but the total of communicants in missions churches worldwide (180,653). Lowrie, *Manual of Missions*, title page and 71. Of course mission churches were not the usual churches American blacks belonged to, so the comparison is difficult.

[37] Clarke, *Dwelling Place*, 158–66; Albert Raboteau, *Slave Religion: The "Invisible Institution" in the Antebellum South* (New York: Oxford University Press, 1978). A particularly fine exposition of the African American prophetic voice to white America is Raboteau's treatment of Francis Grimké in "'Ethiopia Shall Soon Stretch Forth Her Hands': Black Destiny in Nineteenth-Century America," in his *A Fire in the Bones: Reflections on African American Religious History* (Boston: Beacon Press, 1996), 37–56.

Closely allied to Capers- and Jones-style slave missions was one of the most popular benevolent reforms in antebellum America: the establishing of a Christian republic in Liberia, West Africa, from which to spread the gospel and civilization throughout the "Dark Continent." On the face of it, the idea of sending African-Americans to extend Christ's kingdom in Africa may seem a definite step forward from the slave missions at home. The moral compromises necessitated by working within the slave system, the competing interests that beset any combination of mission and conquest, the division of Christ's body along racial lines—these obstacles presumably would vanish. What did remain, however, was the dicey combination of mission work with settlement by cultural outsiders, for African-American emigrants to Liberia quickly found that they were no longer (nor had they ever been) generic Africans, inherently suited to "preach to their own kind."[38]

The American Colonization Society, founded in 1817, was the center of the colonization effort, but many smaller societies existed at the state and local level, especially in the South. Although the idea met decisive rejection from free black communities after about 1830, African Americans had been among the first to propose such a plan—slaves in Massachusetts in 1773; free blacks in Newport, Rhode Island in the 1780s; and the Quaker ship owner Paul Cuffee in 1816. The founding of the British colonization project, Sierra Leone (1787), boosted interest in a similar colony for American ex-slaves. Whites and blacks in favor of the idea saw in it the opportunity for evangelization, black independence, and a straightforward solution to America's race problem by returning the former slaves to Africa.[39] Leading churchmen gave colonization hearty endorsement as part of a package plan with gradual abolition and financial compensation to slaveholders for the loss of their human property. This three-part scheme, they believed, presented the best hope for doing justice all around—and solving the sectional crisis that was threatening the nation with civil war.[40]

A further reason colonization enjoyed such wide appeal was that it enabled one to admit the wickedness of slavery while finding larger purpose in it: in God's providence American slavery would lead to the redemption of Africa. This idea appealed to Christian slaveholders with troubled consciences and to other whites concerned with America's calling as a Christian nation, but just as importantly it helped many black Christians find meaning in the horrors of their enslavement. They could identify with Joseph in Egypt, who told his brothers who enslaved him, "You meant it for evil, but God meant it for good."[41]

---

[38] An opponent of the plan admitted in 1832 that "the Colonization Society is a favorite of the nation, and that our view of it is exceedingly unpopular," and even the Boston editors, in publishing the anti-colonization piece, distanced themselves from its criticisms. "The American Colonization Society," *New England Magazine* 2 (1832): 13.

[39] Cornelius, *Slave Missions*, 160–61. To this list of motives she adds *profit* as well.

[40] Ibid., 172–73; Charles Hodge, review of *The Question of Negro Slavery and the New Constitution of Kentucky*, by Robert Jefferson Breckinridge, *Biblical Repertory and Princeton Review* 21 (1849): 582–607; cf. Allen C. Guelzo, "Charles Hodge's Antislavery Moment," in *Charles Hodge Revisited: A Critical Appraisal of His Life and Work*, ed. John W. Stewart and James H. Moorhead (Grand Rapids, Mich.: Eerdmans, 2002), 299–325.

[41] Cornelius, *Slave Missions*, 161. The providential reading of colonization is hotly contested. Allen C. Guelzo minces no words: "Colonization disguised itself as benevolence to blacks when in fact what it really amounted to

As with Indian missions, colonization attracted government interest, forming a curious collaboration between church and state. Politicians such as Senator Henry Clay and Presidents Jefferson, Madison, Monroe, Fillmore, and Lincoln backed the effort, alongside a host of evangelical ministers and lay slaveholders. Unlike Indian missions, however, the key missionaries in this effort were non-white. Black preachers eagerly promoted the Liberian mission and went there themselves, including pioneers Daniel Coker of the African Methodist Episcopal Church and Baptists Lott Cary and Colin Teague. Episcopalians and Disciples of Christ followed, as did Presbyterians. Disease and disorganization plagued the early years, but between 1822 and 1865 some 13,000 African-Americans emigrated to Liberia. The heyday of emigration came after Liberia became an independent state with an African-American president (1847) and as events of the 1850s made prospects of racial justice in America look dimmer than ever, causing some free black leaders in the United States to take a second look at colonization. Some whites for their part began to view colonization as the best hope to avert a civil war or, when war came, to "mitigate the social effects of emancipation."[42]

As this long list of motivations suggests, the colonization effort often excited interest more for its expected benefits to America than to Africa. The Liberian mission never succeeded in its touted goals on the other side of the Atlantic. Emigrants died of disease within months of their arrival, confounding the hopes and prayers of many. West Africa became "the graveyard of missionaries," black and white—prompting many reflections on God's "strange providences." Presbyterian John Lowrie wrote of one of many failed starts, "Seldom have we known a mission commenced with more deliberate and well-informed judgment, conducted by more devoted and thoroughly qualified men, and resulting in more disastrous and apparently fruitless efforts."[43] Yet some survived and valiantly worked to establish schools and churches, finding as missionaries often do that the people are more interested in acquiring Western advantages like education than in accepting Christ. And the notion that America's Africans were ideally suited to evangelize "their own people" proved illusory as well: Africans thought in terms of tribal identity, not generic "Africanness." West Africans found their new African-American neighbors so profoundly different from themselves that they referred to them as "white men."[44] A two-tiered so-

---

was protectionism for whites, which is why so many antislavery Northerners used it to sugarcoat emancipation." It was "a crude precursor to apartheid." Guelzo, *Lincoln's Emancipation Proclamation: The End of Slavery in America* (New York: Simon and Schuster, 2004), 155. Guelzo's remarks refer to President Lincoln's consideration of colonization as part of his plan for emancipation.

[42] John Saillant, "Missions and Race Relations in the United States, 1822–1860," in *The Foreign Missionary Enterprise at Home: Explorations in North American Cultural History*, ed. Daniel H. Bays and Grant Wacker (Tuscaloosa, Ala.: University of Alabama Press, 2003), 15–17; Cornelius, *Slave Missions*, 172; Guelzo, *Lincoln's Emancipation Proclamation*, 155–61. The quotation is from Cornelius. Eric Burin's new history of the ACS, *Slavery and the Peculiar Solution: A History of the American Colonization Society* (Gainesville, Fla.: University Press of Florida, 2005), gives emigration statistics on pages 169–73. Some 5,888 people emigrated to Liberia under ACS auspices between 1848 and 1860.

[43] Lowrie, *Manual of Missions*, 31–32.

[44] Cornelius, *Slave Missions*, 166.

cial structure developed in Liberia, with blacks of American ancestry as the ruling class. Liberia never became a model Christian republic. Indeed, as early as 1854 mission boards were wondering whether Liberia's republican governmental form hindered the mission's effectiveness, since republics depend upon a populace in whom education and self-command are deeply rooted, and ex-slaves hardly fitted the bill.[45]

Back home in America, despite the basic racism of the colonization project, the Liberian mission did benefit blacks. The proposal that African-Americans undertake the mission meant that they must be trained for it, and so provided a strong challenge to the Southern laws prohibiting slave literacy. Missionaries to slaves in America often favored the colonization project for just this reason, as did free blacks like Arabella Jones of Washington, D.C. Jones promoted her school for black girls by pointing out that "many of our citizens of color are emigrating to Liberia, and it is necessary, as well-wishers of our race, that our children be well educated, in order to impart their knowledge, to the illiterate." Christian slaveholders, too, promoted education for slaves and the repeal of slave literacy bans in view of the Liberian mission.[46]

On the whole, we see in slave missions a mixture of success and failure: success in bringing a large population to Christ in about a generation and awakening many consciences to the evils of slavery, whatever the intentions of particular missionaries; and failure to bring a whole-person gospel to people in bondage when that bondage served the interests of the sending society. As with Indian missions, we see the inherent problems when missions are joined with settlement and domination. While colonization offered to transcend the spiritualization of the gospel and the perpetuation of systematic subordination, its entanglement with political needs in America and use of the settlement strategy in Africa severely limited its success.[47] Yet we can discern ways in which God was indeed able to bring good out of human evil.

The Sandwich Islands Mission

A striking counterexample to "home foreign" missions was the showcase American overseas mission of the early nineteenth century: the Hawaiian or Sandwich Islands Mission of the American Board of Commissioners for Foreign Missions. While this field too had its share of difficulties, it yielded an unusual number of happy providences, confirming the mission's sense of calling. Missionaries encountered a Hawaiian leadership eager not only to receive the words of eternal life, but also to reorder society according to the law of God. William R. Hutchison comments that this "was the venture that best realized

---

[45] Lowrie, *Manual of Missions*, 29.

[46] Cornelius, *Slave Missions*, 166–68. See articles in the ACS journal, *The African Repository* (1825–1892).

[47] For further reflections on the problems inherent in the combination of settlement with mission work, see George Marsden's account of the work among the Stockbridge Indians in his *Jonathan Edwards: A Life* (New Haven: Yale University Press, 2003), 406–409.

early visions of entire tribes and nations entering the Kingdom on something like the urgent millennial schedule."[48]

The Sandwich Islands, as they were then called, had been discovered by Captain Cook in 1770. His account of this exotic locale stirred the imaginations of missions-minded evangelicals keen to take the gospel to the very ends of the earth. But traders got there first, disrupting internal power relations, exploiting the natives for prostitution, introducing alcohol and diseases, and causing the population to decline by more than half. In 1820, when the first modest ABCFM party arrived—headed by only two ordained missionaries—the Hawaiian leaders found them much preferable to the whites they had encountered thus far, and welcomed them to stay. Within twenty years the mission could boast having committed the Hawaiian language to writing, translated parts of the Bible, enrolled thousands in schools, and guided the native government to enact laws against prostitution, drunkenness, profanation of the Sabbath, and gambling. Best of all, almost twenty percent of the population had joined the church, thanks especially to a mass revival in the late 1830s.[49]

This signal success crowned the early work of the ABCFM, a joint effort of Congregationalists, Presbyterians, and Dutch Reformed founded in 1810 in the first flush of nineteenth-century evangelical hopefulness. The zeal of youth started the missionary juggernaut rolling. In an oft-repeated story, a dozen students at Williams College (Massachusetts) were praying outdoors in 1806 when a rainstorm rolled in and the group sought refuge under a haystack. There they pledged themselves, God permitting, to go as missionaries to Asia. The students, led by Samuel Mills (1783–1818), were inspired by the new foreign mission societies in England and especially by William Carey. They dreamed of being the first from America to join the overseas missionary effort—though no foreign missions board, denominational or otherwise, yet existed in the United States. They formed a secret society to encourage each other and "inquire" into the missionary call. Several of them enrolled in the new Andover Theological Seminary and approached the Massachusetts General Association of the Congregational Church for guidance and possible support. Their elders advised them to study and wait—not the most welcome words to eager young visionaries. Only when one of their number, Adoniram Judson, betook himself to England and returned with commissions from the London Missionary Society in case the Americans would not support them, and after a wealthy lady made a generous bequest, did the fledgling Board agree to send the first missionaries off to India.[50]

Judson and his wife Ann Haseltine, members of the first little band of foreign missionaries of the ABCFM, decided while en route to India that infant baptism was unbiblical, and on arrival in India resigned their commissions, joining instead with the English Baptists. Needless to say, this providence read one way to the Baptists, another way to the Congregationalists and Presbyterians. The

---

[48] Hutchison, *Errand to the World*, 69.

[49] Ibid., 69–70.

[50] William E. Strong, *The Story of the American Board: An Account of the First Hundred Years of the American Board of Commissioners for Foreign Missions* (Boston: Pilgrim Press, 1910), 3–16.

Judsons went on to fruitful work in Burma, and other ABCFM missionaries went to India, but by another set of providences a field opened for the ABCFM in the Sandwich Islands.

While these American students were dreaming of foreign missionary work and making preparations for it, half a world away in Hawaii a lad named Opukahaʻia witnessed the brutal murder of his parents and infant brother during King Kamehameha's wars of unification. After some training to be a pagan priest, he and another lad named Hopoʻo left their home islands on an American trading ship, arriving in New Haven in 1809. Sailors on board the ship named the boys Henry and Thomas. At Yale College they met Christian students who, flush with excitement over the college revivals of those years, took the Hawaiians under their wings, brought them to classes, tutored them, and led them to the Lord. Henry lived for some time with the family of Yale president Timothy Dwight.[51]

Samuel Mills, leader of the haystack prayer meeting a few years before, on hearing of these Hawaiians, proposed a boarding school for the training of likely foreign youths who could then bring the gospel back to their homelands. In 1816 the ABCFM established the Cornwall School in the hills of northwestern Connecticut. Along with Henry and Thomas were seven other Hawaiians, eight Cherokees, three Stockbridges, two each of Choctaws, Oneidas, and Caughnowagas, a Tahitian, a Malayan, and a Marquesan. In time Chinese, Greeks, and others came. Though Opukahaʻia died in 1818, his dream of carrying the gospel back to Hawaii inspired the ABCFM to attempt it.[52]

The Cornwall School lasted only about ten years. Interestingly, while the American Indian missions adopted the boarding school system and stuck with it as the best hope for Native Americans after removal, the American Board found the boarding school unsuited to foreign missionary goals. It was costly, and in accustoming the natives to white American ways it alienated them from their home culture, making them less effective communicators to their people. "In short," Rufus Anderson wrote, "the indications of Providence seemed clearly to teach, that the best education for heathen youths, and indeed the only suitable education, having reference to their success as teachers of their uncivilized brethren, must be given through the instrumentality of missionary institutions in their respective countries."[53]

A year after Opukahaʻia's death Thomas Hopoʻo and two other Hawaiians joined as "native helpers" with two ordained missionaries and their wives in the first mission to the Sandwich Islands. The sermon text at their ABCFM com-

---

[51] Edwin W. Dwight, *Memoirs of Henry Obookiah, a Native of Owhyhee and a Member of the Foreign Mission School* (New Haven: Nathan Whiting, 1819), 3–25.

[52] Hiram Bingham, *Twenty-One Years*, 57–59; Rufus Anderson, *History of the Sandwich Islands Mission* (Boston: Congregational Publishing Society, 1870), 10–12.

[53] Anderson, *History of the Sandwich Islands Mission*, 13–15. Another providence coming through this failed venture, Anderson remarked, was the assurance it gave to the Choctaws and Cherokees "of the really benevolent feelings of the whites toward the Indians." (A poignantly misplaced confidence, it turned out.) And among American Christians it provided a "display of native talent," convincing donors that the "heathen" really could be civilized and Christianized.

missioning was Joshua 13:1—"There remaineth yet very much land to be possessed." A doctor, two schoolmasters, a printer, and a farmer, together with their wives and children, completed the band. (This grouping gives a good indication of the breadth of instruction in civilization the missionaries intended.) Hiram Bingham recounted their arrival after more than five months at sea, March 30, 1820:

> As we approached the northern extremity of Hawaii, we gazed successively, upon the verdant hills, and deep ravines, the habitations of the islanders, the rising columns of smoke, the streams cascades, trees, and vestiges of volcanic agency: then, with glasses, stretching our vision, we descried the objects of our solicitude, moving along the shore—immortal beings, purchased with redeeming blood, and here and there, the monuments of their superstition.[54]

The missionaries had every reason to expect to have to deal with the despotic king Kamehameha, who had taken advantage of Western firearms to unify the islands, and with the time-honored traditions of Hawaii: a pagan priesthood staunchly defending its customs and powers, human sacrifice, infanticide, sexual promiscuity, a complex system of taboos that enslaved the common people and threatened them with death for any infraction.[55] But Bingham explained, "How were our hearts surprised, agitated, and encouraged beyond every expectation, to hear the report—'Kamehameha is dead—His son Liholiho is king—the tabus are abolished—the images are destroyed—the heiaus [temples] of idolatrous worship are burned, and the party that attempted to restore them by force of arms has recently been vanquished!' The hand of God! how visible in thus beginning to answer the prayer of his people, for the Hawaiian race!"[56]

"The nation, without a religion, was waiting for the law of Jehovah," concluded ABCFM leader Rufus Anderson. The Hawaiians even told Bingham that a prophet named Kalaikuahulu, a generation before the missionaries' arrival, had predicted "that a communication would be made to them from Heaven (the residence of 'Ke Akua maoli,' the real God) entirely different from anything they had known, and that the tabus of the country would be subverted."[57]

---

[54] Bingham, *Twenty-One Years*, 69.

[55] Bingham describes the taboo system on pages 20–22, painting the priests as wholesale licensed murderers, "seizing men and women at pleasure, binding, strangling, or beating them to death, and offering them up in sacrifice to their malevolent deities." Even as sympathetic an interpreter of Hawaiian traditions as Susanna Moore writes that before the abolition of the taboo system, "Violence, ritualized violence, lay deep at the center of things. To be an ancient Hawaiian was to be terrified most of the time." Susanna Moore, *I Myself Have Seen It: The Myth of Hawai'i* (Washington D.C.: National Geographic Society, 2003), 41. Ruth Tabrah notes that "the ending of kapu [taboo] was met with, jubilation. . . . The freeing from kapu brought a deep inner change to Hawaiians who would never again feel the swift death-dealing blow of a club against the skull for failing to prostrate at the approach of even the shadow of a chief. Never again would a woman who ate with a man, or a girl who tasted banana, coconut, or pork, risk death." Ruth M. Tabrah, *Hawaii: A Bicentennial History* (New York: W. W. Norton, 1980), 35–36.

[56] Bingham, *Twenty-One Years*, 70; Anderson, *History of the Sandwich Islands Mission*, 18–19.

[57] Anderson, *History of the Sandwich Islands Mission*, 19; Bingham, *Twenty-One Years*, 28.

Here was a most remarkable state of affairs, and the missionaries gladly stepped in to a kind of top-down mission reminiscent of the conversion and education of medieval Europe by Benedictine monks. The first great breakthrough came when Thomas Hopoʻo brought the queen mother Keʻopuolani to faith in Christ. Then the very woman who brought about the abolition of the Hawaiian religion, Kamehameha's favorite wife Kaʻahumanu (now prime minister), took ill, and Sybil Bingham patiently nursed her and prayed for her. This forceful royal, so uninterested in Christianity despite the longsuffering attentions of the missionary wives, became convinced that Mrs. Bingham's prayers had brought her healing. Kaʻahumanu became a Christian and directed her considerable power to the Christianization of Hawaii, with Hiram Bingham as her personal mentor in things spiritual and governmental.[58]

With such a wide open door Bingham and his fellow missionaries set about building their idea of a Christian society in Hawaii. An extensive system of schools instructed first the ruling class, and soon the commoners, in reading, writing, arithmetic, and the Bible, all in the Hawaiian language. Like the American Indian boarding school students, Hawaiians learned to adopt Anglo-American gender roles and ideals of domestic life. And a decade and a half after the conversion of key nobles, the "great revival" of 1837–1840 brought thousands into the church through the use of intensive week-long series of meetings, invitations to join inquirers' groups, and other methods that encouraged religious intensity. With some 22,000 communicants in a population of 100,000, the ABCFM pronounced the Sandwich Islands a Christianized nation in 1853.[59]

This mass-inculcation in New England Christian ways benefited the Hawaiians significantly. Not only did they learn the words of eternal life, they became one of the most literate societies on earth. The chasm between noble and commoner narrowed, as missionaries insisted on schooling for common people and the gospel taught spiritual equality and mutual love. Indeed, it was a former slave, Betsey Stockton—the first unmarried American woman to go to the foreign field—who opened the first school for commoners in Hawaii.[60] And while Hawaii remained a monarchy rather than a democratic republic, the natives themselves adopted a written constitution limiting the monarch by a declaration of rights grounded in the gift of God and the exercise of personal responsibility. Bingham, key advisor to the "instructed natives" who produced

---

[58] Tabrah, *Hawaii*, 34–35, 41. On the importance of missionary wives and their modeling of Christian domesticity, see Dana Robert, "Evangelist or Homemaker? Mission Strategies of Early Nineteenth-Century Missionary Wives in Burma and Hawaii," *International Bulletin of Missionary Research* 17 (2004): 4–12.

[59] Lowrie, *Manual of Missions*, 70; Hutchison, *Errand to the World*, 87.

[60] Moffett, "Betsey Stockton"; John A. Andrew III, "Betsey Stockton: Stranger in a Strange Land," *Journal of Presbyterian History* 52 (1974): 157–66. Stockton was not a product of the slave missions of the South. She grew up in the North in the family of Ashbel Green, the first professor of Princeton Seminary, at the time when Pennsylvania and New Jersey were gradually abolishing slavery.

the legislation, urged that the new statutory laws ought not obliterate the existing common law of Hawaii.[61]

But an extreme cultural makeover in the image of New England, however benign in intent, alienated Hawaiians from their own heritage and created a deep loss of identity. "Civilizing" went too far. Wrestling, kite flying, and other traditional Hawaiian amusements were outlawed, along with the hula. This theme has dominated treatments of the Sandwich Island mission ever since, most famously in James Michener's *Hawaii*. The Hawaiians have become poster children against missionary suppression of innocent pleasures, as just about any travel video on Hawaii will attest. Puritanical inhibition, the story goes, stultified native enjoyment of their island paradise.[62] When in the twentieth century Americans replaced the old ethos of restraint with the celebration of release and gratification, the assumed superiority of Western culture gave way to cultural pluralism, and Hawaii became the fiftieth state, the tourist industry remade the islands once again into a garden of earthly delights—the missionary era serving in current retellings only to throw the pleasures of paradise into high relief.

Pleasure-vs.-Puritanism aside, though, the Sandwich Islands mission represents for many modern interpreters, along with foreign missions generally, a deeper problem. It was not just the makeover in the New England mode that alienated the Hawaiians from their identity, leaving "such deep wounds that it would be more than a century before Hawaiians once again began to take pride in who and what they were." It was the change of religions itself. "The freedom that accompanied the emancipation from the ancient myths came with a terrible price," writes Susanna Moore. Few Hawaiians "understood that the abolition of the old rituals would inevitably render the culture weak and porous, ultimately leading to a collective loss of memory, if not annihilation."[63] While students of missions today affirm the importance of preserving cultural practices that do not skew the gospel, we must not imagine that the words of life necessitate psychological and cultural death. How to bring the gospel in its wholeness without engaging in cultural imperialism has become a dominant theme in mission work today.

In 1993 the remains of Henry Opukaha'ia were moved from Connecticut to a hillside on the Big Island overlooking the ocean. The Connecticut Office of State Archaeology viewed it as another instance of "repatriation"—the giving back to native peoples of grave contents and cultural treasures. Hawaiian Christians saw in the event something deeper. They celebrated Opukaha'ia's homecoming, not to make ethnic identity more important than Christian identity, but to claim Christianity as their own. The earthly remains of the man who inspired the Hawaiian mission belong in Hawaii, not New England, to embody

---

[61] Bingham, *Residence of Twenty-One Years*, 561. His translation of the constitution from the original Hawaiian follows.

[62] James A. Michener, *Hawaii* (New York: Random House, 1959); Bradford Smith, *Yankees in Paradise* (Philadelphia: Lippincott, 1956). These were by no means the first to criticize the mission for cultural meddling. Herman Melville and Elizabeth Elkins Sanders had sounded that note already in the 1840s. Hutchison, *Errand to the World*, 74–77.

[63] Tabrah, *Hawaii*, 48; Moore, *I Myself Have Seen It*, 53.

the fact that one need not abandon one people for another to become a follower of Christ.[64]

Conclusion

Early nineteenth-century American evangelicals felt a sense of destiny, not just as a nation but as a vanguard of Christ's church—and with that sense of destiny, a feeling of opportunity and grave responsibility. As one seminarian wrote,

> We are living, we are dwelling in a grand and awful time,
> In an age on ages telling; to be living is sublime.
> Hark! the waking up of nations, hosts advancing to the fray;
> Hark! what soundeth is creation's groaning for the latter day.[65]

The zealous theological student who penned these words was not a fiery Methodist or God-and-country Presbyterian, but an Episcopalian in New York City who would soon become deeply interested in the Oxford movement. And so his expression of early American missionary zeal suggests just how pervasive was the Protestant conviction that the century of progress would herald the coming of Christ's reign on earth.

With this confidence in the coming Kingdom, American missionaries joined those from Britain and Europe—and in some cases indigenous missionary pioneers, as we have seen—in launching the Great Century of missionary expansion. But the very forces that produced the opportunity freighted mission work with attitudes that could work against it. An earlier and more frequently cited missions hymn, "From Greenland's Icy Mountains" (1819), gives voice to the sense of responsibility in a more problematical way:

> Can we, whose souls are lighted
> With wisdom from on high,
> Can we to men benighted
> The lamp of life deny?[66]

It is one thing to sing the responsibility of carrying the word of life to the world's limits, and another to cast that responsibility in terms of Christian

---

[64] "Going Home: Henry Opukaha'ia Returns to Hawaii," *Digging In* (newsletter of the Office of State Archaeology and Connecticut Historical Commission), Fall 1993, no. 2, online at http://archnet.asu.edu/archives/crm/conn/digin/dig2.htm; "Ka 'Ohe Ola Hou Inc.—The Bamboo Lives Again," webpage of "a Big Island-based organization seeking to educate Hawaiians and others about the strong Christian values Opukaha'ia held," at http://www.obookiah.com. The attempt to retain Hawaiian traditions alongside Christianity can occasion controversy: see for example Sandy Simpson, "The Testimony of Heneri Opukaha'ia Regarding the State of Religion and Society in Hawaii Before the Gospel: A Rebuttal to Daniel Kikawa's Book *Perpetuated in Righteousness*," online at http://www.deceptioninthechurch.com/obookiah.html.

[65] Arthur Cleveland Coxe, 1840. Coxe wrote this hymn while a student at General Theological Seminary, New York, at the age of 22. He later became Bishop of Western New York (1865–1896).

[66] The author of this hymn, Reginald Heber, was another Anglican: a rector in Shropshire who later became Bishop of Calcutta (1823–1826). Both hymns are found in the Presbyterian Hymnal of 1933 and elsewhere.

superiority. We are enlightened; they are in darkness. While this captures a basic spiritual truth, it shifts the focus to ourselves and claims the superiority of our souls, and, by implication, of our way of life. The air of condescension was not the hymn writer's main point, but still we come face to face with a dilemma that has confronted the modern missions movement from the start: the problem of bringing the gospel from a position of assumed cultural superiority. Nineteenth-century missions went largely from the developed world to the undeveloped world, mixing the spread of Western civilization with the spread of the gospel—and doing so in situations of decidedly unequal power relations.

These days it is common to arraign missionaries as agents of imperialisms cultural and political, as scholars unable to relate to spiritual motivation seek other explanations for missionary behavior. I hope to have pointed us to the sober fact that God's work in this sin-sick world is not always easy, and to have reminded us that God remains in control and is accomplishing His purposes. Sometimes, as in the case of American Indian missions, the providence behind the setbacks is well-nigh inscrutable to us. Sometimes, as in the case of the slave missions, we can see a glimmer of divine purpose in an apparently insoluble dilemma. And sometimes, as in the case of Hawaiian missions, joyous providences bring with them responsibilities seemingly too big for anyone's shoulders. Missionaries were often their own most searching critics, knowing full well their shortcomings and agonizing over the moral complexities they faced. They labored on in spite of them, setting an example for us today, and launching the global mission effort that we have inherited.

Chapter Five:

BAPTISTS AND THE GREAT COMMISSION

By Thomas J. Nettles

"Young man, sit down. You're an enthusiast. When God pleases to convert the heathen, He'll do it without consulting you or me." So, with some variations and conflations, the script runs. That suggestive line assigned to John Colett Ryland Sr., came as a response to a topic for discussion proposed by a young William Carey—"Whether the command given to the apostles to teach all nations was not binding on all succeeding ministers to the end of the world, seeing that the accompanying promise was of equal extent."[1]

Several ideas involved in that exchange contain in embryo form the major historical questions and conflicts of doing missions the Baptist way. First, what is the relationship between the human and the divine in the means that God will use to save His people? Second, by what authority and to what purpose do present-day ministers seek to fulfill the command to the apostles? That is, is the divine mandate delegated through His churches only? Third, the common assumptions in this apparently conflicting interchange propose a massively complex question: Is the human race fallen, in need of redemption, and dependent upon an accompanying revelation of redemptive truth?

THE OBLIGATION TO USE MEANS

Invoking the Latter-Day Glory

According to J. W. Morris, an ostensible eyewitness, the famous interchange between Ryland Sr. and Carey took place in 1786 subsequent to the Baptist

---

[1] S. Pearce Carey, *William Carey*, 8th ed. (London: The Carey Press, 1934), 54; Timothy George, *Faithful Witness: The Life and Missions of William Carey* (Birmingham, Ala.: New Hope Press, 1991), 53; Michael Haykin, *One Heart and One Soul* (Durham, N.C.: Evangelical Press, 1994), 193–95; John C. Marshman, *The Life and Times of Carey, Marshman, and Ward*, 2 vols. (London: Longman, Brown, Green, Longmans, & Roberts, 1859) 1:10.

ministers' meeting in Northampton, England.[2] The ministers that stayed behind engaged in "desultory conversation" until Ryland Sr. entered the room; he "in his accustomed freedom" asked the young ministers Carey and Morris to "propose questions for general discussion." Morris suggested that the ministers discuss the latter part of 2 Peter 2:1. He records that he "was very ludicrously told to go home and read Gill and Brine . . . and not to come there with his Arminian questions." To Carey's proposal Ryland Sr. responded, without waiting for the rest of the company to pitch in, "that nothing could be done before another Pentecost, when an effusion of miraculous gifts, including the gift of tongues, would give effect to the commission of Christ as at first; and that he was a most miserable enthusiast for asking such a question."[3]

The most recounted event and words of Baptist mission history recede into uncertainty as one seeks to understand precisely what was said, when it was said, why it was said, and what it meant. One thing is certain, however. The event established that the mission efforts of the English Baptists rode on the back of a mammoth struggle for the use of means in worldwide propagation of the gospel. One manifestation, usually but falsely associated with the Ryland-Carey encounter, is hyper-Calvinism. Based on closely argued, but fallaciously conceived, ideas concerning the inability of fallen humanity to repent and believe, hyper-Calvinists concluded that the unregenerate have no duty for such response to the gospel. In the same way, gospel ministers had no warrant to call on the unregenerate to repent of sin and believe in Christ. Thus they constructed their answer to the so-called "modern question."

The real issue between Carey and Ryland Sr., however, concerned another way of construing means. Is the church presently called to send forth gospel laborers to the heathen world in the absence of a sure divine indication that the days of the "latter-day glory" are upon us? Among those Particular Baptist Churches, the "modern question" had been largely settled before Carey's proposal. The "latter-day" question was a matter of serious discussion.

John Ryland Jr., gave no credence to the anecdote of his father's gruff response to young Carey. In a long footnote in his *Life and Death of the Reverend Andrew Fuller* (1816), Ryland demonstrated the improbability of Morris' 1786 date. Modern historian Michael Haykin, reviewing all the data and finding reports of Carey's personal reminiscences sufficiently compelling, concluded that it occurred on September 30, 1785, at Northampton. Given the probability of the younger Ryland's presence at this ministerial meeting, his response stirs confusion: "I never heard of it till I saw it in print, and cannot give credit to it at all."[4]

The younger Ryland's biography of Fuller appeared the same year as the first edition of Morris' account, 1816, and his perplexity at Morris' anecdote

---

[2] Haykin, *One Heart and One Soul*, 194; J. W. Morris, *Memoirs of the Life and Death of the Reverend Andrew Fuller* (London, 1816), 96–97.

[3] J. W. Morris, *Memoirs of the Life and Writings of the Rev. Andrew Fuller*, first American edition from the last London edition (Boston: Lincoln & Edmands, 1830), 84–85.

[4] John Ryland Jr., *The Life and Death of the Reverend Andrew Fuller* (London: Button & Son, 1816), 175.

was fresh on his mind when he wrote the footnote. In all the subsequent events leading to Carey's publication of the *Enquiry* (1792) and in the next twenty-two years of conversation and correspondence with Carey and Fuller, that bit of mission history never fell from Carey's lips or wormed its way even by implication through his pen. In producing his biography of Fuller, Ryland Jr. ran across nothing that would hint at the interchange between his father and Carey, much less confirm its reality. Such lack of awareness of an event by one so intimate with all the principals of the story invites historical reticence. Even Fuller's remarks that "Some of our most aged and respectable ministers" considered Carey's missionary vision "a wild and impracticable scheme" referred to the years 1788–1790. Ryland Sr. apparently attended no ministerial meetings in that Baptist association from 1786–1792. Joshua Marshman, a few hours after talking with Carey in 1832, indited the gist of his remarks that "good old John Ryland denounced" Carey's views as "unscriptural." Eustace Carey, the nephew of the missionary, reported that his uncle mentioned this event to him, but that Ryland Jr. maintained his same mind about it. In light of Morris's testimony, Joshua Marshman's letter, and Eustace Carey's testimony that he heard his uncle reminisce about the rebuke, some kind of rebuke or response of incredulity seems possible.[5]

A more substantial question concerns the motivation for the rebuke. Contemporary writers almost universally discuss it as a rebuke coming from hyper-Calvinist convictions.[6] William R. Estep wrote, "There is no question in the meaning of the exchange. The response was characteristic of both the man and the hyper-Calvinism predominant among the Particular Baptists at the time."[7]

The difficulty with Estep's conclusion is threefold: Ryland Sr. maintained high but not hyper-Calvinist theology and chastened high Calvinists that would "neglect the unconverted"[8]; the Baptist association in which the statement was made was not a hyper-Calvinist association but replete with ministers that took the positive side of the "modern question"; and the content of the rebuke concerned not the duty of calling sinners to repentance and faith, but the means by which the conversions of the latter days would be initiated.

As Morris reported the rebuke, it focused on the necessity of God's restoring extraordinary means before the latter-day glory would begin. The younger Ryland's footnote discussion addressed only the "latter-day glory," not hyper-Calvinism. "No man prayed and preached about the latter-day glory more than my father," Ryland Jr. certified. His father expected that long before Christ reigned personally on the earth "the gospel would be spread all over the world, and the fulness of the Jews and of the Gentiles be brought into the church." Ryland Jr. never recalled his father's anticipation of the restoration of miraculous gifts for that time.[9]

---

[5] Eustace Carey, *Memoir*, 62.

[6] George, *Faithful Witness*, 55; Haykin, *One Heart and One Soul*, 196.

[7] William R. Estep, *Whole Gospel, Whole World* (Nashville, Tenn.: Broadman & Holman, 1994), 7.

[8] Peter Naylor, "John Collett Ryland," in Michael Haykin, ed., *British Particular Baptists* (Springfield, Mo.: Particular Baptist Press, 1998), 192.

[9] Ryland Jr., *The Life and Death of the Reverend Andrew Fuller*, 175.

Carey's *Enquiry* did not discuss the "modern question." Instead, he addressed misguided notions as to what would serve as divine warrant for bringing the message of Christ into all the world. He showed that the Great Commission was not limited to the age of the apostles but still commanded the worldwide spread of the gospel. No special manifestation of providence or restoration of miraculous gifts was needed to justify action.

> It has been said that we ought not to force our way, but to wait for the openings, and leadings of Providence; but it might with equal propriety be answered in this case, neither ought we to neglect embracing those openings in providence which daily present themselves to us. What openings of providence do we wait for? We can neither expect to be transported into the heathen world without ordinary means, nor to be endowed with the gift of tongues, &c. when we arrive there. These would not be providential interpositions, but miraculous ones. Where a command exists nothing can be necessary to render it binding but a removal of those obstacles which render obedience impossible, and these are removed already.[10]

William Ward, one of the celebrated Serampore Trio, wrote in 1817 to Thomas Baldwin, editor of the *American Baptist Magazine and Missionary Intelligencer*, with a report of the progress of the English Baptist Mission at Serampore. "As it respects the conversion of the natives," he wrote, "we have had no Pentecost; yet we dare not say we have caught nothing, nor doubt whether God has done great things for us." As he reflected on the revelation of joy in heaven over one sinner that repents, he commended the American churches for joining their common cause. Ward lamented, "It is indeed marvellous that the wretched and stale excuses offered by those who are unfriendly to missions, should have deluded the people of God so long." Then, invoking the language of those that challenged the English Baptists, he played their lines, "The time is not come; we must first have another Pentecost; God must first produce greater changes in the condition of the heathen nations!"[11] His representation of the problem did not follow the contours of hyper-Calvinism but of a misapplied confidence in the latter-day glory.

Answering the Modern Question

The concept of means in the "modern question" controversy bore a more fundamental relation to individual conversion and evangelism than to worldwide missions. Andrew Fuller already had presented an extended affirmation of the duty of sinners to believe and the duty of ministers actively to evangelize. In

---

[10] William Carey, *An Enquiry Into the Obligations of Christians to use Means for the Conversion of the Heathen* (Leicester, 1792), 10–11.

[11] William Ward, "English Baptist Mission," in *The American Baptist Magazine and Missionary Intelligencer* (January, 1817), 29–30.

recollections of his theological pilgrimage, he mentioned "Edwards on the Will" as pivotal in his thinking. Speaking of himself in third person pronouns, he described this discovery in his preface to *The Gospel Worthy of All Acceptation*.

> He had also read and considered, as well as he was able, President Edwards's *Inquiry into the Freedom of the Will*, with some other performances on the difference between natural and moral inability. He found much satisfaction in the distinction; as it appeared to him to carry with it its own evidence—to be clearly and fully contained in the Scriptures—and calculated to disburden the Calvinistic system of a number of calumnies with which its enemies have loaded it, as well as to afford clear and honourable conceptions of the Divine government. If it were not the duty of unconverted sinners to believe in Christ, and that because of their inability, he supposed this inability must be natural, or something which did not arise from an evil disposition; but the more he examined the Scriptures, the more he was convinced that all the inability ascribed to man, with respect to believing, arises from the aversion of his heart. They *will not* come to Christ that they may have life; *will not* hearken to the voice of the charmer, charm he never so wisely; *will not* seek after God; and *desire not* the knowledge of his ways.[12]

Every member of Fuller's fraternity of ministerial friends read Edwards and embraced the significance of this simple point. He had written the manuscript for *Gospel Worthy* in 1781, but did not publish it until 1786. In the meantime he included this Edwardsean distinction as one of the clear guiding principles in his *Confession of Faith* presented to the church in Kettering in 1783. He believed all people were born "with a vile propensity to moral evil" and, therefore, their only inability, inhering in their fallen natures, was a "moral and a criminal inability." Their only lack is "a right disposition of mind." Had they a heart for it, they would perform the requirements of the divine Law. Only their "wicked aversion to him" presently inhibits such obedience.[13] This reality produces heavy and clear implications for the gospel ministry.

> I believe it is the duty of every minister of Christ plainly and faithfully to preach the gospel to all who will hear it; and as I believe the inability of men to spiritual things to be wholly of the moral, and therefore of the criminal kind, and that it is their duty to love the Lord Jesus Christ and trust in him for salvation though they do not; I therefore believe free and solemn addresses,

---

[12] Andrew Fuller, *The Complete Works of the Rev. Andrew Fuller*, 3 vols. (Philadelphia: American Baptist Publication Society, 1845), 2:330.

[13] Ryland Jr., *The Life and Death of Reverend Andrew Fuller*, 105ff.

invitations, calls, and warnings to them to be not only consistent, but directly adapted, as means in the hand of the Spirit of God, to bring them to Christ. I consider it as a part of my duty which I could not omit without being guilty of the blood of souls.[14]

Fuller presented the full text of this confession before the church with many ministers from the association present and participating. His conclusion concerning the "modern question" was no secret but already well known among his contemporaries and shared by most of them.

Carey's Mature View of Means

Armed with full conviction that sinners must repent, ministers must call them to repentance, and that no new revelation is needed for the church to seek the salvation of the nations, William Carey embarked for India on June 13, 1793. He spent the rest of his life away from England translating the Scriptures, preaching the gospel, teaching at university, and establishing churches. The only surviving son of Carey's only brother chose to come to India as a missionary. On March 12, 1812, the day before the printing office at the mission fell to fire, Carey wrote to his nephew about his convictions of the importance of missionary labors. He expressed a settled conviction that the gospel spread in the world through the means of spiritually gifted individuals sent by the church. Fulfillment of the Great Commission does not at all depend on an extraordinary manifestation of gifts, but on the promise of a perpetual giftedness in the church until all God's people reach unity in the faith and in the knowledge of the Son of God.

> Whether you come to India or not, be assured that the work of publishing the gospel is the most important work you could have chosen. Engage in it with humble dependence on God, and with a single eye to his glory, and I doubt not but he will give a blessing to your undertaking. I am fully of the opinion that every person to whom God has given abilities for the work, is bound to devote himself to the work of the ministry. It is not at the option of such a person, whether he will engage in it or not, nor is it at the option of a church whether it will send one to the work of the ministry upon whom God has bestowed spiritual gifts. If the church neglects to send such a member into the ministry, the guilt lies on them. The number of persons now required to spread the gospel through the earth, is unspeakably great. If fifty thousand ministers, besides those actually employed, were now to go forth, they would be so thinly spread about, as scarcely to be perceived. The harvest is indeed great, but the laborers are very few.[15]

---

[14] Ibid., 106.
[15] Eustace Carey, *Memoir*, 392.

At the same time, embracing the doctrine of the perpetuity of means should not make Christians less conscious of their dependence on the immediate operations of the divine Spirit. In 1831, W. H. Pearce, missionary son of Samuel Pearce, wrote a journal about a preaching tour in Kharee in which he saw the harvest of many souls by the power of the gospel. In his final observations, he summarized a mature viewpoint that sustained the missionary labors: "that in the use of all legitimate means, we ought to feel a more humble dependence upon God for success, and a more ardent spirit of prayer, that success may be granted."[16]

RISE OF BAPTIST MISSIONS IN AMERICA— *JURE DIVINO* ECCLESIOLOGY

A Defining Providence

In 1813 when the American Board of Commissioners for Foreign Missions (ABCFM), the governing committee for the missions effort of Congregationalists, met in Boston, it officially dissolved relations with Adoniram Judson and Luther Rice. These two men had notified the Board that it was no longer compatible with their sentiments to follow its instructions on the matter of baptism. Their missionary brothers sent out with them found this to be a hard blow but nevertheless conceded, "What the Lord means by thus dividing us in sentiment, and separating us from each other, we cannot tell. This we know, the Lord seeth not as man seeth; and it ill becomes us to be dissatisfied with what he does." Likewise, the Board sought to see wisdom in the mysterious permissions of providence: "Instead, however, of inducing discouragement, they should rouse the holy zeal, and quicken the pious exertions, of all the friends of truth; and should they, in the wisdom of God, be so overruled, as to bring an accession of strength to the missionary cause, the event would be joyous."[17]

Though the Congregationalists were mystified at this strange providence and had to fight back the possibility of discouragement, the Baptists had no doubt about the beneficence of this providence and knew precisely it would "bring an accession of strength to the missionary cause." In 1814 when Baptists in America formed the General Missionary Convention, popularly known as the Triennial Convention, Richard Furman addressed the churches with a certainty about the outcome of God's purpose: "The change of sentiment relative to the subject of baptism that has lately occurred in the minds of two respectable characters, who were sent out as Missionaries by another denomination of our christian brethren, appears to have been of the Lord and designed as a means of exciting the attention of our churches to foreign Missions."[18]

---

[16] W. H. Pearce, "Journal of a Visit to Kharee," in *The Annual Report of the Committee of the Baptist Missionary Society* (London, 1832), 44.

[17] *Minutes of the American Board of Commissioners* (September, 1813) 55, 60–61.

[18] Richard Furman, "An Address Given to the Public" (1814), cited in Leon McBeth, *A Sourcebook for Baptist Heritage* (Nashville, Tenn.: Broadman Press, 1990), 209–10.

A Tapestry of Preparation

This striking event provided the final and most compelling motivation for the national organization for missions among Baptists, but other factors also had been operating.

Baptists took special pride in the recently won freedom from state-established religion at the federal level and worked for these same liberties in individual states. They saw republican liberties as expressive politically of a Baptist ecclesiology. The United States, they believed, would become the basis for the spread of Christ's kingdom, Baptist churches being its purest expression.[19]

Adding luster to this vision, the sustained spiritual impact of the Second Great Awakening fostered hope that soon the worldwide spread of gospel truth would be forthcoming as a precursor to the millennial reign of Christ. In a manner similar to the *Connecticut Evangelical Magazine*, the *American Baptist Magazine* reported the progress of revivals of religion in the churches. That, combined with recent events among the Baptists of England, provoked hope that the latter-day glory would look peculiarly Baptist.

In 1803 reports appeared in the magazine from churches and associations about a "great and good work of God," and "a glorious revival of religion that had taken place." There was a "great revival in the upper parts of Georgia," as well as a "happy work of grace" in Savannah. In Kentucky, in the six associations in the state, 14,076 communicants were reported, "10,000 of whom, at least, are young converts." From Wheeling a pastor wrote "the great head of the church is pouring out his Spirit in many places, on this side of those lofty mountains that divide between us and the eastern states." He reported also that "the state of Kentucky abounds with converts flocking to Jesus. Zion's foes have really been astonished."[20]

In addition to material about revival in America, the *American Baptist Magazine* contained an evangelistic address drawn up by William Ward in 1801, translated into Bengalee by Carey, and passed out to the Hindus. Reports of numbers of conversions and baptisms among the "Hindoos" were followed by a baptismal hymn affirming the Baptist viewpoint.

Magazine reports of church revival continued even fourteen years later. George Witherel reported that he baptized sixty-four within a three-month period. Many young people "on the broad road to ruin" had been converted. He also reported that "more than one hundred have hopefully been born into the kingdom of grace, within four weeks" in Wilmington, Vermont. About seventy had been added to the Baptist church in Barnardston and a like number to the Congregational church. "Dear Sir," he concluded after such an encouraging survey, "we have long been praying for that happy era, called the millennium. May we not hope it has already begun? We can say,

---

[19] Thomas Baldwin, "A Sermon Delivered at Boston, on Tuesday, April 2, 1799" (Boston: Manning & Loring, 1799) 9, 20; Samuel Stillman, "A Sermon Delivered at Boston, April 25, 1799" (Boston: Manning & Loring, 1799) 10–12. Sam Strange, "Baptists and Religious Liberty, 1700–1900" (Ph. D. diss., The Southern Baptist Theological Seminary, 2006), 325–88.

[20] *The Massachusetts Baptist Missionary Magazine* (September 1803), 20–26.

Heaven here, heaven there,
Comforts flowing every where."[21]

Of numerous reports of large numbers of conversions and baptisms in several churches, the purging of doctrinal error from churches, the editor also gave information that "to the three Baptist Churches in Boston more than one hundred and twenty have been added the past season." Each report showed interest in the advance of work among the paedobaptist brethren also. Baldwin concluded the report with the auspicious hope, "May the light of divine truth continue to spread, until all the darkness occasioned by error shall be dissipated, and the earth filled with the knowledge and glory of God!"[22]

Another factor disposing Baptists to missions came from the work of the Philadelphia Association. William Staughton, baptized by Samuel Pearce, educated at Bristol Academy, and present in 1792 in Kettering when the Baptist Missionary Society was formed, came to Charleston, South Carolina, in January 1794. He served as pastor in Georgetown for seventeen months and moved to Bordentown, New Jersey, and appeared in the meeting of the Philadelphia Association in 1796. He presented a "Circular Letter" that year on infidelity. Such falsehood will fail, he certified, but the living system of Christianity "must prevail till the kingdoms of this world become the kingdoms of our Lord and of His Christ." When we are pursuing the "interests of Zion, we are fellow workers with God."[23]

Staughton's friend William Rogers regularly shared missionary correspondence with the Association. In 1806 he addressed the delegates on the subject of "Christian Missions." He discussed mission theology, mission history, and the present encouraging signs that the world might soon sing the song of redeeming love. "That the eternal God may be glorified, immortal souls saved, civil society benefited, savage cruelties superseded, and millennial days introduced, are among the many objects contemplated by the industrious sons and daughters of grace." Missionaries know that only Jesus' blood can atone and His righteousness justify. Only the Holy Spirit can change "the stoutest heart." The missionary knows that no other name than that of Jesus can save. "An experimental sense, therefore," that the missionary certainly must have, "of the glory and the worth of the Redeemer, inspires the wish that all the ends of the earth may come and serve him." Even as the Word of God was powerful in the Reformation, so we believe, Rogers asserted, that through the ministration of the Word, "the glory of the latter day will be visible, when the precious sound of evangelical ministers has gone out into all lands and 'their words unto the ends of the world'." Rogers pointed to the work of Carey and the Baptist Missionary Society as pivotal in starting an avalanche of missionary societies and missionary action.[24]

---

[21] *The American Baptist Magazine* (January 1817), 37.

[22] Ibid., (March 1817), 73–77.

[23] *Minutes of the Philadelphia Association 1707–1807*, ed. A. D. Gillette (Philadelphia: American Baptist Publication Society, 1851), 321.

[24] Ibid., 426–33.

The Centennial Sermon in 1807 (the Philadelphia Association had been founded in 1707) had a major mission component. Samuel Jones rehearsed the history of the Association and culminated with a commendation of the missionary spirit and the hope that "before another century will revolve, . . . we hope and expect, that the latter day of glory, the spiritual reign of Christ, will commence. . . . May the Lord hasten and accomplish his holy purpose to the praise of his glory."[25] The Philadelphia Association shared, therefore, the hope of the latter-day glory along with the use of means for its initiation and advance.

Baptists in America also immediately began to form mission societies for the support of Carey and the other missionaries of the English mission. Associations had been engaged formally in home mission activity since 1755 when the Philadelphia Association sent a "ministry that travels" to gospel-starved populations in a broad geographical area. The Charleston Association followed suit along with the Shaftesbury Association. The Massachusetts Baptist Missionary Society, formed in 1802, purposed "to furnish occasional preaching, and to promote the knowledge of evangelistic truth in the new settlements within these United States, or farther if circumstances should render it proper."[26] Accordingly they showed great interest in the English Baptist mission and carried correspondence from the missionaries and reports of other missionary appointments.

Even after the formation of the General Missionary Convention, American Baptists retained such a sense of unity with England that it sent missionaries to meet requests for help. In January 1817, the *American Baptist Magazine* reported, "The brethren at Serampore, having earnestly requested that a paper-maker might be sent out, who should not only be fully competent to the superintendence of their manufactory, but well disposed to the labours of the mission; Mr. Joel Randall, a member of the church at Salisbury, offered himself, and was accepted by the committee as well qualified for the requisite services. His wife, a pious woman, cheerfully consented to accompany him with her only child, and infant daughter." They set him aside with the admonition that he would spread the gospel not only with paper and ink but with conduct and spoken word, and sent him on his way.[27]

And Their Households?

All of these factors having paved the way, one thing was needed. Though broadly catholic in hope and attitude and joyful over the vast expanse of the work of God's Spirit, they still were Baptist and believed that the purest expression of the church and gospel labor would be Baptist. The changed conviction of Adoniram Judson, Ann Judson, and Luther Rice from approval of infant baptism to an acceptance of believers-only baptism rocked both the Congregational and Baptist worlds and thrust Baptists, by divine providence, into the growing missionary enterprise.

---

[25] *Minutes of the Philadelphia Association 1707–1807,* 466.

[26] *Massachusetts Baptist Missionary Magazine,* 1:6.

[27] *American Baptist Magazine* (January 1817), 30.

Upon their appointment by the ABCFM, Judson and Rice heard the following charges: "You are to teach, not the commandments, or the dogmas of men; but the pure doctrines of the gospel, drawn directly from the Scriptures of truth." And again, "In teaching the Gentiles, it will be your business, not vehemently to declaim against their superstitions, but in the meekness and gentleness of Christ, to bring them as directly as possible to the knowledge of divine truth." They received a succinct and carefully articulated word about how to receive converts.

> If God, in his infinite grace, prosper your labors, and give you the happiness to see converts to the truth, you will proceed in regard to them, at once with charity and caution. You will allow sufficient time for trial, and for the reality of conversion to be attested by its fruits; that, as far as possible, the scandal of apostasy may be prevented. You will admit none as members of the church of Christ, but such as give credible evidence that they are true believers; and none to the ordinance of baptism, but credible believers and their households.[28]

These instructions gave clear guidance concerning the priority of conversion and the necessity of pursuing church purity. Judson reasoned, however, that when he faced William Carey and the English Baptists on landing in India, he would be called upon to give a defense of how such care for true conversion was consistent with the baptism of "households." As he studied, he came to doubt the validity of the instructions. He began to suspect that the Baptist side of the question was right. Ann urged him to stop. Nothing could be gained by changing viewpoints now. She solemnly warned that if he became a Baptist she would not. Knowing all that was at stake, however, she began her own study and began to come to the same conclusion. Soon after their arrival in India, where ironically they discovered that the English Baptists had a policy of never discussing that issue with non-Baptist missionaries, they completed their study. They concluded that the Baptists were right. Judson wrote to the Serampore trio a letter of explanation.

> As you have been ignorant of the late exercises of my mind on the subject of baptism, the communication which I am about to make, may occasion you some surprise.
> It is now about four months, since I took the subject into serious consideration. My inquiries commenced during my passage from America, and after much laborious research and painful trial, which I shall not now detail, have issued in entire conviction, that the immersion of a professing believer is the only Christian Baptism.

---

[28] *Minutes of the Third Annual Meeting of the American Board of Commissioners* (November 1812), 41.

> In these exercises I have not been alone. Mrs. Judson has been engaged in a similar examination, and has come to the same conclusion. Feeling, therefore, that we are in an unbaptized state, we wish to profess our faith in Christ by being baptized in obedience to his sacred commands.[29]

Ann wrote her family and friends explaining the change and the circumstances that produced it. One letter she began with the words, "Can you, my dear Nancy, still love me, still desire to hear from me, when I tell you I have become a Baptist?" After a careful narrative of the principal factors in the change, she summarized, "Thus, my dear Nancy, we are confirmed Baptists, not because we wished to be, but because truth compelled us to be."[30]

Luther Rice wrote the Board of Commissioners and sent a copy of his correspondence to Dr. Baldwin of Boston. Explaining both the motive and the means of his study of the question, Rice concluded, "But it is with emotions peculiarly afflicting, that I proceed to inform you, that, in the result of this examination, I am compelled to relinquish a view of that sacred ordinance which I have formerly apprehended to be highly important. I am now satisfactorily convinced that those only who give credible evidence of piety, are proper subjects, and that immersion is the proper mode of baptism."[31]

Rice had the reputation of being "the most obstinate friend of Pedobaptism of any of the Missionaries." On October 19, 1812, William Carey heard of Rice's change. The next day he wrote to William Staughton reporting that the Judsons had been baptized, that he expected Rice to be baptized soon, and that Baptists in America must make good use of this amazing providence of eternal significance. "Is it impossible to form a Baptist Mission Society in America?" At any rate, they should "stir in this business" because it is a "providence which gives a new turn to American relation to Oriental Missions." "I hope," he wrote two months later, "our Baptist friends in America will take these two brethren under their protection, and consider them as their missionaries."[32]

Not only must mission work be advanced, but one must not spoil this triumph of truth by a vain spirit. While Carey considered "their baptism as a glorious triumph of truth over prejudice," and thanked God for it, he expressed hope that "none of our Baptist brethren in America will glory over their Congregational brethren on account of this circumstance." The change is important, "but let us improve it as christians."[33]

The Church, Yes; the Society, No

Just as surely as the regulative principle of biblical interpretation shouldered a specifically Baptist theory of the missionary task, even so that fulcrum

---

[29] *Massachusetts Baptist Missionary Magazine* (March 1813), 266–67.
[30] *Massachusetts Baptist Missionary Magazine* (May 1813), 294.
[31] Ibid., 293.
[32] *Massachusetts Baptist Missionary Magazine* (September, 1813), 322.
[33] Ibid., 322–23.

of Baptist ecclesiology led to a period of intense and widespread opposition to the missionary societies, and preeminently the General Missionary Convention, that had been founded to support the mission effort. Though personal envy, some covert greed, and sectional jealousy fueled elements of the opposition, the self-conscious reason concerned the purity of the Baptist way of doing things. Recurring themes included the apparent usurpation of the prerogative of God by collection of money for accomplishing spiritual ends, requiring of education for qualification to preach, and the employment and hiring of ministers. Another equally forceful objection pointed to the usurpation of the prerogatives of the church, the divinely ordained body to carry out God's commission in the world. Daniel Parker noted, "I have been under the necessity to expose error, and when I find it among my baptist brethren, which I believe is the living church of Jesus Christ, my feelings are worse hurt, and I am apt to strike the harder."[34] Parker objected strenuously to what was implied in the name of the society, The General Missionary Convention for the Baptist Denomination of the United States of America. "This evidently proves," he surmised, "they claim the government of the ministry and consequently arrests the government and authority Christ gave his church."[35] In discussing the terms of the Great Commission, Parker asked, "Was this a missionary society gave this command, or is it the command of our King and King of Zion, or was there a missionary society independent of the church to send them and fix on the field of their labors, and support them?" In another place Parker discussed the calling of Paul and Barnabas. He pointed to "the order of God in his church, and the union that exists between Christ and his church; first his calling his preachers to the work and then the church, (not a missionary society,) sending them out in gospel order to preach and administer the ordinances of the gospel."[36]

Foundational to all the errors of the missionary societies, in John Taylor's estimation, was a blatant disregard for Baptist church government. "I consider these great men are verging close on an aristocracy, with an object to sap the foundation of Baptist republican government." He went on to explain,

> The highest court Christ has fixed on earth, is a worshipping congregation, called a church. An association is a creature of the churches, whose power is only self government while together, and whose work, as to the churches, is to settle differences if possible, and that only by advice, without any kind of coercion. But these men foolishly conclude, if they get the associations to correspond with them, they at once grasp the whole society, consisting of hundreds of thousands, and would fondly make their advisory counsel a great court of appeals to the society. But a Baptist association, from their native style (advisory counsel) has no right to go into a permanent correspondence with any set of

---

[34] Daniel Parker, *A Public Address to the Baptist Society* (Vincennes: Stone & Osborne, 1820), 5.
[35] Ibid., 16.
[36] Parker, *A Public Address*, 29.

men, but by direction from the churches, and especially such a motley tribe as the Board of Foreign Missions. . . . For my own part, I would full as soon be in religious correspondence with the Masonic friends, as this sanctimonious tribe.[37]

Slavery, Missions, and the Board

The ecclesiological impetus also led to the separation of the Baptists in the South from the General Missionary Convention in 1845. The Abolition movement led to increasing tensions within the societies beginning around 1833, the year following the founding of the American Baptist Home Mission Society. As the southern brethren began to feel the pinch of the increasingly intense moral concerns over slavery, they demanded a clear answer on the issue of slavery and missions. When they learned without equivocation that the mission board residing in Boston would not appoint a slaveholder as a missionary nor do anything that would imply approbation of slavery, they took the option of forming a separate way of doing missions. Luther Copeland and a growing number of historians have sought to argue that the Southern Baptist Convention arose purely as a defense of slavery (the original sin of Southern Baptists).[38] The South's defense of slavery was vigorous even among the Baptists, but the burden of the evidence shows that the intersection of missions and ecclesiology finally drove the wedge between the northern and southern brethren. The acting board, in adopting "a new qualification for missionaries," that is, non-slaveholding, assumed "an usurpation of ecclesiastical power quite foreign to our polity."[39]

The Constitution of the Triennial Convention stated clearly the qualifications of the missionaries focusing on zeal, talents, and piety; the churches consented to those qualifications and did not give the power of amendment to the acting board. This action of the board amounted to the writing of a new constitution and a prelatical imposition of its newly constructed qualification. The slavery controversy provided the occasion, but missions and ecclesiology constituted the immediate cause for the division.

The Baptist understanding of a regenerate church and the ongoing conversion work basic to the survival of a Baptist church could be seen as more congenial to the theology of missions than other ecclesiologies. At the same time, its view of the autonomy of the local congregation has caused numerous difficulties in maintaining the full cooperation of its many local congregations in a united action for missions.

---

[37] John Taylor, *Thoughts On Missions* (n.p., 1820), 10.
[38] Luther Copeland, *The Southern Baptist Convention and the Judgment of History* (New York: University Press of America, 1995), 3, 7–16; H. Leon McBeth, *The Baptist Heritage* (Nashville, Tenn.: Broadman Press, 1987), 382.
[39] William B. Johnson, "Address to the Public," *Annual of SBC* (1845), 17–20.

MISSIONS AS AN EXPRESSION OF ORTHODOXY

Lottie Moon and Southern Baptist Orthodoxy

The first test of Southern Baptist determination to maintain theological orthodoxy had immediate implications for its missionary program. Lottie Moon (1840–1912), among the most productive and popular missionaries in Southern Baptist history, had a favored upbringing in antebellum Virginia. She became, according to John A. Broadus, the best-educated woman in the South. In 1873 she went to China where she did children's work, performed evangelistic work among women, and evangelized the region of Ping Tu, which became the most fertile field for conversion among nineteenth-century Southern Baptist theaters of missions. Her work there laid the theological and evangelistic foundation for the great Shantung revival of the twentieth century. She remained at her labors until her death in 1912, in Kobe Harbor, Japan, en route to the United States after it had been discovered that she had starved herself in an effort to relieve the suffering of Chinese Christians.

Crawford Howell Toy had taught Miss Moon at Albemarle Female Institute from 1856–58. His own attempt to enter foreign mission service in Japan failed because of the Civil War. He eventually taught at the Southern Baptist Theological Seminary for ten years, resigning in 1879. His view of biblical inspiration had departed from that of the confession of faith that governed the seminary. A romantic interest between him and Lottie Moon had developed intermittently since the Albemarle days.

When Lottie Moon learned of his resignation, she was not convinced that Toy had disqualified himself for a career in missions. She probably believed that his views had not been represented carefully in the press. Her correspondence about Toy with H. A. Tupper of the Foreign Mission Board seems giddy, and her interest in Toy was not discouraged by Mr. Tupper.[40] Perhaps she really hoped that he had a bright future before him in China or Japan and that that future would be with her.[41]

If Moon harbored that hope, it was crushed in 1881 when she became aware that two young mission volunteers appointed to China, T. P. Bell and John Stout, had their appointments recalled. The Board became aware that both men had studied with Toy and held his views on biblical inspiration, views that Southern

---

[40] Lottie Moon to H. A. Tupper, March 22, 1880. Miss Moon's letters are found in the archives of the International Mission Board in Richmond, Virginia. Also, Keith Harper, *Send the Light* (Macon, Ga.: Mercer University Press, 2002), 93.

[41] Una Roberts Lawrence, *Lottie Moon* (Nashville, Tenn.: Sunday School Board of the Southern Baptist Convention, 1927), 91–96, summarizes the supposed virtual engagement and theorizes that Moon's study of the scientific works in her library prompted her conclusion that Darwinism was "an untenable position, and certainly it could not be so harmonized with the Word of God as to make one who believed it a 'good workman' on a frontier of the Kingdom" [94]. Catherine Allen tells the story in a similar way, but believes that Lawrence might be confused over the chronology about the interest in mission work in Japan. She cites a letter from missionary T. P. Crawford showing that Miss Moon had announced to the mission that she planned to return to the United States to join Toy at Harvard, citing a letter from Crawford to Tupper, September 12, 1881. Catherine Allen, *The New Lottie Moon Story* (Nashville, Tenn.: Broadman Press, 1980), 137–40.

Baptists rejected. This established once and for all that Toy could never join her on the mission field.

Moon's correspondence showed she felt despondent over these developments and even entertained notions about leaving the field to join Toy at Harvard.[42] Long, deliberate, and intense consideration, however, of all involved convinced Lottie Moon that such a change was at best impracticable and at worst disloyal to her redeemer. The critical need for laborers in China, the fatigue and debility of her missionary colleagues, and the clarity of God's prerogative over her life, as well as her increased love for the Chinese people, shoved aside this last shot at romantic and domestic fulfillment. In addition, though slow to accept the verdict of state-side Baptists, her personal study convinced her that loyalty to Toy and loyalty to the gospel could not coexist. She had opportunity to give incarnation to her own words written in 1873: "Could a Christian woman possibly desire higher honor than to be permitted to go from house to house and tell of a savior to those who have never heard this?" She then clinched her exhortation with words that surely must have recurred to her in a personal crisis like this: "We could not conceive a life which would more thoroughly satisfy the mind and heart of a true follower of the Lord Jesus." When in later years a relative asked her if she ever had a love affair, she answered, "Yes, but God had first claim on my life, and since the two conflicted, there could be no question about the result."[43]

Northern Baptist Missions on the Downgrade

The Northern Baptist Convention, in the 1920s, became an object lesson concerning what can go wrong in the relation of orthodoxy to missions. Since A. H. Strong's visit to the mission field and his sounding of the alarm of the dangers of liberal education in its impact on missions in 1918, complaints of liberalism on the mission field had increased.[44] A special committee appointed to investigate these allegations made its report in 1925. They were instructed in particular with reference to the policy of the Board of Managers in the appointment and retention of "missionaries who do not accept or have repudiated or abandoned the evangelical faith as held historically by Baptists."

The difficulty with the specific instruction came from a Convention action in 1922. Cornelius Woelfkin led a victorious liberal movement to reject the adoption of a confession of faith for the single principle, "The Northern Baptist Convention affirms that the New Testament is the all-sufficient ground of our faith and practise, and we need no other statement."[45] The mission board stated

---

[42] H. A. Tupper to Lottie Moon, July 13, 1881.

[43] Lawrence, *Lottie Moon*, 96; Allen, *The New Lottie Moon Story*, 139. After enduring this blow, Lottie suffered through another theological defection. In 1886, N. W. Halcomb resigned his charge because of a theological struggle over the deity of Christ. Lottie and Mrs. T. P. Crawford worked feverishly to dissuade Halcomb from his chosen course of action. He remained firm in his defection and became an employee of the United States government. See Lottie Moon to H. A. Tupper, July 27 and August 7, 1886; Harper, *Send the Light*, 125, 127.

[44] A. H. Strong, *A Tour of the Missions: Observations and Conclusions* (Philadelphia: The Griffith and Rowland Press, 1918), 165, 193ff., 211.

[45] *Annual of the Northern Baptist Convention* (1922), 133.

that "Liberty must be limited . . . by loyalty to Christ as risen Saviour and Lord, loyalty to the gospel of divine grace, loyalty to the great Baptist principles which bind us together" and "must never degenerate into license or into indifference to dangerous error." It should "always be exercised in our denominational sphere within the bounds of the Christian and Baptist faith." The Board sought to define this for itself.

> Guided by the facts that Baptists have always been known as evangelicals, and that the gospel is the most important message of the Scriptures, we have demanded that all our officers and missionaries be loyal to the gospel. We will appoint only suitable evangelical men and women; we will appoint evangelicals and we will not appoint non-evangelicals. And by the gospel we mean *the good news of the free forgiveness of sin and eternal life (beginning now and going on forever) through a vital union with the crucified and risen Christ, which brings men into union and fellowship with God. This salvation is graciously offered on the sole condition of repentance and faith in Christ and has in it the divine power of regeneration and sanctification through the Spirit. The only reason we have for accepting this gospel is our belief in the deity of Christ in whom we see the Father, a faith founded on the trustworthiness of the Scriptures and the fact that we have experienced this salvation in our own hearts.*[46]

While a historic evangelical might respond positively to the doctrinal abstract, the churches of the Convention could only hope that the Board, given arbitrary doctrinal authority, shared their outlook. Officially, however, theological expectation was empty and eventually must give way to latitude of theological expression. Certain facts had to be taken into account that included fair representation of "widely differing theological views."[47]

In spite of such latitude, the committee's investigation did yield some cases that even they had to consider outside the norm, doctrinal divergence "so extreme that in our judgment they do not come within the limits laid down by the Board." Serious issues on the inspiration of Scripture, the atonement, human sinfulness, eternal life, resurrection, and the uniqueness of the person of Christ emerged in their survey of missionaries.[48]

This alarming sprinkling of missionaries with such anti-evangelical ideas prompted some efforts at healing this obviously dangerous doctrinal wound. The committee issued an admonition to schools to take care in their training of ministry and missionary candidates, and conservatives sought to bring in a binding confession of faith by way of the back door.[49] The admonition went

---

[46] *Annual of the Northern Baptist Convention* (1925), 86. Italics in the original.
[47] Ibid., 85–86.
[48] Ibid., 88–91.
[49] Ibid., 93, 95.

unheeded, and the fresh attempt at salvaging a confessional commitment failed. The Convention resembled a gelding commanded to reproduce.[50]

A FELLOWSHIP OF TRUTH

Baptist missionary advance has come into existence by way of overcoming a variety of objections and obstacles. Thousands of missionaries and scores of mission organizations, however, join with Carey, the Judsons, and Lottie Moon in a fellowship of truth. One-time slave Lott Cary, sent out by the Triennial Convention as a pioneer missionary to Africa, served in Liberia from 1822 until his death in 1828 as a missionary, a physician, and a political leader. Carey heard a sermon on John 3 that led to his desire to learn to read and eventually his conversion. He purchased his freedom as well as that of his family through shrewd business deals he made with waste tobacco. His zeal for the gospel led him to forsake a highly lucrative business life as a free man to enter into missionary labors. Though he labored earnestly as a preacher of the gospel, political conditions eventually demanded his increased involvement in the affairs of the colony, and he died in an accident, preparing to defend its liberties.[51] In 1897, his example inspired the founding of the Lott Cary Baptist Foreign Mission Convention, an African-American denomination.[52]

Emerging from twentieth-century conflicts within the American Baptist churches, two other Baptist groups developed that emphasized the work of missions. The General Association of Regular Baptists, founded to avoid compromise in the missionary mandate of the church by promotion of purer doctrine and purer churches with more consistent local autonomy, supported missionaries through independent missionary agencies. They organized and separated from the Northern Baptist Convention in 1932. Many conservatives stayed within the Convention, keeping up the fight for the appointment of conservative missionaries, and established the Conservative Baptist Foreign Mission Society in 1943. When their continued efforts at reformation within the Convention failed, they formed the Conservative Baptist Association of America in 1947. A part of their intention was the promotion of missions among the churches.

Southern Baptist foreign mission work presently maintains over 5,000 missionaries in over 100 countries. Among Southern Baptists, Thomas J. Bowen of Nigeria, the Bagby family in Brazil, Bill Wallace in China, and literally thousands of others have testified to the enduring call of God in Scripture and personal experience to proclaim the glory of Christ's redemptive work in the whole world. Bowen, appointed in 1849 to Africa, produced a dictionary and grammar of the Yoruba language and ruined his physical and mental health in his labors for the gospel, dying in 1875. Six of the nine children of William and Anne Bagby followed them into missionary work in Brazil. Bill Wallace, a physician, after a life

---

[50] Ibid., 274.

[51] G. W. Hervey, *The Story of Baptist Missions* (St. Louis, Mo.: C. R. Barnes, 1885), 199–207.

[52] Bill Leonard, *Baptist Ways* (Valley Forge, Pa.: Judson Press, 2003), 274–75.

of joyful self-sacrifice for the temporal and eternal health of China, was beaten to death after systematic torture in a communist Chinese prison in 1951.[53]

CONCLUSION

Extreme scrupulosity over the use of means tends to produce an overreaction and inclines toward carelessness. Scripture not only admonishes the use of means for the conversion of the lost, but specifies those means. Compromise on biblical means signals a change in one's understanding of authority and, at times, the nature of the gospel.

While contentiousness and a spirit of divisiveness are to be avoided, conscientious ecclesiology must be maintained. Though evangelicals may disagree on issues of the ordinances and church government, those disagreements must not become a pressure for violation of conscience. That we decide not to take seriously the commands of Christ concerning baptism, church discipline, and the Lord's Supper would be more devastating for long-term missions than the apparent divided body fostered by denominational convictions.

Orthodoxy supported by confessional commitment is requisite in any faithful missionary labor. This aspect of mission work takes denominations beyond the ecclesiological differences into the great body of truths around which such striking fellowship and mutual support takes place. Regrettably, the lack of confessional discipline presently is leading to massive confusion, dissatisfaction, division, and decline among several mainline churches, including the American Baptist Churches of the USA.

---

[53] Estep, *Whole Gospel, Whole World*, 94, 127, 128, 282–83; Hervey, *The Story of Baptist Missions*, 598–603.

Chapter Six:

EVANGELICAL MISSIONS IN MODERN AMERICA

By Fred W. Beuttler

On January 19, 1981, Marxist guerrillas from the terrorist cell group M-19 burst into a guest house near the Summer Institute of Linguistics (SIL) head-quarters in Bogota, Colombia. Unable to find the director, the gunmen seized a young translator, Chester A. Bitterman III, who had been staying there with his family. The kidnappers issued an ultimatum: "Chet Bitterman will be executed unless the Summer Institute of Linguistics and all its members leave Colombia by 6:00 p.m. February 19."[1]

Chet Bitterman, 28, had been in Bogota with his wife and two young daugh-ters, preparing for translation work with the Carijona tribe, an Amazonian peo-ple without a written language. During his SIL training, he had told his mentors, "save a hard tribe for us." For forty-eight days the guerrillas held him, in spite of pleas from his wife, a fellow missionary. SIL refused to negotiate with the terror-ists as a matter of policy, but staff fervently prayed for the missionary's release. Finally, on March 7, gunmen shot Bitterman through the heart and left his body on a stolen bus in Bogota.

SIL began its work in Colombia in 1962, working under contract with the Colombian government to transcribe tribal languages and teach literacy. Affiliated with Wycliffe Bible Translators, SIL was the technical branch of a two-part missionary enterprise to bring the gospel to each of the world's 6,900 lan-guages. SIL and Wycliffe were founded by William "Cam" Townsend, who, in 1917 as a young missionary in Guatemala trying to evangelize using a Spanish Bible, was confronted by a Cakchiquel Indian who challenged him, "If your God is so great, why doesn't he speak my language?" Cam Townsend then realized his vision for Bible translation: that every people group, no matter how small, should have a Bible to read in their own language. Townsend divided the task

---

[1] There are numerous press accounts of the Bitterman story. See *Chicago Tribune*, and the *New York Times* from February, 1981; see also http://www.desiringgod.org/library/sermons/84/061084.html. Bitterman's death is in "Colombian Rebels Kill Missionary," *New York Times*, March 8, 1981, p. 1. One fascinating piece is a follow-up by Rogers Worthington, "Death in Colombia gives mission new life," *Chicago Tribune*, Feb. 16, 1982, p. C1.

into two parts: first, the Summer Institute of Linguistics would be responsible for the technical linguistic work of researching language structures, creating alphabets and grammars, and teaching literacy in native languages, often under host government contract; and second, Wycliffe would translate Scriptures into native languages. A missionary would work for both organizations, wearing two hats but with a common goal, to provide Scripture in a tribe's own language.

The Marxist guerrillas accused Chet Bitterman and SIL of being a front for American imperialism, charging that the Institute's activities violated the cultural integrity of indigenous Colombians, a form of "ethnocide," and were looting the country's resources. SIL was a non-political, technical, scientific organization, but it was also part of a broader missions movement, which did seek to proclaim the gospel of Jesus Christ to "all nations," to fulfill the Great Commission. Atheistic Marxist hostility was joined with the harsh criticisms of secular anthropologists, who sought to preserve tribal cultures in their holistic purity.

Why was Bitterman martyred? The martyrdom of Jim Elliot and his four colleagues at the hands of the "Auca" Indians in the Ecuadorian jungle in January 1956 marked one transition point in the history of evangelical missions, a real cultural coming of age, especially after *Life* magazine and *Readers Digest* ran the story.[2] But while Elliot and his companions were martyred by a primitive people, something that had happened numerous times in the past, the Bitterman affair was significantly different. His death was on the front page of the *New York Times*, but few made the connection with its historical antecedents. The Auca martyrs died at the hands of a savage tribe who were suspicious of civilization, but Bitterman was killed by educated, ideologically-driven and anti-imperialist revolutionaries, in many ways like the Chinese Boxers of eight decades earlier.

Why did these Marxist guerrillas target SIL? What about it was threatening? Was Bitterman martyred because of his Christian faith? Or his planned missionary outreach to indigenous peoples? Or for SIL's apparent complicity with the CIA and U.S. foreign policy in Colombia?[3] Was he killed because he was a Christian? Or because he was perceived as an agent of American imperialism? In the Bitterman case it is very hard to separate out the motives of his captors.

There are two stories wrapped up in the Bitterman affair, two competing narratives over the interpretation of the broader movement that his martyrdom represents. Most of us in the Christian community are familiar with the stories of faithful, heroic missionaries, willing to sacrifice their comforts, careers, and

---

[2] See Elizabeth Elliot, *Shadow of the Almighty: The Life and Testament of Jim Elliot*, and *Through Gates of Splendor* (New York: Harper, 1957). A documentary of the same name was released in 2005, and a film *End of the Spear* (2006) told of Missionary Aviation Fellowship pilot Nate Saint, and his son's successful attempt to reach the Indians for Christ.

[3] Several years before the Bitterman kidnapping, CIA director George H. W. Bush publicly said the agency would no longer recruit missionaries for information (admitting that it had been CIA policy before), but would accept information if volunteered. See also, Gerald Colby with Charlotte Dennett, *Thy Will Be Done: The Conquest of the Amazon: Nelson Rockefeller and Evangelism in the Age of Oil* (New York: HarperCollins, 1995). See, however, Deann Alford, "The CIA Myth: Mission agencies still fight 50-year old accusations," *Christianity Today,* January 2006, 58.

even lives for the gospel. The martyrdom of Jim Elliot and his four companions inspired countless missionaries to follow their example of selfless service to the cause of Christ. A generation later, Bitterman's example of service unto death led to hundreds of other believers volunteering to take his place. There is a second interpretation of the missionary encounter, however, and that is its often close association with American foreign policy during and after the Cold War. In addition, secular anthropologists accused missionaries of cooperating with host governments to turn native cultures into national ones, diminishing their native cultures and breaking up holistic peoples through evangelism. Much of this criticism is political, economic, and cultural, centered in an ideological hostility toward Christianity.

What is the history of American evangelical missions from the 1860s to the present? Chet Bitterman's story suggests the complexity of this history, for there is substantial overlap between American history and the history of Christian missions over the last century and a half. One of the main challenges in approaching modern American missions is to connect the internal story of evangelical missions with the larger history of American and world policy as it affects and interacts with those missions. Evangelicals know the early history of John R. Mott of the Student Volunteer Movement, for example, but few realize that Mott shared the Nobel Peace Prize in 1946 for his activities. This chapter will survey the missions activities of American evangelicals from the 1860s to the present, seeking to connect these two histories, missions history with American history, in order to develop a practical framework and draw some lessons for modern missions. For it is only by connecting these competing narratives that we can properly assess possible futures for American evangelical missions.

Modern American Missions

Missionary activity does not take place in a vacuum, for it is embedded in the historical context as the faith is incarnated into a new culture. American evangelicalism shares with popular culture an indifference to history, apart from selective memories of past heroes. One of the chief curricula for missions recruitment, the *Perspectives on the World Christian Movement*, while quite sound in its biblical and theological foundations, is weak in its treatment of missions history, which it virtually omits after World War II.[4]

---

[4] Ralph D. Winter and Steven C. Hawthorne, eds., *Perspectives on the World Christian Movement*, 3rd ed. (Pasadena, Calif.: William Carey Library, 1999). In addition to this introductory work, there are numerous scholarly histories and analyses of modern missions. Especially encouraging is the series by W. B. Eerdmans, "Studies in the History of Christian Missions." See Donald M. Lewis, ed., *Christianity Reborn: The Global Expansion of Evangelicalism in the Twentieth Century* (Grand Rapids, Mich.: Eerdmans, 2004); Brian Stanley, ed., *Missions, Nationalism, and the End of Empire* (Grand Rapids, Mich.: Eerdmans, 2003). Also very helpful is Lamin Sanneh and Joel Carpenter, eds. *The Changing Face of Christianity: Africa, the West, and the World* (New York: Oxford University Press, 2005). See also Andrew Walls, *The Missionary Movement in Christian History: Studies in the Transmission of Faith* (Maryknoll, N.Y.: Orbis Press, 1996). Earlier works, which are still useful, are Joel Carpenter and Wilbur Shenk, eds., *Earthen Vessels: American Evangelicals and Foreign Missions, 1880–1980* (Grand Rapids, Mich.: Eerdmans, 1990), and, from a mainline perspective, is William Hutchison, *Errand to the World: American Protestant Thought and Foreign*

There are numerous ways to tell the story of American evangelical missions in the period under examination, as the "Great Century" is transformed into the "American Century." One could focus on the numerous stories of faithful individuals, the rise and development of various missions institutions, or the phenomenal growth of Pentecostalism, which, in the century since the Azusa Street Revival in 1906, has mushroomed into roughly 600 million people worldwide. Yet the growth of this particular branch of conservative Protestant Christianity is part of a larger context, which is too seldom considered in popular Christian histories.

The material context of the missionary has changed dramatically from 1865 to 2000. The modern Christian missionary is now inescapably part of a global culture, with modern medical care, easy air travel, and instant communications over the Internet. Sociologist Peter Berger has described four major aspects of globalization, which is now the new context of missions activity, and has been with us for over a half-century. The first he calls the "Davos" culture, named after the location of the World Economic Summit, the culture of elite international business, a "yuppie *internationale*." This culture has created a worldwide economic network, a system closely related to what others have described as "McWorld," the spread of American popular culture symbolized by the global reach of the McDonald's restaurant chain. A third major force is what Berger describes as the "faculty club," the internationalization of the Western intelligentsia, its values and ideologies. "To put it graphically, if the 'Davos culture' tries to sell computer systems in India, the 'faculty club culture' tries to promote feminism or environmentalism there—a rather different agenda." This is the world of university education, think tanks, and non-governmental organizations—Westernized elites spread worldwide (picture the anthropologist on his fieldwork).

The fourth globalizing culture, according to Berger, is evangelical Protestantism, especially in its Pentecostal form. This pluralistic and modernizing culture originated in North America, but has become indigenous in numerous cultures, accounting for perhaps three-quarters of the growth of Christianity worldwide.

> What is clear is that this type of Protestantism is creating a new international culture, increasingly self-conscious as such (here the relation to American Evangelicals is relevant), with vast social, economic, and political ramifications. While the new Protestantism should not be misunderstood as a movement of social protest or reform (its motives are overwhelmingly personal and religious), it has large and unintended consequences. These

---

Missions (Chicago: University of Chicago Press, 1987). Many mission agencies have histories available, often published on their websites, along with written histories such as Edwin L. Frizen, *Seventy-Five Years of IFMA, 1917–1991: The Nondenominational Missions Movement* (Pasadena, Calif.: William Carey Library, 1992) [IFMA is the Interdenominational Foreign Missions Association]. These internal histories, however, are usually quite narrow in scope, and thus do not provide the broad overview necessary to understand the larger movement.

are decidedly favorable to pluralism, to the market economy, and to democracy. It should be observed here that there may be other globalizing popular movements, but Evangelicalism is clearly the most dynamic.

Berger suggests that, rather than a continuation of a form of Anglo-Saxon imperialism, evangelicalism has "become a cultural force in itself, with large numbers of people clamoring to share it," a "vital, autonomous movement no longer dependent on support from the outside."[5] This dynamism, though, is in competition with the other three forms of globalization, which are all intensely secular and generally hostile to the Christian faith. Likewise, a resurgent Islam has provided an additional challenge.

The period between 1865 and the present is an immense one, with hundreds of thousands of Christian missionaries and hundreds of millions of new believers. The growth of the Christian faith is astounding from the period from William Carey to the beginning of the twentieth century, in what missions historian Kenneth Scott Latourette called "the Great Century." By 1900, self-professed Christians represented roughly one-third of the world's population. A century later, however, after immense outpouring of resources, self-professed Christians still represent roughly one-third of the world's population, around 2 billion in a world of 6 billion people.[6] However, the center of Christianity has shifted, as now the majority of Christians are no longer in the European-dominated Northern hemisphere, but in the two-thirds world, the global South.[7]

To attempt to connect missions history with the larger American and world history is a difficult task and cannot be resolved by any easy periodization. The world dominated by European empires in the nineteenth century, of which America was just entering with its own colonies in 1898, is now a globalized, decentered world, dominated by a few regional powers and one remaining superpower. One can point to key transitions, such as the various wars of the period, or to the World Missionary Conference at Edinburgh in 1910. But even our interpretation of the Edinburgh conference begets ambiguity. Was it an expression of Christian missions, of Anglo-American imperialism, or of a liberal Christian ecumenical movement? Rather than be limited to strict dates, one should focus on thematic transitions, key watersheds that emerge in different times and places, depending upon which story is emphasized. For example, the end of World War II is a clear transition point in world history, as it is in missions. But where does it fit in the various stories? Is it the end of European imperial domination of the globe, which plays itself out in Third-World independence movements, starting with India in 1947, Indonesia in the 1950s, and Africa in the early 1960s? Or does it mark the rise

---

[5] Peter L. Berger, "Four Faces of Global Culture," *National Interest*, vol. 49, no. 23–29, Fall 1997.

[6] David Barrett and Todd Johnson, eds., *World Christian Trends, AD 30–AD 2200* (Pasadena, Calif.: William Carey Library, 2001).

[7] See Philip Jenkins, *The Next Christendom: The Coming of Global Christianity* (New York: Oxford University Press, 2002).

of Soviet expansionism and the Cold War? World War II is an enormous catalyst for new types of missionary endeavor, everything from former Air Corps pilots forming Mission Aviation Fellowship, to the creation of the National Association of Evangelicals, but what of the transitions afterward?

Evangelical missionaries were caught up in these larger conflicts and transitions, sometimes leading, sometimes responding, to these events. To organize this vast period, we have divided this chapter into six sections. Having already addressed several broad thematic issues, this chapter next focuses on the specific challenges of the "modern" as a new and current context for missions. The third section concentrates on the conflict in the period between roughly the 1880s and the 1930s, between civilizing and Christianizing, among both mainline Protestants and evangelicals. The fourth section discusses the impact of World War II, both as an impetus for decolonization, but also for disestablishment, which opens the way for entrepreneurial evangelicalism and the rise of parachurch movements. Section five addresses several key turning points in the mid-1970s, especially the Lausanne Conference on World Evangelization, where the notion of "unreached peoples" was introduced, providing a new focus for missionary activities. The sixth section briefly examines the emergence of global Christian missions, concluding with some general observations about the continuing challenges to the fulfillment of the Great Commission.

The Challenge of the "Modern"

When does the "modern" period begin in Christian missions? William Carey is considered by many to be "the father of modern missions," as his efforts mark a turning point in the expansion of the Church. Puritans initiated early Protestant missions in North America, committed to extending the Kingdom of God in the wilderness. Yet the shattering of the Puritan commonwealth in the First Great Awakening opened the way toward a distinctively modern development in the 1780s, the doctrine of religious freedom, as enshrined in the First Amendment to the new American Constitution. Too often this amendment has been interpreted through an Enlightenment framework, but this omits the profoundly Christian influences behind it and ignores the many faithful believers who provided the support for its passage. While not often seen as part of the missionary story, the First Amendment helped fulfill Jesus' command to "render unto Caesar," thus limiting the power of the federal government in matters of truth and faith. The United States then is the world's first modern nation and provides a new context for missions—critical for the growth of the Church.

The doctrine of religious freedom enshrined in the First Amendment places Christianity within a voluntary system, an essential encouragement to missions efforts. Rather than rely on the coercive power of the state, for example, in providing financial support through taxation, the Christian faith was now potentially freed from such compromises. The voluntary system began the idea of "church planting" by denominations, rather than the parish system of established churches. Second, it released evangelistic energies and entrepreneurial spirit, first in competition for home missions, then by transference into foreign missions. The disestablishment of Christian churches quickly led to an emphasis upon organization and enthusiasm for the task ahead, freeing numerous individuals from the restrictions of ecclesiastical structures.

This emphasis upon disestablishment appears quickly in the growth of American Protestant missions. One of the first North American missions organizations, the American Board of Commissioners for Foreign Missions (1810), was soon led by Rufus Anderson (1796–1880), who served as foreign secretary of the ABCFM for forty years, from 1826 to 1866. Anderson pointed away from the civilizing mission, a vision of a cultural Kingdom of God, and towards the Great Commission, with the goal of creating churches abroad that would be self-governing, self-supporting, and self-propagating.

The career of D. L. Moody provides an example of how this functioned. Born in 1837, Moody grew up in Northfield, Massachusetts. He became a Christian in a Congregationalist Sunday School, then moved to Chicago in 1856, where he became a successful shoe salesman. He was caught up in the urban revivals of 1858, and soon he entered Christian work full time, becoming an evangelist with the YMCA and also opening a Sunday School for the children of the streets. During the Civil War he broadened his ministries to work with soldiers, and after the war he became president of the Chicago YMCA and started an independent congregation, the Illinois Street Church. Moody's work as a layman was an expression of entrepreneurial evangelism as he expanded his work internationally, using the network of YMCAs to set up a series of preaching tours, first to the British Isles from 1873 to 1875, and then to Brooklyn, Philadelphia, New York, Chicago, and Boston. In 1880 Moody began the Northfield Conferences, which met annually, emphasizing missions and evangelism. In 1886, at one of Moody's conferences, one hundred students pledged to become missionaries. Princeton collegian Robert P. Wilder, the son of missionaries in India, was delegated to recruit additional workers, and two years later, in 1888, the Student Volunteer Movement for Foreign Missions (SVM) was formed, with John R. Mott as chairman and Robert E. Speer as traveling secretary. Moody developed a network of institutions for education and missions training, including the Moody Bible Institute, and encouraged the growth of the SVM.

The institutional structures developed by Moody and others created an entrepreneurial movement that was distinctly modern. Yet other parts of American culture were modernizing as well, introducing significant new challenges to the spread of the gospel. A number of these became most visible in Chicago in the years 1892–93, with significant implications for the Church and the future of missions. At least three major challenges to the Church emerged in Chicago, providing a distinctively modern context for the missionary movement. A century later we are still in the midst of these challenges.

Chicago in the late nineteenth century was the fastest growing city the world had ever seen, with a growth from roughly three thousand people at its founding to over a million and half in a single lifetime. Population densities on Chicago's Near West Side were as dense as in Calcutta, and the death rates, particularly from waterborne diseases, were as high. Slums and squalor were only part of the problem, for many middle-class Protestants had already moved to new suburbs, fleeing the massive migration of Jews and Catholics from Southern Europe who were transforming Chicago. Industrialism and immigration led to urban slums, providing significant further challenges to missions.

The first major challenge was the modern secular research university, represented by the opening of the University of Chicago. Originally a Baptist college, it was rechartered as a secular university with an emphasis upon academic freedom and research. Backed by private philanthropic wealth, the new university emphasized the creation and discovery of new knowledge, part of a pattern of development that numerous other American universities experienced. These institutions were part of a larger secularization of the American elite, as numerous children of Protestant culture moved outside the faith, replacing a broad evangelical faith with a modernist progressive secularism. How does the "faith once delivered" respond to academic institutions focused on the creation and advancement of new knowledge?

The second major challenge was represented by the World's Columbian Exhibition, the World's Fair, which opened in Chicago in 1893. The "Windy City" was visited by over twenty-six million people in the first year, who were awed both by the City Beautiful of the elite, but also by the "midway" of carnival attractions. The lure of progress and modern civilization is a continued challenge to the Christian faith, with the rise of middle-class leisure, technological innovation, and mass consumerism.

For two weeks in the fall of 1893, members of numerous religious traditions met in Chicago at the world's first Parliament of the World's Religions. The advent of religious pluralism, prefigured in this Parliament, has led less to existential angst or concern for one's soul, but rather to the happy pluralism of American culture, a spiritual relativism that raises tolerance to the highest virtue. This challenge also continues to confront the Church today.[8]

These challenges were not, of course, without responses by Christians at the time. D. L. Moody returned to Chicago in the summer of 1893, for a major evangelistic crusade targeted at the tourists then flocking to the World's Fair. British journalist and Christian William T. Stead visited Chicago, publishing the following year the exposé *If Christ Came to Chicago*, with the book's cover of Jesus driving the moneychangers out of Chicago.

Yet to look at Peter Berger's analysis of globalization a century later, these challenges to the Church's missions movement are still present. The secular university has trained thousands of social scientists, most deeply hostile to missionary enterprises; modern consumer culture socializes others away from sacrifice with promises of material prosperity; and religious pluralism leads to confusion, indifference, and the diminishment of missionary fervor.

---

[8] One could add numerous other challenges that Chicago posed for Christians in the 1890s, such as municipal corruption, a white slave trade filling Chicago's red light district, economic depression, labor violence, and desperate poverty.

The Rise and Fall of the Watchword:
Civilizing or Christianizing?

In the summer of 1893, missionary evangelist John R. Mott built a new house in the Chicago suburbs. Mott was not yet thirty years old, but already was the head of the Student Volunteer Movement. Raised in a devout Methodist home, he was led to a "reasonable and vital faith" at Cornell University after hearing C. T. Studd, renowned cricket-player-turned evangelist and one of the "Cambridge Seven" who later worked with Hudson Taylor in China. Studd's words, "Seekest thou great things for thyself? Seek them not. Seek ye first the kingdom of God," deeply affected Mott, who that same year attended Moody's conference and became one of the hundred men who volunteered for foreign missions. In 1888 he had become college secretary of the YMCA and used that network to help organize the SVM as the missions department of the YMCA and YWCA. Mott had chosen Chicago to provide support for Moody's evangelistic crusade during the World's Fair.

In many ways Moody's successor as evangelist, Mott was instrumental in building the Student Volunteer Movement into one of the largest mission sending agencies for a generation. Its watchword, "The Evangelization of the World in This Generation," provided the goal for hundreds of student missionary recruits. By the 1940s, over 20,000 SVM missionaries were engaged in gospel ministry around the world. The Student Volunteer Movement's vision of the gospel, however, blended Christianity with a broader modern culture, which, as American culture secularized in the 1920s, created significant tensions that dramatically transformed the missionary enterprise. Hence, at SVM's Quadrennial conference, from December 28, 1928, to January 1, 1929, SVM leader Sherwood Eddy removed the watchword from the program, substituting for "evangelization of the world in this generation," the phrase "world christianization," by which he meant a social, economic, and political program, rather than one explicitly focused on the gospel of Jesus Christ.

The tensions between civilizing and Christianizing had been present at least since the time of Puritan missionary John Eliot in the seventeenth century, but for this generation the challenges shattered this linkage. Yet this story is not simply a story internal to Christian theology, but part of a larger story of how evangelical Christianity has interacted with Western expansion over the globe. One of the great pioneers in Protestant missions is William Carey, the "father of modern missions," whose book, filled with missions statistics demonstrating the scope of the task, *An Enquiry into the Obligation of Christians to Use Means for the Conversion of the Heathen* (1792), led to the beginning of the Great Century of missionary expansion. Often overlooked in popular accounts, however, is how Carey's mission was closely connected with the British Empire.

Missionaries were often at the forefront of opposition to the worst facets of colonial exploitation and were often resisted and resented by colonial officials, but the Great Century was one which often linked cross and flag. Carey's great work of education and translation of the Scriptures into numerous native languages required financial, technological and scientific support, as well as security, which almost naturally developed into the practice of the mission compound. Dr. David Livingstone, one of the foremost English missionaries in the nineteenth century, considered "civilization" as a key component of the modern missionary agenda, arguing that "civilization, commerce, and Christianity" needed to go hand in hand for any to succeed.[9]

The faith missions movement was in reaction to this linkage of Christianity and Western colonialism. Englishman J. Hudson Taylor (1832–1905) believed that "God's work in God's way will never lack supply," and he was the first really to reject the model of the mission-establishment. His China Inland Mission (CIM), established in 1865, rejected the treaty-port/mission compound model, and went deep into the interior to bring the gospel to the unreached millions. Taylor adopted a financial policy based only on prayer, with no solicitations; he adopted native dress and accepted single women and unordained men as missionaries. As important, he insisted that missions policy be directed from the field, rather than the home country. Before his death, he had established over two hundred mission stations with hundreds of missionaries, and over 125,000 Chinese Christian believers. Half of all missionaries in China by 1900 were affiliated with CIM, and the faith missions movement had been replicated over the globe. The faith missions model became the premier institutional form of evangelical missions by the early twentieth century.

The Student Volunteer Movement was part of a larger expansion of Anglo-American control over the globe. Americans had a troubled relationship with empire, especially after the development of the new European imperialism in the 1870s, with its extraterritoriality, concessions, and indemnities. But they too fell easily into the lure of empire, creating an unofficial, if interdenominational, establishment. The Congregational minister Josiah Strong, in *Our Country: Its Possible Future and Its Present Crisis* (1885), called for a mission of "Anglo-Saxon Christian civilization" to the world. Missionaries to Hawaii helped overthrow the monarchy and facilitated the annexation of the islands by the United States. At the end of the Spanish-American War, President William McKinley struggled over what to do with the Philippine Islands, newly liberated from Spain. As he explained to a group of ministers who had called on him at the White House, after days of struggle he prayed and said that God had told him to take the Philippines, "to educate the Filipinos, and uplift and civilize and Christianize them."

This civilizing and Christianizing language was commonplace among British and American missionaries in the early twentieth century. Christianity then was seen by many indigenous peoples as an expression of Western culture, and this was encouraged by mission schools, many of which used the teaching of English to create a class of native elites to administer a modern state.

The inevitable reaction against Western imperialism and the linkage of Christianity with Western culture led to often violent outbreaks as well as encouraged ideological opposition to the faith. In China, the Boxer Rebellion in

---

[9] Quoted in Carpenter, *Earthen Vessels*, 309.

1900 tragically targeted all Christian missionaries, as well as numerous Chinese Christians. The Boxers lashed out against all that was perceived as foreign, and ironically it was those in China Inland Mission, who were most culturally sensitive and had helped create an indigenous Chinese Christianity, who were martyred in higher percentages than those missionaries who had remained under the protection of Western armies. More than 135 adult Protestant missionaries and 53 Western children were killed by the Boxers during the rebellion in 1900. Forty-seven of the 88 China Inland Mission workers in Shansi province were martyred.

American opposition to European imperialism in China led to the "open door policy," and by the 1920s, after the Chinese Revolution, China became closely linked with the United States and American missionaries. Anglo-American Christian missionaries developed an informal establishment, continuing the training of native elites at such institutions as Peking Union Medical College, and also working with Chiang Kai-Shek and the Nationalist Chinese. As China slipped into civil war and then was attacked by Japan in 1934 and then again in 1937, American Christian missionaries increasingly worked with the Nationalist Chinese leadership, tying their faith to one of the factions that divided country. During World War II Madame Chiang, a Methodist, toured the United States raising support for the Nationalist cause.

The mixture of Christianity and Western civilization, while understandable as a gradual development and constant temptation, increasingly tied the Christian faith to the policies of Western nations. The World Missionary Conference in Edinburgh in 1910, with over 1200 delegates, had virtually no representation from non-Western churches, even though organized Protestant missions had been operating there for over a century. Delegates were also chosen on the basis of finances, that is, the mission agencies with the biggest budgets had the biggest delegations. Continental Europeans saw the Edinburgh conference less as a distinctively Christian conference and more as an expression of Anglo-Americanism, a perception strengthened when, in the next great conference at Versailles in 1919, Christian mission property in German colonies abroad was confiscated and turned over to Allied mission societies.

The conflict over the civilizing vs. the Christianizing mission of the Western missionary was one of the central areas of division leading to the Fundamentalist-Modernist controversy in the 1910s and 1920s. The challenge of religious pluralism, seen at the Parliament of the World's Religions in Chicago, was even stronger for many on the mission field, especially for those in cultures whose traditions antedated Christianity by centuries, such as in India, Japan, and China. The need for humanitarian relief, so pressing in the face of desperate Asian poverty and pestilence, also provided a challenge for missionary motivation and priorities. Cholera killed countless thousands before the missionary could preach the gospel.

Protestant theological liberalism, as it accommodated itself to modern tolerance, relativism, and universalism, flourished among many on the mission field, especially after 1910. Faithful believers, however, were careful to separate mission motives, pointing out that biblical motives had been replaced by the humanitarian. Henry Frost, the director for North America for China Inland Mission, which had led in the indigenization of the Christian faith to local cultural contexts, argued that "While it is always true that Christianity civilizes, it is never true that civilization Christianizes."[10]

Within a few years, theological modernism spread within mainline Protestant denominations and their mission agencies. Unable to preserve the distinctiveness of the Christian faith in the face of religious pluralism and relativism, as well as increasingly seeing the humanitarian mission as their central purpose, missions faced a serious crisis. Mainline Protestants responded with a special commission, the "Layman's Inquiry," which surveyed missions abroad. Under the direction of philosopher William Ernest Hocking, the commission published *Rethinking Missions* in 1932, calling for a reorientation of missions away from individual soul evangelism and instead toward social service, education, and "interreligious dialogue." Hocking wanted the missionary to be seen as an "ambassador," invited and indeed even accredited by the host country, with a task of mutual understanding rather than conversion. The Hocking report raised some important issues, for it called for seeing the Western role as developing partnerships with indigenous churches, rather than continued domination from abroad, but it was premised on theological modernism.

Henry Frost of China Inland Mission wrote in 1933 in response to the Hocking report: "Social reform is good, but it is not the Gospel. Education is good, but it is not the Gospel. Medical work is good, but it is not the Gospel. Indeed these matters, good as they are, may destroy the Gospel."[11] The result of the various dilution of the uniqueness of the gospel was predictable. From a mission force overwhelmingly dominated by mainline denominations in the 1910s and 1920s, by the 1980s only one in ten missionaries abroad were from mainline churches, from over 10,000 in 1925 to around 2500 sixty years later. The decline in missions among the mainline suggests this truth, that action without sound theological reflection leads to apostasy and the end of the missions enterprise.

There were, however, some positive things that emerged from the mainline missions movement. In addition to a clear call for the indigenization of the church, Protestant denominations allowed for specialization and solid financial support for salaried workers with high educational standards, rather than individualistic amateurs. The development of such places like Peking Union Medical College, the "Johns Hopkins of the Orient," provided Western scientific medical training to Chinese physicians and helped save countless lives from epidemics and disease. In addition, the work of the established mainline missionaries helped provide some of the structures that eased the transition to self-supporting churches. The decline in mainline missions was not due to its calls for indigenization of missions, but rather to its modernist theology.

[10] See Henry Frost's "What Missionary Motives Should Prevail?" in *The Fundamentals*, vol. 12 (Chicago: Testimony Publishing Co., 1910–1915), 85–96.

[11] Quoted in Alvyn J. Austin, "Blessed Adversity," in Carpenter, *Earthen Vessels*, 55.

Missions in the American Century: World Wars, Decolonization, and Disestablishment

Theological controversy soon gave way to more pressing issues with the coming of war in the late 1930s. America was reluctant to get involved, especially in Europe, although many urged a vigorous response in Asia. Henry Luce, born in China to Presbyterian missionaries, was one of the century's most important publishers, founding *Time* and *Life* magazines. In a seminal article in 1941, "The American Century," Luce called upon the nation to "undertake now to be the Good Samaritan of the entire world," bringing American abundance to feed all of the world's hungry. "Administered by a humanitarian army" in the service of its ideals, America's role was to spread free economic enterprise, independence, self-reliance, equality of opportunity, and scientific know-how, to be the world's powerhouse for ideals to "do their mysterious work of lifting the life of mankind from the level of the beasts to what the Psalmist called a little lower than the angels."[12]

World War II and its aftermath were a major transition point in the history of missions, although all the implications of this conflict were not fully perceived by American evangelicals. The experience of over twelve million Americans in arms in the first real global war awakened a large number of lay Christians to the vast need abroad, as well as providing them with the skills to develop new organizations that continued the task of world missions. The war also awakened nationalistic spirit among colonized millions worldwide, signaling the end of European empires and forcing the disestablishment of numerous mission churches. Some elements of Luce's vision were becoming a reality, although not in ways he intended.

On September 2, 1945, with an American OSS officer on the dais, Vietnamese revolutionary Ho Chi Min read a statement, modeled on America's, declaring the independence of Vietnam from French colonial rule. From one perspective, the Pacific war was a clash between rivals for the succession of European empires in the Far East, but from another it was the liberation of Asian peoples from foreign power. The American war in the Pacific was caught between both of these positions, as were American missionaries.[13] Many had been imprisoned by the Japanese during the war, faithfully testifying to their Christian faith in prison camps. With the war's end, General Douglas MacArthur called for 10,000 missionaries to help rebuild, reorient, and bring "Christian civilization" to Japan. Only about 2,000 came, but the power of the gospel helped transform individual lives.[14]

---

[12] Henry Luce, "The American Century," in *Life*, Feb. 7, 1941, pp. 61–65.

[13] This was not limited to World War II, however. In the 1960s in Vietnam, missionary translation teams worked with tribal groups in the Central Highlands, but in the Vietnam War, many of these tribes sided with the American military against the communists. During the Tet offensive in 1968, the Viet Cong murdered numerous missionary translators. See Stan Guthrie, *Missions in the New Millennium: 21 Key Trends for the 21st Century* (Carlisle, U.K.: Paternoster Press, 2000), 112.

[14] One of the most moving stories is that of Japanese pilot Mitsuo Fuchida, who led the attack on Pearl Harbor and became a Christian after Hiroshima. He later became a leading Japanese evangelist. See his story at http://www. bli.org/pearlharbor/printmitsuo.htm.

America vacillated between its ideals. In 1946, the Americans granted independence to the Philippines, having been a model colonial power. Within a very few years, however, American opposition to the restoration of European empires had shifted, seeing a new enemy in global Communism. The center of the struggle was in China. Mao Tse Tung's Communists drove the Nationalist party under Chiang Kai-Shek off the mainland, declaring the People's Republic of China on October 1, 1949. The Nationalists, especially Madame Chiang, had close relations with the American missionary community. Within two years, Mao expelled all Western missionaries, leaving scarcely one million Chinese Christians on the mainland. The "China Lobby," including Henry Luce and former medical missionary and Congressman Walter Judd (R-MN), helped shape American foreign policy into the 1970s, supporting anti-communist forces throughout Asia.

The Chinese government moved swiftly to subjugate the church to the state, creating the "Three-Self Patriotic Movement," as the only legal church.[15] Was decolonization, the expulsion of the missionaries, and the creation of a political church the end of Christianity in China? Many of the expelled missionaries thought so in the immediate aftermath. But this was not the case. The church in China grew underground, in house churches, leading to what some estimate as between 50–80 million believers by 2000.

While the Chinese story is exciting, there are parallels in other colonized lands of forced disestablishment. Between 1947 and 1962, most former European colonies became independent. Of the five major imperial systems (British, French, Dutch and Belgian, with independence for the Portuguese colonies coming in the mid-1970s), all had some connections with its established churches. Indeed, as one scholar describes it, on the map of Catholicism and Anglicanism around the world "can be seen a ghostly remnant" of defunct empires.[16] In each former colony there were independence movements that combined Western ideas of state sovereignty with anti-imperialist hatred of foreigners. The first phase of decolonization was in the late 1940s and early 1950s, with such states as India gaining independence. In addition to neutralism in the emerging Cold War, Prime Minister Nehru had four pillars of domestic policy: democracy, socialism, unity, and secularism. Missionaries were soon forced out. Other newly independent nations followed India's lead, meeting at Bandung in Indonesia in 1956 to begin the non-aligned movement. Many new nations followed China and India's lead in expelling missionaries. In this they were joined by some church groups, such as the Asian Conference of Churches and African Council of Churches, which called for a moratorium on missionary personnel and foreign funds. One of the major problems for many missions was that they had linked themselves with colonial governments, often using state aid, like mission schools in East Africa.

---

[15] See Philip Yuen-Sang Leung, "Conversion, Commitment, and Culture: Christian Experience in China, 1949–99," in Lewis, ed., *Christianity Reborn*.

[16] Jenkins, *The Next Christendom*, 58–59.

Some forced disestablishment strengthened churches. As one African leader said after independence, "We need that moratorium so that we can let what is 'rice Christian' in our midst die. We need time to peel off the foreign wrapper and to find what the real message of God is for us. Then we can translate this message into life and action so that we can do effective E-1 evangelism in our midst. Once we have achieved this, then we will again be ready to join hands with the rest of the world to complete the task of world evangelization."[17]

In many ways, the experience of mission churches after the colonial period was similar to that in the American context in the eighteenth and early nineteenth centuries. Just as American Christians flourished after disestablishment, so too did the Christians not linked with colonial regimes. Those missionaries who were successful in translating the gospel cross-culturally, who used incarnational evangelism and pushed the indigenization of local leadership, thrived. Yet in spite of the decline of mainline missions caused by theological liberalism, the efforts of numerous faithful mainline Christians had provided distinct tools for later missionary endeavors.

Much as the First Amendment had freed early American Christians from the debilitating compromises with governmental agencies, at least in principle, so too did the adoption of the UN's Universal Declaration on Human Rights (1948), with committed Christians on the drafting team, create the potential for a non-coercive religious faith and the right of conversion.[18] Article 18 says that:

> Everyone has the right to freedom of thought, conscience and religion; this right includes freedom to change his religion or belief, and freedom, either alone or in community with others and in public or private, to manifest his religion or belief in teaching, practice, worship and observance."[19]

This international freedom, while often ignored by oppressive regimes, is the voluntary principle in religion, removing faith from the realm of the tribal, and instead making it the choice of the individual. This American Protestant principle was elevated to a worldwide principle, a powerful affirmation of human dignity.

Evangelical Missions, 1945 - 2000

The principles initiated in the First Amendment to the U.S. Constitution in the eighteenth century led directly to a new form of religious organization, the

---

[17] Quoted in *Let the Earth Hear His Voice*, J. D. Douglas, ed. (Minneapolis, Minn.: World Wide, 1975), 251.

[18] The provision recognizing the right to change one's religion was insisted upon by Lebanese philosopher Charles Malik, a faithful Christian statesman. See Mary Ann Glendon, *A World Made New: Eleanor Roosevelt and the Universal Declaration of Human Rights* (New York: Random House, 2001), 69–70.

[19] This principle was cited in the Lausanne Covenant, Article 13, as "in accordance with the will of God." See http://www.lausanne.org.

voluntary society, which led to the expansion of foreign missions. After World War II a new wave of organizations, called "parachurches,"[20] fueled the post-war expansion of missions, providing a distinctly American model of ministry. These independent, special-purpose agencies dramatically expanded the opportunities for many entrepreneurial individuals to form their own societies, often based on specific methods. The Gideons are one such association. Founded in 1899 as a network of business and professional men who distribute Bibles, after the war it grew to more than 250,000 laymen in 180 countries, "carrying out the same program using the same methods."[21]

The need to establish relationships among so many independent agencies led to the formation of one of the first coordinating agencies, the Interdenominational Foreign Mission Association (IFMA), in 1917, as accrediting agency for evangelical mission boards. In 2006, it represented 87 different mission boards, with thousands of missionaries. A similar agency, the Evangelical Fellowship of Mission Agencies was established in 1946 as an affiliate arm of the National Association of Evangelicals. Around 100 agencies are members of EFMA, with over 20,000 missionaries from North America in its affiliates. IFMA and EFMA frequently hold missions conferences and training sessions together, coordinating to increase the effectiveness of evangelical missions organizations through partnerships.[22]

There are dozens of examples of entrepreneurial evangelicals setting up parachurch organizations to carry on distinctive ministries. Often started in the United States, they naturally continued abroad. One such ministry is the Navigators. In the 1930s California workingman Dawson Trotman began teaching discipleship principles to sailors in the U.S. Navy, working through individual Bible study onboard ships. Trotman and his colleague Les Spencer incorporated the Navigators in 1943 as a discipleship ministry focused on small-group Bible study and Scripture memorization, using a principle of "spiritual multiplication," as new disciples would be trained by teaching others. During the war thousands of Navigator volunteers discipled within the enlisted ranks in the Navy. After the war the ministry expanded, sending its first overseas missionary to China in 1949. Fifty years later, more than 4000 Navigators staff from 64 nationalities serve in more than 100 countries.[23]

Another, larger parachurch was Campus Crusade for Christ. In 1951 a young businessman, Bill Bright, was inspired to start Campus Crusade as a ministry to college students. Soon it expanded to various "niche ministries," the military, athletes, politicians, businessmen, and so on. A born communicator,

---

[20] Parachurch groups are special-purpose agencies, normally evangelical and outside the control of religious denominations. See article by sociologist Jeff Hadden, at http://religiousbroadcasting.lib.virginia.edu/parachurch.html. See also material from the Hartford Institute for Religious Research, http://hirr.hartsem.edu/org/faith para-church_articles.html.

[21] See http://www.gideons.org.

[22] For IFMA, see http://www.ifmamissions.org, as well as Edwin L. Frizen, *Seventy-Five Years of IFMA*. For EFMA, consult http://efma.gospelcom.net.

[23] See http://www.navigators.org/us/aboutus, under "History." See also Betty Lee Skinner, *Daws: The Story of Dawson Trotman* (Grand Rapids, Mich.: Zondervan, 1974).

Bright developed numerous tools and methods for evangelization. His booklet, *The Four Spiritual Laws*, published in 1956, became the most widely disseminated booklet in history, with more than 2.5 billion distributed worldwide. In 1979 Campus Crusade produced the *Jesus* film, a feature-length movie based on the Gospel of Luke. Translated into more than 800 languages, it is the most widely viewed film in history, with estimates at over 5 billion viewers. In the half-century since its beginning, Campus Crusade boasts that it is "the world's largest Christian ministry," with a staff of 26,000 full-time employees and more than 225,000 trained volunteers in its over sixty ministries.[24]

The expansion of evangelical parachurch ministries after World War II overshadowed the decline in mainline missions in that same period. The story of the Student Volunteer Movement is tragic but also instructive. In 1946, after one of the most devastating wars in all human history, the Nobel Committee gave its peace prize to John R. Mott for his work in missions. Yet it was not so much for his work as an evangelist, but rather for his efforts at organizing the world's youth in peaceful activities. D. L. Moody had been an evangelist for the YMCA, and Mott had been his anointed successor there and with the SVM, but by the late 1930s, both organizations were no longer distinctively Christian. The hopeful enthusiasm of the "watchword" had declined, disappearing from their conference in 1932 due to theological liberalism. Many of the delegates had little knowledge of Scripture or spiritual fervor. Discouraged by the spiritual drift within the SVM, evangelicals within it formed the Student Foreign Mission Fellowship in 1936, which merged in 1945 with InterVarsity Christian Fellowship, becoming its missions department.[25] Starting in 1948, IVCF adopted the SVM practice of triennial missions conferences, holding them traditionally in Urbana on the University of Illinois campus, with around 18,000 attending.

While greatly used by God in the early years of the Student Volunteer Movement, John Mott in the 1920s and 1930s began a "deliberate policy of throwing the net as widely as possible," enlisting men of "good will" in non-Christian lands to build his student movement, rather than focusing on the unique redeeming power of Jesus Christ. As two historians suggest, it "was not a massive hemorrhage; it was a slow leak. It was a gradual downward decline, 'a gentle slope, soft underfoot, without sudden turnings, without milestones, without signpoints.'"[26] Four years after Mott's death in 1955, the SVM merged with the United Student Christian Movement and the Interseminary Movement, forming the National Student Christian Federation. In 1966, it merged with other liberal groups to form the University Christian Movement, which soon voted itself out of existence. The real story is not in organizations, however, for the spirit of evangelical student missions did not end with SVM's death, but continued from the early SVM into IVCF.

---

[24] See http://billbright.ccci.org/public/ and also www.demossnewspond.com/ccci/presskit/bbobit.htm.

[25] InterVarsity had started in Britain a generation earlier, expanding to Canada between the wars and to the United States in 1938. See http://www.intervarsity.org/aboutus/history.php. See also Keith and Gladys Hunt, *For Christ and the University: The Story of InterVarsity Christian Fellowship in the USA, 1940–1990* (Downers Grove, Ill.: InterVarsity Press, 1992).

[26] Keith and Gladys Hunt, *For Christ and the University*, 56–57.

In addition to new methods and organizations, new thinking developed in evangelical missions after World War II as missions increased in complexity and sophistication. Strategic assessments of the task ahead combined with careful mobilization of resources helped shape the next phase of the movement. Cam Townsend's work with Wycliffe applied advanced anthropological and linguistic techniques to the furtherance of gospel ministry. One strategic thinker was Donald McGavran. Born in India of missionary parents and influenced by SVM, McGavran served in India, where his experiences led to his book *The Bridges of God* (1955), where he argued for missionaries to examine individual people groups. One village, for example, while having only one language, had fifty different caste-groups. McGavran would later develop his insights into his principles for "church growth," establishing an Institute for Church Growth in Oregon and then becoming the founding dean of the School of World Mission at Fuller Seminary.

Another key missions strategist was Ralph Winter, whose career paralleled many in the post-war evangelical missions movement. Trained in engineering through accelerated methods by the Navy during the war, Winter then attended Princeton Seminary, where he met Bill Bright. He hitchhiked to the first InterVarsity missions conference, then attended an SIL training program the summer of 1948. He finished his Ph.D. in structural linguistics at Cornell in 1953, later moving with his family to Guatemala, where he served as a missionary to the Mayan Indians for ten years. In 1967 he helped create the Theological Education by Extension program, which has been used by more than a thousand schools to train over 100,000 local church leaders in their home communities. He joined McGavran at Fuller's School of World Missions and developed several other special-purpose agencies, such as the William Carey Library (1969) to publish missionary books. In 1976 he left Fuller to create the U.S. Center for World Missions to build "a church for every people by the year 2000."[27]

Significant as all these individuals and organizations are, it is impossible to tell the story of evangelical missions without evangelist Billy Graham. Originally an American evangelist working for one new post-war parachurch agency, Youth For Christ, Graham developed his international mission slowly. He became a national figure after anti-communist newspaper magnate William Randolph Hearst urged his papers to "puff Graham" during the 1949 Los Angeles Crusade, but it was only in 1956 that Graham ventured on a preaching tour to India and East Asia. After that, Graham became the first international evangelist, taking the revivalist theology and methods of Edwards, Finney, and Moody to a worldwide audience. The Billy Graham Evangelistic Association (BGEA) carefully organized its crusades through close preparation with local churches and ministries. Graham began developing an international network, bringing church leaders first to a small conference in Montreux, Switzerland, in

---

[27] There are several sources on Ralph Winter's life. See the article in John D. Woodbridge, ed,. *Ambassadors for Christ* (Chicago: Moody Press, 1994), 314–19. See also Roberta H. Winter, *I Will Do A New Thing: The US Center for World Mission ... and Beyond* (1987; rev. ed., Pasadena, Calif.: William Carey Library, 2002), and http://www. uscwm.org.

1960 and later to the World Congress on Evangelism in Berlin, in 1966, with regional conferences thereafter.

Graham and the BGEA were responsible for one of the most important turning points in post-war evangelical missions, the International Congress on World Evangelization, held in Lausanne, Switzerland, in July 1974. In his opening address, Graham traced the roots of the Lausanne conference to John R. Mott, arguing that the first great missionary conference in Edinburgh in 1910 combined two streams, the "evangelical" and the "ecumenical," but theological drift had led the ecumenical to predominate. "Since then, the world church has floundered," as evangelism was replaced by "humanization - the reconciliation of man with man, rather than of man with God."[28] Instead, Graham affirmed the orthodox and universal gospel of Jesus Christ.

Lausanne marked the internationalization of evangelicalism, where, for one of the first times, "the division between missionary-sending and missionary-receiving nations disappeared." Whites were outnumbered, as the majority of the delegates were from the Third World, representing more than 150 countries.[29] Out of Lausanne emerged an ongoing agency, the Lausanne Committee on World Evangelization, which continued to coordinate world missions, taking as its motto, "The Whole Church Taking the Whole Gospel to the Whole World."[30] Lausanne was in many ways a conference of international missions strategists, the generals and staff officers, rather than "the foot-soldiers of the faith." Graham sponsored three additional worldwide conferences for these "Itinerant Evangelists," in 1983, 1986, and 2000, encouraging and training over 20,000 indigenous evangelists.

One of the most important outcomes of the Congress was the adoption of the Lausanne Covenant, where the delegates committed themselves to make disciples of all nations. The Covenant expressed a clear link between evangelism and social responsibility, and it rejoiced "that a new missionary era has dawned," as the dominance of Western missions was "fast disappearing," opening the way to evangelistic partnerships with the "younger churches." Also emphasized was the "urgency of the evangelistic task," with a goal "that every person will have the opportunity to hear, understand, and receive the good news."

In the sessions, new strategic thinking emerged, which shaped how Christians would fulfill that task. Ralph Winter argued forcefully for the concept of "unreached peoples." "I'm afraid that all our exultation about the fact that every *country* of the world has been penetrated has allowed many to understand that every *culture* has by now been penetrated," a serious misunderstanding that limited the spread of the gospel. Winter insisted that the word *ethnē* in the Great Commission referred to "peoples," distinct cultural communities, rather than nations.[31] He called for a paradigm shift from "winning souls in

---

[28] Billy Graham, "Why Lausanne?" in *Let the Earth Hear His Voice*, 26–27.

[29] John Pollack, "Billy Graham," in Woodbridge, ed., *Ambassadors for Christ*, 284.

[30] See http://www.lausanne.org. The Lausanne Covenant is accessible under the "documents" section, at http://www.lausanne.org/Brix?pageID=12891.

[31] Ralph Winter, "The Highest Priority: Cross-Cultural Evangelism," in *Let the Earth Hear His Voice*, 213, 221.

all countries" to thinking of "planting pioneer church movements in all of the remaining Unreached People Groups."[32] Winter later developed these insights through training programs, including the *Perspectives* course, programs which dramatically transformed the focus of numerous mission agencies, leading to such conceptual tools as the "10/40 Window."[33]

Lausanne also elevated social ministry as a part of the missionary's task: "We affirm that evangelism and socio-political involvement are both part of our Christian duty. For both are necessary expressions of our doctrines of God and man, our love for our neighbour and our obedience to Jesus Christ." A year after Lausanne, theologian John Stott published *Christian Mission in the Modern World*, where he argued that the critical statement for missions was not the Great Commission, but rather John 20:21 "As the Father has sent me, I also send you," with a call to do the works Jesus did, such as preaching good news to the poor, from his call in Luke 4:18–19. To Stott, evangelism and social action were two sides to the same coin: "Neither is a means to the other, or even a manifestation of the other. For each is an end in itself." This means for Stott that mission describes "everything the church is sent into the world to do." Unlike the earlier Social Gospel, however, the foundation was on changing the heart of the individual, then structural change.[34] Tetsunao Yamamori, head of the relief and development agency Food for the Hungry, codified this into the concept of "the two hungers," shorthand for those doubly burdened by physical hunger and by a spiritual hunger for salvation. Yamamori proposed a "symbiotic strategy" which would integrate evangelism with social action, often using tent-making personnel, as a way to combine the resources of social justice ministries with evangelism, not by merging agencies, but by working for individual conversions first, and then watching reforms occur like yeast through dough.[35]

The Task Ahead: Challenges in the Era of Global Christianity

Sometime around the 1990s, the majority of self-professed Christians in the world shifted from the North to the South. In 1900 and in 2000, the percentage of self-identified Christians remained about the same, at roughly one-third of world population, but these figures hide an enormous change over the century. Christianity is now most dynamic outside of Europe and even North America. Over the past one hundred years, evangelical church attendance in Latin America grew 5000 percent; African attendance, 4000 percent, and Asian

---

[32] Ralph Winter, quoted in Tetsunano Yamamori, *Penetrating Missions' Final Frontier: A New Strategy for Unreached People* (Downers Grove, Ill.: InterVarsity Press, 1993).

[33] The 10/40 Window refers to the area of the world between the latitudes 10 degrees and 40 degrees north of the equator, in Africa, the Middle East, and Asia, which has the largest numbers of unreached peoples and greatest physical and spiritual needs. See Patrick Johnstone and Jason Mandryk, *Operation World* (Carlisle, UK: Paternoster Press, 2001), 17, 755.

[34] Quoted in Guthrie, *Missions in the Third Millennium*, 126.

[35] Yamamori, *Penetrating Missions' Final Frontier*, 37, 135–36.

evangelical church attendance grew by 2000 percent. In Africa alone, the number of Christians increased from around 10 million in 1900 to 360 million a century later. The Church now worldwide is the first universal religion, a multitude from *almost* every tribe and nation.

Some missions scholars are pointing out the profound changes that will take place in the Church worldwide. Historian Philip Jenkins describes "the next Christendom" in glowing terms as a global revolution whose implications we are only beginning to perceive. Andrew Walls argues that "the center of Christianity has moved to the southern world, to Africa and Asia," but that has yet to really affect how theology is done in the West. While he "wouldn't say there's no future for Western Christianity or no important task for Western theologians, it and they will be less and less significant for the future of Christianity."[36]

In spite of such optimistic accounts, there still are significant challenges for the Church worldwide. The first challenge remains the vast numbers of unreached peoples. In spite of the global advance of the Christian faith, there is still an enormous task remaining. The percentage of professed Christians actually declined in the decade of the 1990s, due to the large number of births, a situation that continues as world population rises. Only 2,500 languages have Bible translations, out of roughly 6,900 language groups. There are still around four billion non-Christians worldwide, and of that around 1.6 billion have never even heard the gospel. Many missions groups are targeting not these vast numbers of unreached, but rather nearby groups easily reached.

A second problem is a seeming decline in missions interest on the part of American Christians. For all the public emphasis on missions, it remains a small portion of evangelical budgets. Less than 6 percent of global Christian giving goes to support world missions, with outreach, evangelism, and translation work among non-Christians attracting the least money. "The average church member donating his $2.75 a week, gives out of this only $0.15 (fifteen American cents) to support Christian foreign missions." In fact, the annual total amount of church money embezzled is $16 billion, more than the $15 billion spent on foreign missions![37] Indeed, as global travel has become cheaper, there has been a shift away from long-term, career missionaries to short-termers, a trend that has exploded among American evangelicals. From around 22,000 in 1979, by 1990 it had swollen to around 120,000, and by 1998 to almost a half-million. But too often, short-term missionaries do not yield long-term results. Two large agencies, Operation Mobilization and Youth With A Mission, have provided much of the training and infrastructure that has increased the emphasis on short-term missionaries, but as missions funding has remained static, this has led to the decline in career missionaries on the field.[38]

Missions statisticians argue that the problem is the same as with world hunger—"the supply is vastly more than adequate, but distribution is criminally inadequate." The distribution of "the benefits of Christianity . . . is uneven,

---

[36] Andrew Walls, *Missionary Movement.*
[37] Barrett and Johnson, *World Christian Trends,* 660.
[38] Guthrie, *Missions in the Third Millennium,* 87.

unfair, unplanned, chaotic, counterproductive." The billion Christians in the developed world get 95 percent of Christianity's tangible benefits, while over a billion non-Christians in the developing world get nothing. "Yet we as missionary-minded Christians continue to direct 84 percent of all our evangelizing activity at other Christians."[39] In the 30 years after Lausanne, evangelical mission agencies have been increasingly targeting unreached peoples, but much still remains to be done in this area.

A third challenge, one that is not often perceived by evangelicals, is the shift in global populations away from rural areas and into massive cities. The perception of American Christians of foreign missions all too often involves a small tribe in the bush, rather than the global reality of teeming millions in vast urban slums. The "unreached" increasingly are uprooted rural people rather than tribes in the jungles. However, there has been a decline in interest among Western churches in investing in missions to those areas. "For whatever reason, Western investment in missions has been cut back dramatically at just the point it is most desperately needed, at the peak of the current surge in Christian numbers."[40] Perhaps we need to return to the missionary model of D. L. Moody on the streets of Chicago in the 1860s, where he ministered to the hordes of street urchins living hand to mouth, providing Bible studies and Sunday Schools for the urban poor.

A fourth challenge is that posed by the European situation. After the ravages of the first half of the twentieth century, Europe, once the origin of Protestant missionary movements, has become a mission field. The number of atheists and agnostics in Europe grew from a little over one million in 1900, to over 130 million in 2000. The secularization of Western Europe paralleled the growth of communism in the East, and while the end of the Soviet Union opened up a vast mission field with hundreds of missionaries flowing in after 1991, Europe remains secular. While mission agencies strategically shifted focus toward unreached peoples, optimistically hoping to fulfill the task by some arbitrary date like the year 2000, Europeans were leaving the faith in the millions, the first culture to become "post-Christian." If Christianity could become marginal where once it was the center of the culture, what does that mean for the future of the Church worldwide?

A related challenge is the corrosive influence of the modern university, one of the most secularizing agents in history. One "missionary" to the secular was Francis Schaeffer, who believed that, in many ways, as Europe goes, so goes the world. Establishing an intentional community, L'Abri in Switzerland, Schaeffer ministered to the disaffected youth adrift in a post-Christian culture. Schaeffer's disciple Ranald Macaulay, argued that, "As much as the United States influences the developing world technologically, so much does Europe influence the world intellectually." One of Europe's great exports has been the university, now a global institution, "the most far reaching major cultural tradition ever developed

---

[39] Barrett and Johnson, *World Christian Trends*, 683.
[40] Jenkins, *Next Christendom*, 213.

in history."[41] Merely evangelized believers are no match for the disciples of the modern secularizing university.

Just as evangelicals need to rethink our image of the missionary to the unreached as one from rural village to urban slum, so too should we rethink the implications of the growth of the Church in the global South. The newly evangelized youth in his village soon migrates to the city, where he comes under the authority of those trained in modern universities. Soon the faith drifts away, as he is ill-equipped to meet those intellectual challenges. This may not take place immediately, of course, but over a generation it looks all too plausible, as ambitious sons of converted believers struggle to enter the global economy. Missionaries are often ill-equipped for such challenges. One missions strategist sees "a tragic amateurization of missions," with short-termers on "tourist-mission jaunts" and career missionaries with simple Bible institute backgrounds. "Today, the average missionary to, say, India, is very poorly prepared to answer the questioning of honest intellectuals who have heard that Christianity was a drag on scholarship, science and enlightenment ... the missionary's secular education has already told him the same thing. To answer with an outline of Romans is not enough."[42]

It seems that many of the challenges to Christian missions at the beginning of the twenty-first century are the same as in 1890s Chicago, with the industrial city, religious pluralism which undermined the distinctiveness of the faith,[43] and the secular university. What then was local is now global. Since Lausanne, missions strategists have focused the Church's efforts on "unreached peoples," but perhaps this category needs to be expanded conceptually. Rather than envisioning the prototypical tribe in the jungle, one should think of what has happened to that tribe over the past two generations. Pushed out of ancestral lands, they drift to the margins of a large urban center, filled with other uprooted peoples. Their children drop their mother tongue for a new language and aspire to education to enable them to enter the global economy.

This abstract example illustrates that increasingly in the future, along with the cities, the universities should be seen as a new strategic missions frontier. That was the direction that Lebanese ambassador Charles Malik pointed to back in 1980: "The problem is not only to win souls but to save minds. If you win the whole world and lose the mind of the world, you will soon discover that you have not won the world. Indeed it may turn out that you have actually lost the world."[44]

---

[41] Ralph Winter, *Mission Frontiers*, Summer 2003.

[42] Ralph Winter, "Twelve Frontiers of Perspective," 7–8, in *Missions Frontiers*, online at http://www.uscwm.org, link to *Missions Frontiers*.

[43] The challenge of religious pluralism to the mission enterprise has contributed to a decline in emphasis on missions among evangelicals. See the works of James Davidson Hunter, especially *Evangelicalism: The Coming Generation* (Chicago: University of Chicago Press, 1987).

[44] Malik spoke at the Dedication Ceremony of the Billy Graham Center at Wheaton College, Illinois. Charles Malik, *The Two Tasks* (Westchester, Ill.: Cornerstone, 1980), 32; and *A Christian Critique of the University* (Downers Grove, Ill.: InterVarsity Press, 1982).

One place where this challenge presents itself most strongly is in sub-Saharan Africa, which has seen such phenomenal growth in the faith in the last century. For all of the excitement over the spiritual dynamism, however, it may be that much of this growth is a mile wide and an inch deep. The genocide in Rwanda in 1994 is a tragic example, for it was one of the most "evangelized" countries in Africa. One penetrating analysis of the Rwandan case was that while the nation was "converted," it was not discipled "at the profound level of culture." Tribalism remained preeminent, and "the blood of Christ was not applied to the breaking down of the divided wall of hostility between Hutu and Tutsi," resulting in mass murder. "The task given to the church in the Great Commission was nothing less than to disciple nations. If the church does not disciple the nation, the nation will disciple the church. Rwanda is an extreme example of this principle."[45]

It may be time for evangelicals to move beyond, or rather build upon, the insight that the word *ethnē* in the Great Commission means "peoples," and not countries, to realize that we are also to win the minds of all structures, the *ethnē* of the tribes as well as the culture of the state, as a means of true transformation.

This chapter began with a call to integrate the two competing stories of American and missions history, and it is necessary to sketch out some possible overlap, for they point to continuing themes in American evangelical missions. The first is the context of the American political tradition. As mentioned earlier, the principle of religious freedom as enshrined in the First Amendment was one of the great charters for the missionary, as it enabled the voluntary principle in religion to expand outside of state interference.[46] This has changed the context of modern missions, a distinctly American contribution to the history of the Church. This principle of religious freedom was written into the Universal Declaration of Human Rights. In 1998, religious freedom became, for the first time, a pillar of American foreign policy. Passed almost unanimously by Congress, the International Religious Freedom Act of 1998 requires the U.S. State Department to report on the conditions of religious freedom in every country of the world, an area where American Christians are helping to change the condition of persecuted believers worldwide.[47] This is not just an opposition to religious persecution and advocacy for the release of religious prisoners, but also for a positive expression of religious freedom, which would include the right to change one's religion and participate as a believer in public life.

The second major story involves the challenges implicit in the martyrdom of Chet Bitterman. Critics of missionaries, either from the communist left or the secular anthropological community, denounce the missions enterprise as an ex-

---

[45] Darrow Miller with Stan Guthrie, *Discipling Nations: The Power of Truth to Transform Cultures* (Seattle, Wash.: YWAM Press, 2001), 191–92.

[46] Indeed, the First Amendment can even protect the missionary abroad, as he or she can truthfully explain that America is not a "Christian" nation, an essential point in the midst of an unpopular war.

[47] See Allen D. Hertzke, *Freeing God's Children: The Unlikely Alliance for Global Human Rights* (Lanham, Md.: Rowman & Littlefield, 2004). The United States and Vatican City are the only two governments in the world that have the extension of religious freedom as an explicit principle of their foreign policy.

pression of imperialism and modernization, a narrative that is dominant among the international community. In a postmodern context, however, it is the larger narrative that wins—the one that is able to incorporate all the truths within competing narratives that has the best explanatory power. The secular story of anthropologists trying to preserve the pristine primitivism of a Stone Age tribe against the "cultural imperialism" of the missionary is a simplistic morality tale, especially when seen in the larger context of the anthropologist's semester-long field work versus the missionary spending a decade of his or her life creating the grammars and vernacular Scriptures, developing the very tools that will empower that tribe to engage the modern world on its own terms. The act of translation and literacy training is the means by which indigenous peoples can preserve their culture and survive in the face of pressures from multinational corporations and government bureaucrats. That is the larger story, one that is seldom told in our segregated histories.

The twenty-first century is now the century of global Christianity, a worldwide faith without a single geographical center. The American evangelical contribution to this expansion has been, and continues to be, profound. It developed the model for the church growth movement in the modern world, for the explosive increase of Christianity in the Two-Thirds World continues the earlier American pattern, where political disestablishment and the voluntary principle led to the development of indigenous churches, which were incarnated in local cultures. While by no means exclusive, the global expansion of evangelical Christianity is in large part an expression of American Christian influence.

The great progress of the past century of American evangelical missions has stressed evangelism and individual conversion, illustrated by one recent sermon in a Pentecostal congregation interpreting the Great Commission as "evangelism, evangelism, evangelism." But evangelism is not mentioned in Matthew 28:19–20; rather it is a call to "make disciples." Over the past generation the Church has learned the meaning of *ethnē*. Perhaps this generation will focus on the discipling task as we seek to obey for the next "great century."

In 1957, at InterVarsity Christian Fellowship's Urbana missions conference, evangelist Billy Graham told the story of how, when Standard Oil was looking for a man to run their entire Far East operation, they approached a missionary to be their representative. The company offered him ten thousand dollars, and he turned it down; twenty-five thousand, and he turned it down; fifty thousand, and he turned it down. They asked, "What's wrong?" He said, "Your price is all right, but your job is too small. God has called me to be a missionary." The calling of the missionary, like the calling of the missions historian, is not a small job. But we are merely co-workers in fulfilling the command to make disciples of all nations, for we follow One who is with us always, "to the very end of the age."

PART THREE:
MAJORITY CHURCH MISSIONS

Chapter Seven:

THE GREAT COMMISSION IN LATIN AMERICA

By J. Daniel Salinas

> *Today, the twenty Latin American nations may well be classified as Protestant, in the sense that in each one of them the Evangelical community is already too numerous to be regarded as a minority and strong enough to cause the general public to stop and look and listen. In any event, that community is not a feeble congregation of outcasts hanging around the philanthropic skirts of foreign missionaries, but rather a very powerful ferment with sufficient energy of radiation to alter for good the social atmosphere and the spiritual climate of a whole continent.*[1]

Historiography of the Latin American church has concentrated on the efforts of foreign missionaries and preachers and mostly ignored the fact that Latin Americans have been active since the beginning of evangelical presence in the continent in the preaching of the gospel both within Latin America and to other continents. In recent years, it has been Latin American historians themselves who have developed this area of research. However, historiography from this part of the world looks different since it relies chiefly upon oral sources. Yet, this does not mean it has nothing to contribute to the global history of missions and evangelism.

Latin American ecclesiastical history is part of the Western missionary movement. Our lands were conquered by European countries, we speak European languages, our political systems follow European models, and so on.[2] As a Latin

---

[1] Alberto Rembao, "The Presence of Protestantism in Latin America," *International Review of Missions* 21.1 (1948): 57.

[2] The argument for Latin America being Western is implicit in *Certeza* 3.47, (1972) with a cover title for the issue of *América Latina: Occidental . . . ¿Y qué más?* See especially the article, Samuel Escobar, "Reto Al Cristianismo," *Certeza* 3.47 (1972).

American I have always considered myself a Westerner. In this sense, the Latin American missionary movement is part of the Western missionary movement because it has generally followed the same patterns and models brought by missionaries to Latin America. But in missiological circles Latin America is considered to be non-Western. Missiologists must be the only ones saying that! Everywhere else— the United Nations, the World Bank, UNICEF, and the Organization of American States, for example—Latin America is included in the Western hemisphere.

In the mid 1980s, figures on Latin American missionaries were scarce and included mostly those in remote tribal and rural work. The situation is now different. According to 2002 data, there are 6,455 registered Latin American missionaries, 134 mission agencies, 177 church initiatives, and 30 missionary training centers in the region.[3] The number of Latin American missionaries might be as high as 10,192.[4] These numbers reflect career missionaries and do not include tent-makers nor the great number of evangelicals who have left the region for socio-economic reasons and have taken the message of the gospel wherever they have gone.

Continuous evangelical presence in Latin America is over a century old. Colombia's evangelical church, for example, celebrated in 2006 a century and a half of history.[5] It would not be fair to say that missionary involvement is only recent. This is a clear example of how historiography has maintained a false impression. Many foreign mission agencies have published biographies and anthologies of their missionaries in the region.[6] The literature of what those mission agencies have done and are doing in Latin America is extensive. Most of them publish a periodical magazine with stories of their missionaries. By contrast, the amount of literature available on the missionary involvement of Latin Americans in the expansion of the evangelical faith in their own countries is limited to a few sketchy monographs and some articles in local magazines with limited distribution. The biographies published on Latin Americans have been about famous outlaws, political figures, or the liberators and patriots of Latin America. Since local missionaries do not fit into any of those categories, their lives have gone without any recognition.[7]

Most of the history of the evangelical church in Latin America has been lost because no one has written it down. Peruvian historian Juan Inocencio Silva describes the situation in the following terms:

> Over time, God's people have forgotten the ultimate importance of transmitting and keeping the collective memory of the new and many significant experiences obtained throughout his-

---

[3] COMIBAM, *Catálogo de Organizaciones Misioneras de Iberoamérica*, ed. Ted Limpic (Guatemala: COMIBAM Internacional, 2002), 221.

[4] Patrick J. Johnstone, *Operation World*, 21st century ed. (Carlisle, U.K.: Paternoster, 2001), 35.

[5] The actual date of its founding is March 8, 1886. Francisco Ordóñez, *Historia del Cristianismo Evangélico en Colombia* (Armenia, Colombia: Alianza Cristiana y Misionera, 1956), 28.

[6] One of the best known is Elisabeth Elliot, *Through Gates of Splendor* (New York: Harper, 1957).

[7] An exception worth mentioning is Victor Landero. See Bob Owen and David M. Howard, *The Victor: The Victor Landero Story* (Old Tappan, N. J.: F.H. Revell, 1979).

tory. This situation has led to a process of ecclesiastical anomie whose final product is a church without memory which continues to lose its identity and a correct sense of its life and mission. The fragile oral memory of evangelicals has been diluting itself over time with the irreparable loss of the first, second and third generations as it has received scarce or no importance. In this way, willingly or unwillingly, we have been slowly destroying the collective memory of evangelicals. If we do not preserve the oral and collective memory of the evangelical people we run the risk of becoming a memory-less church, sick with historical amnesia . . . and this is very serious.[8]

An early missionary who has attracted the attention of biographers and researchers is Francisco Penzotti (1851–1925). His is one of the better-documented ministries from the second half of the nineteenth century.[9] Francisco Penzotti emigrated from Italy to Uruguay as a thirteen-year-old boy. After reading the New Testament he became an evangelical Christian. He developed his ministry under the tutelage of Dr. Thomas Wood from the Methodist church in Montevideo. From 1883 to 1906 Penzotti traveled by ship, mule, foot, and whatever other means from Chile all the way to Mexico, opening offices for the American Bible Society and starting churches. On January 10, 1889, in El Callao, a harbor near Lima, Peru, Penzotti founded the first evangelical church officially established in the country, the Iglesia Metodista Episcopal del Callao. However, evangelical ministry in those days had many perils. Penzotti spent eight months in a Peruvian prison accused of preaching a different faith than the official one. Immediately after his imprisonment, the country was torn by civil strife between allies and enemies of Penzotti. The uproar was so intense that it reached the highest officials. This episode was instrumental in changing the laws of the country to allow freedom of religion and the opening of the country to the gospel. During his time in Central America, Penzotti preached constantly and opened offices for the American Bible Society in every country. He became known as the Apostle of the Central American churches. In a time of fierce persecution and religious intolerance, under Penzotti's leadership more than a quarter of a million Bibles were given away and over two million excerpts of Scripture were distributed. When he died in 1925, his name was directly associated with the evangelical history of at least twelve countries in Latin America. The scholarship on Penzotti is exceptional because he left extensive records and

[8] Juan Inocencio Silva, *La Ciencia Histórica y la Misión de la Iglesia* (accessed February 27, 2006); available from http://ekeko2.rcp.net.pe/fratela/ponencias/juan-inocencio-silva.htm.
[9] Claudio Celada, *Un Apóstol Contemporáneo: la Vida de F. G. Penzotti* (Buenos Aires: Libreria La Aurora, 1900); Margarette Daniels, *Makers of South America* (New York: Missionary Education Movement of the United States and Canada, 1916); Samuel E. Escobar, *Precursores Evangélicos: Cartas de Diego Thomson, Memorias de Francisco Penzotti*, Serie Presencia (Lima: Ediciones Presencia, 1984); Francisco Penzotti, *Spiritual Victories in Latin America*, Centennial Pamphlets No. 16 (New York: American Bible Society, 1916); Luis D. Salem, *Francisco G. Penzotti, Apóstol de la Libertad y la Verdad*, Colección Historia 2 (México: Sociedades Bíblicas en América Latina, 1963).

diaries of his ministry. However, this has not been the case in the great majority of people.

In 1912 the Central American Mission reported having twenty-four missionaries on the field and "about fifty native workers, male and female, giving their whole time to the spread of the gospel, and about fifty more giving a portion of their time."[10] These people also "made possible the work of the Bible Societies, being employed as colporteurs. Their spiritual discernment is most marked and they become mighty preachers."[11] Besides these words on the ministry of Latin Americans, there are no explicit references—with a handful of exceptions—to who they were, what their actual work was, where exactly they were located, or how they supported themselves. They remain anonymous. Therefore, it is understandable that most people think the Latin American missionary movement is of recent making. Many, including some Latin Americans, would assume that Laura Heikes's assessment is correct: that the "movement from Latin America got a late start in comparison with Asia and Africa, which have been sending out missionaries over the past 50 years. Although the Latin American movement began in the 1970s, it did not experience significant growth until the 1990s."[12] Such a statement, however, does not do justice to the almost two centuries of incredible missionary efforts of Latin American evangelicals to cross many kinds of borders in order to reach their continent for Christ.

Missiologist Samuel Escobar has noted that for each foreign missionary in Latin America there have been tens of anonymous national missionaries. Then he added,

> In each country the missionaries Diego Thomson or Francisco Penzotti visited in the nineteenth century soon appeared a nucleus of national volunteers to help them with the educational and evangelistic task. At the dawn of the twentieth century, just one congregation in Peru, the Iglesia Evangélica de la calle Negreiros, had ninety nuclei of missionary extension in three countries . . . During the 1930s Argentinian Baptists sent missionaries to southern Peru to work alongside Irish missionaries. These are just small samples. Currently, in the sierras of the Andean countries, in the native Mexican and Guatemalan communities, among the communities of the Amazon jungle with Bible translations there are spontaneous movements of constant and sacrificial missionary extension. The fact that they have an oral and not a written tradition, or that their lives do not call the attention of the well-known missionary press, should not deceive the most attentive scholars.[13]

---

[10] CAM, *The Central American Bulletin* 18.3 (1912).

[11] Ibid., 18.4 (1912).

[12] Laura Heikes, "Una Perspectiva Diferente: Latin Americans and the Global Mission Movement," *Missiology: An International Review* 31.1 (2003): 70.

[13] Samuel Escobar, *Una Decada en Tiempo de Misión* (Quito: Ediciones Comunidad, 1987), 19.

For example, in 1865 Manuel Paniagua became the first evangelical in Colombia sent as a colporteur to remote places around the country.[14] In 1879 another Colombian, Heraclio Osuna, went to Caracas, Venezuela, also as a colporteur and to start a congregation.[15] In 1911 João Jorge de Oliveira and his wife were sent by the Brazilian Baptist Convention as missionaries to Portugal. The Igreja Presbiteriana do Brasil sent Rev. João Marques da Mota in 1920 as their first Brazilian missionary to Portugal. Four years later the general assembly of the Igreja Presbiteriana do Brasil decided to close Portugal as a mission field. Consequently, Erasmo Braga together with his father Rev. Carvalho Braga started the first Brazilian missionary agency, the Sociedade Missionária Brasileira de Evangelização em Portugal.[16]

Juan Fonseca, writing the history of the Church of God in Peru, comes to the conclusion that the beginning of that denomination was the result of "joint efforts between the North American mission and national groups." He concludes that it would be "unfair to attribute to one person the merit of founding the Church of God" in Peru.[17] Regarding the involvement of local people, Fonseca adds,

> Another mechanism that permitted the expansion of the denomination consisted in the work, at times heroic, of those who went to new fields and formed new congregations. Those doing this work lacked monetary remuneration and, in general, they went as self-supported missionaries. The Church of God did not have a program or a Missions Department. Evangelization was done by men and women who were convinced that God had called them to live with all type of privations and risk all for the sake of the gospel.[18]

Fonseca mentions the involvement of Latin American women in the missionary enterprise, a "face" of the mission endeavor that has been even more ignored. Doubtless there have been Latin American parallels to female workers such as Gladys Aylward and Elisabeth Elliot, but their lives, ministries, and achievements were never recorded. In the late 1970s the denomination that I was part of in Bogota sent Mrs. Beatriz Díaz, a widow with children, as missionary to Spain to work among gypsies. Not long ago I inquired about her. I called the sending church. I also called the headquarters of the denomination. Nobody was able to tell me the exact date, not even the year, she had departed for Europe. They told me she was still in Spain. The initial plan to reach the gypsies did not work out, but that had not discouraged her. She went on and started a church

---

[14] Ordóñez, *Historia del Cristianismo Evangélico en Colombia*, 41.

[15] Ibid., 45.

[16] Bárbara Burns, "Missões Brasileiras: O Gigante Começa a Despertar," in *". . . Até Aos Confins da Terra": Uma História Biográfica Das Missões Cristãs*, ed. Ruth A. Tucker (São Paulo: Vida Nova, 1996); Júlio Andrade Ferreira, *História da Igreja Presbiteriana Do Brasil*, 2 ed., 2 vols. (São Paulo: Casa Editora Presbiteriana, 1992).

[17] Juan A. Fonseca Ariza, "La Misiología de la Iglesia de Dios en Perú: Una Perspectiva Histórica" (Lima: Paper presented at the Latin American Theological Fraternity, 1997), 9.

[18] Ibid., 25.

that is growing and supporting her. Now there are three churches of that denomination in Spain, with their own Spanish missionary to northern Africa. To write Beatriz Díaz's story one would have to rely solely on oral sources. If this is the case with a missionary that has gone abroad supported by a well-established denomination, how much worse is the available information for the hundreds of women who remained as missionaries in their own countries or went to another country in the region with no denominational support?

Latin Americans have been involved as missionaries since the very beginning of the history of the evangelical church in the continent in the nineteenth century. They have undertaken the responsibility of taking the gospel to every corner of their continent with sacrifice and commitment. Their life stories are recorded only in heaven's annals. A challenge remains for historians to sort through the scarce oral traditions and to find local deposits of documents scattered throughout the continent to uncover the rich and multifarious webs of personal and denominational stories. The Centro Evangélico de Misiología Andina (CEMAA) in Lima, Peru, has encouraged several projects of this sort. Also commendable is the contribution of Lindy Scott, a North American historian, to Mexican evangelical history.[19] In Mexico, the work of Carlos Martinez-García and Carlos Mondragón of the Centro de Estudios del Protestantismo Mexicano has been a catalyst for historical research on evangelical presence not only in their country but for the whole continent.[20] Samuel Escobar and other historians have worked on systematization and research on the evangelical history in Peru.[21] These are but an indication of a broader historical trend that will not only benefit the evangelical church in Latin America but also the Church around the world.[22]

[19] Lindy Scott, "Economic Koinonia within the Body of Christ" (M.A. Thesis, Trinity Evangelical Divinity School, 1975); Idem, *Los Evangélicos Mexicanos en el Siglo Veinte* (Mexico, D. F.: Editorial Kyrios, 1980); Idem, "Salt of the Earth: a Socio-Political History of Mexico City Evangelical Protestants (1964–1991)" (Ph.D. Dissertation, Northwestern University/Garrett Evangelical Theological Seminary, 1991); Idem, *La Sal de la Tierra* (Santo Domingo, Mexico: Editorial Kyrios, 1994); Idem, "The Christian Transformation of Latin America Culture: Otilio Montaño, Gonzalo Báez-Camargo, and Gabriela Mistral" (Paper presented at the Point Loma Nazarene University on April 8, North American Christian Foreign Language Association: 2000); Lindy Scott and Titus F. Guenther, *Del Sur Al Norte: Aportes Teológicos Desde la Periferia*, Fraternidad Teológica Latinoamericana 13 (Buenos Aires: Kairos, 2003).

[20] See for example, Carlos Martinez-García, "Secta: Un Concepto Inadecuado Para Explicar el Protestantismo Mexicano," *Boletín Teológico* 23.41 (1991); Idem, "La Biblia en la Nueva España," *Boletín Teológico* 24.47/48 (1992); Idem, "Protestantismo, Derechos Humanos y Tolerancia en Los Pueblos Indios de Chiapas," *Revista Electrónica Espacio de Diálogo* 1.1 (2004); Carlos Mondragón, "El Ensayo Heterodoxo en América Latina," *Boletín Teológico* 26.56 (1994); Mondragón, "Protestantismo y Paramenicanismo en América Latina," in *Protestantismo y Política en América Latina y el Caribe*, ed. Tomás J. Gutierrez S. (Lima: CEHILA, 1996); Mondragón, "Historia de Las Ideas Protestantes en América Latina, 1920–1950" (M.A. Thesis, Universidad Nacional Autónoma de México, 2000); Mondragón, *Leudar la Masa: el Pensamiento Social de Los Protestantes en América Latina, 1920–1950*, Colección Fraternidad Teológica Latinoamericana 22–23 (Buenos Aires: Kairos Editiones, 2005); Carlos Monsiváis and Carlos Martínez García, *Protestantismo, Diversidad y Tolerancia* (Mexico, D. F.: Comisión Nacional de los Derechos Humanos, 2002).

[21] Escobar, *Precursores Evangélicos*; Samuel Escobar and others, *Protestantismo en el Peru: Guía Bibliográfica y de Fuentes* (Lima: Ediciones Puma del Centro de Investigaciones y Publicaciones [CENIP], 2001).

[22] For example, Tomás Gutiérrez S, *Los Evangélicos en Perú y América Latina: Ensayos Sobre Su Historia* (Lima: Ediciones AHP, 1997). See also, Comunidad, *Cristianos en Las Luchas Revolucionarias. Taller de Teología* 11 (Mexico, D. F.: Comunidad Teológica de México, 1982); Comunidad, *Contribuciones Para Una Historia del*

More recently, Latin American missionary history has been documented differently and with more resources even though it has focused primarily on numerical quantification. Numbers are not bad in themselves. The problem is when one believes they give a complete picture. Who defines the parameters for what is included in the numbers? Samuel Escobar has alerted North American and European centers of missionary research, warning them of the error of believing that "there is missionary work only where their computers register it, or that there is missionary activity only when there is the type of missionary society they consider proper."[23] There is also pressure from some organizations in Latin America to fulfill certain quotas for missionaries.[24] Since anonymity has been the way of doing missions in the Latin American church in the past, there is enough evidence to believe that it continues to be the norm. The evangelistic task on the continent is being done by foreign missionaries and Latin American missionaries who remain outside of the databases: simple men and women who work quietly, sacrificially, and boldly.

There are various responses to the current missionary enterprise in Latin America. First, a considerable number of evangelical churches do not participate in the missionary enterprise. Estimates in 2000 were that only 5 percent of the churches in Latin America had a missionary program.[25] I remember talking to a friend in charge of raising missionary interest in the congregations of his denomination. He shared his difficulty to convince pastors and churchgoers of their missionary responsibility. Besides two of the largest congregations, the others presented several reasons not to get involved. They argued that they were still small and had scarce resources. They said they were still in need of receiving missionaries instead of thinking about sending or supporting them. They mentioned their small budgets and the fact that the majority of their members were poor. My friend's comments hold true across denominational and economic lines.

However, the fact that a church does not send missionaries does not mean evangelism is absent. Churches are generally committed to reach their neighborhoods and towns with the gospel. The primary reason for not sending missionaries has to do with the scarcity of finances. I have visited many of these congregations, both rural and urban. Their passion for Christ is evident. Their hearts ache with the spiritual needs of their relatives and acquaintances. Many congregations do not have the resources to support their pastor with a decent salary. Therefore, most of the pastors are bi-vocational. These are the churches that comprise the majority of evangelical congregations across the continent,

---

Protestantismo en América Latina. 14 (Mexico, D. F.: Comunidad Teológica de México, 1984). On the methodological challenge, see Eduardo Hoornaert and others, *História de Igreja na América Latina e No Caribe, 1945–1995: o Debate Metodológico* (Petrópolis, RJ and São Paulo, SP: Vozes; CEHILA, 1995).

[23] Escobar, *Una Decada en Tiempo de Misión*, 20.

[24] Bertil Ekström, "Informe de la Presidencia 1997–2000. 1 Asamblea Internacional de COMIBAM-Lima, Perú 13–18 Noviembre 2000" (Cooperación Misionera Iberoamericana COMIBAM, 2000), 1.

[25] Ibid., 4.

but would never appear in missionary statistics or in the "500 most successful businesses."[26]

Second, there is a group of churches that plan to send, have sent, or are currently supporting their missionaries. Most of these churches have followed the trends and practices of foreign mission agencies. They have added numbers to the missionary force but have not produced an indigenous reflection on the topic. Samuel Escobar explains that although "Latin America is experiencing missionary winds, almost in its entirety what is being done is a repetition of the traditional and historical patterns."[27] Escobar, therefore, challenges evangelical churches to think about mission, "forging a missiology that will not be a simple copy or servile translation of what is done in other parts."[28] Many of these churches and organizations are strongly committed to programs like "adopt a people group," the 10/40 window, AD2000, and the like. In many of these programs, Latin American missionaries are expected to blend in and to go with the flow defined by foreign missions. These churches are faithfully and sacrificially supporting their missionaries. However, many of them have had to learn along the road how to support their missionaries in an effective manner. Very few of these churches have an organized missions department. Nevertheless, what they lack in organization they make up for in sincerity and desire to obey the Lord. This group of churches is quite vocal about promoting missionary programs, and this is the group with the largest number of formal missionaries on the field. These churches are of all economic and social conditions, some with more financial resources than others.

Among this second group of churches there are two different trends. First, some churches send their missionaries through an established agency like *Pueblos Musulmanes* (PM), Frontiers, WEC International, New Tribes, Latin America Mission, Latin Link, and the like. Missionaries sent this way are part of an international team and are expected to follow the structural and logistical procedures of the agency. They are trained in transcultural and missiological schools, either in Latin America or abroad. Missionaries of this sort are involved in a variety of ministries like education, health, street children, community development, church planting, camping, and so on.

A second trend among these mission-active churches is to employ their own missionaries to start extensions of the mother church. These churches function like transnational companies that export their own version of Christianity.[29] Most of these churches are mega-churches that have developed their own variety

[26] Several scholarly studies have appeared on this group of churches. For example, Miguel Alvarez, "The South and the Latin American Paradigm of the Pentecostal Movement," *Asian Journal of Pentecostal Studies* 5.1 (2002); Jean Pierre Bastian, "The Metamorphosis of Latin American Protestant Groups: A Sociological Perspective," *Latin American Research Review* 28.2 (1993); Michael Bergunder, "The Pentecostal Movement and Basic Ecclesia Communities in Latin America: Sociological Theories and Theological Debates," *International Review of Mission* 91, no. 361 (2002); John Marcom Jr., "The Fire Down South," *Forbes*, October 15, 1990; David Martin, "Speaking in Latin Tongues," *National Review*, September 29, 1989; Sergio Matviuk, "Pentecostal Leadership Development and Church Growth in Latin America," *Asian Journal of Pentecostal Studies* 5.1 (2002).

[27] Escobar, *Una Decada en Tiempo de Misión*, 1.

[28] Ibid., 9.

[29] Mauricio Cardoso, "Fe Tipo Exportação," *Veja*, April 1997.

of prosperity theology supported by their own marketing methodology. The "owner" or founder is usually a charismatic man with absolute control over all aspects of the church, including finances. Missionaries sent by these churches must follow to the smallest detail the methodology defined by their "anointed" leader. Newly planted congregations soon enlarge the assets of the "company." Unproductive missionaries are removed and replaced at any time. For example, the *Igreja Universal do Reino de Deus* from Brazil claims to have work in over ninety countries,[30] yet, it is "lamentable that the theology of that church is not balanced."[31] The phenomenon these churches has created has caught the attention of the secular press as examples of successful companies and as an expression of young Latin American entrepreneurs.[32]

A third group of churches and organizations in Latin America have developed an indigenous Latin American theology of mission and evangelism. The rest of this chapter is dedicated to this group. This group exists mainly within the context of the *Fraternidad Teológica Latinoamericana* (FTL) and the university student movements related to the International Fellowship of Evangelical Students (IFES).[33] This group has considered critically and constructively the methods and theory of evangelism and missions that have come from North America and Europe. The main emphasis has been to develop a contextual evangelism that would be sensitive to the idiosyncrasies and culture of the particular situation in Latin America. Samuel Escobar explains this task as follows:

> The condition of the churches in Latin America differs quite a bit from that in other latitudes. Therefore, the "packages" of concepts, techniques and customs that so enthusiastically are translated from English should undergo a careful evaluation in light of the Word of God. The fact that we look for a way we can call our own and that we neglect to accept submissively foreign missionary models, some of which have already shown their unusefulness, does not mean we do not have missionary passion and vocation.[34]

Puerto Rican missiologist Orlando Costas provides a model within this third group. He worked to develop a contextual evangelization. For Costas, evange-

---

[30] http://www.igrejauniversal.org.br/

[31] Alderi Souza de Matos, "História Das Missões na Igreja Brasileira Do Século XX" (unpublished paper).

[32] Mónica Andrea Cabarcas, "La Explosión de la Fe," *Semana*, March 7, 2005; Cabarcas, "Cristianos: ¿Divide y Reinarás? *El Tiempo*, August 28, 2005; D'Artagnan, "Cristianos: ¿Misión Pastoral o Electoral?," *El Tiempo*, March 5, 2006; Andrés Garibello, "Iglesias Colombianas Que Exportan Fe. ¿Cuáles Son y Cómo Nacieron Los Cultos Nacionales Que Están Llegando a Los Rincones del Planeta?," *El Tiempo*, March 5, 2006; Garibello, "¿A Qué Obedece el Auge de Las Iglesias Cristianas? Online Discussion," *Semana*, July 7, 2005. See also, David Neff, "Market-Driven Missions? *Christianity Today*, December 6, 1999.

[33] For a brief history of the FTL see, Samuel Escobar, "La Fundación de la Fraternidad Teológica Latinoamericana: Breve Ensayo Histórico," *Boletín Teológico* 59/60 (1995). For an introduction to the work of IFES in Latin America, see Samuel Escobar, *La Chispa y la Llama. Breve Historia de la Comunidad Internacional de Estudiantes Evangélicos en América Latina* (Buenos Aires: Certeza, 1978).

[34] Escobar, *Una Decada en Tiempo de Misión*, 22.

lization is a thoroughly contextual action for three reasons: evangelism always relates to a specific historical situation; the people being evangelized are not abstract persons, separated from reality, but men and women of flesh and bones who are immersed in concrete historical situations; and evangelization has as its fundamental goal the transformation of all peoples.[35]

However, evangelization has not always been contextualized properly. Costas evaluated the evangelization actually being practiced in Latin America as "spurious" and "embarrassing,"

> [b]ecause it not only has reflected and produced confessional and denominational divisions, but it has also been accompanied by the "metaphysical sin"—the negation of our mutual existence as witnesses of the gospel. While we Christians and churches do not open ourselves one to the other at least to interchange ideas and experiences, even contradictory and conflictive ones; while we do not recognize that in this parcel of the Third World there are others who, even though they have a way of thinking and a practice that is different to ours, are also preoccupied with the Great Commission of our Lord, evangelization will continue being an embarrassing scandal.[36]

Likewise, Ruben Lores, former president of the Latin America Biblical Seminary in San José, Costa Rica, believes "the churches that directly or indirectly owe their origin to foreign missionary societies have received a body of attitudes, ethical stances, critical postures, economic ideas and sectional loyalties that are more substantially related to the ideology of 'manifest destiny' than to the Gospel of Christ."[37] This "manifest destiny" is a "dynamic ideology," a mixture of both politics and theology, which North Americans carry with them wherever they go to evangelize, making them more the "ambassadors of Anglo-Saxon Christianity and the American way of life than of the Gospel of the Lord Jesus Christ."[38] Lores perceived that a theology mixed with "manifest destiny" produced "the best kind of supporters of the *status quo* that any ruler can expect," and especially at the level of international relationships.[39] The insights of Lores present huge implications for evangelism and missions, both for the foreign missionaries who come to Latin America and for Latin Americans who go to the ends of the earth. More careful reflection must be done on what the pure gospel is without cultural trappings.

---

[35] Orlando Costas, "Por Una Auténtica Evangelización Contextual," *Pastoralia* 2.3 (1979).

[36] Ibid., 6.

[37] Lores defines ideology as a system of conceptual formulations, more or less coherent, which is intrinsically related to and becomes a program of action in a given historical situation. Ruben Lores, "Manifest Destiny and the Missionary Enterprise," *Study Encounter* 11.1 (1975): 1.

[38] Ibid., 15.

[39] Ibid., 9.

The Argentinian theologian and Methodist pastor José Míguez Bonino has voiced similar concerns about this dangerous "cocktail" of theology and politics brought by missionaries to Latin America.

> Missions and missionaries came to Latin America as—conscious or unconscious—expressions and agents of a world view in which Protestant faith was integrated with a political philosophy (democracy in its American version), an economic system (free enterprise capitalism), a geopolitical/historical project (the United States as champion and center of a "new world" of progress and freedom), and an ideology (the liberal creed of progress, education, and science).[40]

Míguez considers the close tie between Latin American and North American Protestants as "basically harmful" since "Protestantism has helped to create a benevolent and idealized image of the colonial powers—mainly of the United States—which disguised the fact of their domination."[41] The harm is due to the image Latin Americans have of the United States and consequently of Protestantism itself. This is the image of "a strong tradition of imperialistic domination, arbitrary interventions in the life of Latin American countries, abuse of economic power, [and] support of the most reactionary and inhuman forces in Latin American countries."[42]

Costas presents the example of his native Puerto Rico as a case study. Protestantism arrived on the island accompanying the troops of the United States during the Spanish American War at the end of the nineteenth century. After the war, "the United States converted the island into a sugar-colony and worried little for the pathetic social and economical situation of its people. Had it not been for the missions and the churches that they established, the majority of islanders would have died of hunger—and in fact many died that way!"[43] However, all the work of the churches, in spite of their humanitarian efforts, "caused lots of damage" to the reception of Protestantism, "because they served as ideological instruments of the colonial power."[44]

Another criticism voiced by this third group of Latin American Protestants is the ideological link between Christian mission and the world of free enterprise. Costas is adamant about the issue:

---

[40] José Míguez Bonino, "How Does the United States' Presence Help, Hinder or Compromise Christian Mission in Latin America?" *Review and Expositor* 74.2 (1977): 176. For a Catholic approach, see Joseph Gremillion, *The Church and Culture since Vatican II: The Experience of North and Latin America* (Notre Dame, Ind.: University of Notre Dame Press, 1985). See also, Samuel Escobar, "The Two-Party System and the Missionary Enterprise," in *Re-Forming the Center* (Grand Rapids, Mich.: Eerdmans, 1998).

[41] Míguez Bonino, "How Does the United States Presence Help, Hinder or Compromise Christian Mission in Latin America?" 178.

[42] Ibid.

[43] Orlando Costas, "Compromiso y Misión" (San José, Costa Rica: Caribe, 1979), 115.

[44] Ibid. See also Samuel Silva Gotay, "Protestantismo y Política en Puerto Rico a Partir de la Invasión de Estados Unidos," in *Protestantismo y Política en América Latina y el Caribe*, ed. Tomás J. Gutiérrez S. (Lima: CEHILA, 1996).

Christian mission was not only made to depend on the model of the "colonial-mercantile-imperial" or "neo-colonial-liberal-capitalist" enterprise, but also on its goal to reorganize society in terms of an economy free from state control, of a governmental structure based on voting rights, and of universal vision founded in the idea of progress.[45]

Costas observed that mission societies and other related ministries have adopted the same strategies developed in the world of business, bringing significant regions of the Third World to the new mode of international capitalism. However, Costas does not doubt the sincere commitment of Christians involved in the modern missionary movement. "Nevertheless, they are part of a world-wide system that often uses people, movements, and institutions for purposes other than the communication of the gospel and its liberating power."[46]

Keeping this in mind, the identification of missions and the missionary task with expansionistic and imperialistic ideologies has created suspicion among many Latin Americans of the validity of the evangelical version of Christianity. It has been aggravated by the impression given by foreign missionaries working in Latin America that missionary work requires huge amounts of money, high-power technology, and grandiose programs. These two elements have influenced both the reception of the gospel by unbelievers and the direct involvement of believers in ministry. During the era of the Cold War, Latin American evangelicals, in general, experienced the effects of the "black legend" which considered them subjects of a foreign empire.[47] It is not a surprise to see that the growth of the evangelical church has increased exponentially after the fall of the Berlin Wall and the globalization of economics. This, however, is still a subject for further research.[48] As Latin Americans cross many borders they need to be aware of their own "additions" to the message of the gospel.

The process of contextualization and Latin Americanization of evangelism and of the mission of the church also has its constructive side. Ecuadorian New Testament scholar René Padilla has defined and articulated the concept of *Misión Integral,* integral or holistic mission. In a nutshell, integral mission is the integration of two elements of the gospel that have been historically severed— social action and proclamation.

---

[45] Orlando Costas, *The Church and Its Mission: A Shattering Critique from the Third World* (Wheaton, Ill.: Tyndale House, 1974), 76.

[46] Ibid., 77.

[47] Bastian, "The Metamorphosis of Latin American Protestant Groups," 34. See also, Samuel Escobar, *Los Evangelicos: ¿Nueva Leyenda Negra en America Latina?,* Serie Protestantismo y Nacion (Mexico: Casa Unida de Publicaciones, 1991).

[48] For several works that point in that direction, see Daniel H. Levine, "Religion, Society, and Politics: States of the Art," *Latin American Research Review* 16.3 (1981); Levine, ed., *Churches and Politics in Latin America* (Beverly Hills, Calif.: SAGE Publications, Inc., 1979); Edward Lynch, "Reform and Religion in Latin America," *Orbis* 42.2 (1998); Catalina Romero, "Globalization, Civil Society and Religion from a Latin American Standpoint," *Sociology of Religion* 62.4 (2001).

The social action that does not have its roots in the Gospel is not evangelical in the sense of being an answer to the love of God in Christ. It could be just a secular endeavor, but it should not pretend to be Christian, since it does not put Christ in the center. On the other side, what good is it to preach a Gospel that limits itself to the individual experience of salvation and does not lead the believer to live out that salvation in love to the neighbor as an answer to the love of God in Jesus Christ?[49]

Therefore, integral mission is oriented to the satisfaction of all the basic needs of human beings—need of God, love, food, shelter, clothing, physical and mental health, and the sense of human dignity. It also considers that human beings are social, created to live in communion with God and with their neighbors. Consequently, integral mission forms persons "who do not live for themselves but rather for others, persons with the capacity to receive and to give love, persons who are 'hungry and thirsty for justice' and who 'work for peace.'"

Mission does justice to the biblical teaching and the concrete situation only when it is *integral*. In other words, when it is a *crossing of frontiers* (not only geographic frontiers, but also cultural, racial, economic, social, political, and so on) with the purpose of transforming human life in all its dimensions, according to God's purpose, and to empower men and women to enjoy the plentiful life that God has made possible through Jesus Christ and the power of the Spirit.[50]

However, there is still a lot of ground to cover in order for churches and Christian institutions to adopt an integral or holistic approach to evangelization and mission. After a study of the churches in Buenos Aires, Argentina, the Kairos Foundation divided the churches into three groups:

1. A predominant number of churches do not see themselves as part of the area in which they are located. They can ignore the city and the needs of people. Their efforts are centered on self-preservation.
2. Only a few churches are really concerned for their respective neighborhoods. Most do not listen to outsiders and are not interested in the real needs of people around them. Yet they regard themselves as saviors of the city because they do some work for people.
3. It is rare to find churches that see themselves as part of, or partners with, their respective neighborhoods, working with them in the solution of common problems, as incarnate in their communities.[51]

---

[49] C. René Padilla, *Mission Between the Times: Essays on the Kingdom* (Grand Rapids, Mich.: Eerdmans, 1985), 35.

[50] Ibid.

[51] C. René Padilla, "Integral Mission Today," in *Justice, Mercy and Humility: Integral Mission and the Poor*, ed. Tim Chester (Waynesboro, Ga.: Paternoster Press, 2002), 61.

As Padilla explains, the slow process of assuming and practicing integral mission has to do with the fact that "a narrow view of mission has been taken for granted."[52] Yet, integral mission has become the ministry agenda for a good number of people around the world. Integral or holistic mission is, to date, the major contribution of Latin America to the theory and practice of evangelism and cross-cultural missions. This approach has been embodied in the formation of organizations like the Micah Network with representatives from all the continents and every sort of denominational background.[53] In Latin America, the *Red el Camino* unites churches, mission agencies, NGOs, and other similar evangelical organizations that minister to different sectors of society with a holistic concept of evangelism and mission.[54] It is not an exaggeration to say that integral or holistic mission has been a theory of mission that Latin America has exported to the whole globe.[55]

Within the student movements affiliated with the International Fellowship of Evangelical Students (IFES) there has also been a similar holistic approach to evangelism and missions. For example, a seminal idea of integral mission was present at the First Latin American Missionary Congress with the theme "Jesus Christ: Lordship, Purpose, and Mission," held in Curitiba, Brazil, January 23–30, 1976. This congress was convened by the *Aliança Bíblica Universitária do Brasil* (ABUB) with more than 500 participants, mostly university students from throughout Latin America.[56] The final document of the congress, *El Pacto de Curitiba*, states,

> We recognize that mission cannot be an isolated department of the life of the church, rather it is an essential part of its essence, because "the church is a missionary church or it is no church at all." Therefore, the mission involves every Christian in the totality of their life, substituting the wrong concept of the "professional missionary labor" with the universal priesthood of all believers. We are profoundly concerned for the lack of this missionary vision of the church within the Latin American context.[57]

---

[52] Ibid., 62.

[53] Steve Bradbury, "Introducing the Micah Network," in *Justice, Mercy and Humility: Integral Mission and the Poor*.

[54] Robert Guerrero, "Networking for Integral Mission: El Camino Network, Latin America," in *Justice, Mercy and Humility: Integral Mission and the Poor*. For a presentation of various holistic ministries in Latin America, see C. René Padilla, "Holistic Mission in Theological Perspective," in *Serving with the Poor in Latin America*, ed. Tetsunao Yamamori et al. (Monrovia: MARC Publications, 1997). See also C. René Padilla and Tetsunao Yamamori, *El Proyecto de Dios y Las Necesidades Humanas: Más Modelos de Ministerio Integral en América Latina* (Buenos Aires: Kairos, 2000).

[55] See Samuel Escobar, *The New Global Mission: The Gospel from Everywhere to Everyone* (Downers Grove, Ill.: InterVarsity Press, 2003), 142–54.

[56] See Escobar, *Una Década en Tiempo de Misión*, 1–8; Linda Sellevag, "Jesucristo: Señorío, Propósito, Misión. Congreso Misionero - Curitiba 1976," *Certeza* 16.62 (1976).

[57] CIEE, "El Pacto de Curitiba," in *Teología del Camino: Documentos Presentados en Los Últimos Veinte Años Por Diferentes Comunidades Cristianas de América Latina*, ed. Pedro Arana Quiroz (Lima: Presencia, 1987), 46.

The *Pacto* reminded the participants that "as in the past Jesus' calling and mission demanded to cross geographical borders, today the Lord challenges us to cross the borders of inequality, injustice and ideological idolatry." The commitment was to "work in such a way that the same missionary vocation would lead us to penetrate into all the areas of the Latin American societies."[58] And they have. From the Rio Grande all the way to the Patagonia, graduates are part of a mostly silent missionary movement. They are found in politics, positions of influence in their countries making efforts to write just laws and reduce rampant corruption. They are in the best hospitals and clinics. Hundreds of them are in pastoral and other related ministries, providing a contextualized model of ministry. Others have started their own organizations to reach the poor and to work alongside the communities in the many facets of development.[59] Some work with family ministry, others with youth, still others with children at risk. The list continues indefinitely. Evangelicals are doing Christian mission in the midst of the normal intricacies of life and making a difference for the kingdom of God in Latin America and beyond.

In conclusion, from the beginning, Latin American evangelicals have participated in the expansion of the church and the propagation of the gospel within and outside the continent. The majority of Latin American evangelists and missionaries have gone unnoticed by historians. Their oral stories have been forgotten and the details of their lives are largely unknown because they did not leave a paper trail. Current historiography is recognizing that there has been a closer cooperation between foreign missionaries and local believers in the evangelistic and missionary task than previously thought. There are ongoing efforts to recover and discover those stories that remain in the memories of older generations and those that are "hidden" under the dust in ecclesiastical deposits of documents. Even today, anonymous Latin American believers are involved in obeying the Great Commission inside their own countries and around the world.

---

[58] Ibid., 48.

[59] Two examples: Through the leadership of Eugenio Ariaza, the *Asociación Mexicana de Tranformación Rural y Urbana* (AMEXTRA) from 1984 has served over 75,000 people in ten states. COMPA, "Todo Empezó en la Universidad," *En Contacto*, Verano 2005. Also in Mexico, Saúl and Pilar Cruz founded Armonía Ministries to work in severely deprived slums. See Saúl and Pilar Cruz, "Integral Mission and the Practioner's Perspective," in *Justice, Mercy and Humility: Integral Mission and the Poor*.

Chapter Eight:

THE GREAT COMMISSION IN ASIA

By Richard R. Cook

Asia is a continent of contrasts. Christian missions in Asia in the twenty-first century is also complex. No other continent has greater need for missionary activity, but the churches in Asia themselves may soon have the resources to meet these needs. For instance, there have never in history been more Christians in China than today, with somewhere between 30–70 million believers. Yet, at the same time, there have never been more non-Christians in China, with over one billion people who do not yet profess Christ.

Asia is vast and vibrant.[1] It contains around thirty countries, including Japan in Northeast Asia, numerous nations in Southeast Asia and South Asia such as the Philippines, Indonesia, and India, and Turkey in West Asia. Many regions in Asia enjoy a rich cultural heritage stretching back 5,000 years. At least three major cultural blocks have emerged in Asia: Mesopotamia, India, and China. Asia is the birthplace of the major living religions of Christianity, Islam, Hinduism, and Buddhism. Today, about 60 percent of the world's population resides in Asia, numbering around three billion people. Economic development also varies dramatically, with Japan as an established economic super power, surging economies in India and China, as well as persistent pockets of poverty in some areas. In this explosive context, the growth of Christian churches in the twentieth century often occurred in competition with Marxism and secularism, alongside the revitalization of Islam, Buddhism, Hinduism, and various folk religions. Urbanization is also changing the face of the continent. The remaining task of missions to Asia is overwhelming, but it is just this task that Asian Christians are now mobilizing to achieve with unprecedented concern and commitment. For Christian missions in the twenty-first century, Asia contains both unprecedented opportunities as well as challenges. As will be argued, China and Korea in particular could play a historic role not only in missions in Asia but also globally during the next century.

---

[1] The continent of Asia is massive and complex, and might be variously defined. This chapter will focus primarily on the region of East Asia, with less consideration of South Asia, Southeast Asia, and Central Asia.

Within this dynamic context of rapid church growth, exploding global economies, and expanding political clout, evangelical churches in Asia may soon lead the world in missionary activity. Missions from Asia cannot be understood apart from this vital context. Therefore, this chapter first scans the broad context in Asia during the first years of the twenty-first century. The explosive growth of the Asian church, including a brief examination of its history past and present, will be considered second. With these major trends in view, the final section of this chapter will explore the Asian churches' important role in the modern missionary enterprise.

Context of Missions from Asia

The global center of the church has shifted several times during Christian history. And that center may now be shifting to Asia, most of all to East Asia. At the forefront of the economic resurgence of Asia today is China. China scholar Oded Shenkar forcefully argues that the transformation occurring in China is unique, signaling the rise of a new global superpower. Several exceptional factors set the emergence of China apart from the economic growth of India, Japan, and other Asian economies. Shenkar contends,

> China's rise has more in common with the rise of the United States a century earlier than with the progress of its modern-day predecessors and followers. What we are witnessing is the sustained and dramatic growth of a future world power, with an unmatched breadth of resources, lofty aspirations, strong bargaining position, and the financial and technological wherewithal of an established and business-savvy Diaspora. The impact of a rising China on the countries of the world—both developed and developing—will be enormous....[2]

As its economy has grown in the past several years, China has been aggressively engaged in the global market, particularly in the pursuit of sources of energy. For instance, the BBC News reported on China's growing influence in Africa, noting that "China's rapacious energy needs are increasingly shaping its foreign policy," particularly in Africa. Chinese companies are already involved in numerous projects in Africa, such as building a railway line in Angola and roads and bridges in Rwanda.[3] China has been aggressively developing ties around the world, especially in Asia. For instance, China has been mending its relations with Cambodia, and it emerged in 2004 as the number one foreign investor in Cambodia.[4] The implications of these momentous economic developments for Christian missions will be considered in the next section.

---

[2] Oded Shenkar, *The Chinese Century: The Rising Chinese Economy and Its Impact on the Global Economy, the Balance of Power, and Your Job* (Upper Saddle River, N.J.: Wharton School Publishing, 2006), 1.

[3] "China's Growing Focus on Africa," BBC News, January 17, 2006. http://news.bbc.co.uk/go/pr/fr/-/2/hi/africa/4619956.stm

[4] "China turns on charm, wins friend," *Chicago Tribune*, March 30, 2006, front page.

Economics and geo-politics throughout history have often played a key role in the growth and expansion of churches. Vital Christian churches in politically and economically powerful regions frequently provided leadership for potent missions movements. Although the Christian Church has never had a formal global "center," churches from different regions of the world have wielded exceptional influence at different times during the past two millennia. These regional churches often became missionary "centers" for evangelizing other parts of the world. The Mediterranean basin served as the ecclesiastical and economic center during the first several centuries of church history, a center that gradually shifted north to Europe during the Middle Ages. A momentous transition occurred around the sixteenth century, however, as the center of both the global economy and Western Christianity shifted to the Atlantic region. Led initially by Roman Catholic Spanish and Portuguese explorers, merchants, and missionaries, tri-lateral trade in the Atlantic between Europe, Africa, and the New World significantly enriched the nations of Western Europe. Over time, the wealth created by trade and the new global economy particularly served the political fortunes of Protestant powers such as Britain and the United States. Missionaries from these Protestant countries—oftentimes raised up by evangelical revivalism and working in tandem with Western commercial interests—spread the Christian gospel around the globe.

The economic dominance of Atlantic nations may now be waning, however, and the Pacific Rim appears poised to emerge as the new center of global trade and the global economy. Significantly, if Pacific Rim nations follow the pattern of the Spanish and Portuguese and the British and North Americans before them, then as this region prospers economically, vibrant missions movements will emerge among the churches of East Asia. Churches from the United States, Canada, and Australia with established missionary institutions will be challenged to partner effectively with Christians in Asian countries such as China, South Korea, and Japan. The potential shift of the center of the global economy to the Asia Pacific region may be the most significant trend of the early twenty-first century, and it will likely have tremendous impact on Christian missions.

Influential diaspora communities in the West also complement the economies of Asia. While early immigration to the United States from Asia was mostly halted in the 1920s, the Hart-Celler Act of 1965 again opened the doors. The new immigration laws favored skilled and highly educated workers and also allowed a provision for family reunification, provisions that allowed post-1965 Asian American populations to be "disproportionately found near the top of the occupational, and therefore economic, ladder."[5] While the religious makeup of these communities is difficult to determine, R. Stephen Warner contends that, "migration is not random, so even the relatively evenhanded Hart-Celler provisions do not produce a religious cross section of each sending country among its emigrants."[6] For instance, due to a variety of reasons, about 75

---

[5] R. Stephen Warner, *A Church of Our Own: Disestablishment and Diversity in American Religion* (New Brunswick, N.J.: Rutgers University Press, 2005), 254.

[6] Ibid.

percent of Korean-Americans are Christian, mostly Protestant. While many post-1965 Chinese immigrants profess no religion, including thousands who come as graduate students, many of them convert to Christianity after they arrive in the United States. Christian churches, remarkably, may have become the "predominant religious institutions among the Chinese in America."[7] While this generation of immigrants may in itself represent an impressive missions force, the second generation, their children, may prove to be even more potent. Throughout American history, the children of immigrants from various parts of the world have often thrived. They share, it seems, their parents' drive for success, but unlike their parents they are also fluent in the English language and are comfortable with American culture. The children of Asian immigrants are now coming of age, and as highly educated and motivated professionals they can influence both the economy in the United States and, in some cases, in Asia. Furthermore, as many members of this outstanding generation of Asian Americans grew up in Christian churches, they also have the potential to impact global missions, particularly missions to Asia. The confluence of burgeoning economies and Christian churches in Asia along with these powerful Asian-American communities could change the face of missions.

Perhaps no other continent evinces such extraordinary spiritual need while offering such unprecedented opportunity for effective Christian missionary activity. Yet significant problems must be overcome. Global markets are sensitive to dramatic variation, and the future of Asian economies is by no means certain; likewise, political instability is a dangerous, ever-present reality in some Asian countries. Additionally, rapid church growth now evident in many regions of Asia might not continue, and missionary zeal in Asia could decline. Bold predictions made at the end of the nineteenth century that China and Asia would emerge during the following century as a world powerhouse should give all pundits reason to pause, as these predictions did not come to pass (at least not until the very end of the twentieth century).

From the perspective of evangelicals, the explosive growth of several Asian economies may indicate that God desires to bless Asia in order that the churches in Asia may be a blessing to others. As Psalm 67:1–2 states, "May God be gracious to us and bless us… that Your way may be known on earth, Your salvation among all nations." Evangelicals in Asia and throughout the world look forward to the growing impact of Asian churches on world missions.

The Church in Asia

The growth of Christianity in Asia might best be seen as the re-emergence of an ancient church. Christianity spread into Asia from Palestine during the first decades of the Christian era. By some accounts, Christianity was introduced by the apostle Thomas into India as early as A.D. 52. There is also evidence of two major migrations of Syrian Christians into South India with a contin-

---

[7] Ibid.

ued Christian presence there. By A.D. 150 there were Christians in modern-day Iran/Persia. Nestorian Christians following the silk trade route from Persia arrived in China no later than A.D. 635. The reigning emperor of the Tang Dynasty welcomed the Nestorians, and the faith spread to several major cities. Although the Nestorians won thousands of converts, their greatest success was probably among the foreign community in China. In 845 there was a severe persecution, and although the Nestorians lost a foothold in China, they continued among tribes on the northern frontier (such as among the Uighur). John of Montecorvino, an Italian Franciscan missionary, arrived in Beijing in 1291. The Mongolian emperor had asked the European traveler Marco Polo for one hundred missionaries, but Pope Nicholas IV dispatched a much smaller contingent. The emerging Catholic Church clashed with the remnants of the Nestorian church, and the latter was finally destroyed with the fall of the Mongol Dynasty and the advent of the Ming Dynasty in China in 1368.[8]

While the number of Christian churches grew most rapidly around the Mediterranean basin, and later in Europe and North America, Asia has had a consistent Christian witness. As nations in Europe achieved global dominance in the fifteenth and sixteenth centuries, missionaries from those countries penetrated the New World, Africa, and Asia. In Asia, a number of churches were planted, both Protestant and Roman Catholic. Catholic missions in the sixteenth century, for instance, returned to China under the initial leadership of the Jesuit Matteo Ricci. Catholic missions established a church in China that has survived to the present, but the initial success was hampered by the arrival of several other Catholic missionary orders that undermined the unity of the missionary movement in China.

The Protestant churches that grew out of missions during the imperial era tended to remain closely tied to Western missions and denominations. The period from about 1900 to 1920, however, might be identified as the pivotal moment of the move from "missions" to "movement." That is, during these decisive decades one witnesses a shift from the eighteenth- and nineteenth-century Western missions enterprise to the twentieth-century indigenous church movement in Asia and throughout much of the majority world.

In 1910 as Protestant mission agencies amassed thousands of pages of documents, compiled multiple volumes, and devised complex strategies to fulfill the Great Commission, grassroots indigenous Christians around the world were embracing not only the gospel, but also the commission to reach all peoples. With their focus often on formal church structures, the planners of the 1910 World Missionary Conference in Edinburgh seemed to overlook the tremendous shift occurring in the Christian world. Although Edinburgh was the culmination of previous missionary conferences and paved the way for the formation of the World Council of Churches, the planners did not comprehend adequately the already vibrant Christian activity outside the West. While the conference planners did invite a small number of Christian leaders to represent "younger

---

[8] See Samuel Hugh Moffett, *A History of Christianity in Asia: Beginnings to 1500*, vol. 1 (San Francisco, Calif.: HarperSanFrancisco, 1992).

churches," the explosion of indigenous Christian movements does not seem to have been on their radar screen.

Christians in Africa and Asia were seeing visions and receiving anointing from the Holy Spirit to bring the gospel message to their people and to the world. Some of these prophets and self-proclaimed church leaders were orthodox, and some were not. But they were not waiting for the blessing of Western church leaders before they began their ministries. While each story of the rise of indigenous church leaders and churches is unique, the story of Wang Mingdao in China will be presented as a representative example of the emergence of a highly orthodox, independent church in China.

Wang Mingdao's story starts, typically, mired in Western imperialism and the missions complex of the period. At the height of the Boxer uprising in 1900, Wang's father, a Methodist medical doctor, was sheltered with hundreds of other Chinese Christians in the foreign legations of Beijing. Apparently fearing that he would have to witness the Boxer armies killing his wife and daughter, Dr. Wang committed suicide. Several weeks after the conclusion of the Boxer hostilities, Wang Mingdao was born in 1900 and raised in poverty by his widowed mother. Wang, however, enjoyed many of the advantages offered by Western imperialism and foreign missionaries. Although extremely poor, he received a free Western education in missionary schools, and, in 1919, he was gainfully employed in a mission school several hours outside of Beijing. The British missionary principal of the school noted Wang's intelligence and talent, and he offered to sponsor Wang's further education in China and, eventually, doctoral studies in Great Britain. All the doors of opportunity offered by Western imperialism and missions were open to the young Wang, doors that many of his Chinese contemporaries used to attain education and pursue wealth.

A friend of Wang's, however, challenged him to be re-baptized. The friend suggested that the Bible taught believers' baptism by immersion, and Wang decided to investigate the claim. Armed with his own Bible, just recently published in vernacular Chinese, Wang immersed himself in the Scriptures. When he concluded that he must be re-baptized, the British missionary principal of the school informed Wang that if he went through with his new convictions he would be fired. Wang realized that his dream of a Western-sponsored education would also be over. Wang wanted to be certain about his new convictions, but he did not consult other missionaries or pastors; rather, he spent several more days searching his own Bible. The morning after his decision to be re-baptized, he and a small troop of students were expelled. They left the school building, trudging through the snow in northern China. Wang himself dramatically describes the scene in his 1950 autobiography. They searched along the frozen river for a place they could baptize one another by immersion. Wang says that his long hair and thin baptismal garments froze immediately as his body emerged from the frigid water. Although the story may be embellished, it provides an apt metaphor. When Wang emerged from the water, he had broken all ties to Western imperialism and the Western missions movement based on his personal interpretation of the Bible, and he embarked on his own independent path.[9]

After several years of quiet Bible study at home, Wang emerged in the mid-1920s as a prominent national Bible teacher, and he eventually would publish his own widely read quarterly journal and establish the largest church in Beijing that survived into the 1950s. Significantly, Wang and his contemporaries personify a larger shift from missions-dominated churches to the emergence of indigenous Christian movements around the world. Certainly many majority-world Christians are still associated with missions-related churches and Western denominations, but the emergence of indigenous movements can also have an effect on them. For instance, with the growth of indigenous churches, missions-related churches have been forced to speed the process of contextualization, and the perception that Christianity is a Western-related movement has, at least in some cases, abated.

Despite challenges from secularism and the sometimes fierce persecution during the twentieth century, churches in Asia have continued to grow. Between 1900 and 1970 the number of Christians in Asia rose from just over 20 million to a remarkable 96 million. Then, after 1970, the churches exploded. By 2000, the Christian Church had grown to over 300 million adherents, and growth continued with an estimated 344 million by 2005. Projections are that by 2025 there will be nearly 500 million Christians in Asia alone.[10] As Philip Jenkins argues, demographic considerations suggest that Christianity will continue to grow in numbers and influence. That is, Christian growth in Asia, Africa, and Latin America is often occurring in the same places where there is dramatic population growth.[11] In Asia, the convergence of population growth, Christian growth, and economic growth may herald a new age of Christian missions from Asia.

Missions from Asia

Evangelical churches in Asia have seized the challenge of missions. In this, the churches in Asia are following historic patterns. Missions have been a central concern since the Apostle Paul demonstrated that the mission to the Gentiles was the fulfillment of the promise to make Abraham a father of many nations (Rom 15; Gen 12). The mandate to reach out in missions has been embraced by successive generations of Christians, and the younger churches in Asia, Africa, and Latin America naturally take on the task of the Great Commission with zeal. For example, house church Christians in rural China with minimum education and Bible training share a passion to tell others. One rural house church leader, in an interview discussing his rejection of the government-approved churches,

---

[9] See Richard R. Cook, "Fundamentalism and Modern Culture in Republican China: The Popular Language of Wang Mingdao, 1900–1991" (Ph.D. Dissertation, The University of Iowa, 2003).

[10] David Barrett, "Missiometrics 2005: A Global Survey of World Mission," *International Bulletin of Missionary Research*, 29.1 (January 2005): 29.

[11] See Jenkins, *The Next Christendom*.

pointed to the importance of the Great Commission, saying, "Who is the head of the church, the government or Christ? This is a matter of conscience. If we are faithful to Christ, we will be obedient to the Great Commission—making disciples of all peoples…. Moreover, it is a responsibility and calling for every child of God."[12] This section will first briefly survey the remaining task of missions in Asia and beyond, then it will explore the mission vision advocated by Asian church leaders, and finally it will provide a sampling of the mission organizations that have been emerging in Asia.

The spiritual needs of Asia are stunning. Samuel Moffett, professor emeritus at Princeton Theological Seminary and author of *History of Christianity in Asia*, notes that after 2,000 years of missions work the population of Asia is still largely not Christian. He states that one problem is that Asians perceive Christianity as a foreign religion even though "Jesus was born in Asia." Nonetheless, Moffett insists that Asia represents "the future of missions."[13] Much of the so-called "10/40 Window" falls in Asia. It is estimated that around two billion people from the continent are part of 11,000 remaining unreached people groups. Of the one billion Muslims in the world, most live in Asia, and it is estimated there are 4,000 unreached Muslim people groups there. There are 700 million Hindus, mostly in India and Nepal, another 2,000 unreached people groups. Southeast and Northeast Asia contain about 300 million Buddhists, some of them in about 1,000 unreached people groups. Indonesia, with a population of over 240 million, has the largest number of Muslims in the world. China alone has a population of about 1.2 billion people and 1,000 unreached people groups.[14] Recognizing these immense needs, churches in Asia are creating plans and organizations to mobilize Christians to proclaim the gospel throughout the continent.

As some of the over 300 million Asian Christians become involved in missions, they have many choices. Many, especially in large and culturally diverse countries such as India and Indonesia, choose to participate in cross-cultural missions within their own national borders. Indonesia, for instance, counts 130 unreached people groups, with a need to reach Muslim, Hindu and animist peoples. There are extensive opportunities, and, in many cases, the indigenous Christians are the best qualified to reach unreached people groups in their own countries.

As Asians join in missions a number of practical issues and problems arise. Only a tiny sample of the complex issues can be mentioned here. Asian Christians may choose to start and operate indigenous missions, or they may choose to partner with existing Western organizations. Each model contains numerous

---

[12] Min-Fu Hsu, "Understanding Christian Conversion in Late-Socialist China: Rural Peasants versus Urban Intellectuals" (PhD Dissertation [draft], Trinity Evangelical Divinity School, 2006). Used with permission.

[13] Quoted in Rob Moll, "Missions Incredible," *Christianity Today*, March 2006, 30.

[14] Statistics cited in A. Scott Moreau, ed., *Evangelical Dictionary of World Missions* (Grand Rapids, Mich.: Baker Books, 2000), 82. Although the term is difficult to define, an "unreached people group" may be defined as "a significantly large sociological grouping of people who perceive themselves to have a common affinity one for another…. From the viewpoint of evangelization, this is the largest possible group within which the Gospel can spread without encountering barriers to understanding or acceptance" (745).

challenges, and the decision can be difficult. For missionaries joining Western missions, complex economic and cultural considerations arise. For instance, the question of language can be difficult: does a seminary-educated missionary from Korea need to be fluent in English to minister in China? America- and Britain-based missions, for practical reasons, often require English as a common language for missions business.

Financial support structures can also present thorny challenges as majority world missionaries join Western missions agencies. Should Filipino missionaries, for instance, be required to raise the same amount of money as American missionaries in order to serve in Japan? Can Western-based agencies impose a lower pay scale for missionaries from Asia than for Western missionaries? If not, then can these agencies require missionaries from poorer countries to raise the same funds as missionaries from wealthy Western countries? Western missions agencies have worked hard to address these issues, and many Asians are serving effectively in these organizations. Asian missionaries are also rising to leadership in Western missions agencies. For instance, Overseas Missionary Fellowship (formerly China Inland Mission), founded in Britain by J. Hudson Taylor in 1865, recently appointed an ethnic Chinese as Executive Secretary. At the same time, Asian churches have also been establishing their own missions agencies, sending out their own missionaries.

Indigenous missions from Asia also face challenges. They must, for example, establish administrative organizations, develop missionary training centers, build up financial structures, and cultivate leadership. Indigenous missions are arising, however, and they are using numerous models. Indian Christians, for instance, can be deployed cross-culturally, but within the vast country. In Indonesia, missionaries with a passion to reach Muslims can remain in the country, and the ethnic and religious complexity of Indonesia also makes it possible for a variety of cross-cultural ministries. In one innovative approach to missions, church leaders in the Philippines have been working to train a portion of the numerous maids from the Philippines and send them out as trained evangelists. Taiwan desires to use historic, cultural, and linguistic ties with China to deploy missionaries to the mainland. Missionaries from Japan and other parts of Asia come to Taiwan to learn Mandarin and prepare for missions to China. Chinese diaspora communities around Asia have also become involved in missions to China. There are missionaries from everywhere going everywhere.

South Korean churches desire to position themselves as a "potent vanguard" of this missions movement from Asia.[15] As the country that already sends the second largest number of missionaries in the world, the goal of some Korean church leaders is to surpass the United States.[16] Students from Korea are well-represented in many missions training schools in the United States and around the world, and Korean church leaders are also training many missionaries in their own seminaries and training centers. The number of missionaries from Korea is rocketing, as the churches are sending out 1,100 new missionaries each

---

[15] Moll, "Missions Incredible," 30–34.

[16] The number of U.S. and Canadian long-term Protestant missionary personnel is estimated at over 110,000.

year, as many new missionaries annually as all the countries of the West combined. The terrific growth of the Korean missions movement is fairly new, as the opportunity for South Koreans to venture out in missions can be traced back to the 1988 Seoul Olympic games which helped force the country to open politically.[17] Today almost 13,000 Korean missionaries are serving long-term around the world.[18] With the 2008 Olympics scheduled for Beijing, many Christians hope to bring the gospel into China, but many Chinese Christians hope for increased political relaxation so they may bring the gospel to the world.

Some of the important missionary training centers in Korea include the Global Missionary Training Center and the Graduate School of World Mission at Chongshin University in Seoul. Many seminaries are training missionaries; there are also more and more centers throughout Asia specifically dedicated to missionary training, such as Mission India Bible Institute in Nagpur, India, Evangelical Theological Seminary of Indonesia in Yogyakarta, and China Missions Seminary in Hong Kong. Asian missions bring not only new personnel to the global missions force, but also fresh insights and a new zeal. Referring to the Korean missions movement, David Lee, Director of the Global Missionary Center in Korea, states, "In terms of theology and missiology, in terms of methods, we may not be unique. But it's uniquely Koreans doing this with Korean structure, with Korean church support, with Korean zeal and Korean spirituality, which is willing to suffer and willing to shout to God with perseverance."[19]

Korean churches have already experienced some setbacks, however. While Korean missionaries are often well-educated and well-trained, they have occasionally been accused of lacking cultural sensitivity and of fostering financial dependency in some mission fields. Alas, many of the standard criticisms of Western missions may sometimes be relevant to the emerging Korean movement. Some countries in the Middle East, according to anecdotal stories, have recognized the presence of missionaries among the expatriate Korean communities in their countries and have quietly moved to block Koreans from entering their countries. Paul Freston suggests that South Korea is a regional Protestant "superpower," with a position comparable to Brazil's in Latin America. Nonetheless, Freston notes that Korea has a unique history in the region and is "probably not a forerunner of developments in other Asian countries."[20]

The astonishing complexity of missions from Asia can be seen from the case of the now well-known "Back to Jerusalem" movement. Back to Jerusalem is a slogan that dates before the 1940s in China when Christians dreamed of sending missions back along the ancient silk route to Jerusalem. They believed that missions had encircled the world during the nearly two thousand years since the time of Christ, and it was the responsibility of Chinese Christians to complete the task of circumnavigating the globe. Missionaries were sent to China's west-

---

[17] Rob Moll, "Prophecy and Politics," *Christianity Today*, March 2006, 32.

[18] Ibid., 30–34.

[19] Moll, "Missions Incredible," 30–34.

[20] Paul Freston, *Evangelicals and Politics in Asia, Africa, and Latin America* (New York: Cambridge University Press, 2001), 61.

ern provinces, and some were even stranded in western China in 1949 after the Communist Revolution in China.[21] With the advent of communism in China, the vision faded into the shadows and was largely unknown around the world.

By the 1990s, house churches in China were experiencing tremendous growth, and Chinese Christians desired to take the gospel to all parts of China. The revivals also brought a desire to renew the Back to Jerusalem vision. In the West, the movement became prominent with the publication in 2003 of the book *Back to Jerusalem* by Paul Hattaway.[22] At about the same time, Hattaway published the sensational account of a Chinese Christian, "Brother Yun," also known as the "Heavenly Man." Among other extraordinary stories, the book details Brother Yun's own account of his miraculous survival from a fast of food and water lasting over 70 days.[23] The books seem to have reached a broad audience, and the movement gained further notoriety when journalist David Aikman discussed Back to Jerusalem in his widely read account of the churches in China, *Jesus in Beijing*.[24]

These works publicized the goal of Brother Yun and other Chinese house church leaders to mobilize 100,000 Chinese missionaries to march across Asia, sweep into the Middle East, and back into Jerusalem. The audacious goal captured the attention of both supporters and critics. Supporters desired to help China mobilize these forces of fearless Chinese Christians who had been trained in the context of persecution. Critics suspected that the millions of dollars reportedly raised under the banner of "Back to Jerusalem" could not be well-used in the current political climate in China; they also in some cases questioned the integrity of the leaders of the growing Back to Jerusalem movement and the credibility of some of the miraculous accounts from Brother Yun. More friendly critics pointed out that 100,000 was an unreasonably high goal, and, more importantly, wondered what the impact of 100,000 missionaries would be even if they could be mobilized. That is, 100,000 largely illiterate Chinese peasants marching on Jerusalem through the Middle East with minimal Bible training and even less missionary training, with no fear of death, might conjure up images of a new crusade.

Several meetings of prominent Chinese church leaders have been held outside of China to try to sort out the controversy and determine who, if anyone, can claim a right to the "Back to Jerusalem" moniker. Those meetings, it would seem, have been inconclusive, and some church leaders may decide to abandon using the slogan. The situation is even more complex, however, as some Korean churches have also embraced the slogan. Inspired by Back to Jerusalem, some missions groups in Korea decided to sponsor a Peace March in 2004, calling for

---

[21] China church researcher Wang Ruijen recently published a book in Chinese in Taipei, Taiwan, that discusses the early years of the Back to Jerusalem movement.

[22] Paul Hattaway, *Back to Jerusalem: Three Chinese House Church Leaders Share Their Vision to Complete the Great Commission* (Waynesboro, Ga.: Piquant, 2003).

[23] Paul Hattaway, *The Heavenly Man: The Remarkable True Story of Chinese Christian Brother Yun* (London: Monarch Books, 2002).

[24] David Aikman, *Jesus in Beijing: How Christianity is Transforming China and Changing the Global Balance of Power* (Washington, D.C.: Regnery, 2003).

over 2,000 Koreans to march in Jerusalem. The multilateral religious and political tensions were heightened when months before the Peace March a Korean missionary, Kim Sun Il, was taken hostage in Iraq. Terrorists connected to Abu Musab al-Zarqawi demanded that the Korean government abandon its plan to send 3,000 troops to join the United States-led forces in Iraq. On June 22, 2004, Kim's beheaded body was found in Baghdad. According to AsiaNews, the terrorists had explained the kidnapping on their website: "We killed an infidel who tried to propagate Christianity in Iraq. This infidel studied theology and was preparing to become a missionary in the Islamic world."[25] Some Koreans argued that the Peace March in Jerusalem should be canceled or postponed, as the AsiaNews reported, "The government of South Korea strongly urged South Korean Christian groups to cancel or postpone a peace march in Jerusalem scheduled for next month, arguing that such a step was necessary to forestall possible terrorist attacks by Islamist groups," a spokesperson adding, "there is credible evidence that Christian missionaries going to Jerusalem will likely be targets of terrorist attacks."[26] But the event was held with little incident, and it was repeated in 2005. In sum, this march demonstrated the complexity of missions from Asia, as South Korean Christians, inspired by a Chinese house church movement, decided to gather in Jerusalem, but the march was complicated by the Korean government's cooperation with U.S. military activity in Iraq!

In China, while many Chinese Christians mobilize for missions to the Islamic world and the Middle East, more cautious voices urge that the churches should first focus on reaching the minority groups in China, including the Muslim areas in western China, and then, in the future, consider how the churches might reach beyond the borders of China.

As Chinese Christians do look to move beyond the borders of China, they may find they hold an unexpected advantage over their Western counterparts. Observers have ironically noted that China enjoys a "moral advantage" over Western competitors when seeking out markets and oil in the Middle East. That is, while Western nations may be imposing an embargo on a Middle Eastern or African country because of, for example, human rights violations, China may be able to exploit the restrictions on Western companies and develop new markets at the expense of the rest of the world. In light of China's closed doors for decades, it is now intriguing to find, for instance, in 2005, Beijing welcomed Zimbabwe's controversial president Robert Mugabe to China. Chinese Christian professionals and tent-making missionaries may be able to take advantage of these opportunities to go where Western missionaries are not permitted to go.

Western missions have been keen to partner with majority-world Christians, and maybe sometimes too anxious. For instance, a portion of the Western and Korean money invested in the Back to Jerusalem movement may, in some cases, have caused more harm than help. Indigenous movements that arise spontaneously are attractive to many Christians who desire to support majority-world

[25] AsiaNews, "Government Warns Again Jerusalem Jesus March" July 22, 2004, http://www.asianews.it/view.php?l=en&art=1184.
[26] Ibid.

churches and missions. But these relationships must be made carefully. Obvious concerns include fraud and dependency, but additional problems can arise that hurt both the donors and the recipients of aid. For instance, various divisions among the majority-world churches may entangle Western partners. Issues that do not exist in the West, or at least do not cause divisions, can sometimes cause bitter schisms in churches in the majority world. Thus, by supporting one group, the Western sponsor may unwittingly alienate another key partner in ministry. As in the West, churches in Asia divide along any number of lines, including theological, philosophical, ecclesiastical, and political lines.

Churches in the West may have tended to romanticize the churches in the majority world. House churches in China, in particular, have often been idealized among evangelicals in the West. However, as the house churches are becoming better known in the West, such as through the Back to Jerusalem movement, the various controversies and divisions are also becoming well-known. Through the 1970s and 1980s, while very little was known of the house churches, many in the West imagined a purified and holy church living in harmony and empowered by the Holy Spirit. One song written by Sister Ruth, the prolific songwriter from the house churches, feeds this notion. It is titled, "5:00 a.m. in China." The lyrics speak movingly about the faithful brothers and sisters who rise early each morning for sweet moments of prayer. When Sister Ruth spoke about the song during her visit to the 2003 Christmas Conference sponsored by Christian Life Press in Chicago, she humorously mentioned an anecdote about a dear and faithful house church sister who was learning the song. This sister, when she heard in the song that she and the other house church Christians were supposed to be rising for prayer each day at 5:00 a.m., commented wittily, "Oh, dear... do we have to get up that early? Can't we pray at 6:30 or 7:00?!!"[27] To idealize Christians in the majority world and suppose that they would be any less susceptible to human frailty and sinfulness than Christians in the West seems to indicate, possibly, a very subtle form of chauvinism.

In addition to the powerful missions movement arising in Asia, there are also the dynamic diaspora communities outside Asia. These communities can sometimes be involved in ministries not possible for Christians in Asia. For instance, the prominent Chinese Christian leader Yuan Zhiming is based in the United States. Yuan gained notoriety in China through his participation in a recognized television production in the 1980s, and he was converted to Christianity after he immigrated to the United States in the 1990s. In 2003, through his organization ChinaSoul, he put out a powerful DVD series entitled *The Cross: Jesus in China*. While evangelicals in the West may wonder who the next "Billy Graham" of China will be, the next great evangelist may not be a preacher at all. With the current political climate in China, the most effective means for evangelism may be through multimedia. Chinese people may not be allowed to attend large Christian gatherings, but, with the surging economy, televisions and video players are readily available. *The Cross* is a powerful collec-

---

[27] The author witnessed Sister Ruth's comments at the 2003 Christmas Conference sponsored by Christian Life Press in Chicago.

tion taped on location in China of interviews and testimonies of Christians from all walks of life. Yuan Zhiming brilliantly combines his talents as a filmmaker, philosopher, and apologist as he weaves the dozens of various stories together into a coherent montage, in which the whole is more powerful than each of its parts. He begins, for instance, with the stories of several families that were near collapse before family members embraced a personal relationship with Christ. Although later interviews will be with prominent media stars in Beijing—actors, singers, writers, etc.—and key house church leaders, Yuan chooses to start with the stories of average Chinese. He desires, it seems, to show the relevance of Christ to everyday Chinese struggling to find meaning, value, and love in their bankrupt family life. The wide-ranging stories and testimonies build upon one another to create ever-increasing power and impact. One account, for instance, is of an orphanage of abandoned children managed at great cost but with much love by several Christian sisters who claim to be motivated by the love of Jesus. The video is designed not only to document the stories of Christians from all over China, but also to touch the hearts and minds of Chinese and lead them into a relationship with Jesus Christ. Like Yuan Zhiming, the large number of immigrants from all parts of Asia, many who are joining Christian churches in the U.S. and in other countries, will continue to have a profound impact in their home countries. They can increasingly provide critical links for mission cooperation among the diaspora communities, the churches in Asia, and churches in the West.

Not only are immigrants from Asia going to have an increasing role in missions, but their children, second generation Asian-Americans, may represent the most dynamic potential missions force in the coming decades. At this time they are increasingly filling university Christian student groups and having significant influence on college campuses. With high motivation, impressive educational backgrounds, and fluency in English and often second and third languages, Asian-Americans are poised to influence both America and the world.

CONCLUSION

The current growth of the churches in the majority world may be one of the most exciting developments of the twenty-first century. Evangelicals observe this growth with both awe and trepidation. The phenomenal growth contests the conventional wisdom that materialism and secularism will eventually dominate around the globe. These new churches, in the eyes of many evangelicals, demonstrate that God is still building His kingdom. There is fear, also, as these groups often do not resemble churches in the West, and, more importantly, some hold extreme and even heretical teachings. While Western evangelicals celebrate the growth of the church, there is also concern about schisms and the further splintering of the body of Christ.

Important theological issues remain for the churches in Asia. For instance, as churches continue to work out their own identity, they will also need to consider how much dialogue they will pursue with other churches both inside and outside of Asia. Churches in Asia will have important decisions to make. For instance, do they perceive their own churches to have continuity with the early church, with Western church history, or with other majority-world Christians? Can they challenge the received orthodoxies from the Reformation, Augustine, and the early church? Must they maintain allegiance to the early ecumenical councils and fundamental Christian doctrines? Or, rather, do they believe they are autonomous movements independent of previous church history and independent from the historic framework of God dealing with the Christian Church? Further, can they look at their own histories and uncover evidence that God dealt with their ancestors in ways similar to the way God revealed Himself to Israel? If the body of Christ is not further to fragment into a vast array of competing factions, many of these issues must be addressed. The New Testament does not only require missions (Matt 28), but also unity (John 17). While maintaining unity will be difficult, the potential for cooperation is powerfully illustrated by a joint statement of faith signed by several of China's large nationwide house church networks in 1998.[28]

Also important for consolidating the gains of recent church growth is the important issue of ecclesiology. Churches must ask which structures can best match the cultural context and also remain faithful to biblical teaching. These church bodies will also increasingly need to address the question of the relationship of the church and the state. While churches in Latin America have already pursued this question more vigorously with mixed results,[29] the churches in Asia, as they gain in size and influence, will also be forced to wrestle with this issue.

The history and growth of majority-world Christian churches is a particularly fertile field for academic research and writing. As the historian Luke preserved in the New Testament the remarkable record of the Apostle Paul and the story of the early Church and the early Church's missions to the Gentiles, historians today must also record events before they are lost. Records and materials should be collected. The historical record of the rapid expansion of the churches over the past 50–100 years must be preserved for future generations. Through the final decades of the twentieth century, the most electrifying story may have been the story of the explosion of the churches in the majority world. Historians are just now taking up the critical task of telling that story with greater commitment and detail. During the first decades of the twenty-first century, the most electrifying story may be the growth of cross-cultural missions from these burgeoning majority-world churches. Cutting edge research is needed now to chart these developments.

---

[28] See Aikman, *Jesus in Beijing*, for both a discussion of the genesis of the statement and a complete translation.
[29] See Freston, *Evangelicals and Politics in Asia, Africa, and Latin America.*

Chapter Nine:

THE GREAT COMMISSION IN AFRICA

By Tite Tiénou

This chapter examines the participation of African evangelicals in world missions in the nineteenth and twentieth centuries, with a particular focus on selected individuals. The work of these individuals shows that Africans' involvement in "fulfilling the Great Commission" of Matthew 28 began soon after they accepted the gospel. It will be argued that this involvement focused primarily on the evangelization of the African continent in the nineteenth and early part of the twentieth centuries and that African involvement in Christian missions extended to the rest of the world in the latter part of the twentieth century. I will first briefly consider the nature of *evangelicalism* in order to establish some common ground and minimize misunderstanding. Secondly I will describe the role of "native workers" in the evangelization of Africa. Thirdly, I will examine African evangelicals' mission vision for the continent and beyond. I will conclude with a few remarks about the prospects for the continued involvement of Africans in world mission.

Evangelicalism in Africa

I begin this study of the participation of African evangelicals in world mission with a brief look at the word *evangelicalism*. A definition of *evangelicalism* may seem superfluous in this particular book, but I provide the following in order to establish the broader context of the present task and also to minimize misunderstanding. The intention here is to offer perspectives guiding the present endeavor. For our purposes, *evangelicalism* is used as Timothy George defines it. For him:

> Evangelicalism . . . is a renewal movement within historic Christian orthodoxy with deep roots in the early Church, the Reformation of the sixteenth century, and the great awakenings of

164

the eighteenth century (and it includes puritanism, pietism, and pentecostalism as well as fundamentalism).[1]

If one accepts George's definition, as I do, then evangelicalism would be viewed as a movement focused on fidelity to God's gospel. Also, with this definition, nearly all Protestant mission societies working in Africa in the nineteenth century and into the early part of the twentieth could, and should, be considered *evangelical*. Consequently, one must resist the tendency to restrict *evangelicalism* to contemporary usages of the term. Evangelicalism is not located in specific organizations or ecclesiastical bodies; it is rather a community of Christians who purpose to live the gospel and promote it in this world. For the African continent this means that every effort must be made not to restrict evangelicalism to the Association of *Evangelicals* of Africa or to churches and schools castigated for what is presented as their defining characteristic, namely their "refusal of ecumenical dialogue."[2] In this regard it is worth noting that Tokunboh Adeyemo, third General Secretary of the Association, then known as the Association of Evangelicals of Africa and Madagascar, states that "an evangelical is one who believes in [the] good news, who has experienced ... redemption, who is committed to its propagation; and who lives steadfastly in obedience to the authority of the Book—the Word of God—as his rule of faith and practice".[3] Based on this, the label *evangelical* can and should be applied to millions of Christians in Africa, regardless of their church or denominational affiliation. These are people who have believed the gospel and propagated it with zeal and often sacrifice and suffering. Many of these Christians from the past will forever remain nameless and faceless because no one recorded their contributions. There is, however, sufficient evidence of African evangelical involvement in advancing the gospel. This chapter reviews some of the evidence of the missionary activities of African evangelicals. We begin with the role of "native workers."

"Native Workers" and the Planting of Christianity in Africa

The significance and importance of Africans in the evangelization of the continent has been noted in numerous publications and by various authors. Notable contributions to this literature include: Lamin Sanneh's *West African*

---

[1] Timothy George, "Evangelicals and Others," *First Things* 160 (February 2006): 15. For other definitions of evangelical or evangelicalism, see page 2 above, as well as David W. Bebbington, *Evangelicalism in Modern Britain*; Alister McGrath, *Evangelicalism and the Future of Christianity* (Downers Grove, Ill.: InterVarsity Press, 1995) and Douglas A. Sweeney, *The American Evangelical Story*.

[2] Tharcisse Gatwa, "Theological Education in Africa: What Prospects for Sharing Knowledge?" *Exchange* 32.3 (2003): 203. It is rather telling that an article published on theological education in Africa in 2003 fails to take seriously self-described evangelical theological institutions, stating without proof or nuance that "[t]hese churches represent trends in Christianity which have always kept their distance from those who joined the ecumenical movement. These divisions that were exported by the Europeans to Africa, a past into which Africans should no longer identify with, are being perpetrated today" (203–4). ("Perpetrated" should, perhaps, have been rendered *perpetuated*). This is an astonishing statement in light of the complexity of history and the reality on the ground.

[3] Tokunboh Adeyemo, "What and who is an Evangelical?" in *AEAM: Association of Evangelicals of Africa and Madagascar: History and Ministries* (Nairobi: AEAM, n.d.), 6.

Christianity (1983) and *Abolitionists Abroad* (1999), Andrew F. Walls's *The Cross-Cultural Process in Christian History* (2002), Paul V. Kollman's *The Evangelization of Slaves and Catholic Origins in East Africa* (2005), and Jean-Paul Messina and Jaap van Slageren's *Histoire du christianisme au Cameroun* (2005). These authors, among others, document the often-neglected "African agency" in the propagation of the gospel and the establishment of the Church (in its multiple dimensions) in Africa. Indeed, as Andrew F. Walls notes, "the first church in tropical Africa was an African, not a missionary creation. Most Africans have always heard the gospel from Africans, and virtually all the great movements towards the Christian faith in Africa have been African led."[4] Yet, in many North American and European evangelical circles, the story of the evangelization of Africa (especially that which occurred in the so-called pioneer era) continues to be told with little acknowledgment of the Africans' participation. Evidence of this viewpoint can be seen in a 1964 article in *Christianity Today* entitled "Africa: Continent in Crisis," or in the section devoted to Africa in J. Herbert Kane's *Understanding Christian Missions* (Fourth Edition, 1986), or in a recent issue of *Christianity Today* (March 2006) illustrating the impact of South Korea's missions by showing a Korean missionary preaching to a small group of Ghanaians under a tree in rural Ghana.[5] "Africans are the *missionized* not the *missionaries*" seems to be the consistent view expressed in these publications.

Let us turn to J. Herbert Kane and Al Snyder for specific examples of evangelical perceptions of the evangelization of Africa. According to Kane, "Christianity has made more converts in Black Africa than all the rest of the Third World combined. In spite of the fact that we got off to a late start in Africa as compared with Asia, we have made converts much faster."[6] There is little doubt in Kane's text that the "we" refers to outsiders and not to African Christians inclusive. Focusing his attention on West Africa, Al Snyder informed readers of *Christianity Today* in 1964 that the evangelization of this region occurred in three phases or "periods": the *"evangelization"* phase (from the early nineteenth century to about 1914), the *"institutionalization"* phase (from World War I to World War II), and the *"nationalization"* phase (from the end of World War II onward) during which "[t]he symbol of Christianity is becoming less and less the foreign missionary and more and more the consecrated national leader."[7] It is worth noting that this is the same region where, according to Lamin Sanneh,

---

[4] Andrew F. Walls, *The Cross-Cultural Process in Christian History* (Edinburgh: T&T Clark, 2002), 45.

[5] The March 2006 issue of *Christianity Today* is especially noteworthy in light of the known role of Ghanaian evangelicals in world evangelization, both in Africa and beyond. One can read about this in Peter Barker and Samuel Boadi-Siaw, *Changed by the Word: The Story of Scripture Union Ghana* (Accra: Scripture Union Ghana, Africa Christian Press, and Asempa Publishers, 2003). Gottfried Osei-Mensah, one- time pastor of Nairobi Baptist Church and the first international director of the Lausanne Committee for World Evangelization, is a Ghanaian whose roots are in Scripture Union Ghana. Certainly Koreans are very active in missions, even in Ghana and other African countries. What I find distressing is the message (perhaps unintentional) conveyed by the report in this *Christianity Today* article: Ghanaians (and Africans?) are *objects* not *subjects* of Christian mission.

[6] J. Herbert Kane, *Understanding Christian Missions*, 4th ed. (Grand Rapids, Mich.: Baker Book House, 1986), 215.

[7] Al Snyder, "Western Africa: National Impetus," *Christianity Today*, July 31, 1964, 8. Names of the phases and italics appear in the original.

"the diffusion of Christianity between 1787 and about 1893" was essentially done by Africans. Sanneh writes, "The religious map of Africa was permanently changed as the new religion was carried into numerous communities by the wide-ranging activities of African agents."[8]

Thus far, we have seen two viewpoints on the role of Africans in the evangelization of the continent. For Sanneh and Walls, African Christians have been part of the story of African evangelization and Christianity from the very beginning. By contrast, Africans are somewhat invisible in how Kane and Snyder describe the growth of Christianity in Africa. What should one think? What actually happened? For this one needs to pay attention to the activities of the people known in various missionary documents as "native workers" or "native agents."

The many documents written by early North American and European missionaries about their life and work in Africa (including chronicles, letters, magazines, pamphlets, journals, and books) are replete with references to "native workers," "native evangelists," "native agents," or, more rarely, "native clergy." A variety of individuals are given this label. These individuals have varying levels of responsibility in the structures of mission organizations. Bernard Salvaing notes that between 1840 and 1891 the term "native workers" could refer to three kinds of personnel in a missions context: first, well-educated clergy such as Samuel Ajayi Crowther; second, less well-educated clergy; and third, many other workers such as catechists, Bible readers, and teachers.[9] Salvaing shows that on the Western coast of Africa (from present-day Sierra Leone to Nigeria) missionary societies such as the Wesleyans and the Church Missionary Society used the services of African personnel even if they sometimes called for European supervision as much as possible.[10] The African personnel made a significant contribution to the work of gospel proclamation and church planting. Indeed, as Phyllis L. Garlick observes, "[t]he West Africa history of the C. M. S. is an epic of partnership. It is the story of African and European missionaries."[11] Writing about the Presbyterian Church of Ghana, a church established by the Basel Mission, David Kpobi states that this church "quickly moved to being a missionary church characterized by *sending* and *giving*.... This is a characteristic the church had right from the beginning."[12] In light of the preceding, the African factor in the evangelization of West Africa is undeniable.

The African factor was not unique to West Africa. Africans were also involved in evangelization in Central Africa and East Africa. In Central Africa, Mrs. Alexander [Grace Anna Main] Macaw's 1937 book entitled *Congo: The First Alliance Mission Field* is dedicated to "All those who have labored for the

---

[8] Lamin Sanneh, *West African Christianity: The Religious Impact* (Maryknoll, N.Y.: Orbis Books, 1983), 53.

[9] Bernard Salvaing, *Les missionnaires à la rencontre de l'Afrique au XIXe siècle: Côte des esclaves et pays yoruba, 1840–1891* (Paris: Editions l'Harmattan, 1994), 99–100.

[10] Ibid., 121.

[11] Phyllis L. Garlick, *With the C. M. S. in West Africa: A Study in Partnership* (London: Church Missionary Society, 1935), 12.

[12] David Kpobi, "The PCG, a church in Mission in the 21st century: Renewal and Reformation," *Akrofi-Christaller Centre News* 25 (July-December 1999): 8, 9. Italics in the original.

167

evangelization of the Congo including the native pastors and evangelists but especially to that long roll of our HONORED MISSIONARY DEAD."[13] In the chapter on the church in Congo, Macaw writes: "Native Christians took up the torch and passed it to others. Many of them endured great hardships for the sake of the gospel, 'being destitute, afflicted, tormented,' and many of them joined the noble army of martyrs, 'of whom the world was not worthy.'"[14] Roland Oliver notes a similar pattern in East Africa. He shows that from 1891 to 1913, in various Ugandan districts, the "vast developments [of] the foreign missionary expansion, both Catholic and Anglican, had followed and not preceded the expansion of the faith through indigenous channels," Apoloyo Kivebulaya and Tomasi Semfuma being two specific examples of "African Anglican evangelists" of this period.[15]

For the remainder of this section of our study, let us return to West Africa for a closer scrutiny and with a deliberate focus on the Francophone and interior area because the story of this region is seldom mentioned in the literature in English. This approach will allow us to look beyond the abundant scholarly work in English that focuses on the countries of Ghana, Liberia, Nigeria, and Sierra Leone in West Africa. Christians from Sierra Leone have had a significant role in the evangelization of this region.

Andrew Walls has noted that the Krio Church of Sierra Leone, "built on recaptive Africans," was "of incalculable importance in Christian expansion in West Africa" and that "[i]n area after area, well into the twentieth century, the first contact of African peoples with Christian faith was through an itinerant or immigrant Sierra Leonean."[16] Robert S. Roseberry of the Christian and Missionary Alliance devotes a chapter to a man called Julius the Cobbler, a Sierra Leonean in Côte d'Ivoire, who, as "a lay worker in the Dimbokro church," helped in the advance of Alliance work.[17] The story of Sierra Leonean Christians in gospel proclamation must therefore go beyond well-known and well-documented cases such as that of Samuel Ajayi Crowther (c.1806–1891). Crowther had strong evangelical commitments, a solid education, and good credentials. Although Ghanaians J. E. J. Capitein (who died in 1747) and Philip Quaque (who served as an ordained Anglican clergyman in West Africa from 1765 to 1816) are the first Africans known to be ordained by Protestants,[18] Samuel Ajayi

[13] Mrs. Alexander Macaw, *Congo: The First Alliance Mission Field* (Harrisburg, Pa.: Christian Publications, 1937), iii.

[14] Ibid., 131.

[15] Roland Oliver, *The Missionary Factor in East Africa* (London: Longmans, Green and Company, 1952), 182–83 and 193.

[16] Andrew F. Walls, *The Missionary Movement in Christian History* (Maryknoll, N.Y.: Orbis Books, and Edinburgh: T &T Clark, 1996), 103, 105.

[17] Robert S. Roseberry, *The Soul of French West Africa* (Harrisburg, Pa.: Christian Publications, 1947), 7–12. This man, referred to by his first name only, is believed to have been born in 1890. The dates of his work in Dimbokro are not specified but, given the fact that the Christian and Missionary Alliance began its work in Côte d'Ivoire in 1930, he most likely labored there in the 1930s and 1940s.

[18] Stephen Neill, *Survey of the Training of the Ministry in Africa*, Part I (London: International Missionary Council, 1950), 5.

Crowther has the distinction of being the first African Anglican Bishop. He had an undeniable role in the spread of the gospel in Nigeria.[19]

The work of Julius the Cobbler in Côte d'Ivoire in the 1930s (a French colony at the time) shows that Sierra Leoneans took the gospel beyond the colonial boundaries-in-the-making. Sierra Leonean Christians did not restrict themselves to British zones of influence or colonies; they proclaimed the gospel wherever they happened to be in West Africa. William Wadé Harris (1865–1929), though he was not from Sierra Leone, is a well-known English-speaking West African whose legacy in Côte d'Ivoire continues to the present day. Harris, a Liberian Methodist/Anglican, preacher, teacher, and catechist, established the foundations for subsequent missionary work in Côte d'Ivoire through his preaching in 1912–1914 and 1914–1915, as he journeyed on foot from Liberia to Ghana. Robert S. Roseberry writes of what he saw of Harris' work in 1923 and speaks of the "mass movement" that came out of it and how "[t]his remarkable movement changed our whole outlook of missions and the power of God. We saw that the Lord could get along without us by putting His power upon a simple native."[20] Moreover, in the chapter devoted to Harris in *The Niger Vision,* entitled "The Black Prophet," Roseberry states that the Wesleyan missionaries in Côte d'Ivoire and "[e]very other Missionary Society, including the Catholic, is reaping in the harvest" of Harris' labor.[21] In "The Need of Laborers," a short article published in *The Alliance Weekly* (1945), it is noted, "God is not limited to the foreign worker.... Out of the races and tribes of the dark lands He can and will call whole-hearted workers with the burden of their people's salvation upon their hearts."[22] This was certainly the conviction of Robert S. Roseberry (1863–1976)—who served in Sierra Leone and helped open the French West Africa field of the Christian and Missionary Alliance, of which he was chairman for many decades—as his comments on Harris indicate. Yet Harris is but one of many "native workers" mentioned by Roseberry in his writings. Let us meet several others.

We begin with Bokari Saba, to whom much space will be given. The ministry of Bokari Saba is mentioned in Roseberry's major works *The Niger Vision* (1934) and *The Soul of French West Africa* (1947), as well as in numerous articles appearing in *The Alliance Weekly* and *The Alliance Witness.* Bokari Saba is one of the few Africans and "native workers" whose first and last names are provided in missionary literature. He was Bozo in ethnicity (from the "Boso Tribe" in

---

[19] On Samuel Ajayi Crowther, the following may be consulted: J. F. A. Ajayi, *Christian Missions in Nigeria, 1841–1891: The Making of a New Élite* (Burnt Mill: Longman, 1965); Garlick, *With the C. M. S. in West Africa;* John Loiello, "Bishop in Two Worlds: Samuel Ajayi Crowther (c.1806–1891)," in *Varieties of Christian Experience in Nigeria,* ed. Elizabeth Isichei (London: The MacMillan Press, Ltd., 1982), 34–61; Lamin Sanneh, *Abolitionists Abroad* (Cambridge: Harvard University Press, 1999), 150–70 and 243–46; Andrew F. Walls, "Samuel Ajayi Crowther (1807–1891)," in *The Cross-Cultural Process in Christian History* (Maryknoll, N.Y.: Orbis Books, and Edinburgh: T & T Clark, 2002), 155–64.

[20] Robert S. Roseberry, *Black Magic... the Challenge* (Chicago: World Wide Prayer and Missionary Union, 1935), 11.

[21] Robert S. Roseberry, *The Niger Vision* (Harrisburg, Pa.: Christian Publications, 1934), 169.

[22] "The Need of Laborers" *The Alliance Weekly,* September 8, 1945, 275.

Roseberry's words), from Mali, a boatman,[23] and "had a command of at least four languages."[24] He had been Muslim prior to his conversion to Christ.[25] Bokari Saba's date of birth is not indicated in the available documents, but his date of death was reported by Roseberry in *The Alliance Weekly* of September 8, 1945: "We were sorry to hear that Bokari Saba, the great evangelist, went to be with the Lord on Sunday, July 18."[26] Given the date of this periodical, the year can only be 1945. Yet, in *The Soul of French West Africa*, Roseberry states Saba's date of death as July 18, 1946.[27] This latter date, unfortunately, seems to have become the official one because it is the one readily available to readers of Roseberry's books![28]

Bokari Saba came to Christian faith most likely in 1921 or 1922, through missionary Harry Wright, in Ouagadougou (Burkina Faso) and helped build the first mission station of the Assemblies of God in that city and country.[29] In this regard, Bokari Saba's conversion was like that of many early adherents to evangelical faith in that region of Africa: they heard the gospel while working for missionaries. Harry Wright provides one of the first written accounts of Bokari Saba's evangelistic efforts in his article entitled "The Lord Will Provide" published in *The Alliance Weekly* in 1930.[30] The following year, another article in *The Alliance Weekly* described Saba as "a self-supporting native evangelist in the Mopti area of the French Soudan."[31] For his part, Roseberry emphasized that "Bokari was not drafted; he was a volunteer for God from the very first."[32] When Roseberry announced Bokari Saba's death in 1945 he wrote, "He has turned more people to God than any other man in our French West Africa Mission. His zeal, courage, and faithfulness in presenting a living Christ set town after

---

[23] Roseberry, *The Niger Vision*, 226. In Burkina Faso and Mali the Bozo are known for their expertise in fishing.

[24] Roseberry, *The Soul of French West Africa*, 16.

[25] Roseberry, *The Niger Vision*, 226, and *The Soul of French West Africa*, 13.

[26] "The Need of Laborers," *The Alliance Weekly*, September 8, 1945, 275.

[27] Roseberry, *The Soul of French West Africa*, 13.

[28] See for example, Milton and Nancy Pierce, *The Triumphs, Trials, Tidbits and Trivia of History (Seventy-five Years of Alliance Ministry in Burkina Faso)* (Bobo-Dioulasso: n.p., 1997), 23, where Bokari Saba's year of death is listed as 1946.

[29] Roseberry, *The Niger Vision*, 226–230; Roseberry, *The Soul of French West Africa*, 13–14; Roseberry, *75ème anniversaire des Assemblées de Dieu du Burkina Faso: 1921–1996* (Ouagadougou: Imprimerie des Assemblées de Dieu, n.d.), 6. In *The Soul of French West Africa* (p. 14), Roseberry indicates that Bokari Saba's conversion took place in Ouagadougou where he had accompanied "pioneers." Although Roseberry never provides the identity of these "pioneers," we know that this team of "pioneers" was led by Harry Wright, who had served with the Christian and Missionary Alliance in Sierra Leone, that they arrived in Ouagadougou on January 1, 1921, and that they began the work of the Assemblies of God in Burkina Faso (*75ème anniversaire*, 6, 10). Harry and Grace Wright left Burkina Faso in 1922 to serve with the Christian and Missionary Alliance in Guinea (ibid., 11). They finished their missionary service in Mali with the Christian and Missionary Alliance. It is worth noting that Saba himself acknowledges Harry Wright as the person who led him to Christ as Wright renders his testimony thus for readers of *The Alliance Weekly*: "Mr. Wright showed me the way to Christ" (H. M. Wright, "The Lord Will Provide," *The Alliance Weekly*, April 26, 1930, 264).

[30] H. M. Wright, "The Lord Will Provide" *The Alliance Weekly*, April 26, 1930, 264, 267–68. Wright refers to Saba as "the evangelist Bokari" and concludes, "[t]he spontaneous expansion of the native church is an assured fact when men have a living experience of Jesus Christ" (268).

[31] "Bokari Saba's Testimony," *The Alliance Weekly*, January 10, 1931, 24.

[32] Roseberry, *The Soul of French West Africa*, 13.

town on fire."[33] Bokari Saba was the first to preach the gospel in certain cases, as in the towns of Youdiou and Zamblela in Mali.[34] He also preached in Burkina Faso, Côte d'Ivoire, and Guinea.[35] Roseberry notes that Bokari Saba's "ministry in Ntorosso helped lay the foundation of the Bible School"[36] which "opened in 1936 and has been mightily used in the training of young men and women who have given effective witness for Christ."[37]

Bokari Saba, this remarkable layperson whose life and work helped establish the foundation of evangelical Christianity in present-day Burkina Faso and Mali, was but one of numerous African Christians noted for their contributions in documents written by European and North American missionaries. Let us also mention the important evangelistic ministries of Jacques Diassana in Mali, Mary Prow in Côte d'Ivoire, and Ba Hawa in Mali as we conclude this section of our study. Jacques Diassana, converted to Christ when he was a schoolboy, led the church district of Sanékuy in Mali with courage, wisdom, and determination at a time when outside missionaries were sent home because of war.[38] He, with others in the district, took the gospel beyond the borders of their own ethnic group and into adjacent western Burkina Faso.[39] In Côte d'Ivoire, Mary Prow was a Liberian woman who helped in the evangelization of Bouaké.[40] In Mali we find Ba Hawa, a remarkable Fulani woman who had a key role in winning the whole village of Kolo, near San, to Christ. This woman, who was sixty years of age in 1942, was also instrumental in encouraging the Christians of the village to build their church without outside help.[41]

William Wadé Harris, Julius the Cobbler, Bokari Saba, Jacques Diassana, Mary Prow, and Ba Hawa are some of the "native workers" who advanced the gospel and helped in establishing what we today call "mission" churches and

---

[33] "The Need of Laborers," *The Alliance Weekly*, September 8, 1945, 275. Roseberry also writes that "[a]t a recent conference in Habbeland [French Soudan (Mali) 1947], the staff of native evangelists working there said, 'We have not yet reached all the towns in the district that were visited by Bokari'" (*The Soul of French West Africa*, 19).

[34] Francis McKinney, "A Trip to Youdiou," *The Alliance Weekly*, July 17, 1943, 457: "In 1935 we made our first trip as a family to Youdiou. Bogkari Saba, the evangelist, had preceded us with the news of salvation." Roseberry, "Touring in the Soudan," *The Alliance Weekly*, July 19, 1947, 457: "A conference with the different church groups in the Koutiala district was called to meet at Zamblela. Bokari Saba was the first witness in this town, and it was through his energy and consecration that the first church was built." See also Roseberry, *The Soul of French West Africa*, 15.

[35] Roseberry *The Soul of French West Africa*, 18–19.

[36] Ibid., 15.

[37] J. H. Hunter, *Beside All Waters: The Story of Seventy-five Years of World-Wide Ministry of the Christian and Missionary Alliance* (Harrisburg, Pa.: Christian Publications, 1964), 34.

[38] Roseberry, *The Soul of French West Africa*, 136–43, where he is simply referred to as "Jacques the school boy." His full name is provided in Marius Bonjour, *Le désert refleurira* (n.p., 1987), 81–87.

[39] Bonjour, *Le désert refleurira*, 84–85; Alfred C. Snead, *Missionary Atlas: A Manual of the Foreign Work of The Christian and Missionary Alliance* (Harrisburg, Pa.: Christian Publications, 1950), 28. My father and mother, who became Christians in the 1940s, did so by hearing the gospel through the evangelization done by Christians of the Sanékuy district. My father later went to the N'Torosso Bible School and became a "native worker" in the 1950s.

[40] Roseberry, *The Soul of French West Africa*, 78–82. Roseberry tells of Mary Prow's desire to take the gospel to an "untouched section" and missionaries saying to her "that she could still be a missionary; one must witness in Jerusalem and Judea as in the uttermost parts of earth" (81). This is one the very few instances in Roseberry's writings where a "native" is called "missionary," Roseberry adds, "[t]hat Mary was ministering in Jerusalem there was no doubt."

[41] G. Mabille, *L'appel du soudanais* (Paris: Société des Mission Evangéliques de Paris, n.d.), 43–47.

their institutions in the countries of Burkina Faso, Côte d'Ivoire, and Mali. They represent numerous other African Christians throughout the continent, known and unknown, who labored for the cause of the Christian faith with full confidence in the gospel, personal sacrifice, and much suffering. They frequently engaged in "power encounter" as they established churches and led new converts in the burning of their "fetishes."

African Christians also developed a vision for mission beyond the borders of their locations almost as soon as they became Christian themselves, as we have seen in the case of the Presbyterian Church of Ghana or the Sanékuy district of the Christian and Missionary Alliance. In some instances, African Christians sent money outside of the continent of Africa for the support of missionary efforts. For example, in 1929, in a brief note entitled "Self-Support - And More" published in *Pioneer Advance,* one reads that:

> Our hearts were rejoiced at the end of January to receive a check for $72.97 from the native church at Kwimba, Congo, Africa. This amount was sent in by the African church, half of which was to go for the Porto Rico [sic] Relief fund and the other half to the work among the Jews in New York City.... This church is self-supporting in that it supports its own teachers, no funds being sent from this land for such purposes. This money is, therefore, real missionary work for them.[42]

In general, however, the newly (and barely) established evangelical churches in Africa sent and supported gospel-proclaiming personnel in the continent. This was the case for the Assemblies of God of Burkina Faso, which sent "workers" to Togo (1936), Ghana (1931), Niger (1935), Senegal (1945), and Côte d'Ivoire (1958).[43] Later, in 1985, the legacy of this vision for mission would be structured and organized into a formal agency of the church called VIMAB (Vision Missionnaire des Assemblées de Dieu du Burkina).[44] The missionary vision and practice of African evangelicals continued in the continent and extended beyond it as the twentieth century progressed.

African Evangelicals and Mission in Africa and Beyond

From the mid-twentieth century African evangelicals have become much more intentional about their participation in world missions, beginning with evangelization in the continent. *New Life for All*, an evangelistic program which began in Northern Nigeria in 1963, spread to Bénin, Burkina Faso, Côte d'Ivoire, Ghana, Mali, Niger, and Sierra Leone in West Africa and Cameroon and Chad

---

[42] *Pioneer Advance*, bulletin 1 (1929): 4.
[43] Roseberry, *75ème anniversaire des Assemblées de Dieu du Burkina Faso*, 33–34.
[44] Ibid., 31.

in Central Africa.[45] It was instrumental in convening the July 1968 West African Congress on Evangelism in Ibadan, Nigeria, "attended by over 450 delegates ... from every country in West and East Africa and some from South Africa."[46] Yakubu Yako, from Nigeria, "[a]n experienced evangelist and arresting speaker, [who] had served for a number of years under the indigenous African Missionary Society" was especially important in *New Life for All.*[47]

It was Nigerian evangelicals who established what was probably the first intentional mission agency in West Africa: the Evangelical Missionary Society founded in the 1950s. This agency of the Evangelical Church of West Africa (Nigeria) currently has more than 1,200 missionaries in Africa and beyond. Panya Baba (1932–) is perhaps its best-known leader, having directed it from 1970 to 1988. Moreover, in 1985 a consultation on missions was held in Jos, Nigeria. This consultation was sponsored by the Nigeria Evangelical Mission Association (NEMA). The fact that participants came from five countries in Africa (Nigeria, Ghana, Cameroon, Kenya, and Uganda) as well as Britain, Guatemala, and the United States, signaled a new level of intent.[48]

The intentional participation of African evangelicals in missions can be seen in continent-wide bodies such as the Association of Evangelicals in Africa. Consequently, no study of African evangelicals' involvement in missions can be complete without mention of the Evangelism and Missions Commission of the Association of Evangelicals in Africa. This Association, founded in 1966, has issued a variety of statements regarding the necessity of gospel communication over four decades.[49] The Evangelism and Missions Commission was, however, "officially inaugurated on December 12, 1990," even though its creation was discussed in 1979 and its creation ratified by the Fourth General Assembly held in Lilongwe, Malawi, in 1981.[50]

The evangelistic activities of Africans in the diaspora, together with their other ministries, had added another dimension to the missionary involvement of African evangelicals beyond the continent by the end of the twentieth century. In the past decade African Christians in the diaspora have founded, and continue to found, many churches in Europe, Canada, and the United States. These churches, labeled "African churches" by outsiders and "international churches or ministries" by their founders, are quite visible in Europe but mostly "invisible" in the United States. They proclaim the gospel to Africans of the diaspora, of course, but they sometimes focus specifically on reaching the population of the host country. This is the case for the "Embassy of God Church" in Kiev,

---

[45] Eileen Lageer, *New Life for All* (Chicago: Moody Press, 1970), 144.

[46] Ibid.

[47] Ibid., 17.

[48] Matthews A. Ojo, "The Dynamics of Indigenous Charismatic Missionary Enterprises in West Africa," http://www.geocities.com/Missionalia/ojo1.htm?200613. Accessed on 4/13/2006.

[49] See, for example, the "Introduction" in *AEAM: Association of Evangelicals of Africa and Madagascar* (n.p., n.d.), 2, where item 4 of the Association's reasons for existence reads: "To further the Gospel, serving as a catalyst for world evangelization (Phil. 1:12)."

[50] Christina Maria Breman, *The Association of Evangelicals in Africa: Its History, Organization, Members, Projects, External Relations, and Message* (Zoetermeer: Uitgeverij Boekencentrum, 1996), 142–43.

Ukraine, which focuses on evangelizing Ukrainians, not Africans.[51] African Christians also participate in missions in Europe and North America through their work in Christian unions on university campuses or their service in established denominations of these regions of the world.

Missiologists and other students of the worldwide expansion of the Christian faith have observed the increasing participation in missions of Christians from countries perceived primarily as recipients of missionaries. As we have seen in this chapter, African evangelical Christians are part of the story of the so-called "Third World" missionary force even though, in Africa, "the missions introduced a clear dichotomy: mission is the foreigners' affair, the church is for the 'natives.'"[52] What are the lessons of, and prospects for, the continued involvement of African Christians in missions?

Prospects

In this chapter I have provided evidence that African Christians have always been active participants in "fulfilling the Great Commission." Especially in the evangelization of the continent, these Christians did not wait for injunctions like the one Pope Paul VI made to the Catholic Bishops of Africa in Kampala, Uganda, in 1969: "By now, you Africans are missionaries to yourselves. 'Missionaries to yourselves': in other words, you Africans must now continue, upon this Continent, the building up of the Church."[53] If the involvement of Africans in Christian missions is a fact, and far from recent, why was it possible for John Mbiti to write in 1971, "The Church in Africa has far too long been missionary-minded, but only in terms of receiving missionaries and depending on them. This philosophy must change"?[54] The contribution of Africans to the evangelization of the diverse population of the continent is certainly an important dimension of missions. It is for this reason that Mbiti's view must be re-assessed. Nonetheless, his statement places in bold relief one of the greatest unresolved missiological questions of our day: Why should Africa be perceived as mission receiving and not mission sending when most observers agree that it is a continent with a significant Christian and evangelical population? Practitioners and students of missions who seek an adequate answer to this question must take into account the historical contributions of African Christians as well as their present involvement in worldwide evangelization. As this chapter has shown, lay workers have played a significant role in this largely untold account of the history of Africans in mission. More than fifty years ago,

---

[51] See J. Kwabena Asamoah-Gyadu, "An African Pentecostal on Mission in Eastern Europe: The Church of the 'Embassy of God' in the Ukraine," *Pneuma: The Journal of the Society for Pentecostal Studies* 27.2 (Fall 2005): 297–321; and same author, "Africa Initiated Christianity in Eastern Europe: Church of the 'Embassy of God' in Ukraine," *International Bulletin of Missionary Research* 30.2 (April 2006): 73–75.

[52] Klaus Fiedler, *The Story of Faith Missions* (Oxford: Regnum Books International, 1994), 364.

[53] Pope Paul VI, "Address to the Closing of the All-African Bishops' Symposium," *AFER: African Ecclesial Review* 11.4 (1969): 403.

[54] John Mbiti, *The Crisis of Mission in Africa* (Mukono: Uganda Church Press, 1971), 4.

Stephen Neill described the historical situation correctly: "the village catechist, with slender qualifications and very modest pay, is the real hero of the Christian situation in Africa."[55]

As they study the present mission involvement of African Christians, missiologists must still wrestle with the idea that "[t]he agency by which, and probably by which alone, we can Christianize Africa, is the African himself, but he must first be trained to that work by the European in Africa."[56] In the past the evangelization of the continent was done by Africans and non-Africans. This is true in the present and will be so in the future. As for the requirement that Europeans must train Africans for evangelization, the present reality in Europe should dissuade any person from advocating that idea today. God does not distribute His gifts according to continent or ethnicity. Furthermore, Europe is in need of re-evangelization, and African Christians are participating in this effort. This is not to suggest that Africans have the solution to the problem of Europe's evangelization. After all, African evangelicals presently involved in cross-cultural mission in Africa face challenges similar to those faced by earlier generations of European and North American missionaries on the continent, imperialistic tendencies being one of the most common.[57] African Christians should participate in missions, not because their continent is the future or the laboratory of Christianity,[58] but out of love for God and obedience to Him[59] since they have no special calling in Christian missions than that of faithfully proclaiming the gospel in word and deed. Full consecration to God, wholehearted and unashamed commitment to His gospel, and sacrificial work in its proclamation are the best tributes that contemporary African evangelicals in missions can pay to their predecessors.

---

[55] Jean-Dominique Durand, "La missiologie, un vaste monde. A propos d'un recueil du Crédic sur vingt-cinq ans de recherches missiologiques," *Mémoire Spiritaine* 22 (2005): 148; Stephen Neill, *Survey of the Training of the Ministry in Africa*, 9.

[56] Douglas M. Thornton, *Africa Waiting or The Problem of Africa's Evangelization* (New York: Student Volunteer Movement for Foreign Missions, 1902), 139.

[57] Both David Kpobi ("The PCG, a Church in Mission in the 21st century: Renewal and Reformation," 11) and Matthews A. Ojo ("The Dynamics of Indigenous Charismatic Missionary Enterprises in West Africa," 19) mention the imperialistic tendencies of African Christians engaging in cross-cultural ministries in their own countries or in neighboring ones.

[58] The idea of Africa being the continent of the future or a laboratory of Christianity is both old and current. It can be seen in the following publications: Kwame Bediako, *Christianity in Africa: The Renewal of a Non-Western Religion* (Maryknoll, N.Y.: Orbis Books, 1995); William Coppinger, "The Continent of the Future," *Word, Work and World*, 1.5 (June 1882): 221–29; Kä Mana, "L'Afrique, une chance pour le christianisme mondial," *Perspectives missionnaires* 34.2 (1997): 45–57; and Cornelius H. Patton, *The Lure of Africa* (New York: Missionary Education Movement of the United States and Canada, 1917), especially chapter VII, entitled "Africa the Laboratory of Christianity."

[59] Samuel Hugh Moffett, "Theology of Missions," *Ashland Theological Journal,* 18.1 (1985): 21–22.

CONCLUSION:

ONGOING IMPERATIVE FOR WORLD MISSION

By D. A. Carson

Granted the interests and character of our honoree John Woodbridge, granted the focus of the essays in this *Festschrift*, and granted the title assigned me—"The Ongoing Imperative for World Mission"—I should relieve your suspense and tell you right away that I'm for world mission. I hope that doesn't come as too big a surprise.[1]

Yet what shall I do with this title? To show something of the sweep of possible discussions the title might call forth, I shall begin by outlining some of the roads I might have traveled in this address, but chose to resist resolutely, before pursuing another way.

The Roads Not Traveled

I shall offer an apostolic number of such roads. Granted "the ongoing imperative for world mission," we might have usefully surveyed:

(1) *An array of "Great Commission" texts*.[2] We might have begun with Matthew 28:16–20. Here we observe that the controlling verb is "make disciples," not "make decisions" or "entertain the sheep." The three supporting participles, all carrying some imperatival force from the context, require us to go, baptize, and teach the disciples everything Jesus has commanded—which sounds as if there might be some further propositional and imperatival content, and not just the biblical storyline. The form of the Great Commission in Luke 24:46–49 is cast as fulfillment and prediction—fulfillment, in that Jesus Christ's passion and

---

[1] As this paper was presented at a banquet honoring Dr John D. Woodbridge, and not as one of the technical papers of the conference, I have decided to preserve the slightly chatty nature of the presentation, and to keep footnotes to a minimum.

[2] Most recently, see the competent survey by Robert L. Plummer, "The Great Commission in the New Testament," *The Southern Baptist Journal of Theology* 9.4 (2005): 4–11.

resurrection were predicted in Scripture, and prediction, for in consequence of Jesus' death and resurrection, "repentance for the forgiveness of sins will be preached in his name to all nations, beginning at Jerusalem."[3] The disciples are witnesses of these things, and Jesus further promises "to send what my Father has promised"—doubtless a reference to the Holy Spirit—so that these believers will be "clothed with power from on high." Similar themes are developed in Acts 1, with the geographical extension of the ministry of the witnesses spelled out rather more clearly: "in Jerusalem, and in all Judea and Samaria, and to the ends of the earth" (Acts 1:8). John's form of the Great Commission (John 20:19–23) is prefaced by Jesus' appearance to the disciples in a closed and locked room and His greeting "Peace be with you." Doubtless this is meant to be more than a casual *Shalom*; it is meant to be evocative of a huge theological structure. For John's Gospel has made clear that the person who does not obey the Son stands under the abiding wrath of God (John 3:36), while in His death and resurrection the Son fulfills His role as the ultimate sin-bearing "Lamb of God" (1:29, 34). The peace that Jesus promised His followers just a few days earlier, on the night He was betrayed—"Peace I leave with you; my peace I give you. I do not give to you as the world gives" (14:27)—is anchored in His own death and resurrection. And now, risen from the grave, Jesus tells the ten disciples gathered in the room, "As the Father has sent me, I am sending you" (20:21). Some have bled the dramatic parallelism in this commission for more than it can carry,[4] yet the power of this standard of sacrifice and service will never be matched by even the most heroic missionary. And once again, the commission is tied to the gift of the Holy Spirit and the forgiveness of sins.

Of course, the theme of the Great Commission extends beyond these specific texts. For instance, we cannot forget the instructions of the Spirit to commission Paul and Barnabas for the work of the first missionary journey; nor can we forget the apostle's self-understanding—he is an ambassador of the Great King, conveying His message, "Be reconciled to God" (2 Cor 5:20). But although such texts clamor for attention, for our purposes they must remain a road not traveled.

(2) *The biblical theology of "Great Commission" texts.* Very often Christians have studied the Great Commission texts in isolation from the books or corpora in which they are embedded, and thus unwittingly denuded them of some of their power. To take but one example—before reading Matthew 28, we are expected to read Matthew 1–27. The very first verse announces the ancestry of Jesus through David back to Abraham. Abraham figures elsewhere in Matthew's Gospel. In Matthew 3, John the Baptist tells us that God is able to "raise up children for Abraham" out of the stones themselves. Apparently genetics does not control the locus of the people of God, despite the covenant with Israel. A

---

[3] Scripture taken from the HOLY BIBLE, TODAY'S NEW INTERNATIONAL VERSION®. TNIV®. Copyright© 2001, 2005 by International Bible Society. Used by permission of Zondervan. All rights reserved.

[4] See the careful treatment by Andreas J. Köstenberger, *The Missions of Jesus and the Disciples According to the Fourth Gospel: With Implications for the Fourth Gospel's Purpose and the Mission of the Contemporary Church* (Grand Rapids, Mich.: Eerdmans, 1998).

little later, Jesus Himself tells us that "many will come from the east and the west, and will take their places at the feast with Abraham, Isaac and Jacob in the kingdom of heaven" (Matt 8:11). We are not far from anticipating the theology of the apostle Paul, who says that the real children of Abraham are those who share Abraham's faith (e.g., Rom 4). The genealogy of Jesus, in Matthew 1, draws attention, among other things, to the non-Hebrews, including Ruth, a Moabitess who, according to the law, should have been excluded from Israel. The name of Jesus is carefully parsed for us—it is nothing other than the Greek form of Joshua, which means "Yahweh saves"—and so Jesus comes to save His people from their sins (Matt 1:21). Coming as it does in the opening lines of the book, this explanation provides a grid for the rest of this first Gospel. This is the book which shows us how Jesus comes to save His people from their sins—by His teaching, by the inauguration of the kingdom, by His death and resurrection, by His consummating return. Small wonder there is a trainee mission (Matt 10) to prepare His disciples for the work of outreach they will have to undertake, in both Jewish and Gentile contexts (and thus cross-culturally), after Jesus' resurrection and ascension. The eschatological discourse reminds us that "this gospel of the kingdom will be preached in the whole world as a testimony to all nations, and then the end will come" (Matt 24:14). Much more could be said, but you get the idea—the Great Commission is not simply tacked on at the end of the Gospel of Matthew. Rather, it brings to a climax one of the themes that drives through the entire book. Similar things could be said, with various emphases, of every book and corpus in the New Testament, anchoring our Great Commission texts to the very structure of the new covenant. And of course, precisely because such themes have been marvelously probed in recent years by, on the one hand, Andreas Köstenberger and Peter O'Brien,[5] and, on the other, by Eckhard Schnabel,[6] little needs to be said about them here.

(3) *The still larger biblical storyline.* Rather myopically, I have limited myself so far to New Testament texts. Yet the New Testament documents nestle within an entire canonical framework. The first responsibility of sentient creatures, not least of God's image-bearers, is to recognize their creatureliness, with all that creatureliness entails. Failure to do so is the beginning of idolatry, and therefore of condemnation and death. The most spectacular evidence of God's grace is His pursuit of rebels. Despite the amount of space devoted to God's choice of Israel and to all of the history that flows from this choice, Paul is entirely right to point out that the history of Israel is itself nestled within the still larger history of humanity's creation and fall. That is why we need a New Adam Christology, as much as, say, a high priestly Christology; and that is why we must recognize that the promise to Abraham that through his seed all the nations of the earth would be blessed is not done away by the Mosaic covenant. It would be enriching to tease out the countless Old Testament anticipations of the cultural

---

[5] *Salvation to the Ends of the Earth: A Biblical Theology of Mission* (NSBT 11; Downers Grove, Ill.: InterVarsity Press, 2001).

[6] *Early Christian Mission.* Vol. 1: *Jesus and the Twelve.* Vol. 2: *Paul and the Early Church* (Downers Grove, Ill.: InterVarsity Press, 2004).

and racial open-endedness of the people of God in the last times—texts such as Isaiah 19:23–25: "In that day there will be a highway from Egypt to Assyria. The Assyrians will go to Egypt and the Egyptians to Assyria. The Egyptians and Assyrians will worship together. In that day Israel will be the third, along with Egypt and Assyria, a blessing on the earth. The Lord Almighty will bless them, saying, 'Blessed be Egypt my people, Assyria my handiwork, and Israel my inheritance.'" But these massive biblical structures of thought and expectation I must reluctantly set aside—though I will briefly return to this specific passage a little later.

(4) *Responses to objections: alternative exegeses.* Despite the apparently straightforward nature of the Great Commission texts, some have argued that the commission applied only to the apostles, or only to the first generation of believers, so it has no ongoing mandate today. Certainly the apostles enjoyed some unique functions. Nevertheless, if the Great Commission itself tells the apostles to teach *their* disciples to obey *everything* that Jesus commanded them, presumably the command inherent in the Great Commission should not be excluded. Matthew's version of the Great Commission does not read, "All authority in heaven and on earth has been given to me. Therefore go and make disciples of all nations, baptizing them in the name of the Father and of the Son and of the Holy Spirit, and teaching them to obey everything I have commanded you, except for this commandment to make disciples. Keep their grubby hands off that one, since it belongs only to you, my dear apostles. And surely I am with you always, to the very end of the age." The ludicrousness of this reading merely has to be spelled out; the laughter will handle the rest. Moreover, Paul can instruct a Timothy to find reliable men who will be able to teach others (2 Tim 2:2) He certainly does not mean, ". . . teach others everything except the gospel, of course, since that job was given to apostles only." The believers in Revelation 12 overcome the devil himself by three means—and one of them, as we shall see, is the word of their testimony. But enough—there is little value in exploring that particular objection further.

(5) *Responses to objections: the job's already done.* This objection is grounded in a peculiar reading of a handful of texts. Jesus had predicted that the gospel would be preached to all nations. Paul, writing to the Colossians, happily asserts that the gospel "has been proclaimed to every creature under heaven" (Col 1:23; a handful of texts express similar thoughts: e.g., Rom 10:17–18; 1 Tim 3:16). Lest we succumb too quickly to pedantry, it is worth recalling that elsewhere Paul asserts, "It has always been my ambition to preach the gospel where Christ was not known" (Rom 15:20), and as a result plans to head to Spain (15:24). The sweeping claim that the gospel has already been preached in all nations and to every creature, then, must be qualified by Paul's own assessment. More importantly, the claim must be read in the light of the Bible's handling of salvation-historical developments. For two millennia, the focus of much of God's redemptive work was among the Israelites; now, Paul is saying, in fulfillment of God's ancient purposes, the gospel has gone to all the nations, to every creature. That is precisely the point Paul makes, among others, when he addresses the

Athenian intelligentsia (Acts 17:30). But once again, we cannot pause to focus on this question.

(6) *Responses to objections: postmodern predilections*. I have no intention of taking cheap shots at postmodernism, partly because I'm still trying to figure out what it is. If it is tied to our finiteness, and thus to the insistence that we cannot escape the narrowness of our vision, then it is hard to deny its cogency. Surely it is true to say that there are two kinds of perspectivalist—those who admit it and those who do not. Of beings that can be said to know, only an omniscient God is free from perspectivalism.

Nevertheless, the harder voices of postmodernism raise two objections to the Great Commission. The *first* is nicely articulated by Brian McLaren. In the light of the cultural move from modernism to postmodernism, he argues, we should stop thinking so antithetically and join hands with co-religionists such as Muslims, Hindus, and Buddhists, refusing to proselytize each other's members as we stand, shoulder-to-shoulder, against the far greater dangers of injustice, social evils, and secularism.[7] Indeed, in his most recent book, McLaren says that what he calls "the secret message of Jesus," stripped of events in Jesus' life such as the cross, is potentially of great benefit to all the world's religions: "This reappraisal of Jesus' message may be the only project capable of saving a number of religions, including Christianity, from a number of threats, from being co-opted by consumerism or nationalism to the rise of violent fundamentalism in their own ranks."[8] I confess I am finding it difficult to decide whether McLaren more seriously misunderstands and misrepresents Islam, Hinduism, and Buddhism, or Christ.[9]

---

[7] E.g., see Brian D. McLaren, *The Church on the Other Side* (Grand Rapids, Mich.: Zondervan, 2003), 83: "The church must present the Christian faith not as one religious army at war against all other religious armies but as one of many religious armies fighting against evil, falsehood, destruction, darkness, and injustice."

[8] Brian D. McLaren, *The Secret Message of Jesus: Uncovering the Truth that Could Change Everything* (Nashville, Tenn.: W Publishing Group, 2006), 7–8.

[9] McLaren believes that "it's significant to note that all Muslims regard Jesus as a great prophet, that many Hindus are willing to consider Jesus as a legitimate manifestation of the divine, that many Buddhists see Jesus as one of humanity's most enlightened people, and that Jesus himself was a Jew" (ibid., 7). This is formally correct, and profoundly misleading. (a) Although "Muslims regard Jesus as a great prophet," none of them sees Him as the greatest prophet. That is strictly reserved for Muhammad. Moreover, they think that Trinitarianism is ridiculous at best and blasphemous at worst, deny that Jesus rose from the dead, and, for the most part, deny that He died on the cross. (b) True, "Hindus are willing to consider Jesus as a legitimate manifestation of the divine," but this willingness extends equally to seeing all religious leaders as a manifestation of the divine. Indeed, some Hindus think of *all* human beings as manifestations of the divine. This has nothing to do with the uniqueness of the incarnation. Moreover, the structure and assumptions of Hinduism mean that Hindu perception of where the human dilemma lies is radically different from that found in biblically faithful Christianity, so it is not surprising that the "answer" lies in cycles of improvement as one gains the karma to make each reincarnation a little more favorable—not in a sin-bearing substitute. (c) Yes, "many Buddhists see Jesus as one of humanity's most enlightened people," but the "Jesus" they thus evaluate is a carefully winnowed Jesus far removed from the historical reality. No religion is more offended by the uniqueness of Jesus' claims or by His insistence—not to say the insistence of His followers—that salvation is found in no other name than His, than is Buddhism. (d) Of course "Jesus himself was a Jew." Moreover, all of His earliest followers were Jews. Yet virtually all of the conflicts Jesus endured during the days of His flesh were with Jews. At the end of the day, Jews and Christians have a fundamentally different reading of *Tanakh* (what we call the "Old Testament"). As undiplomatic as it is to say so in a culture of kosher pluralism, passages like Matthew 23 and John 8 and the letter to the Galatians—and there are many others—will not go away. If McLaren understands these things, then he is misrepresenting these religions; if he does not, then he is making pronounce-

The *second* hard voice ties postmodernism to anti-colonialism, anti-cultural-hegemony, and the like, and is either suspicious of all proselytization in principle (and evangelism is viewed as merely one species of proselytization), or stands against any proselytization undertaken by people from countries with a colonial heritage. Certainly we are on the cusp of massive transformations of perspective.[10] We have expected the majority of world Christian leaders to be white and Western, to be (relative to most of the world) affluent and capable. But there are now far more believers in the Two-Thirds world than in the West. I have preached in churches of 30,000 people in Asia; a big church in France draws 150 people. The West still produces more well-trained theologians than any other part of the world, but this owes much to economic factors, and I suspect it will change in the years ahead. It is only a matter of time until the leaders of Christians in the Two-Thirds world become better known around the world. Witness, for example, the courageous and influential stance of the Anglican Archbishop of Nigeria, Peter Akinola, on the debate over homosexuality within the world Anglican communion. Many churches in São Paulo, Brazil, have something to teach us about energetic racial integration. When we in the West go somewhere as missionaries, even if we ourselves come from humble backgrounds, we are perceived as coming from the affluent world; our ministry is naturally read as "reaching down." When someone from a Two-Thirds world country becomes a missionary to a country of similar socio-economic level, that missionary is naturally read as a peer. When that same missionary serves in a more affluent country, he or she is naturally read as "reaching up." As a result, expectations change, social dynamics change, modes of influence change. Moreover, for better and for worse, Christian missionaries bring some of their culture with them. In recent decades, there have been more efforts by Western missionaries than in the past to disentangle the gospel from the export of American and other Western cultures, but the challenge is considerable. Now, however, with missionaries coming from many different countries, we are finding pockets of churches served by, say, Korean missionaries that have absorbed not only the gospel but also substantial dollops of Korean culture. It is all very fascinating, sometimes confusing, invariably complicated. It's a grand thing that Jesus is building His Church—often by means of His people, sometimes despite us. What is undeniable, however, is that massive changes lie just ahead.

But none of these developments argues against the ongoing imperative for world evangelism. They merely suggest that in the future, we will be less inclined to think of missionaries going from "us" to "them," and more inclined to think of missionaries going from everywhere to everywhere. Korea (to mention but one prominent mission-sending country) sends out a formidable number of missionaries (at the moment, between twelve and fifteen thousand). In addition, Korea sends "tent-makers" into other Asian countries that would otherwise be

---

ments where his misunderstandings are troubling. Either way, his argument is manipulative and, ironically, as offensive to deeply committed and knowledgeable Muslims as to deeply committed and knowledgeable Christians.

[10] Several paragraphs here and under subheading #8 in this address are taken from my earlier essay, "The *SBJT*-Forum: Being Missions-Minded," *The Southern Baptist Journal of Theology* 9.4 (2005): 86–89.

completely "closed." Many African churches send missionaries cross-culturally to other tribes and to other African countries—and, increasingly, to Western countries, primarily to serve those who have emigrated from African countries to the West. Worldwide statistics are complicated and not always easy to come by, and one is not always sure how accurate they are—but in any case, this development is not in dispute, and one must rejoice over it, even if some of the reasons for getting to this point (e.g., the decline of the West) are disappointing. Jesus has told us He will build His Church. He has not told us that such building will necessarily take place in our hometown or school district. It helps to get things into perspective if we take time to read up on worldwide developments in order to gain a worldwide appreciation for what God is doing. Two or three decades ago, missiologists and other Christian leaders were endlessly debating the precise nature and limits of "contextualization," which was understood to go beyond the well-known indigenous principle by demanding not only that churches in any area be self-governing, self-supporting, and self-propagating, but also that their theology be shaped, in measure, by the local cultural context. Nowadays, however, debates over contextualization sound faintly old-fashioned. In the era of global, instantaneous, digital communication, pressures are rising to think through what "globalization" might mean, for good and ill, in the theological arena.[11]

In any case, I cannot take time to run down these related rabbit warrens, as interesting as they are.

(7) *Fundamental skepticism about God, Christ, and the Bible.* In many theological seminaries and universities, not to say in the broader culture, prominent thinkers dismiss what the Bible says about itself, about God, about Christ, and therefore inevitably about the gospel. Transparently, where the gospel is disbelieved, no one will feel the weight of the mandate to proclaim that gospel. Because many of these skeptical voices are influential throughout our culture, some of their strong distaste for anything that smacks of "evangelism" or "world mission" sloshes over into the church itself. That makes no sense, of course, but it is what happens. The skepticism of some parts of our world about the truth of the gospel becomes, among believers, not exactly skepticism, but a sort of waning confidence.

Clearly this is not the place to confront these skeptical voices head-on. But I cannot resist one small observation. From the perspective of Christians whose confidence in the gospel is unwavering, the siren voices of unbelief, far from chilling their fervor for evangelism, constitute a fresh call to evangelize. After all, these siren voices of unbelief need conversion, repentance, faith. Not a little of twentieth-century Western Christian thought has been directed toward meeting exactly that need—whether in biblical scholars like F. F. Bruce, who paved the way for many successors, or in apologists like E. J. Carnell and Francis Schaeffer, who taught us to be orthodox while addressing men and women deeply embedded in contemporary culture, or in popular speakers such as Ravi

---

[11] See Craig Ott and Harold A. Netland, ed., *Globalizing Theology: Belief and Practice in an Era of World Christianity* (Grand Rapids, Mich.: Baker, 2006).

Zacharias, who continues to challenge the shoddy thinking that infects so many minds with pernicious idolatry. The improving quality of Christian books during the past three-quarters of a century—despite the sad sluice of rubbish—is cause for a great deal of quiet thanks to God. But this aspect of the ongoing mandate of world evangelism I must set aside.

(8) *Nuanced judgments as to what "world mission" includes.* It is perennially important to work hard at the proper relation between ministry of the Word and other ministries, including social concern. Exclusive focus on the former is in danger of fostering a docetic view of the Christian life; exclusive focus on the latter is in danger of abandoning the actual proclamation of the good news. Although there are some important principles to work out, the actual balance of time allotment must depend in part on the local situation. When people are crying on a devastated beach after a tsunami, it is not the best time to distribute Bibles, absent fresh water, food, and shelter. Yet an ostensibly Christian organization which, decade after decade, distributes tons of blankets and food, founds orphanages, and combats HIV, without ever offering Bible studies or explaining what doing this in Jesus' name *means*, and what the gospel is about and how important it is for time and eternity, is indistinguishable from UNICEF or *Médecins sans Frontières*, and is no more Christian than they. Around the world, organizations are wrestling with these and related issues. Always there should be two overlapping circles to the discussion: first, what the Bible actually says about these matters, so far as we can discern it aright; and second, how it applies in any particular context. As a rule, we are most impressed by Christian witness that is full of the Bible, full of Jesus, full of the gospel, full of excellent teaching, full of sacrificial service, full of ministering to the whole person, and, where possible, the community itself, in the conscious outworking of the transforming gospel. For obvious reasons, this can vary enormously around the world. To discuss these matters at length here would take us into an expanding debate.

In fact, this debate has in recent years become far more complex than it had been, owing to renewed interest in the study of culture. Such study shows that, while we may wrestle over what it means to penetrate the culture, or to transform the culture, or to contribute to the time when the glory and honor of the nations will be brought into the city of God (Rev 21:26), we cannot afford to forget that we ourselves are part of the culture. We may constitute a sub-culture with a distinguishable profile from the larger surrounding culture, but we cannot avoid the fact that, for better and for worse, we ourselves belong to that larger culture. The notion of doing good to the city and seeking its prosperity is irrefragably tied to the fact that we are part of the city (Jer 29:7). But from all this important discussion, we will reluctantly turn aside.

(9) *Strategies to fulfill the ongoing imperative for world mission.* In a remarkably penetrating paper, still unpublished (as far as I know), Tim Keller reads Acts very carefully[12] to learn some of the strategies of the early church as the first generation of believers sought to evangelize the Roman world. Apart from

---

[12] Tim Keller, "Reaching the 21st Century World for Christ," unpublished paper prepared for The Gathering, San Antonio, TX, September 2005.

observing the much-noted fact that the apostle Paul planted churches in urban centers, from which the gospel spread out into the surrounding regions,[13] Keller draws attention to the centrality of the gospel, rightly conceived; to the transformation of human life under the gospel (e.g., freeing the slave girl in Acts 16); to the power of communal life and the integrity of corporate worship. These and other themes in Acts contribute to the drama of the Church's rapid expansion. All of them are worth exploring, and I hope Keller's paper will achieve wide circulation. But I shall not take that road here.

(10) *Statistics.* With my background in chemistry and mathematics, I am probably more impressed by numbers than I ought to be. Moreover, because Trinity Evangelical Divinity School stands at the hub of a worldwide network of Christian leaders, it is fairly easy to tap into a great deal of interesting data.[14] Christians interested in the worldwide church eagerly note that in the late 1970s Cambodia could boast of only 2,000 Christians; today the number is about 150,000. As recently as 1989, there were only four known Christians in Mongolia; today, there are about 20,000, meeting in over 100 churches and 500 house churches. The first church in Nepal began in 1959 with twenty-nine members. Today there are more than half a million believers meeting in 5,000 congregations. The number of Christians, broadly defined, in Asia as a whole, has grown from 22 million in 1990 to over 300 million today, of whom 140 million are evangelicals. In South America, there are more than 8,000 Ibero-missionaries to other parts of that continent. The megalopolises of the world are becoming more and more cosmopolitan. London, for instance, boasts 440 spoken languages, and 51 percent of the churchgoers in that city are non-English-speaking. Europe is by far the "darkest" continent, as measured by the percentage of the population without evangelical faith—certainly under 3 percent (by contrast, the percentage in Latin America is 14.5 percent). Vienna has more registered prostitutes than evangelicals; Belgium has more Muslims than Protestants. Other statistics are no less disturbing. Brazil alone has 12 million children living on the streets. It is estimated that more than eight million children in Latin America are victims of pornography and sexual trafficking.

These and many other statistics tell their own stories. Transparently, they have a bearing on how we think about missions. But once again, I shall shunt such information to one side.

(11) *Pragmatic tips, "how to"-style instructions.* These are not always bad. Some time ago, J. Herbert Kane, who taught missions for many years here at Trinity, wrote a book titled *Life and Work on the Mission Field.*[15] The work is rather dated now, of course, but in its time it was wonderfully helpful at the level of practical advice and insight. Many books of a more specialized nature, but

---

[13] On the church of the first century being an urban movement, see, not least, Wayne Meeks, *The First Urban Christians: The Social World of the Apostle Paul* (New Haven: Yale University Press, 1983).

[14] Many of the following figures were reported at the most recent summit of the World Evangelical Alliance (2005).

[15] (Grand Rapids, Mich.: Baker Book House, 1980).

belonging to the same species, have been published since then. It would be a useful exercise to scan and summarize such work. But once again, I forbear.

(12) *The training needed to sustain and nurture world mission.* Once again, this is a huge topic, and what place better than Trinity to explore it? Our doctoral programs in education and in intercultural studies are constantly exploring such matters, and our resident missiologists doubtless know far more about such matters than I do.[16] So I have additional reason to avoid this topic.

Having listed a dozen roads not traveled, I turn at last to where I want to spend the remaining space of this essay.

The Way of Fundamentals

I wish to highlight three fundamental biblical truths as they relate to the ongoing mandate for Christian missions.

(1) *The sheer desperate lostness of human beings.* We dare not overlook how implacably opposed our culture is to viewing human beings in this way. I still manage to engage in university missions from time to time. By and large, university students display an awesome ignorance of matters biblical and theological. They have never heard of Abraham or Isaiah, do not know the Bible has two Testaments, and are considered gifted if they can remember three of the Ten Commandments. If, then, I set out to explain the doctrine of the Trinity to them, or say something about the incarnation, or insist on the historical reality of the resurrection of Jesus, a lot of the terrain is new to them—and there are very few objections. Initially, at least, their response is mild curiosity more than anything else: "Oh, is that what Christians believe? Very interesting." But the one topic almost guaranteed to ignite their ire is sin. Even for many Christians, the catena of biblical quotations collected by the apostle Paul sounds a bit over the top:

> "There is no one righteous, not even one;
>> there is no one who understands;
>> there is no one who seeks God.
> All have turned away,
>> they have together become worthless;
> there is no one who does good,
>> not even one."
> "Their throats are open graves;
>> their tongues practice deceit."
> "The poison of vipers is on their lips."
>> "Their mouths are full of cursing and bitterness."
> "Their feet are swift to shed blood;
>> ruin and misery mark their ways,

---

[16] See also the brief but thoughtful essay by Benjamin L. Merkle, "The Need for Theological Education in Missions: Lessons Learned from the Church's Greatest Missionary," *The Southern Baptist Journal of Theology* 9.4 (2005): 50–61.

and the way of peace they do not know."
"There is no fear of God before their eyes."[17]

What we must perceive is that the unfolding of the Bible's entire plotline is bound up with human sin, and God's utterly righteous wrath against it. Paul argues at length that human beings did not have to await the arrival of the Mosaic legislation before becoming guilty. The proof of our guilt, from the fall on, is our death: "death reigned from the time of Adam to the time of Moses" (Rom 5:14). Our guilt is tied to the fundamental idolatry. The deep significance of Genesis 3 is not the outcome of choosing one fruit over another, but the outcome of defying God, of de-godding God. The temptation put to Eve was this: "God knows that when you eat of it your eyes will be opened, and you will be like God, knowing good and evil" (Gen 3:5). The expression "to know good and evil" commonly means more than simply "to discern the difference between good and evil," but something like "to establish the difference between good and evil." That was exclusively God's role. During the creation, God alone pronounced that what He made was good: "he saw all that he had made, and it was very good" (Gen 1:31). Thus, if He forbids the fruit of a certain tree, it can only be because the prohibition is good. To defy it is not mere transgression; it is to make human beings the ultimate arbiters of good and evil, as God Himself recognizes (Gen 3:22). This is the beginning of all idolatry.

The first responsibility of sentient, moral creatures, as we have already stated, is to recognize their creatureliness. It is not enough to recognize, in some abstract fashion, that God is the Creator. Rather, we must recognize that we are His creatures—made by Him and for Him, obligated to Him not only in our origin but in our ongoing existence, utterly dependent on Him, joyfully thankful to Him. The only alternative is the most appalling idolatry. Thus the rebellion of Genesis 3 touches off the drama that unfolds throughout the rest of the Bible—our fundamental alienation is alienation from God. The most heinous thing about sin is that we have offended God. That is why David, after the affair with Bathsheba, confesses to God, "Against you, you only, have I sinned and done what is evil in your sight" (Ps 51:4). At one level, of course, this is not true. David sinned against Bathsheba, he certainly sinned against Bathsheba's husband, he corrupted the military high command, he sinned against his family, he sinned against the nation, he even sinned against the baby in Bathsheba's womb. In fact, it is difficult to think of anyone against whom David had *not* sinned. Whence, then, this anguished cry, "Against you, you only, have I sinned and done what is evil in your sight"? But at a deeper level, of course, that is exactly right—what makes sin heinous, what makes it grotesquely offensive, is that it is first and foremost sin against God. If you cheat on your income tax, the party most offended is God; if you puff yourself up with pride, or slander a neighbor, or become profane, the person most offended is God.

What is it in Scripture that is repeatedly said to be most offensive to God, to anger God? What is it that characteristically brings down the wrath of God—in

---

[17] Rom 3:10–18, citing Pss 14:1–3; 53:1–3; Eccles 7:20; Pss 5:9; 14:3; 10:7; Isa 59:7–8; Ps 36:1.

many hundreds of passages? It is not rape, or murder, or lying, or theft, even though some passages, in Isaiah and Amos for instance, display God's wrath because of social injustice. No, the thing that is characteristically portrayed as bringing down the wrath of God is idolatry. The human stance that prompts God to send the devastation of the flood, or send His covenant people into exile, is repeated and determined idolatry.

Does not Paul say as much? In his letter to the Romans, he devotes two and a half chapters to demonstrating how all humankind, Jews and Gentiles alike, are wrapped up in sin. His exposition ends with the catena of Old Testament quotations I have already cited, and it begins with the somber words, "The wrath of God is being revealed from heaven against all the godlessness and wickedness of human beings who suppress the truth by their wickedness" (Rom 1:18). One of the most striking elements of the wrath of God in the Scriptures is the intensely personal element in it. God's wrath is not characteristically presented as the impersonal outworking of a kind of tit-for-tat moral structure—do bad stuff, and bad stuff happens to you, and God feels sorry about that. Rather, God's anger is personal and real because God Himself is the One who has been offended; our sin attempts to de-god God. The efforts of some recent writers to re-cast the massive biblical evidence in this regard, perhaps most notoriously Steve Chalke,[18] reflect at best an abysmal inattentiveness to what Scripture actually says. The tragedy, of course, is that if we cannot see clearly the nature of the problem, we will not see clearly the nature of the solution. If we refuse to see what the Bible says about the wrath of God, we will certainly fail to see what the cross achieves. If we turn away embarrassed from what the Bible teaches of God's wrath, we will never glimpse the glory of what the Bible says about God's love, supremely manifested in Christ Jesus, especially in His cross and resurrection. We will stumble back to the distortions of 1920s liberalism, so memorably mocked by H. Richard Niebuhr in his 1937 book, *The Kingdom of God in America*: "A God without wrath brought men without sin into a kingdom without judgment through the ministrations of a Christ without a cross."

The consequences of our rebellion against God are beyond calculation. They include not only death, what Paul calls "the last enemy," but the degradation of the entire cosmos. That is why "all things" must be reconciled to God (Col 1), for "all things" are alienated from Him. Temporal judgments are not the mechanical result of evil's automatic return, but the sanction of God. Read Jeremiah and Ezekiel to be reminded how carefully God Himself wants His people to know that if Nebuchadnezzar and the Babylonians destroy Jerusalem and raze the temple, it is not because their gods or their armies are superior, but because God Himself, out of outraged justice and holiness, has decreed the judgment. God "gives us over" to the outcome of our undisciplined self-focus and self-love In other words, even the outworking of what we perceive to be historical cause

---

[18] In particular his book *The Lost Message of Jesus* (Grand Rapids, Mich.: Zondervan, 2003). Chalke uses the plentiful biblical affirmation of the love of God to dissolve the equally plentiful biblical depictions of the wrath of God. It is worth reading the book carefully. See also the accurate and penetrating review by Mike Gilbart-Smith on the http://9marks.org website.

and effect is nothing other than the entailment of God's wrath "being revealed from heaven" (Rom 1).

But there is more. Jesus Christ demands that we think in terms of heaven and hell. Sheep and goats do not end up at the same destination (Matt 25:46). If the judgments of the Old Testament Scriptures seem horrific, they are considerably less than the barrage of pictures that Jesus Himself deploys to describe hell (see also Rev 14:14–20). No thoughtful reader of the Bible can ever forget that "people are destined to die once, and after that to face judgment" (Heb 9:27). That is precisely why Jesus urges his followers to store up treasure in heaven (Matt 6:19–21).

By and large, our culture does not begin to recognize the abject seriousness of the human condition, the mounting guilt of human rebellion, the sheer, desperate lostness that characterizes unforgiven human beings. Even death itself has to be sanitized, marginalized, domesticated—and never, ever, speak of judgment to come.

> Go, bury death in limousines; dispel
> Inevitable death in transient mirth,
> Acquire toys and earthly wealth from birth;
> Pursue position, luxuries, and tell
> Your mortal colleagues of your virtues; sell
> Your future for the present; measure worth
> In prominence, and seek the highest berth;
> Send flowers, and do not think of death and hell.
>   Appalling folly, attitude perverse—
>   Before the one great certainty, to play
>   The ostrich and ignore hard facts, or worse,
>   Transform the corpse by euphemism's play.
> Still more: as surely as a mortal dies,
> His certain death portends the great assize.[19]

And what shall we do with bold and terrifying biblical language, like the following? "But the cowardly, the unbelieving, the vile, the murderers, the sexually immoral, those who practice magic arts, the idolaters and all liars—their place will be in the fiery lake of burning sulfur. This is the second death" (Rev 21:8).

> There are no friends in hell: the residents
> With zeal display self-love's destructive art
> In narcissistic rage. The better part,
> The milk of human kindness, no defense
> Against a graceless world, robbed of pretence,
> Decays and burns away. To have a heart
> Whose every beat demands that God depart—
> This is both final curse and gross offense.

---

[19] The four sonnets in this address are drawn from D. A. Carson, *Holy Sonnets of the Twentieth Century* (Grand Rapids, Mich.: Baker, 1994), one of them slightly adapted.

> Say not that metaphor's inadequate,
> A fearful mask that hides a lake less grim:
> Relentless, pain-streaked language seeks to cut
> A swath to bleak despair, devoid of him.
> This second death's a wretched, endless thing,
> Eternal winter with no hope of spring.

The first fundamental in the ongoing mandate for Christian missions, then, is the sheer, desperate lostness of human beings.

(2) *The sheer glory of God.* We need to recapture how often the glory of God is bound up with God's love for His otherwise damned image-bearers. The same Bible that underscores God's holy wrath repeatedly insists that God is slow to anger, plenteous in mercy. He entreats rebels to return to Him; He continues to provide sun and rain to the just and the unjust. The tension is palpable in passage after passage, perhaps nowhere more so than in Exodus 32–34: "You are a stiff-necked people. If I were to go with you even for a moment, I might destroy you. . . . The LORD, the LORD, the compassionate and gracious God, slow to anger, abounding in love and faithfulness, maintaining love to thousands, and forgiving wickedness, rebellion and sin. Yet he does not leave the guilty unpunished; he punishes the children and their children for the sin of the parents to the third and fourth generation" (33:5; 34:6–7). Hosea the prophet dares apply to God the image of a betrayed husband—God is the Almighty cuckold, still wooing the cheap hussy that is His bride.

And all of this dramatic insistence on the love and mercy of God is nestled within a still larger theme. God acts in love and holiness to display His glory, to bring glory to Himself. The glory of God is woven into the fabric of the Bible's storyline. Here I can draw attention to only a few of the strands.

Begin with Isaiah. In connection with one of the so-called "Servant Songs," the Servant cries,

> And now the LORD says—he who formed me in the womb
> to be his servant to bring Jacob back to him and gather Israel to
> himself, for I am honored in the eyes of the LORD and my God
> has been my strength—he says: "It is too small a thing for you to
> be my servant to restore the tribes of Jacob and bring back those
> of Israel I have kept. I will also make you a light for the Gentiles,
> that you may bring my salvation to the ends of the earth" (Isa
> 49:5–6).

In other words, God is determined to bring maximum glory to His Servant, and He determines that He will achieve this by extending His salvation beyond Israel to the ends of the earth. Small wonder Isaiah elsewhere declares, as we have seen, that on the ultimate day of the Lord,

there will be a highway from Egypt to Assyria [two nations pro-
verbial for their paganism, guilt, and oppression of the Israelites].
The Assyrians will go to Egypt and the Egyptians to Assyria. The
Egyptians and Assyrians will worship together. In that day Israel
will be the third, along with Egypt and Assyria, a blessing on the
earth. The LORD Almighty will bless them, saying, "Blessed be
Egypt my people, Assyria my handiwork, and Israel my inheritance" (Isa 19:23–25).

The New Testament Scriptures articulate the same reality in slightly different
ways, but with no less stress on the glory of God. Thus the form of the Great
Commission in Acts 1:8 impels the believers to be witnesses "to the ends of the
earth." Ephesians 2 insists that "by the blood of Christ" (2:13) Jews and Gentiles
have been reconciled and have been constituted one new humanity. God's purpose is "to reconcile both of them to God through the cross, by which he put
to death their hostility" (2:16). Jews and Gentiles alike are "members of God's
household, built on the foundation of the apostles and prophets, with Christ
Jesus Himself as the chief cornerstone" (2:19–20). Moreover, in the preceding
chapter Paul makes it clear that God has brought all of this about through His
loving predestination, "to the praise of his glorious grace" (1:6), which He has
freely given us in Christ, in the One He loves. Everything that flows from Christ,
including God's intention "to bring all things in heaven and on earth together
under one head, even Christ" (1:10 NIV), the promulgation of "the word of
truth, the gospel of your salvation" (1:13), and the gift of the Holy Spirit as the
promised seal (1:13)—all, all is "to the praise of his glory" (1:14). Thus the
glory of God is irrefragably tied to the extension of the gospel to the end of the
age.

Earlier I mentioned Exodus 32–34, with its tension-filled amalgam of righteous wrath and tender mercy. These chapters depict the dreadful debauchery
of the golden calf episode—Moses is receiving the law on the mountain while
the people have returned to idolatry on the plains below. When Moses returns,
he smashes the tablets of the law. Horrific judgment ensues. Moses feels desperately abandoned, for even his brother Aaron has been implicated in the moral
disaster. As Moses seeks the face of God in the tense and theologically rich
prayers that follow, he cries at one point, "Now show me your glory" (Exod
33:18). He knows full well that the only thing sufficient to stabilize him in this
wretched apostasy is a renewed and deepened vision of God Himself, of the
glory of God. But God replies, "I will cause all my goodness to pass in front of
you, and I will proclaim my name, the LORD, in your presence. I will have mercy
on whom I will have mercy, and I will have compassion on whom I will have
compassion. But . . . you cannot see my face, for no one may see me and live"
(Exod 33:19–20).

What follows is the stuff of drama. Moses is hidden in a cleft of a rock. The
Lord passes by, and Moses is then permitted to peek out and witness something
of the trailing edge of the afterglow of the glory of God (Exodus 34). But while

the Lord is actually passing by, while Moses is still hidden in the rocks and unable to peek out, the Lord himself intones, "The LORD, the LORD, the compassionate and gracious God, slow to anger, abounding in *love and faithfulness* . . ." (34:6)—words that could equally well be rendered, "abounding in *grace and truth.*"

Christians have long recognized that the events of these three chapters, Exodus 32–34, are picked up and developed in the last five verses of John's Prologue (John 1:14–18). There are many points of contact between the two passages. In Exodus, Moses has been up on the mountain to receive the law, including the detailed prescriptions regarding the building of the tabernacle; John tells us that the Word became flesh, and (lit.) "tabernacled" among us (1:14). The supreme meeting-place between God and His community of redeemed sinners was no longer a tent, but the tent of the Word's humanity. In Exodus, God intones that He abounds in love and faithfulness, in grace and truth; John tells us that Jesus, the Word made flesh, is full of grace and truth. Indeed, John himself points out that "the law was given through Moses" (1:17), the very theme of Exodus 32–34. Yet the giving of the law was accompanied by debauchery and idolatry. The display of "grace and truth" was in God's word to Moses; and now, the supreme display of "grace and truth" is in the ultimate Word, the Word made flesh: "grace and truth came through Jesus Christ." Exodus reminds us that no one can look on God and live; John concurs, for he writes, "No one has ever seen God" (1:18). But he instantly adds that, nevertheless, "God the One and Only [the reference is to Jesus Christ, the Word made flesh], who is at the Father's side, has made him known" (1:18). Small wonder that a little later in this Gospel, Jesus can say, "Anyone who has seen me has seen the Father" (14:9).

In short, the parallels between Exodus 32–34 and John 1:14–18 are many. But there is one more that bears directly on our theme. In Exodus, as we have seen, Moses cries out to God, "Now show me your glory"—and God promises to display His goodness. In John's Prologue, the apostle boldly declares of the Word made flesh, "We have seen his glory"—and then in the rest of his Gospel he unpacks the theme of glory. In what way have the disciples seen the glory? After the first sign, the turning of the water into wine in Cana of Galilee, the evangelist declares that Jesus "thus revealed his glory, and his disciples put their faith in him" (2:11). The theme develops along similar lines until chapter 12. There, suddenly, we discover that Jesus will be "glorified" by being lifted up on the cross in hideous death (John 12:20–33).

> "Show me your glory!"
> "I will cause all my goodness to pass in front of you."

And nowhere is there a more moving demonstration of the glory of God in the goodness of God than in the Gospel of John. For here in this God-glorifying death, Christ "will draw all people to [him]self" (12:32). The glory of God in Christ Jesus is the foundation of Christian missions.

Or consider the great vision of Revelation 4–5. Revelation 4 is to Revelation 5 what a setting is to a drama. In other words, Revelation 4 sets the stage with colorful apocalyptic imagery that sets forth the brilliant transcendence and sovereignty of God, who is praised as the Creator: "You are worthy, our Lord and God, to receive glory and honor and power, for you created all things, and by your will they were created and have their being" (Rev 4:11). Even the highest orders of angels voice their utter dependence on Him. And then the drama unfolds. In the right hand of Him who sits on the throne is a scroll, sealed with seven seals. In the imagery of the time, the scroll contains all of God's purposes for judgment and blessing for the entire universe, and these purposes will come into effect only if someone is found who can break the seals. But who in all the universe could possibly approach such a God and serve as His agent in the bringing to pass of all of God's purposes? In fact, no one is found who is worthy, and John the seer weeps. He weeps, not because he is a nosey parker who is frustrated by his inability to peer into the future, but because, in the symbolism of the time, this means that God's purposes will *not* be brought to pass. Life and history have alike become directionless, purposeless, meaningless. But as John weeps, the interpreting elder approaches him and declares, "Do not weep! See, the Lion of the tribe of Judah, the Root of David, has triumphed. He is able to open the scroll and its seven seals" (5:5).

So John looks, and he sees—a Lamb. This does not mean that two animals are parked side by side, a lion and a lamb. Rather, because apocalyptic literature delights to deploy mixed metaphors, the Lion is the Lamb. Indeed, the Lamb itself is simultaneously a sacrifice (it has been slaughtered) and a conqueror—it has seven horns, i.e., a perfection of kingly authority. He comes from the very throne of God—He alone is worthy to open the seals, and thus to serve as God's agent to bring about God's purposes in redemption and judgment. The way He brings about these great ends is made clear in the paean of praise that now erupts in His honor: "You are worthy to take the scroll and to open its seals, because you were slain, and with your blood you purchased for God members of every tribe and language and people and nation. You have made them to be a kingdom and priests to serve our God, and they will reign on the earth" (5:10). The scene ends with the entire universe joining in praise to "him who sits on the throne and to the Lamb" (5:13), who are jointly worshipped throughout the rest of the book.

Thus the sheer glory of God is tightly bound not only to God as Creator, but even more spectacularly to God's redemptive purposes, His missiological purposes, effected by His Son, the vision's Lion-Lamb. The same tie between the gospel and the glory of God is often portrayed in the New Testament, usually in less apocalyptic terminology. For instance, when Paul depicts his ministry and the proclamation of the death and resurrection of Jesus, he tells the Corinthians, "All this is for your benefit, so that the grace that is reaching more and more people *may cause thanksgiving to overflow to the glory of God*" (2 Cor 4:15).

The sheer God-centeredness of the Bible reaches its climax in the closing vision. Revelation 21–22 brings together many strands of biblical thought and exposition into spectacular consummation. The new Jerusalem, obviously symbol-laden, is huge—a cube, about 1,400 miles on edge. But there is only one cube in the Old Testament, viz., the Holy of Holies, into which only the High Priest could enter, and that but once a year on the Day of Atonement, carrying the blood of bull and goat to atone for his own sins and for the sins of the people. But now all of God's redeemed people are living within the cube—the entire new Jerusalem *is* the Holy of Holies, and all of God's people enjoy the bliss of His unshielded presence. No wonder the seer declares, "I did not see a temple in the city, because the Lord God Almighty and the Lamb are its temple" (21:22).

> I saw no temple in the city: there
> The Lord Almighty and the Lamb, his Son,
> Together constitute the temple: Sun
> And moon had disappeared in deep despair,
> Forever obsolete beside the glare
> Of Deity's unshaded glory. None
> Remembers night; for night and darkness shun
> Such light, consigned to self-love's filthy lair.
>> The nations bring their splendor, as the sole
>> Response appropriate to holiness
>> Transfixing. Nothing, no one in the whole
>> Fair city harbors shame or wickedness.
> The city's sons with vibrant joys abound;
> For in the book of life their names are found.

The second fundamental in the ongoing mandate for Christian missions, then, is the sheer glory of God.

(3) *The sheer power of the gospel of Christ crucified.* We tend to overlook how often the gospel of Christ crucified is described as "power." Paul is not ashamed of the gospel, he declares, "because it is the *power* of God that brings salvation to everyone who believes" (Rom 1:16). Writing to the Corinthians, Paul insists that "the message of the cross is foolishness to those who are perishing, but to us who are being saved it is *the power of God*" (1 Cor 1:18). He takes painstaking care not to corrupt the gospel with cheap tricks like manipulative rhetoric, what he dismissively sets aside as "words of human wisdom"—"lest the cross of Christ be emptied of its *power*" (1:17). The "incomparably great power" that is working in those who believe is tied to the exercise of God's mighty strength when He raised Jesus from the dead (Eph 1:19–20).

There is superb irony in all this, of course. When Jesus was executed in the first century, the cross had no positive religious overtones. The Romans had three methods of capital punishment, and crucifixion was the most painful and the most shameful. Yet here were the Christians, their leader executed as a damned malefactor, talking about Him with gleeful irony as if He were reigning from the cross.

So central was the cross in Paul's estimation that he could write, "For I resolved to know nothing while I was with you except Jesus Christ and him crucified. I came to you in weakness and fear, and with much trembling. My message and my preaching were not with wise and persuasive words, but with a demonstration of the Spirit's *power*, so that your faith might not rest on men's wisdom, but on God's *power*" (1 Cor 2:2–5). But this stance, of course, is not exclusively Paul's. Martin Hengel and others have shown that in the first century, the four canonical books we refer to as "Gospels" did not use the word "gospel" as if it were a literary genre. In the first century, no one spoke of "the Gospel of Matthew" or "the Gospel of Mark" or the like. Rather, each of the four relevant books was "*the* gospel *according to* Matthew," "*the* gospel *according to* Mark," and so forth. In other words, there was only one gospel, the gospel of Jesus Christ, the gospel of the kingdom, with multiple witnesses. This one gospel included the good news of Jesus' coming, ministry, teaching, and miracles, but it necessarily culminated in His death and resurrection to redeem lost sinners to God. Otherwise it was not "the gospel." That is why the recent book by Brian McLaren, *The Secret Message of Jesus*, is so misguided. McLaren thinks he can accurately unpack the teaching of Jesus *apart* from consideration of the cross and resurrection. But that is precisely what the four canonical "Gospels" will not allow us to do.[20] Indeed, some wag has said that Matthew, Mark, Luke, and John might almost be considered four passion narratives with extended introductions. That is why the second- and third-century heretical so-called "gospels"—*The Gospel of Thomas*, *The Gospel of Peter*, *The Gospel of Judas*, and others—are not really "gospels" at all—these late, pseudonymous documents leave out the cross and resurrection of Jesus. *Thomas* is merely a collection of 114 sayings, with two snippets of narrative. This is certainly not the one gospel of Jesus Christ, according to Thomas. At the end of the day, it is not by Thomas, and it does not bear witness to the gospel. It is a late document forged in gnosticism, perhaps of Syrian provenance. It is embarrassingly far removed from the emphasis in the New Testament on the gospel of the crucified Redeemer.

Apocalyptic imagery comes to our aid once more. In Revelation 12, the ancient serpent, Satan himself, makes war on the offspring of the "woman," on the people of God—in short, on Christians. He is filled with fury, we are told, because he knows he is doomed and his time is short. How, then, do Christians overcome him? First, they overcome him on the ground of "the blood of the Lamb" (12:11). This takes us back inexorably to the great vision of Revelation 4–5, to the gospel, to the cross and resurrection of Jesus. Second, they overcome him "by the word of their testimony" (12:11). This does not mean they give their testimonies a lot; rather, it means they bear testimony to Jesus and to what He has done. So there it is again—the ongoing mandate for Christian missions, this bearing of public testimony to the triumph of Christ on the cross, is irreducibly tied to the conquest of Satan, and to our own security. Here is where real power lies—in the ignominy and odious shame of the cross. This is

---

[20] Contrast the careful reading of Mark's Gospel by Peter Bolt, who shows how the entire narrative moves toward the cross and resurrection and richly anticipates these events: *The Cross from a Distance: Atonement in Mark's Gospel*, NSBT 18 (Downers Grove, Ill.: InterVarsity Press, 2004).

so stunningly important to Christians that "they do not love their lives so much as to shrink from death" (12:11).

Christians know, above all people, that by nature we were all objects of God's wrath (Eph 2:3). But we have been reconciled to God by Christ Jesus, and we urge others to be reconciled to Him too (2 Cor 5:11–21), for in the cross, "God made him who had no sin to be sin for us, so that in him we might become the righteousness of God" (2 Cor 5:21). Thus we see ourselves, like Christian in *Pilgrim's Progress*, somewhere between the City of Destruction, which by God's grace we have abandoned, and the Celestial City, toward which we press, urging people all around us to join us on our pilgrimage. We have tasted so much; there is so much more to come. The power of God in the cross of Christ has begun its transforming work, but we long for the consummation of all things, the dawning of the new heaven and new earth, the home of righteousness. We long for consummated resurrection existence, when the sheer God-centered-ness of everything will be our incalculable delight. At that point we will experience worship as we ought to experience it, and God will be all in all. Until then, precisely because we have tasted something of the power of the cross, we implore men and women from every tribe and language and people and nation, "Be reconciled to God."

> O let us see your glorious face, perceive
> Shekinah brilliance shining in the gloom
> Behind the veil, transcend the sacred room
> And pierce the Paradise of bliss. We leave
> Our worship hungry yet: can we achieve
> The beatific sight? Dare we presume
> To beg for more, outpace the trailing plume
> Of glory, and pure rays of light receive?
>> It's not that we feel cheated by the grace
>> You freely give: each glimpse of your divine
>> Perfection crushes us—yet gives a taste
>> For holiness transcendent, pure, refined.
> Our worship's still a poor discordant thing;
> But one day we shall see, and we shall sing.

John D. Woodbridge

APPENDIX:
JOHN D. WOODBRIDGE BIBLIOGRAPHY

By Alice Ott

Dissertation:

"L'influence des philosophes français sur les pasteurs réformés du Languedoc pendant la deuxième moitié du dix-huitième siècle" (Doctorat de Troisième Cycle, University of Toulouse, 1969).

Books in European History:

Revolt in Pre-Revolutionary France: The Prince de Conti's Conspiracy against Louis XV, 1755–1757. Baltimore, Md.: The Johns Hopkins University Press, 1995.

> Woodbridge argues that, after becoming estranged from his cousin Louis XV, the Prince de Conti was involved in a plot to wrench the throne from the king. The prince took advantage of a number of different political and religious controversies on the eve of the Seven Years' War (1755–1757)—the denial of the Eucharist to the Jansenists, the challenge to Louis XV posed by the *parlement* of Paris, the revocation of the Edict of Nantes (1685), and the efforts of the English to spark a Huguenot revolt—in an attempt to incite armed rebellion. Although the conspiracy was unsuccessful, it had the unexpected result of Louis XV granting some measure of toleration to obedient Huguenots in 1757–58.

Reventlow, Graf Henning, Walter Sparn and John D. Woodbridge, eds. *Historische Kritik und biblischer Kanon in der deutschen Aufklärung.* Wiesbaden: Otto Harrassowitz, 1988.

> The volume is a collection of papers given at the Eighteenth Wolfenbütteler Symposium at the Herzog August Bibilothek in Wolfenbüttel, Germany (December, 1985). The goal of the Symposium was to examine from a philological, philosophical, and theological-historical standpoint the development of a historical-critical exegesis and hermeneutic of the Bible in Germany.

Special attention in the articles is given to the reception of the critical methodologies of Spinoza, Richard Simon, Jean le Clerc, and Pierre Bayle in Protestant Germany since the beginning of the eighteenth century.

Le Brun, Jacques, and John D. Woodbridge, eds. *Richard Simon. Additions aux Recherches curieuses sur la diversité des langues et religions*. Paris: Presses Universitaires de France, 1983.

This critical edition of Richard Simon's *Additions* was made possible by Woodbridge's chance discovery of a "lost" manuscript copy of this document in the library of the University of Leiden. Simon's *Additions* was written in the 1670s to supplement and update Edward Brerewood's *Enquiries touching the Diversity of Languages and Religions through the cheife parts of the world* (1614; French translation 1640). Simon's work describes the religious beliefs, customs, and ceremonies of primitive Christians, Jews, and Muslims in the East; at the same time, he indicates ways in which the "evolution" of Christianity over time introduced "novelties" and "innovations" into the Roman Catholic Church. Woodbridge and Le Brun provide a substantial introduction that describes the background and significance of this precious manuscript.

Articles in European History:

"La 'grande chausse aux manuscripts,' la controverse eucharistique et Richard Simon." In *Conflits Politiques, Controverses Religieuses. Essais d'histoire européenne aux 16e-18e siècles*, edited by Ouzi Elyada and Jacques Le Brun, 143–76. Paris: Éditions de L'École des Hautes Études en Sciences Sociales, 2002.

Woodbridge describes the fascinating "manuscript chase" by French Catholic (especially Jansenist) and Protestant apologists in the 1660s and 1670s, in search of documentary proof of whether or not Orthodox Christians in the East subscribed to the "Catholic" doctrines of Christ's real presence in the Eucharist and transubstantiation. Catholic apologists believed that demonstrating a common Eucharistic theology with the Eastern Church would prove the antiquity—and apostolic origins—of their doctrine. Woodbridge demonstrates that it was the scholarship of the Catholic (!) savant Richard Simon that in large part undermined Catholic efforts by raising questions about the apologists' linguistic competence and the authenticity of their manuscripts and by calling attention to ways in which the Roman church had diverged from the belief and practice of the primitive Church.

"An Eighteenth Century Fronde? The Conspiracy of the Prince de Conti against Louis XV, 1755–1757." In *De l'Humanisme aux Lumières: Bayle et le protestantisme Mélanges en l'honneur d'Elisabeth Labrousse*, edited by Michelle Magdelaine, Cristina Pitassi et al., 77–93. Oxford: The Voltaire Foundation and Éditions Universitas, 1995.

> This article summarizes key findings from Woodbridge's 1995 monograph, *Revolt in Pre-Revolutionary France* (see above).

"Richard Simon, le père de la critique biblique." In *Le Grande Siècle et la Bible*, edited by Jean-Robert Armogathe, 193–206. Paris: Beauchesne, 1989.

> Woodbridge surveys Richard Simon's biblical scholarship and the intense controversy that it engendered during his lifetime. He argues that Simon deserves the title "father of biblical criticism" in that he not only ascribed errors to the Bible (which others had done before him), but also tried to identify various layers of composition and different authors of the biblical text.

"German Responses to the Biblical Critic Richard Simon from Leibniz to J. S. Semler." In *Historische Kritik und biblischer Kanon in der deutschen Aufklärung*, edited by Graf Henning Reventlow, Walter Sparn, and John D. Woodbridge, 65–87. Wiesbaden: Otto Harrassowitz, 1988.

> Woodbridge interacts with the "pervasive" historiography of Stuhlmacher and others which states that Richard Simon was virtually unknown in Germany until the 1770s when J. S. Semler published several of his works. Woodbridge shows that Leibniz in the 1670s, Carpzov in the 1680s, and Rambach in the 1720s interacted with and then branded the French priest as a dangerous, anti-Christian critic. By the 1750s, however, opinion had changed, and German theologian J. D. Michaelis and a decade later Semler were hailing Simon as the founder of the new exciting field of biblical criticism.

"La conspiration du prince de Conti (1755–1757)." In *Dix-huitième siècle* 17 (1985): 97–109.

> This article contains Woodbridge's preliminary research on the Conti conspiracy.

"The reformed pastors of Languedoc face the movement of dechristianiza-tion (1793–1794)." In *Sécularisation*, edited by Michèle Mat, 77–89. Brussels: Éditions de l'Université de Bruxelles, 1984.

> Woodbridge examines the response of Reformed pastors in the southeastern corner of France to the demand of the "dechris-tianizers" that they discontinue their pastoral functions. Utilizing the abdication statements and other allusions to Protestant pas-toral activities in the departmental records, the author dem-onstrates that the vast majority (between 80–97 percent) of Reformed pastors in Languedoc abdicated their pastoral func-tions in 1793–1794. The chief reasons for these abdications were fear, a moral obligation to obey the "law," acceptance of the "cult of Reason," and financial gain. The movement of dechristianiza-tion thus successfully eliminated the pastoral leadership of the "Church of the Desert" and struck a devastating blow to French Protestantism in the province.

"Richard Simon's Reaction to Spinoza's *Tractatus Theologico-Politicus*." In *Spinoza in der Frühzeit seiner religiösen Wirkung*, edited by Karlfried Gründer and Wilhelm Schmidt-Biggemann, 201–26. Heidelberg: Verlag Lambert Schneider, 1984.

> The discovery by Woodbridge and Jacques Le Brun of Richard Simon's *Brerewood Additions,* a manuscript "lost" for 240 years, provides fresh data to the scholarly debate about Spinozan influ-ence on Simon. Woodbridge argues against Auvray that Simon knew of Spinoza's *Tractatus* by 1675, that is, prior to his com-pleted revision of his monumental work, *The Critical History of the Old Testament* (1677). Simon, despite protestations to the contrary, shared a similar critical approach to the Scriptures as Spinoza, although he balked at the latter's conclusions.

"The Parisian book trade in the early Enlightenment: an update on the Prosper Marchand project." In *Transactions of the Fifth International Congress on the Enlightenment, 1763–1772.* Oxford: The Voltaire Foundation, 1980.

> The article opens with a brief introduction to the person and work of the Parisian *libraire* Prosper Marchand. Marchand penned a 2,000-page manuscript catalogue of the legal book pro-duction of Paris between 1650–1705. Woodbridge along with three other scholars formed the Marchand book project to evalu-ate the significance of this manuscript for understanding the le-gal Parisian book trade at the beginning of the Enlightenment.

Here Woodbridge offers an update on the progress of this project with regard to the purpose, methodology, and immediate uses of the catalogue.

"Censure royale et censure épiscopale: Le conflit de 1702." In *Dix-huitième siècle*, 8 (1976): 333–55.

Woodbridge takes a new look at the conflict between the French royal chancellor Pontchartrain and the archbishop of Paris Louis-Antoine de Noailles over the publication of Richard Simon's *Nouveau Testament de Notre-Seigneur Jésus-Christ* in 1702.

"An 'Unnatural Alliance' for Religious Toleration: The *Philosophes* and the Outlawed Pastors of the 'Church of the Desert'." In *Church History* 42 (1973): 502–23.

The Calvinist pastors of the "Church of the Desert" in the province of Midi operated from a worldview entirely antithetical to that of the spokesmen of the Enlightenment, the *philosophes*. Nevertheless, after approximately ten years of contact the two groups reluctantly came to an "unnatural alliance" in the 1760s around the issue of religious toleration. The event that forged the alliance was the intervention on behalf of the Protestants by Voltaire and other *philosophes* after the execution of Protestant Jean Calas. This alliance would prove important in the ultimate drafting of the Edict of Toleration of 1787.

Books in Church History:

Woodbridge, John D., Sinclair Ferguson, and Frank James III, editors. *Zondervan History of the Christian Church*. Forthcoming.

Woodbridge, John D., editor. *Ambassadors for Christ*. Chicago: Moody Press, 1994.

Winner of the Gold Medallion Award, this volume contains biographical sketches of well-known nineteenth- and twentieth-century missionaries and evangelists, as well as lesser known men and women who served as "ambassadors for Christ" in secular vocations. The inclusion of the stories of a large number of non-Western Christians reflects the exciting reality that Christianity has indeed become a global phenomenon.

Woodbridge, John D., editor. *More Than Conquerors: Portraits of Believers from All Walks of Life.* Chicago: Moody Press, 1992.

> This volume, which was awarded the Gold Medallion Award, contains short biographies of nineteenth- and twentieth-century Christians from many nationalities and walks of life, including politics, literature, sports and entertainment, academics, industry and commerce, and Christian ministry. The common thread in the selected biographical sketches is a vibrant and convincing Christian faith that "more than conquered."

Woodbridge, John D., editor. *Great Leaders of the Christian Church.* Chicago: Moody Press, 1988.

> Winner of the Gold Medallion Award, this volume includes sixty-four short biographical sketches that span the centuries from Peter, Paul, and John in the first century to Billy Graham and Francis Schaeffer in the twentieth. Though biographical in structure, the articles intentionally make the connection between "great leaders" and intellectual and historical trends within Christian history (e.g., Catholic mysticism, Pietism, and revivalism). Contributors include many well-respected British and American authors.

Marsden, George M., Mark A. Noll, and John D. Woodbridge, editors. *Eerdmans' Handbook to Christianity in America.* Grand Rapids, Mich.: Eerdmans, 1983.

> This sequel to the *Eerdmans' Handbook to the History of Christianity* continues the format and style of that volume while focusing on the development of Christianity on American soil from the colonial era to the present. It received the Gold Medallion Award.

Hatch, Nathan A., Mark A. Noll, and John D. Woodbridge, editors. *The Gospel in America.* Grand Rapids, Mich.: Zondervan, 1977.

> The book sheds light on the present American phenomenon of evangelicalism by examining its past in light of several themes. Woodbridge contributed the fourth and fifth chapters on evangelical attitudes to the Bible and revivalism.

Wells, David F. and John D. Woodbridge, editors. *The Evangelicals.* Nashville, Tenn.: Abingdon Press, 1975; Baker, 1977.

Essays by distinguished racially and theologically diverse scholars are arranged around three dimensions of evangelicalism. The first section seeks to define broadly what evangelical belief constitutes, both in the Reformed and Arminian traditions. A second section identifies the history and sociological makeup of this branch of American Protestantism and appropriately includes a discussion of black evangelicals. The final section of essays examines the changing response of evangelicals to social, political, scientific, and cultural trends from 1925 to 1975.

Books in Theology and Biblical Studies:

George, Timothy and John Woodbridge. *The Mark of Jesus*. Chicago: Moody Press, 2005.

> The authors interact with Francis Schaeffer's concept of the "final apologetic," which he proposed in his 1970 work, *The Mark of the Christian*. Schaeffer argued that although non-Christians can rightfully expect Christians to put into practice Christ's teaching on love and peace, this "apologetic" is seldom observed. In the *Mark of Jesus* the authors explore Schaeffer's apologetic and apply it concretely to situations that evangelicals face—loving different or estranged persons, seeking unity with Christians of differing convictions, and avoiding hypocrisy. The book ends with a call for all Christians to authentically bear the "mark of Jesus" and thus earn the right to share the good news of Christ.

Akers, John N., John H. Armstrong, and John D. Woodbridge, editors. *This We Believe: The Good News of Jesus Christ for the World*. Grand Rapids, Mich.: Zondervan, 2000.

> In June 1999 *Christianity Today* published a detailed statement, "The Gospel of Jesus Christ: An Evangelical Celebration." Drafted by leading evangelicals, the statement explains the content of the gospel afresh for the contemporary generation. This volume of essays, published by the Committee on Evangelical Unity in the gospel, serves as "a commentary of sorts" (20) on that statement. Each chapter explains one aspect of the gospel in a manner accessible to both pastors and laymen.

Carson, D. A. and John D. Woodbridge, editors. *God and Culture: Essays in Honor of Carl F. H. Henry*. Grand Rapids, Mich.: Eerdmans, 1993.

This collection of essays interacts with a number of distinct elements in American and Western culture from a decidedly Christian perspective. The approach used is both theological and practical and aims "to help Christians think their way through huge swaths of contemporary culture." An elite roster of contributors tackles such topics as God and economics, the Christian response to media, literature and the arts, the use of leisure, bioethics and human sexuality.

Carson, D. A. and John D. Woodbridge. *Letters Along the Way.* Wheaton, Ill.: Crossway, 1993.

The authors adopt a compelling, fictional literary style for this "novel of the Christian life." The book consists of letters between a younger Christian, Timothy Journeyman, and his mentor, the seminary professor, Dr. Woodson, addressing topics such as biblical inerrancy, Reformed epistemology, evangelicalism, prayer, and coping with death.

McComiskey, Thomas and John D. Woodbridge, editors. *Doing Theology in Today's World: Essays in Honor of Kenneth S. Kantzer.* Grand Rapids, Mich.: Zondervan, 1991.

The premise of this volume of essays in honor of Kenneth Kantzer is that, despite common opinion to the contrary, the doing of theology is "pertinent and spiritually uplifting" and can "contribute much to the spiritual health of the Christian churches." The first section explores how the neighboring disciplines of systematic theology, exegesis, church history, and philosophy contribute to the doing of theology. The second section includes contemporary evangelical perspectives on the topic, and the third section the approach to theology of other traditions (Roman Catholic, Eastern Orthodox, feminist, liberation theology). The volume closes with an essay by Kantzer in which he interacts with the other essays and depicts his own approach.

Carson, D. A. and John D. Woodbridge, editors. *Hermeneutics, Authority and Canon.* Grand Rapids, Mich.: Zondervan, 1986; Baker 1995.

This collection of nine essays serves as a companion volume to the earlier *Scripture and Truth.* The essays address important topics relevant to the doctrine of Scripture that were not included in the earlier volume, including literary genre, harmonization, Barth's doctrine of scriptural authority, the problem of *sensus ple-*

nior, and the formation of the biblical canon. Woodbridge also contributes an article entitled "Misconceptions concerning the impact of the 'Enlightenment' on the doctrine of Scripture."

Woodbridge, John D., editor. *Renewing Your Mind in a Secular World*. Chicago: Moody Press, 1985.

> This collection of essays addresses the challenge of "bringing every thought captive to Christ" in today's secular society. The massive onslaught of Western culture requires that the Christian return to basics: prayer, Scripture meditation, devotional Bible study, and a commitment to the local church. Woodbridge contributed the introduction and an article on Martin Luther's practical advice for Christians experiencing the battle between God and Satan in their daily lives.

Carson, D. A. and John D. Woodbridge, editors. *Scripture and Truth*. Grand Rapids, Mich.: Zondervan, 1983; Baker 1992.

> This widely-acclaimed book consists of twelve essays penned by prominent evangelical scholars, who both individually and collectively argue that "the Bible is the Word of God written." The topic of "Scripture and truth" is examined biblically, historically, and theologically in the three sections of the book. This volume includes an essay co-written by Woodbridge and Randall H. Balmer entitled "The Princetonians and *biblical authority*: an assessment of the Ernest Sandeen proposal."

Biblical Authority. A Critique of the Rogers/McKim Proposal. Grand Rapids, Mich.: Zondervan, 1982.

> Woodbridge in this book successfully lays to rest the thesis proposed by Jack Rogers and Donald McKim in their book *The Authority and Interpretation of the Bible* (1979). The central proposal made by Rogers and McKim was that prior to innovations in the seventeenth century, the historic position of the Church was that the Scriptures were infallible for faith and practice alone and not in the areas of history, science, and geography. Woodbridge points out the logical flaws of the Rogers/McKim proposal and then aptly demonstrates through the use of primary sources that the Church has historically maintained that infallibility extended to historical and scientific detail in the Scriptures.

Articles in Church History and Theology:

"The Role of 'Tradition' in the Life and Thought of Twentieth-Century Evangelicals." In *Your Word Is Truth*, edited by Charles Colson and Richard John Neuhaus, 103–46. Grand Rapids, Mich.: Eerdmans, 2002.

> The volume, *Your Word Is Truth*, contains a statement by the project group Evangelicals and Catholics Together, on the relationship of Scripture and tradition, as well as essays by evangelical and Catholic scholars on that theme. In his contribution, Woodbridge points out that twentieth-century evangelicals have consistently rejected the Counter-Reformation's definition of "tradition" in favor of *sola scriptura*. Evangelicals have, however, their own beliefs, practices, and interpretive grids that function as "traditions." Nevertheless, evangelicals have consistently upheld that the Bible alone is infallible, not their interpretations of it.

"Setting the Compass on Christ." In *Trinity International University 1897–1997: A Century of Training Christian Leaders*, edited by David V. Martin, 203–20. Deerfield, Ill: Trinity International University Press, 1998.

> Woodbridge draws upon John Henry Newman's arguments in *The Mark of a University* in favor of a liberal arts education and applies them to the mandate of Trinity International University. In spite of utilitarian, market-driven pressures to abandon this form of education, Woodbridge challenges the university not to falter in its course. A Christian liberal arts education ideally integrates Scripture into the entire curriculum, so that students not only learn to think, but develop as well a Christian worldview and the intellectual resources to become better servants of Christ. To achieve this goal, the faculty and administration must "set their compass on Christ."

"Why Words Matter." *Christianity Today*, June 19, 1995, pp. 31–32.

> In response to Woodbridge's *Christianity Today*'s article "Cultural War Casualties" (see below), Focus on the Family president James Dobson defended in this issue the legitimacy of using "fighting words" in the battle for Christian values. Woodbridge's response, "Why Words Matter," stresses that while it is important for Christians actively to defend Christian values in the public sphere, the use of "war talk" and "cultural war rhetoric" should be avoided, since incautious words have the power to "inflame passions, needlessly discourage or wound."

"Culture War Casualties." *Christianity Today*, March 6, 1995, pp. 20–26.

The concept of "cultural war" is found in a plethora of contemporary secular and Christian books to describe the conflict over values that is currently taking place in American society. In this article, Woodbridge warns that "adopting uncritically the friend-or-foe, either-or rhetoric of war" leads to a distortion and hardening of positions on both sides, as well as divisions between Christians. A more biblical approach is humbly to seek to understand and love our "enemies," and then to clearly and courteously share the "transforming Gospel of Christ."

"Some Misconceptions of the Impact of the 'Enlightenment' on the Doctrine of Scripture." In *Hermeneutics, Authority and Canon,* edited by D. A. Carson and John D. Woodbridge, 241–70. Grand Rapids, Mich.: Zondervan, 1986; Baker, 1995.

In recent decades, both Roman Catholic scholars and Protestant historians frequently maintain that the doctrine of biblical inerrancy was an innovation associated with the "Enlightenment." Woodbridge argues that prior to the Enlightenment both Catholics and Protestants believed that the Bible's chronological, historical, and scientific allusions were accurate. Biblical inerrancy is therefore not "Fundamentalist doctrine" or an innovation due to the impact of Newtonian science, Baconianism, or Common Sense Realism.

"Recent Interpretations of Biblical Authority, part 1: A Neoorthodox Historiography under Siege." In *Bibliotheca Sacra* 142 (1985): 3–15.

The following four articles, published in *Bibliotheca Sacra* (1985), were first presented by Woodbridge as W. H. Griffith Thomas Memorial Lectures at Dallas Theological Seminary in November 1984. In the first article, Woodbridge challenges the neoorthodox interpretation of biblical authority as proposed by Karl Barth's disciples (Bizer, etc.). It states that the roots of biblical inerrancy extend back only to the second generation of Reformers in the late sixteenth century, and not to Calvin and Luther. This historiography has been under siege since the 1970s by non-evangelical and evangelical scholars alike. Recent research has underscored Woodbridge's contention that Luther and Calvin upheld the doctrine of biblical infallibility.

"Recent Interpretations of Biblical Authority, part 2 : The Rogers and McKim proposal in the balance." In *Bibliotheca Sacra* 142 (1985): 99–113.

> This article provides a brief summary of Woodbridge's critique of the Rogers/McKim proposal, which is found in more detailed form in his *Trinity Journal* review (1980) and his monograph, *Biblical Authority* (1982).

"Recent Interpretations of Biblical Authority, part 3 : Does the Bible teach Science?" In *Bibliotheca Sacra* 142 (1985): 195–208.

> Roman Catholic scholar Bruce Vawter argues that the Bible's teachings with regard to salvation and ethics are alone infallible; biblical statements concerning history and science are accommodated to man's weakness and contain error. John Woodbridge, in this article, musters an impressive sampling of vignettes from the history of Western thought to counter this claim in favor of the view that the Bible's infallibility extends to the natural world.

"Recent Interpretations of Biblical Authority, part 4 : Is biblical inerrancy a fundamentalist doctrine?" In *Bibliotheca Sacra* 142 (1985): 292–305.

> Evangelical historian George Marsden claims that biblical inerrancy is an innovative belief that came about in the late nineteenth century due to American Fundamentalism's commitment to Common Sense philosophy and Baconian inductive science. Woodbridge gives examples of the Western church's commitment to the "pivotal Augustinian tradition" of an inerrant Bible, which persisted until the late seventeenth century. This evidence demonstrates that biblical inerrancy is not a recent Fundamentalist innovation, but the central tradition of the Church throughout the centuries.

Balmer, Randall H. and John D. Woodbridge, "The Princetonians and biblical authority: an assessment of the Ernest Sandeen proposal." In *Scripture and Truth*, edited by D. A. Carson and John D. Woodbridge, 251–86. Grand Rapids, Mich.: Zondervan, 1983; Baker 1992.

> Woodbridge and Balmer critique Ernest Sandeen's contention that the doctrine of biblical inerrancy in the original autographs emerged first in a joint article written by Princeton theologians A. A. Hodge and B. B. Warfield in 1881. Sandeen's proposal, according to the authors, misunderstands the history of biblical authority in the Reformed tradition and at Princeton Theological

Seminary, as well as wrongly ignores the "wider context of American and European evangelical thought." The view of biblical inerrancy was widely held centuries before the Princetonians, as the examples of sixteenth-century Protestant theologians William Whitaker and William Ames indicate.

"Biblical authority: towards an evaluation of the Rogers and McKim proposal." In *Trinity Journal* 9 (1980): 165–236.

> This seventy-page review of Jack Rogers and Donald McKim's book *The Authority and Interpretation of the Bible* forms the foundation of Woodbridge's 1982 book, *Biblical Authority. A Critique of the Rogers/McKim Proposal* (see above).

"History's Lessons and Biblical Inerrancy," in *Trinity Journal* 6 (1977): 73–93.

> Woodbridge uses two eighteenth-century case studies, the influence of the French Remonstrant Bible critic, Jean Le Clerc, and the effect of Enlightenment thought at Yale College in the 1790s to demonstrate historically the danger to individuals and institutions when the doctrine of biblical inerrancy is abandoned. Nevertheless, Christian hope implies the possibility of reversing a slide toward an errant Bible. Therefore, the analogy of a door hinge is preferable to the domino image. This article forms the basis of and is quoted at length in chapter five of his later book *Biblical Authority*.

BIBLIOGRAPHY

Adeyemo, Tokunboh. "What and who is an Evangelical?" In *AEAM: Association of Evangelicals of Africa and Madagascar: History and Ministries*. Nairobi: AEAM, n.d.

Aikman, David. *Jesus in Beijing: How Christianity is Transforming China and Changing the Global Balance of Power*. Washington, D.C.: Regnery, 2003.

Ajayi, J. F. A. *Christian Missions in Nigeria, 1841–1891: The Making of a New Élite*. Burnt Mill: Longman, 1965.

Allen, Catherine. *The New Lottie Moon Story*. Nashville, Tenn.: Broadman Press, 1980.

Alvarez, Miguel. "The South and the Latin American Paradigm of the Pentecostal Movement." *Asian Journal of Pentecostal Studies* 5.1 (2002): 135–53.

Anderson, Rufus. *History of the Sandwich Islands Mission*. Boston: Congregational Publishing Society, 1870.

Andrew III, John A. "Betsey Stockton: Stranger in a Strange Land." *Journal of Presbyterian History* 52 (1974): 157–66.

Asamoah-Gyadu, J. Kwabena. "An African Pentecostal on Mission in Eastern Europe: The Church of the 'Embassy of God' in the Ukraine." *Pneuma: The Journal of the Society for Pentecostal Studies* 27.2 (Fall 2005): 297–321.

Axtel, James. *After Columbus: Essays in the Ethnohistory of Colonial North America*. Oxford: Oxford University Press, 1988.

Barker, Peter and Samuel Boadi-Siaw. *Changed by the Word: The Story of Scripture Union Ghana*. Accra: African Christian Press, 2003.

Barrett, David. "Missiometrics 2005: A Global Survey of World Mission." *International Bulletin of Missionary Research* 29.1 (January 2005): 27–30.

———, ed. *World Christian Encyclopedia: A Comparative Study of Churches and Religions in the Modern World, A.D. 1900–2000*. Nairobi: Oxford University Press, 1982.

Barrett, David and Todd Johnson, eds. *World Christian Trends AD 30–AD 2200*. Pasadena, Calif.: William Carey Library, 2001.

Bastian, Jean Pierre. "The Metamorphosis of Latin American Protestant Groups: A Sociological Perspective." *Latin American Research Review* 28.2 (1993): 33–61.

Baudert, S. "Zinzendorf's Thought on Missions Related to His Views of the World." In *International Review of Missions* 21 (July 1932): 390–401.

Bays, Daniel H. and Grant Wacker, eds. *The Foreign Missionary Enterprise at Home: Explorations in North American Cultural History.* Tuscaloosa, Ala.: University of Alabama Press, 2003.

Beaver, R. Pierce. *Church, State, and the American Indians: Two and a Half Centuries of Partnership in Missions Between Protestant Churches and Government.* St. Louis, Mo.: Concordia, 1966.

_____. "Methods in American Missions to the Indians in the Seventeenth and Eighteenth Centuries: Calvinist Models for Protestant Foreign Missions." *Journal of Presbyterian History* 47.2 (1969): 124–48.

_____. ed. *Pioneers in Mission.* Grand Rapids, Mich.: Eerdmans, 1966.

Bebbington, David W. *Evangelicalism and Modern Britain: A History from the 1730s to the 1980s.* London: Unwin Hyman, 1989.

Bediako, Kwame. *Chrisianity in Africa: The Renewal of a Non-Western Religion.* Maryknoll, N.Y.: Orbis Books, 1995.

Berger, Peter L. "Four Faces of Global Culture." *National Interest* 49 (Fall 1997): 23–29.

Bergunder, Michael. "The Pentecostal Movement and Basic Ecclesia Communities in Latin America: Sociological Theories and Theological Debates." *International Review of Mission* 91.361 (2002): 163–86.

Beyreuther, Erich. *Bartholomaeus Ziegenbalg.* Madras: Christian Literature Society, 1955.

Bingham, Hiram. *Residence of Twenty-One Years in the Sandwich Islands, or, The Civil, Religious, and Political History of Those Islands.* 3rd ed. Canandaigua, N.Y.: H. D. Goodwin, 1855.

Bobé, Louis. *Hans Egede: Colonizer and Missionary of Greenland.* Copenhagen: Rosenkilde and Bagger, 1952.

Bradbury, Steve. "Introducing the Micah Network." In *Justice, Mercy and Humility: Integral Mission and the Poor,* edited by Tim Chester. Waynesboro, Ga.: Paternoster Press, 2002.

Bremen, Christina Maria. *The Association of Evangelicals in Africa: Its History, Organization, Members, Projects, External Relations, and Message.* Zoetermeer: Uitgeverij Boekencentrum, 1996.

Burin, Eric. *Slavery and the Peculiar Solution: A History of the American Colonization Society.* Gainesville, Fla.: University Press of Florida, 2005.

Capers, William. *Catechism for the Use of Methodist Missions.* Charleston, S.C.: John Early, 1853.

_____. "Missions Among the Creek Indians." *Methodist Magazine* 5 (1822): 232–36.

Cardoso, Mauricio. "Fe Tipo Exportação." *Veja,* April 1997, 84–86.

Carey, S. Pearce. *William Carey.* 8th ed. London: The Carey Press, 1934.

Carey, William. *An Enquiry Into the Obligations of Christians to use Means for the Conversion of the Heathen.* Leicester, 1792.

Carpenter, Joel and Wilbur Shenk, eds. *Earthen Vessels: American Evangelicals and Foreign Missions, 1880–1980.* Grand Rapids, Mich.: Eerdmans, 1990.

Carson, D. A. *Holy Sonnets of the Twentieth Century.* Grand Rapids, Mich.: Baker Books, 1994.

_____. "The *SBJT*-Forum: Being Missions-Minded." *The Southern Baptist Journal of Theology* 9.4 (2005): 86–89.

Celada, Claudio. *Un Apóstol Contemporáneo: la Vida de F. G. Penzotti.* Buenos Aires: Libreria La Aurora, 1900.

CIEE. "El Pacto de Curitiba." In *Teología del Camino: Documentos Presentados en Los Últimos Veinte Años Por Diferentes Comunidades Cristianas de América Latina*, edited by Pedro Arana Quiroz, 44–48. Lima: Presencia, 1987.

Clark, Michael P. *The Eliot Tracts*. Contributions in American History, number 199. Westport, Conn.: Praeger, 2003.

Clarke, Erskine. *Dwelling Place: A Plantation Epic*. New Haven: Yale University Press, 2005.

Cogley, Richard. *John Eliot's Mission to the Indians before King Philip's War*. Cambridge: Harvard University Press, 1999.

Colby, Gerald and Charlotte Dennett. *Thy Will Be Done. The Conquest of the Amazon: Nelson Rockefeller and Evangelism in the Age of Oil*. New York: HarperCollins, 1995.

COMIBAM. *Catálogo de Organizaciones Misioneras de Iberoamérica*, edited by Ted Limpic. Guatemala: COMIBAM Internacional, 2002.

Comunidad. *Contribuciones Para Una Historia del Protestantismo en América Latina. Taller de Teología 14*. Mexico, D. F.: Comunidad Teológica de México, 1984.

Conforti, Joseph. "Jonathan Edwards' Most Popular Work: 'The Life of Brainerd' and 19th Century Evangelical Culture." *Church History* 54 (1985): 188–201.

Cook, Richard R. "Fundamentalism and Modern Culture in Republican China: The Popular Language of Wang Mingdao, 1900–1991." Ph.D. diss., The University of Iowa, 2003.

Copeland, Luther. *The Southern Baptist Convention and the Judgment of History*. New York: University Press of America, 1995.

Cornelius, Janet Duitsman. *Slave Missions and the Black Church in the Antebellum South*. Columbia, S.C.: University of South Carolina Press, 1999.

Costas, Orlando. *The Church and Its Mission: A Shattering Critique from the Third World*. Wheaton, Ill.: Tyndale House, 1974.

————. "Compromiso y Misión." San José, Costa Rica: Caribe, 1979.

————. "Por Una Auténtica Evangelización Contextual." *Pastoralia* 2.3 (1979): 3–7.

Cowen, Charles L. "Conversion among Puritans and Amerindians: A Theological and Cultural Perspective." In *Puritanism: Transatlantic Perspectives on a 17th Century Anglo-American Faith*, edited by Francis J. Bremer, 223–56. Boston: Northeastern University Press, 1993.

Cressy, David. *Coming Over: Migration and communication between England and New England in the 17th century*. Cambridge: Cambridge University Press, 1987.

Cruz, Saul and Pilar. "Integral Mission and the Practioner's Perspective." In *Justice, Mercy and Humility: Integral Mission and the Poor*, edited by Tim Chester, 89–101. Waynesboro, Ga.: Paternoster Press, 2002.

D'Artagnan. "Cristianos: ¿Misión Pastoral o Electoral?" *El Tiempo*, Marzo 5, 2006, 1–35.

DeJong, J. A. *As the Waters Cover the Sea: Millennial Expectations in the Rise of Anglo-American Missions 1640–1810*. Kampen: J. H. Kok, 1970.

Douglas, J. D., ed. *Let the Earth Hear His Voice*. Minneapolis, Minn.: World Wide, 1975.

Durand, Jean-Dominique. "La missiologie, un vaste monde. A propos d'un recueil du Cédric sur vingt-cinq ans de recherches missiologique." *Mémoire Spiritaine* 22 (2005): 135–55.

Dwight, Edwin W. *Memoirs of Henry Obookiah, a Native of Owhyhee and a Member of the Foreign Mission School*. New Haven: Nathan Whiting, 1819.

Edwards, Jonathan. *The Life of David Brainerd*. Edited by Norman Pettit. Vol. 7 of *The Works of Jonathan Edwards*; edited by Harry S. Stout. New Haven: Yale University Press, 1985.

_____. "Faithful Narrative of the Surprising Work of God." In *The Great Awakening*. Edited by C.C. Goen. Vol. 4 of *The Works of Jonathan Edwards*. New Haven: Yale University Press, 1972.

_____. *Religious Affections*. Edited by John Smith. New Haven: Yale University Press, 1959.

_____. *The Works of Jonathan Edwards*. 2 Vols. Edited by Edward Hickman. Edinburgh: Banner of Truth Trust, 1974.

Elliot, Elisabeth. *Shadow of the Almighty: The Life and Testament of Jim Elliot*. New York: Harper, 1958.

_____. *Through Gates of Splendor*. New York: Harper, 1957.

Elsbree, Oliver Wendell. *The Rise of the Missionary Spirit in America, 1790–1815*. 1928. Reprint edition, Philadelphia: Porcupine Press, 1980.

Erlank, Natasha. "Jane and John Philip: Partnership, Usefulness and Sexuality in the Service of God." In *The London Missionary Society in South Africa, 1799–1999*, edited by John de Gruchy. Athens, Ohio: Ohio University Press, 2000.

Escobar, Samuel. *La Chispa y la Llama. Breve Historia de la Comunidad Internacional de Estudiantes Evangélicos en América Latina*. Buenos Aires: Certeza, 1978.

_____. *Una Decada en Tiempo de Misión*. Quito: Ediciones Comunidad, 1987.

_____. *Los Evangelicos: Nueva Leyenda Negra en America Latina?* Serie Protestantismo y Nacion. Ciudad de México: Casa Unida de Publicaciones, 1991.

_____. *The New Global Mission: the Gospel from Everywhere to Everyone*. Downers Grove, Ill.: InterVarsity Press, 2003.

_____. "The Two-Party System and the Missionary Enterprise." In *Re-Forming the Center*, 341–60. Grand Rapids, Mich.: Eerdmans, 1998.

Estep, William R. *The Anabaptist Story*. Grand Rapids, Mich.: Eerdmans, 1975.

_____. *Whole Gospel, Whole World*. Nashville, Tenn.: Broadman & Holman, 1994.

Ferreira, Júlio Andrade. *História da Igreja Presbiteriana Do Brasil*. 2 vols. 2nd ed. São Paulo: Casa Editora Presbiteriana, 1992.

Fiedler, Klaus. *The Story of Faith Missions*. Oxford: Regnum Books, 1994.

Forrester, Duncan. *Caste and Christianity: Attitudes and Policies on Caste of Anglo- Saxon Protestant Missions in India*. London: Curzon Press, 1980.

Freston, Paul. *Evangelicals and Politics in Asia, Africa, and Latin America*. New York: Cambridge University Press, 2001.

Frizen, Edwin L. *Seventy-Five Years of IFMA, 1917–1991: The Nondenominational Missions Movement*. Pasadena, Calif.: William Carey Library, 1992.

Frost, Henry. "What Missionary Motives Should Prevail?" In vol. 12 of *The Fundmentals*. Chicago: Testimony Publishing Co., 1910–1915.

Garlick, Phyllis L. *With the C. M. S. in West Africa: A Study in Partnerships*. London: Church Missionary Society, 1935.

Gatwa, Tharcisse. "Theological Education in Africa: What Prospects for Sharing Knowledge?" *Exchange* 32.3 (2003): 193–213.

George, Timothy. "Controversy and Communion: The Limits of Baptist Fellowship from Bunyan to Spurgeon." In *The Gospel in the World*, edited by D. W. Bebbington. Carlisle, Pa.: Paternoster Press, 2002.

_____. "Evangelicals and Others." *First Things* 160 (February 2006): 15–23.

_____. *Faithful Witness: The Life and Mission of William Carey*. Birmingham, Ala.: New Hope, 1991.

Gomez, Michael A. *Exchanging Our Country Marks: The Transformation of African Identities in the Colonial and Antebellum South*. Chapel Hill, N.C.: University of North Carolina Press, 1998.

Gremillion, Joseph. *The Church and Culture since Vatican II: The Experience of North and Latin America*. Notre Dame, Ind.: University of Notre Dame Press, 1985.

Guelzo, Allen C. "God's Designs: The Literature of the Colonial Revivals of Religion, 1735–1760." In *New Directions in American Religious History*, edited by Harry S. Stout and D. G. Hart, 141–72. New York: Oxford University Press, 1997.

Guerrero, Robert. "Networking for Integral Mission: El Camino Network, Latin America." In *Justice, Mercy and Humility: Integral Mission and the Poor*, edited by Tim Chester, 78–86. Waynesboro, Ga.: Paternoster Press, 2002.

Guthrie, Stan. *Missions in the Third Millennium: 21 Key Trends for the 21st Century*. Carlisle, UK: Paternoster Press, 2000.

Gutiérrez S, Tomás. *Los Evangelicos en Perú y América Latina: Ensayos Sobre Su Historia*. Lima: Ediciones AHP, 1997.

Hamilton, J. Taylor and Kenneth G. Hamilton. *History of the Moravian Church: The Renewed Unitas Fratrum 1722–1957*. Bethlehem, Pa.: Moravian Board, 1967.

Hare, Lloyd C. M. *Thomas Mayhew, Patriarch to the Indians*. New York: D. Appleton and Co., 1932.

Harper, Keith. *Send the Light*. Macon, Ga.: Mercer University Press, 2002.

Hart, D. G., S. M. Lucas and S. J. Nichols, eds. *The Legacy of Jonathan Edwards*. Grand Rapids, Mich.: Baker Books, 2003.

Hattaway, Paul. *Back to Jerusalem: Three Chinese House Church Leaders Share Their Vision to Complete the Great Commission*. Waynesboro, Ga.: Piquant, 2003.

_____. *The Heavenly Man: The Remarkable True Story of Chinese Christian Brother Yun*. London: Monarch Books, 2002.

Heikes, Laura. "Una Perspectiva Diferente: Latin Americans and the Global Mission Movement." *Missiology: An International Review* 31.1 (2003): 69–85.

Hertzke, Allen D. *Freeing God's Children: The Unlikely Alliance for Global Human Rights*. Lanham: Rowman & Littlefield, 2004.

Hervey, G. W. *The Story of Baptist Missions*. St. Louis, Mo.: C. R. Barnes, 1885.

Heyrmann, Christine Leigh. *Southern Cross: The Beginnings of the Bible Belt*. New York: Knopf, 1997.

Hoornaert, Eduardo, Ephraim Ferreira Alves, Jaime Clasen, and Lúcia Mathilde Endlich Orth. *História de Igreja na América Latina e No Caribe, 1945–1995: o Debate Metodológico*. Petrópolis, RJ and São Paulo, SP: Vozes, CEHILA, 1995.

Howlett, David. "Historians on Defining Hegemony in Missionary-Native Relations." *Fides et Historia* 37.1 (2005): 17–24.

Hsu, Min-Fu. "Understanding Christian Conversion in Late-Socialist China: Rural Peasants versus Urban Intellectuals." Ph.D. diss. (draft), Trinity Evangelical Divinity School, 2006.

Hudson, D. Dennis. *Protestant Origins in India: Tamil Evangelical Christians 1706–1835*. Grand Rapids, Mich.: Eerdmans, 2000.

Hunt, Keith and Gladys. *For Christ and the University: The Story of InterVarsity Christian Fellowship of the USA, 1940–1990*. Downers Grove, Ill.: InterVarsity Press, 1992.

Hunter, J. H. *Beside All Waters: The Story of Seventy-Five Years of World-Wide Ministry of the Christian and Missionary Alliance*. Harrisburg, Pa.: Christian Publications, 1964.

Hutchison, William R. *Errand to the World: American Protestant Thought and Foreign Missions*. Chicago: University of Chicago Press, 1987.

Hutton, J. E. *A History of Moravian Missions*. London: Moravian Publications Office, 1922.

Jenkins, Philip. *The Next Christendom: The Coming of Global Christianity*. New York: Oxford University Press, 2002.

Jeyaraj, Daniel. *Inkulturation in Tranquebar: der Beitrag der frühen dänisch-hallischen Mission zum Werden einer indischen-einheimischen Kirche (1706–1730)*. Erlangen: Ev.-Luth. Mission, 1996.

Johnstone, Patrick J. *Operation World. 21st Century Edition*. Carlisle, UK: Paternoster Lifestyle, 2001.

Kane, J. Herbert. *A Concise History of the Christian World Mission*. Grand Rapids, Mich.: Baker Books, 1978.

_____. *Life and Work on the Mission Field*. Grand Rapids, Mich.: Baker Books, 1980.

_____. *Understanding Christian Missions*. 4th ed. Grand Rapids, Mich.: Baker Books, 1986.

Kellaway, William. *The New England Company 1649–1776*. New York: Barnes & Noble, 1962.

Kingdon, Robert M. *Geneva and the Coming of the Wars of Religion in France 1555–1563*. Geneva: Droz, 1956.

Kling, David W. and Douglas A. Sweeney, eds. *Jonathan Edwards at Home and Abroad*. Columbia, S.C.: University of South Carolina Press, 2003.

Kollman, Paul V. *The Evangelization of Slaves and Catholic Origins in East Africa*. Maryknoll, N.Y.: Orbis Books, 2005.

Köstenberger, Andreas J. *The Missions of Jesus and the Disciples According to the Fourth Gospel: With Implications for the Fourth Gospel's Purpose and the Mission of the Contemporary Church*. Grand Rapids, Mich.: Eerdmans, 1998.

Köstenberger, Andreas J. and Peter O'Brien. *Salvation to the Ends of the Earth: A Biblical Theology of Mission*. NSBT 11. Downers Grove, Ill.: InterVarsity Press, 2001.

Landero, Victor, Bob Owen, and David M. Howard. *The Victor: The Victor Landero Story*. Old Tappan, N.J.: F. H. Revell, 1979.

Latourette, Kenneth Scott. *A History of Christianity*. Vol. 2, *Reformation to the Present*. Revised ed. New York: Harper and Row, 1975.

_____, *The History of the Expansion of Christianity*. Vols. 1–7. 1937–45. Reprint ed. Grand Rapids, Mich.: Zondervan, 1970.

_____. *These Sought a Country*. New York: Harper and Brothers, 1950.

Lawrence, Una Roberts. *Lottie Moon*. Nashville, Tenn.: Sunday School Board of the Southern Baptist Convention, 1927.

Lehmann, E. Arno. *It Began at Tranquebar*. Madras: Christian Literature Society, 1956.

Léry, Jean de. *History of a Voyage to the Land of Brazil*. Translated and introduction by Janet Whately. Berkeley, Calif.: University of California Press, 1990.

Levine, Daniel H, ed. *Churches and Politics in Latin America*. Beverly Hills, Calif.: SAGE Publications, Inc., 1979.

Lewis, Donald M., ed. *Christianity Reborn: The Global Expansion of Evangelicalism in the Twentieth Century*. Grand Rapids, Mich.: Eerdmans, 2004.

Littell, Franklin Hamlin. *The Anabaptist View of the Church: A Study in the Origins of Sectarian Protestantism*. 2nd ed. Boston: Starr King Press, 1958.

Loiello, John. "Bishop in Two Worlds: Samuel Ajayi Crowther (c. 1806–1891)." In *Varieties of Christian Experience in Nigeria*, edited by Elizabeth Isichei. London: The MacMillan Press, Ltd., 1982.

Lores, Ruben. "Manifest Destiny and the Missionary Enterprise." *Study Encounter* 11.1 (1975): 1–16.

Lynch, Edward. "Reform and Religion in Latin America." *Orbis* 42.2 (1998): 263–81.

Lowrie, John C. *A Manual of Missions, or, Sketches of the Foreign Missions of the Presbyterian Church*. New York: Anson D. F. Randolph, 1854.

Macaw, Mrs. Alexander. *Congo: The First Alliance Mission Field.* Harrisburg, Pa.: Christian Publications, 1937.

Mana, Kä. "L'Afrique, une chance pour le christianisme mondial." *Perspectives missionnaires* 34 (1997): 45–57.

Marsden, George. *Jonathan Edwards: A Life.* New Haven: Yale University Press, 2003.

Marshman, John C. *The Life and Times of Carey, Marshman, and Ward.* 2 vols. London: Longman, Brown, Green, Longmans, & Roberts, 1859.

Martin, Roger H. *Evangelicals United: Ecumenical Stirrings in Pre-Victorian Britain, 1795–1830.* London: Scarecrow Press, 1983.

Martinez-García, Carlos. "Secta: Un Concepto Inadecuado Para Explicar el Protestantismo Mexicano." *Boletín Teológico* 23.41 (1991): 55–72.

Mather, Cotton. *The Great Works of Christ in America.* 1702. Reprint, Edinburgh: Banner of Truth, 1979.

Matviuk, Sergio. "Pentecostal Leadership Development and Church Growth in Latin America." *Asian Journal of Pentecostal Studies* 5.1 (2002): 155–72.

Mayhew, Experience. *Indian Converts: or, Some Account of the Lives and Dying Speeches of A Considerable Number of the Christianized Indians of Martha's Vineyard.* Boston: Samuel Gerrish, 1727.

Mbiti, John. *The Crisis of Mission in Africa.* Mukono: Uganda Church Press, 1971.

McBeth, Leon. *The Baptist Heritage.* Nashville, Tenn.: Broadman Press, 1987.

_____. *A Sourcebook for Baptist Heritage.* Nashville, Tenn.: Broadman Press, 1990.

McGrath, Alister. *Evangelicalism and the Future of Christianity.* Downers Grove, Ill.: InterVarsity Press, 1995.

Meeks, Wayne. *The First Urban Christians: The Social World of the Apostle Paul.* New Haven: Yale University Press, 1983.

Merkle, Benjamin L. "The Need for Theological Education in Missions: Lessons Learned From the Church's Greatest Missionary." *SBJT* 9.4 (2005): 50–61.

Messina, Jean-Paul and Jaap van Slageren. *Histoire du christianisme au Cameroun.* Paris: Karthala, 2005.

Míguez Bonino, José. "How Does United States Presence Help, Hinder or Compromise Christian Mission in Latin America?" *Review and Expositor* 74.2 (1977): 173–82.

Miller, Darrow and Stan Guthrie. *Discipline Nations: The Power of Truth to Transform Cultures.* Seattle, Wash.: YWAM Press, 2001.

Moffett, Eileen F. "Betsey Stockton: Pioneer American Missionary." *International Bulletin of Missionary Research* 19 (1995): 71–76.

Moffett, Samuel Hugh. *A History of Christianity in Asia: Beginnings to 1500.* Vol. 1. San Francisco: HarperSanFrancisco, 1992.

_____. "Theology of Missions." *Ashland Theological Journal* 18.1 (1985): 17–23.

Moll, Rob. "Missions Incredible." *Christianity Today.* March 2006, pages 30–34.

Mondragón, Carlos. "Historia de Las Ideas Protestantes en América Latina, 1920–1950." M.A. thesis, Universidad Nacional Autónoma de México, 2000.

Monsiváis, Carlos, and Carlos Martínez García. *Protestantismo, Diversidad y Tolerancia.* México, D.F.: Comisión Nacional de los Derechos Humanos, 2002.

Moreau, A. Scott, ed. *Evangelical Dictionary of World Missions.* Grand Rapids, Mich.: Baker Books, 2000.

Morison, Samuel Eliot. *Builders of the Bay Colony.* Boston: Houghton Mifflin, 1930.

Morris, J. W. *Memoirs of the Life and Writings of the Rev. Andrew Fuller.* Boston: Lincoln & Edmands, 1830.

Neill, Stephen. *A History of Christianity in India 1707–1858.* Cambridge: Cambridge University Press, 1985.

_____. *A History of Christian Missions*. The Pelican History of the Church, revised ed., New York: Viking Penguin, 1986.

_____. *Survey of the Training of the Ministry in Africa*. Part 1. London: International Missionary Council, 1950.

Newbigin, Lesslie. *The Gospel in a Pluralist Society*. Grand Rapids, Mich.: Eerdmans, 1989.

Niebuhr, H. Richard. *Christ and Culture*. New York: Harper and Row, 1951.

Noble, Walter J. "Wesleyan Evangelicalism and the Modern Missionary Movement." In *Christian World Mission,* edited by William K. Anderson. Nashville, Tenn.: Commission on Ministerial Training, 1946.

Oliver, Roland. *The Missionary Factor in East Africa*. London: Longmans, Green and Company, 1952.

Olmstead, Earl P. *Blackcoats Among the Delaware: David Zeisberger on the Ohio Frontier*. Kent, Ohio: Kent State University, 1991.

Ordóñez, Francisco. *Historia del Cristianismo Evangélico en Colombia*. Armenia, Colombia: Alianza Cristiana y Misionera, 1956.

Oomen, George and Hans Raun Iversen, eds. *It Began in Copenahagen: Junctions in 300 Years of Indian-Danish Relations in Christian Mission*. Delhi: ISPCK, 2005.

Ott, Craig and Harold A. Netland, eds. *Globalizing Theology: Belief and Practice in An Era of World Christianity*. Grand Rapids, Mich.: Baker, 2006.

Padilla, C. René. *Mission between the Times: Essays on the Kingdom*. Grand Rapids, Mich.: Eerdmans, 1985.

_____. "Holistic Mission in Theological Perspective." In *Serving with the Poor in Latin America*, edited by Tetsunao Yamamori, Bryant L. Myers, C. René Padilla and Greg Rake. Monrovia, Calif.: MARC Publications, 1997.

_____. "Integral Mission Today." In *Justice, Mercy and Humility: Integral Mission and the Poor*, edited by Tim Chester, 59–64. Waynesboro, Ga.: Paternoster Press, 2002.

Patton, Cornelius H. *The Lure of Africa*. New York: Missionary Education Movement of the United States and Canada, 1917.

Petite, Norman. "Prelude to Mission: David Brainerd's expulsion from Yale." *New England Quarterly* 49.1 (1986): 28–50.

Pierce, Milton and Nancy. *The Triumphs, Trials, Tidbits and Trivia of History (Seventy-Five Years of Alliance Ministry in Burkina Faso)*. Bobo-Dioulasso: n.p., 1997.

Piggin, Stuart. *Making Evangelical Missionaries 1789–1858*. London: Sutton Courtenay Press, 1984.

Plummer, Robert L. "The Great Commission in the New Testament." *The Southern Baptist Journal of Theology* 9.4 (2005): 4–11.

Pope Paul VI. "Address to the Closing of the All-African Bishops' Symposium." *AFER: African Ecclesial Review* 11.4 (1969): 402–5.

Raboteau, Albert. *A Fire in the Bones: Reflections on African American Religious History*. Boston: Beacon Press, 1996.

_____. *Slave Religion: The "Invisible Institution" in the Antebellum South*. New York: Oxford University Press, 1978

Reichel, William C., ed. *Memorials of the Moravian Church*. Philadelphia: J. B. Lippincot, 1870.

Rembao, Alberto. "The Presence of Protestantism in Latin America." *International Review of Missions* 21.1 (1948): 57–70.

Roberts, Dana. "Evangelist or Homemaker? Mission Strategies of Early Nineteenth-Century Missionary Wives in Burma and Hawaii." *International Bulletin of Missionary Research* 17 (2004): 4–12.

Romero, Catalina. "Globalization, Civil Society and Religion from a Latin American Standpoint." *Sociology of Religion* 62.4 (2001): 475–90.

Roseberry, Robert S. *The Niger Vision.* Harrisburg, Pa.: Christian Publications, 1934.

_____. *75éme anniversaire des Assemblées de Dieu au Burkina Faso: 1921–1996.* Ouagadougou: Imprimerie des Assemblées de Dieu, n.d.

_____. *The Soul of French West Africa.* Harrisburg, Pa.: Christian Publications, 1947.

Rowse, Ruth. "William Carey's 'Pleasing Dream.'" *International Review of Missions* 38 (1949): 181–92.

Ryland, Jr., John. *The Life and Death of the Reverend Andrew Fuller.* London: Button & Son, 1816.

Salem, Luis D. *Francisco G. Penzotti, Apóstol de la Libertad y la Verdad.* Colección Historia 2. México: Sociedades Bíblicas en América Latina, 1963.

Salvaing, Bernard. *Les missionnaires à la rencontre de l'Afrique au XIXe siècle: Côte des esclaves et pays Yoruba, 1840–1891.* Paris: Editions l'Harmattan, 1994.

Sanneh, Lamin. *Abolitionists Abroad.* Cambridge, Mass.: Harvard University Press, 1999.

_____. *West African Christianity: The Religious Impact.* Maryknoll, N.Y.: Orbis Books, 1983.

Sanneh, Lamin and Joel Carpenter, eds. *The Changing Face of Christianity: Africa, the West, and the World.* New York: Oxford University Press, 2005.

Sawyer, Edwin A. *These Fifteen: Pioneers of the Moravian Church.* Bethlehem, Pa.: Comenius Press, 1963.

Schattschneider, David A. "'Souls for the Lamb': A Theology for the Christian Mission According to Count Nicolaus Ludwig von Zinzendorf and Bishop August Gottlieb Spangenberg." Ph.D. diss., University of Chicago, 1975.

Schaufele, Wolfgang. "The Missionary Vision and Activity of the Anabaptist Laity." In *Anabaptism and Mission,* edited by Wilbert R. Schenk. Scottdale, Pa.: Herald Press, 1984.

Schnabel, Eckhard. *Early Christian Mission.* Vol. 1: *Jesus and the Twelve.* Vol. 2: *Paul and the Early Church.* Downers Grove, Ill.: InterVarsity Press, 2004.

Scott, Lindy. *Los Evangélicos Mexicanos en el Siglo Veinte.* Mexico, D. F.: Editorial Kyrios, 1980.

_____. "Salt of the Earth: a Socio-Political History of Mexico City Evangelical Protestants (1964–1991)." Ph.D. diss., Northwestern University/Garrett-Evangelical Theological Seminary, 1991.

Shenkar, Oded. *The Chinese Century: The Rising Chinese Economy and Its Impact on the Global Economy, the Balance of Power, and Your Job.* Upper Saddle River, N.J.: Wharton School of Publishing, 2006.

Sherring, M. A. *The History of Protestant Mission in India.* London: Religious Tract Society, 1884.

Silva Gotay, Samuel. "Protestantismo y Política en Puerto Rico a Partir de la Invasión de Estados Unidos." In *Protestantismo y Política en América Latina y el Caribe,* edited by Tomás J. Gutiérrez S., 235–62. Lima, Peru: CEHILA, 1996.

Singh, Brijraj. *The First Protestant Missionary to India: Bartholomaeus Ziegenbalg (1683–1719).* Oxford: Oxford University Press, 1999.

Skinner, Betty Lee. *Daws: The Story of Dawson Trotman.* Grand Rapids, Mich.: Zondervan, 1974.

Smith, Bradford. *Yankees in Paradise.* Philadelphia: Lippincott, 1956.

Sneed, Alfred C. *Missionary Atlas: A Manual of the Foreign Work of the Christian and Missionary Alliance.* Harrisburg, Pa.: Christian Publications, 1950.

Spangenberg, August G. *An Account of the Manner in which the Protestant Church of the Unitas Fratrum, or United Brethren, preach the Gospel and carry on the Missions among the Heathen.* London: H. Trapp, 1788.

"Special Issue on Missionaries, Multiculturalism, and Mainline Protestantism." *Journal of Presbyterian History,* Summer 2003.

Stanley, Brian. *The Bible and the Flag.* Leicester: InterVarsity Press, 1990.

_____, ed. *Christian Missions and the Enlightenment.* Grand Rapids, Mich.: Eerdmans, 2001.

_____, ed. *Missions, Nationalism, and the End of Empire.* Grand Rapids, Mich.: Eerdmans, 2003.

Stevens, Laura M. *The Poor Indians: British Missionaries, Native Americans and Colonial Sensibilities.* Philadelphia: University of Pennsylvania Press, 2004.

Strong, A. H. *A Tour of the Missions: Observations and Conclusions.* Philadelphia: The Griffith and Rowland Press, 1918.

Strong, William E. *The Story of the American Board: An Account of the First Hundred Years of the American Board of Commissioners for Foreign Missions.* Boston: Pilgrim Press, 1910.

Sweeney, Douglas A. *The American Evangelical Story: A History of the Movement.* Grand Rapids, Mich.: Baker Academic, 2005.

Tabrah, Ruth M. *Hawaii: A Bicentennial History.* New York: W. W. Norton, 1980.

Thompson, Augustus. *Moravian Missions.* New York: Scribner, 1883.

Thornton, Douglas M. *Africa Waiting or The Problem of Africa's Evangelization.* New York: Student Volunteer Movement, 1902.

Tise, Larry E. *Proslavery: A History of the Defense of Slavery in America, 1701–1840.* Athens, Ga.: University of Georgia Press, 1987.

Tucker, Ruth A. *From Jerusalem to Irian Jaya: A Biographical History of Christian Missions.* Grand Rapids, Mich.: Zondervan, 1983.

Van den Berg, Johannes. *Constrained by Jesus' Love: An Inquiry into the Motives of the Missionary Awakening in Great Britain in the Period Between 1698 and 1815.* Kampen: J. H. Kok, 1956.

Varg, Paul A. "Motives in Protestant Mission, 1890–1917." *Church History* 23 (1954): 68–89.

Walls, Andrew F. *The Cross-Cultural Process in Christian History.* Edinburgh: T&T Clark, 2002.

_____. "The Evangelical Revival, the Missionary Movement, and Africa." In *Evangelicalism,* edited by Mark A. Noll, David W. Bebbington, and George A. Rawlyk. New York: Oxford University Press, 1994.

_____. *The Missionary Movement in Christian History: Studies in the Transmission of Faith.* Maryknoll, N.Y.: Orbis Press, 1996.

Ward, William. "English Baptist Mission." In *The American Baptist Magazine and Missionary Intelligencer.* January 1817.

Warner, R. Stephen. *A Church of Our Own: Disestablishment and Diversity in American Religion.* New Brunswick, N.J.: Rutgers University Press, 2005.

Williams, Leighton and Mornay, eds. *Serampore Letters.* New York: G. P. Putnam's Sons, 1892.

Winslow, Ola. *John Eliot, Apostle to the Indians.* Boston: Houghton Mifflin Co., 1968.

Winter, Ralph D. and Steven C. Hawthorne, eds. *Perspectives on the World Christian Movement.* 3rd ed. Pasadena, Calif.: William Carey Library, 1999.

Winter, Robert H. *I Will Do A New Thing: The U.S. Center for World Missions ... and Beyond.* Revised edition. Pasadena, Calif.: William Carey Library, 2002.

Wood Jr., John Halsey. "John Livingston Nevius and the New Missions History." *Journal of Presbyterian History* 83 (2005): 23–40.

Woodbridge, John D., ed. *Ambassadors for Christ*. Chicago: Moody Press, 1994.

Yamamori, Tetsunano. *Penetrating Missions' Final Frontier: A New Strategy for Unreached People*. Downers Grove, Ill.: Intervarsity Press, 1993.

Ziegenbalg, Bartholomaeus. *Propagation of the Gospel in the East: Being an Account of Two Danish Missionaries Lately sent to the East Indies for the Conversion of the Heathens in Malabar*. London: J. Downing, 1709.

_____. *Propagation of the Gospel in the East: Being a Collection of Letters from the Protestant Missionaries*. London: J. Downing, 1718.

_____. *34 Conferences between the Danish Missionaries and the Malabarian Bramans (or heathen priests)*. London: H. Clements, 1719.

Zinzendorf, Nikolaus Ludwig von, *Nine Public Lectures on Important Subjects in Religion Preached in Fetter Lane Chapel in London in the Year 1746*. Edited and translated by George W. Forell. Iowa City, Iowa: University of Iowa Press, 1973.

_____. *Texte zur Mission*. Edited by Helmut Bintz. Hamburg: Friedrich WittigVerlag, 1979.

Person & Subject Index

Scripture Index

Genesis

1:31	186
3:5	186
3:22	186
12	155

Exodus

32–34	189, 190, 191
33:5	189
33:18	190
33:19–20	190
34	190
34:6–7	189

Joshua

13:1	84

Psalms

5:9	186
10:7	186
14:1–3	186
14:3	186
36:1	186
51:4	186
53:1–3	186
67:1–2	152
90:17	xi

Ecclesiastes

7:20	186

Isaiah

19:23–25	179, 190
40:8	x
49:5–6	189
54	46
54:2–3	46
59:7–8	186

Jeremiah

29:7	183

Ezekiel

37	27

Zechariah

12:10	27, 40

Matthew

1	178
1:21	178
3	177
6:19–21	188
8:11	178
10	178
13:24–30	17
13:36–43	17
19:25–26	25
23	180
24:14	178
25:46	188
28	13, 164, 177
28:16–20	1, 176
28:19–20	132

Luke

4:18–19	127
24:46–49	176

John

1:14	191
1:14–18	191
1:17	191
1:18	191
1:29	177
1:34	177
2:11	191
3	106
3:36	177
8	180
12	191
12:20–33	191
12:32	191
14:9	191
14:27	177
17	163
17:21	55
20:19–23	177
20:21	127, 177

Acts

1	177
1:8	177, 190
8	40
10	40
16	184
16:9	25
17:30	180

Romans

1	188
1:14	60
1:16	193
1:18	187
3:10–18	186
4	178
5:14	186
10:17–18	179
10:18	34
11:23	27
15	155
15:20	179

1 Corinthians

1	58
1:17	193
1:18	193
1:26–28	58
2:2–5	194

2 Corinthians

4:15	192
5:11–12	195
5:11–21	8
5:14	61
5:20	177
5:21	9, 195

Ephesians

1:10	190
1:13	190
1:14	190
1:19–20	193
2	190
2:3	8, 195